Mao Tse-tung ON REVOLUTION AND WAR

MOSTAFA REJAI is associate professor of political science at Miami University, Oxford, Ohio. He was associated with the Institute of Government and Public Affairs at U.C.L.A. where he received his Ph.D. In addition to contributions to professional and scholarly journals, and to *The New Communisms*, Mr. Rejai has published *Democracy: The Contemporary Theories* and *Ideas in Action: Modern Political Ideologies* (coauthor).

Mao Tse-tung

★

ON REVOLUTION

★

AND WAR

Edited with an Introduction and Notes by
M. Rejai

DOUBLEDAY & COMPANY, INC.
GARDEN CITY, N.Y.
1969

Library of Congress Catalog Card Number 68–18082
Copyright © 1969 by Mostafa Rejai
All Rights Reserved
Printed in the United States of America
First Edition

CONTENTS

335.43
M29

PREFACE

In 1965–68 a great political upheaval swept Communist China, a revolution employing "Mao Tse-tung's thought" as its guiding principle. In those years, the Chinese press insisted, "The world entered the era of Mao Tse-tung's thought." "Chairman Mao" emerged as the "Red sun in the heart of the peoples of the world"; his "thought" acquired the alleged potency—quite literally—to facilitate scientific discoveries, help crops grow bigger, and perform a variety of other diverse functions. The "little red book" of *Quotations from Chairman Mao Tse-tung,* published in Peking in 1966, quickly became a symbol of ideological unity. Millions of copies were distributed throughout China in an attempt to turn the entire country into "a great school of Mao Tse-tung's thought."

In a striking description of Mao Tse-tung's contribution to Marxism-Leninism, *Jen-min Jih-pao* (People's Daily) editorialized on July 1, 1966: "Mao Tse-tung's thought is Marxism-Leninism inherited and developed with genius, creatively and in an all-round way in the era in which imperialism is approaching complete collapse and socialism is advancing to victory all over the world; it is the acme of Marxism-Leninism in the present era; it is living Marxism-Leninism at its highest. Comrade Mao Tse-tung is the greatest Marxist-Leninist of the present era."[1] Indeed, Mao appears to consider his own stature equal only to that of Marx and Lenin. Although he seems greatly to respect Stalin, this appears due to the latter's status as a symbol of orthodoxy, not to his contributions to Marxism-Leninism.

This volume offers an analytical treatment of the principal elements of "Mao Tse-tung's thought." The grasp of Mao's system of ideas has become indispensable to understanding recent developments in Communist China and their implications for world politics. The volume is specifically designed as a general introduction

---

[1] English text in *Peking Review,* July 1, 1966, pp. 5–8. This is a far more glorified conception of "Mao Tse-tung's thought" than the one set forth in 1945 (see pp. 260–62).

to the works of Mao; as such, it should prove useful to student and layman alike.

Although the book is organized around the writings of Mao Tse-tung himself, six other documents, credited either to the Central Committee of the Chinese Communist Party or to high-ranking Communist officials, proved exceedingly important to the completeness and unity of the volume. These are: (1) Liu Shao-ch'i, *The Political Report* of the Central Committee of the Communist Party of China to the Eighth National Congress of the Party (September 15, 1956); (2) Resolution of the Central Committee of the Chinese Communist Party on the Establishment of People's Communes in the Rural Areas (August 29, 1958); (3) Decision of the Central Committee of the Chinese Communist Party Concerning the Great Proletarian Cultural Revolution (August 8, 1966); (4) "An Epoch-Making Document [Concerning the Cultural Revolution]" (May 16, 1968); (5) "Long Live the All-Round Victory in the Great Proletarian Cultural Revolution!" (September 7, 1968); and (6) Lin Piao, *Long Live the Victory of People's War* (September 3, 1965).

The first five documents are used in Chapter II, while the last one is included in Chapter VI. The 1956 work contains the first authoritative proclamation that the dictatorship of the proletariat had been established in China, a proposition that received formal sanction in the resolution of the eighth party congress on September 27, 1956.[2] The second document announces the creation of the commune system as a stage in the progressive unfolding of communism in China. The third, fourth, and fifth works are important for understanding the cultural revolution and the multiplicity of problems and issues it entailed; they were drawn up, according to the Chinese press, under the "personal leadership" of Mao Tse-tung. The final document is a significant pronouncement on the future of world communism and the appropriate strategy for defeating the "imperialist powers"; it seeks to project on a global level the revolutionary strategy of Mao Tse-tung.

The dual concern of the editor with the authenticity of source material and the uniformity of language and style led him to draw all selections from official Communist Chinese publications of the last few years. This decision entailed some difficulties. To begin with,

[2] See "Resolution of the Eighth National Congress of the Communist Party of China on the Political Report of the Central Committee" (September 27, 1956), in *Eighth National Congress of the Communist Party of China,* I (Peking: Foreign Languages Press, 1956), esp. p. 126.

it is well known that Mao Tse-tung's works have been extensively revised and rewritten to give them greater coherence and unity, and a prophetic quality. At the same time, there is some agreement that relatively little change has been made in the *substance* of most of Mao's writings.[3] This agreement does not extend to Mao's "philosophical" essays—particularly "On Practice" and "On Contradiction"—which, although briefly discussed in the Prologue, are not included in this volume. In any case, wherever appropriate, discrepancies between the older and newer versions of Mao Tse-tung's writings have been pointed out.

The reliance on the authorized translations created another problem, that of readability. There are two language barriers when Mao Tse-tung's works are translated into English: the Chinese barrier and the Communist barrier.[4] The Chinese language differs from English in grammar and syntax. It is characterized by a conciseness and economy of expression that is extremely difficult to render into graceful English. Communist terminology adds further difficulties because it is not even Chinese. The vocabulary and phraseology are often new to the older Chinese intellectuals unless they made a special effort to master them. The official translations often seem stilted, awkward, and curiously shrill in tone, particularly when ideological considerations are injected into them.

The aphoristic quality of the Chinese language and its constant use of hyperbole lend themselves to a high degree of sloganeering. The Chinese Communists appear quite conscious of the fact that a language takes on certain qualities depending on the way in which it is used. The beginning reader should not be surprised that the party line in Communist China is characteristically stated in such terms as "Hundred Flowers," "Great Leap Forward," "Red and Expert," "Politics in Command," and so on. A related consideration is that in a country still largely populated by uneducated peasants it is far easier to capture, communicate, and popularize the essence of a policy in a slogan than to try to explain it in tedious

[3] Donald M. Lowe notes, for example, that "These revisions and rewritings, though not fundamentally altering the content of Mao's thought, make his thought appear more systematic and consistent than it actually was." *The Function of "China" in Marx, Lenin, and Mao* (Berkeley and Los Angeles: University of California Press, 1966), p. 160, n. 1. Cf. Jerome Ch'en, *Mao and the Chinese Revolution* (New York: Oxford University Press, 1967), p. 14; Ralph L. Powell, "Maoist Military Doctrines," *Asian Survey*, VIII:4 (April 1968), p. 247.

[4] I owe this insight to my colleague Byron S. Weng.

technical jargon. The masses are more receptive to language they easily understand; they may retain more, and their sense of commitment is more easily touched. The use of slogan is also consistent with traditional Chinese practice, wherein the emperors' orders were communicated in similar, easily understandable terms.

The reader will note that some of the quotations used in the introductory sections are not immediately documented. These quotations reappear in the reading selections, whereas the documented ones do not. This practice helped avoid cluttering the introductory texts with unnecessary notes.

Certain footnotes appearing in the original works have been deleted. The bibliography of the major recent works at the end of this book will help those who wish to pursue the subject further. The chronology provides a convenient point of reference for some important events in recent Chinese history.

I am much indebted to H. Arthur Steiner of the University of California, Los Angeles, for generating my initial interest in Chinese Communism and for guiding my early studies of the subject. I am grateful to Thomas P. Jenkin of the University of California, Riverside, whose incisive comments and criticisms sharpened and hopefully improved my understanding of Chinese Communist thought.

Cynthia H. Enloe and Byron S. Weng have been generous friends and colleagues, particularly helpful with problems of Chinese communist ideology and of the Chinese language. James R. Woodworth of Miami University has provided consistent moral and material support. Judith Dollenmayer and Lucy Marr of Doubleday & Co. have contributed mightily to whatever readability this volume may have. The Committee on Faculty Research, Miami University, has extended financial support toward the preparation of the manuscript. Thomas Caulwell and Arlene Ferris have rendered competent research and secretarial assistance. My wife Cynthia has assumed major responsibility toward the completion of this book. Needless to say, any shortcomings remain my own responsibility.

M. R.

October, 1968
Oxford, Ohio

PROLOGUE

Marxism-Leninism and the Chinese Revolution

The most decisive feature of "Mao Tse-tung's thought" is the way in which Marxist-Leninist revolutionary theory—originally designed for use in advanced industrial societies—is applied to the "colonial, semicolonial, and semifeudal" country of China.[1] Mao's objective is nothing less than a rewriting of Chinese history from the Marxist-Leninist point of view.

But what, in precise terms, does Mao understand by "Marxism-Leninism"? His response to this question has been explicit and unequivocal: "Marxism-Leninism is the crystallization of the most correct and most revolutionary scientific thought of the world proletariat."[2] Marxism-Leninism is the "science of revolution" and Marxist-Leninists are "revolutionary realists."

The persistent attempt to fuse Marxism-Leninism with Chinese history and conditions is consonant with the communist assertion —first enunciated by Lenin—that the "categorical demand"[3] of Marxism in approaching social problems is that theory be integrated with the actual circumstances in which it exists. Marxism, Lenin repeatedly asserted, is not "a lifeless dogma but a guide to action." Accepting Lenin's propositions, Mao insists that Marxism-Leninism must be fused with specific historical conditions and given "a definite national form" before it can be put into practice. He wrote as early as 1938:

> Another of our tasks is to study our historical heritage and use the Marxist method to sum it up critically. Our national history goes back several thousand years and has its own characteristics and in-

[1] As compared to a "colony," which is controlled by a single imperialist country, a "semicolony" is one under the simultaneous influence of several imperialist powers. A "semifeudal" country is one in which elements of feudalism exist side by side with elements of capitalism.

[2] "On Coalition Government" (April 1945), *Selected Works*, III (Peking: Foreign Languages Press, 1965), p. 314.

[3] See, for example: "On the Right of Nations to Self-Determination" (February 1914), *Selected Works*, IV (New York: International Publishers, 1943), p. 255; "Letter on Tactics" (April 1917), ibid., VI, p. 32.

numerable treasures. . . . Contemporary China has grown out of the China of the past; we are Marxist in our historical approach and must not lop off our history. We should sum up our history from Confucius to Sun Yat-sen and take over this valuable legacy. . . . Being Marxists, Communists are internationalists, but we can put Marxism into practice only when it is integrated with the specific characteristics of our country and acquires a definite national form. The great strength of Marxism-Leninism lies precisely in its integration with the concrete revolutionary practice of all countries. For the Chinese Communist Party, it is a matter of learning to apply the theory of Marxism-Leninism to the specific circumstances of China. For the Chinese Communists . . . , any talk about Marxism in isolation from China's characteristics is merely Marxism in the abstract, Marxism in a vacuum. Hence to apply Marxism concretely in China so that its every manifestation has an indubitably Chinese character . . . becomes a problem which it is urgent for the whole Party to understand and solve.

Marxist-Leninist revolutionary theory must be unified with actual practice. All theory must have an aim: it must seek to bring about a desired state of affairs. The correct approach to learning, according to Mao Tse-tung, is to learn those things that are useful for a particular time and place. Wholesale imitation must be replaced by critical adaptation.

The central core of Marxist philosophy is of course "dialectical materialism," meaning, in simplified terms, class struggle based on divergent economic interests. Marx stressed the primacy of material forces in human society; all else was derivative and secondary. He identified certain stages in human history (e.g., the slave, the feudal, the capitalist), each characterized by a distinctive mode of production, a distinctive set of classes, and conflict among those classes. Class division, according to Marx, is a division between those who own and those who do not own; the criterion is private property. Each phase of history is characterized by tension between an exploited class (the majority) and an exploiter class (the minority); each phase follows a determined course; each phase ends with conflict. The class struggle becomes increasingly acute with every historical phase and greater and greater numbers of people become involved. In capitalist society, class conflict reaches a peak of intensity and culminates in a cataclysmic revolution marking the overthrow of the exploiter class. A period of proletarian dictatorship is followed by the establishment of a "classless society" and the permanent abolition of exploitation and oppression from man's experience. It is important to note that in Marx's vision the proletarian revolution necessarily begins in advanced capitalist societies (Britain, France, and Germany, for example) and spreads to engulf the entire globe.

Mao Tse-tung fully subscribes to the Marxist view that history must be looked upon as a mirror reflecting class activity. "Dialectically" considered, classes and class struggle form the fundamental motive force of historical development. The social sphere can be understood only in terms of class: "Classes struggle, some classes triumph, others are eliminated. Such is history, such is the history of civilization for thousands of years."[4] Revolutions are developmental processes whereby social classes overthrow one another. The unfolding of revolution is determined by fluctuations in class contradictions and the shifting of class forces.

Mao's commitment to Marxist philosophy prompts him to see everything in terms of the juxtaposition of opposing forces or tendencies. This, he insists, is the "law of contradiction" and the "essence" of the dialectic. Contradiction is a concept of central importance in Mao Tse-tung, a more complex and undeviating idea than is commonly recognized. The eternal "unity and struggle of opposites" is presumably absolute and universal, existing in all things and determining their character and development. Every phenomenon is said to embrace two contradictory components or tendencies (e.g., negative-positive, action-reaction), these tendencies are in simultaneous unity and struggle, and this unity-struggle determines the way in which a particular phenomenon develops. Mao writes: "Opposites in contradiction unite as well as struggle with each other, and thus impel all things to move and change."[5]

Every situation, according to Mao, is characterized by the simultaneous existence of many contradictions that are not equally important or significant; the principal and satellite contradictions must be identified. In a capitalist society, for example, the main contradiction is between the proletariat and the bourgeoisie. Other contradictions are secondary. Mao discusses a further distinction between "antagonistic" and "non-antagonistic" contradictions, the difference being that the former can be resolved only through violence, though the latter may be settled by peaceful means.

[4] "Cast Away Illusions, Prepare for Struggle" (August 1949), *Selected Works,* IV (Peking: Foreign Languages Press, 1961), p. 428.
[5] *On the Correct Handling of Contradictions Among the People* (Peking: Foreign Languages Press, 1957), p. 21.

Mao's "theory of contradictions," far from being an "original" contribution to dialectical materialism, is largely a repetition and exposition of the Marx-Engels-Lenin propositions—as a glance at his two major philosophical works, "On Practice" and "On Contradiction," would readily demonstrate.[6] The dialectical materialist philosophy was fully spelled out by Marx and Engels. The pragmatic content of Marxist philosophy was explicit in Marx's insistence (throughout the "Theses on Feuerbach," for example) on the primacy of practice in knowledge, as well as in Lenin's repeated insistence that theory is a "guide to action." Written in 1915, Lenin's four-and-one-half-page essay, "On Dialectic,"[7] touches virtually every idea discussed by Mao Tse-tung. This essay was a highly concentrated statement of Lenin's massive philosophical-polemical work *Materialism and Empirio-Criticism,* written in 1908. In this volume, as in the *Philosophical Notebooks* of 1914–18, the many intricacies of Marxist philosophy were treated in exhaustive detail.

The most persistent claim for the "originality" of Mao Tse-tung has centered upon his distinction concerning antagonistic and non-antagonistic contradictions. As Arthur A. Cohen has shown, however, this proposition was clearly stated by Lenin as early as 1914 and further developed by Soviet writers in the 1930s.[8] Mao himself cites Lenin to the effect that "Antagonism and contradiction are not at all one and the same. Under socialism, the first will disappear, the second will remain."[9] Mao differs from Lenin in insisting that

[6] "On Practice" (July 1937), *Selected Works,* I (Peking: Foreign Languages Press, 1964), pp. 295–309; "On Contradiction" (August 1937), ibid., pp. 311–47. See also *On the Correct Handling of Contradictions . . . ,* op. cit.; "Reform Our Study" (May 1941), *Selected Works,* III (Peking: Foreign Languages Press, 1965), pp. 17–25; "Rectify the Party's Style of Work" (February 1942), ibid., pp. 35–51. On the first two works, July 1937 and August 1937 are the dates officially given, but some scholars now think that they were probably written (or substantially revised) just before their publication in 1950–52. (See Arthur A. Cohen, *The Communism of Mao Tse-tung* [Chicago: University of Chicago Press, 1963], esp. pp. 22 ff.) Mao himself denied this in an interview with Edgar Snow on January 9, 1965. (See Snow, "Interview with Mao Tse-tung," *The New Republic,* February 27, 1965, pp. 20–21.) Compare these views with Donald M. Lowe, *The Function of "China" in Marx, Lenin, and Mao* (Berkeley and Los Angeles: University of California Press, 1966), p. 162, n. 28; and Stuart R. Schram, *The Political Thought of Mao Tse-tung* (New York: Frederick A. Praeger, 1963), pp. 43–46.

[7] "On Dialectic" (1915), *Selected Works,* XI (New York: International Publishers, 1943), pp. 81–85.

[8] Cohen, op. cit., pp. 139 ff.

[9] "On Contradiction," op. cit., p. 345.

antagonistic contradictions continue to exist even in a socialist society, although perhaps in limited and milder form.

There is little doubt that Mao's status as an innovator in Marxist philosophy is at best marginal; the various claims for his originality appear to be unfounded. Though not original in his contribution to the substance of Marxist philosophy, Mao is highly original—indeed heterodox—in applying this philosophy to the concrete conditions of China. This originality consists primarily in four things: (1) shifting the locus of revolution from the urban centers to the rural areas, (2) developing a communist party based on the peasantry, (3) systematic attention to class alliance and "united front" tactics, and (4) emphasis on a protracted military conflict based on peasant guerrilla warfare. In these ways Mao's "model" of the communist revolution departs from its Soviet counterpart.

It is important to note that the united front tactic is not new with Mao Tse-tung, his departure from Lenin and Stalin being a matter of degree (see Chapters II and III). A major difference between a communist revolution in advanced societies and one in backward countries lies in the classes on which revolutionaries must necessarily rely. In advanced industrial societies there are presumably two main classes, the proletariat and the bourgeoisie. In colonial, semicolonial, and semifeudal countries, by contrast, capitalist classes exist side by side with precapitalist classes: there is a vast peasantry, a strong landlord class, a small bourgeoisie, and a comparatively insignificant proletariat. In China, for example, Mao put the urban proletariat at a mere two million people as late as 1926, when the communist movement was well under way (see p. 142). Being exceedingly small, the proletariat cannot engineer a revolution on its own strength alone; it must rely on all other classes, forces, and groups that may, for whatever reason, support its cause.

Mao's extensive analyses of classes in Chinese society are presented in Chapter III. Particularly important is the division of the bourgeoisie into three groups: the petit (lower or petty) bourgeoisie, the middle (or national) bourgeoisie, and the big bourgeoisie. The petty bourgeoisie includes lower government functionaries, lower intellectuals, primary and secondary school teachers, small merchants and traders, and the handicraftsmen. Since these groups are exploited and oppressed by both the domestic and foreign "reactionaries," they constitute a potential revolutionary force.

The national bourgeoisie consists in general of the more liberal and patriotic segments of the bourgeois class who have no ties

with foreign imperialism. It includes middle level owners, industrialists and merchants, and managerial and professional groups.
The national bourgeoisie is a "flabby," ambivalent class, vacillating
between revolution and reaction. Since it supports the capitalist
system but is against imperialist and feudal oppression, it can be
relied upon to a certain degree in the revolutionary movement.

The big bourgeoisie is further subdivided into a comprador segment and a non-comprador segment. The comprador bourgeoisie
has betrayed the country by its collusion with the imperialist
powers; it maintains close ties with them and is their agent. It has
sold its soul, as it were, to the imperialists because it profits from
their policies.[10] When the big bourgeoisie penetrates the governmental structure, when capitalism is combined with state power, a
"bureaucrat-capital" class also comes into being. However, Mao
points out, the big bourgeois traitors, far from constituting a cohesive, homogeneous political force, are divided and fragmented in
their allegiance to the various imperialist powers which vie for the
same colony.

The process of applying Marxism-Leninism to the revolutionary
situation in China involves, to be sure, revision, modification, and
change in the original theory. However, the fundamental nucleus
of that theory—the concept of revolution—remains intact. It is the
basic foundation of the political thought of Mao Tse-tung, and is
intimately related to the concept of war (defined as "the highest
form of revolution"). Every statement of Mao can be comprehended
within the framework of a series of questions, all bearing on revolution. These include:

1. How do revolutions begin? What are the initial forces that pre-
   cipitate revolutionary movements?
2. How do revolutionary movements unfold? What are the stages
   of development through which they move?
3. What keeps revolutions going? What are the dynamic forces that
   push them forward?
4. What functions do revolutions perform? What are the objectives
   they seek to attain?

[10] During the Anti-Japanese War of 1937–45 (see Introduction), Mao subdivided the comprador bourgeoisie itself into two main "cliques." The pro-
Japanese clique ("the capitulators") was considered totally unreliable, while
the pro-American and pro-European clique ("the die-hards") was thought to
have a dual tendency opposing both Japanese imperialism and the Chinese
revolution. Both cliques were considered untrustworthy, although, Mao thought,
it may be possible to play one against the other under certain conditions.

These questions combine to make "revolution" the unifying theme of the political thought of Mao Tse-tung. Accordingly, they are employed as focal points in the organization of this volume.

Before proceeding, it is necessary to place "Mao Tse-tung's thought" in historical context, for Mao's theory of revolution, though imbued with the spirit of Marxism-Leninism, is adapted to and directed by the conditions in China; the two are inseparable. The historical sketch that follows is necessarily selective; it treats only the most important developments and intends to build a historical framework for an analytical treatment of Mao's political thought.

Mao Tse-tung ON REVOLUTION AND WAR

★

INTRODUCTION
Communist China
in Historical Perspective

Communism in China

The Communist takeover of mainland China was the final act in a series of complex and intricate events dating back to the middle of the nineteenth century. Specifically, the following deserve attention: the Taiping Rebellion of the 1850s; the reform movement of the 1890s; the republican movement of the turn of the century and the establishment of the Republic of China in 1912; the anti-republican (warlord) period of 1916–28; the May 4 Movement of 1919 and the gradual evolution of Communist strategy; the Kuomintang (National People's Party) period of 1928–37; the Japanese invasion of 1937–45; and the civil war of 1945–49.

The Taiping Rebellion. The Taiping Rebellion consisted of a series of mass (mainly peasant) uprisings against foreign and domestic oppression. It lasted over a decade (1851–64) and resulted in the loss of millions of lives. The Rebellion was chiefly a reaction against the British penetration of China, the Opium War of 1839–42, and the ensuing embarrassment and humiliation of the Chinese people. Thwarted in attempting to sell opium freely in China and to use it as a medium of exchange for Chinese goods (silk and tea, for example), the British began smuggling the drug into Chinese ports. Chinese efforts to halt this traffic were consistently defeated by Britain's superior naval power. The 1842 Anglo-Chinese Treaty of Nanking ceded Hong Kong to Great Britain and opened Chinese ports to foreign trade. Thus began a century of exploitation under a system of "unequal treaties" that divided China into foreign concessions outside Chinese jurisdiction and immune to Chinese law. Shattered to pieces was the ancient conception of the Middle Kingdom: China as the mighty center of the world.

The failure of the Manchu rulers to throw out the foreign "barbarians," and to meet the growing economic discontent caused by famines and floods, seriously undermined domestic stability. The fact that the Manchus were foreigners themselves (nomadic people who came from the northeast, conquered China in 1644, and ended the Ming dynasty) further aggravated the revolt. The continued demand for social, political, and economic reform fell on deaf Manchu ears; the regime became increasingly authoritarian and oppressive. The sheer power of the Manchus and foreign mercenaries, combined with the absence of organization and leadership in the revolutionary ranks, led to the eventual collapse of the Taiping Rebellion.

The Reform Movement. The reform movement was led by the literati (many educated and trained by Western missionaries) who sought to undermine Manchu authoritarianism, destroy foreign influence in China, and strengthen the country politically and economically. The system of unequal treaties had opened the door to British, French, American, Japanese, and Russian trade. Western penetration of China and the introduction of foreign capital and products led to increasing foreign exploitation, economic maldistribution, and widespread discontent. Defeat at the hands of Japan in the war of 1894–95, which disputed the control of Korea and Taiwan, further humiliated the Chinese people and highlighted the ineptness of the Manchu regime. The conviction grew that only massive reform could return to China its strength, integrity, and self-respect. There followed, in the summer of 1898, the abortive One Hundred Days of Reform and the initiation of changes in the economic, political, military, and educational fields. However, the Empress Dowager (Tzu Hsi) emerged from twelve years of retirement, staged a coup with military support, and deposed the reform-minded Emperor Kuang Hsu.

The Republican Movement. The republican movement was the work of the Western-educated intellectuals who sought to move from dynastic rule to democratic practices and institutions, though the latter were never given a real chance. The continued popular demand for the expulsion of outsiders led to the anti-foreign Boxer Rebellion of 1900 in which hundreds of foreign civilians and missionaries were killed. The Rebellion was led by members of the fanatical secret Society of the Harmonious Fist ("Boxers"), who were soon joined by other anti-foreign and anti-Manchu elements. It took foreign troops—American, British, French, German, Japanese, and Russian—to end the Rebellion. Eventually, however, the pressure for reform gained such momentum that the One Hundred Days was revived and the Empress Dowager forced to accept such unorthodox ideas as parliamentarianism and constitutionalism, which led—at least on paper—to the establishment of a cabinet and a system of representation.

The key figure in the republican movement was Sun Yat-sen, who brought to the revolutionary process the ideological, political, and organizational leadership it thus far had lacked. Educated in Hong Kong and Hawaii, converted to Christianity at the age of eighteen, impatient with Chinese traditions, Sun sought to create a new China representing a fusion of Oriental and Western values—a China free of foreign rule, politically strong, and economically prosperous. His objectives were spelled out in the Three People's Principles of "nationalism," "democracy," and "people's welfare." The first meant political independence and national unity, to be attained by eliminating imperialism and warlordism. The second called for a responsible, popular, republican government in China. The third involved redistribution of land held under feudal arrangements, nationalization of the basic industries, and creation of a modern and efficient economy. These objectives were to be accomplished in three successive stages: military unification, political tutelage, and constitutional democracy.

Ten times did Sun and his associates plan to engineer a revolution and ten times they failed. An eleventh attempt was scheduled for late October 1911. But the accidental explosion of a bomb in the revolutionaries' warehouse on October 10 ignited a popular uprising in Hankow that spread rapidly across many provinces and eventually marked the overthrow of the Manchu regime. Sun Yat-sen, who at the time happened to be on a fund-raising mission in the United States, returned to China and was inaugurated provisional president of the Republic on January 1, 1912. On February 12 of the same year he stepped down in favor of Yuan Shih-k'ai, the military despot who had played a key role in the Empress Dowager's coup of 1898 and whose presidency marked a step backward from republicanism and constitutionalism. Yuan saw himself as the new emperor and in 1915 attempted to found and legitimize a new dynasty. He died a year later, having failed to accomplish this objective.

The Warlords. Yuan's death plunged the country into a period of disunity and warlordism. With the Manchu dynasty overthrown, and the unifying focus of the 1911 revolution removed, there was now room for rivalry and conflict among contending factions. Moreover, warlordism was based upon, and facilitated by, the natural geographic formations of the country, which in many instances were easily grouped into districts organized for military purposes. Warlordism was also encouraged by the relative availability of mercenaries due to unemployment and overpopulation and the attractiveness of a military career in the atmosphere of continuing strife.

Early in the 1920s, Sun Yat-sen renewed his efforts to unify China, create a viable national government, and revitalize the Kuomintang (KMT), which had gone into eclipse since 1912. In this he asked for support from the West, including Great Britain and the United States. Having been refused, he called upon the Soviet Union—which enjoyed considerable prestige in China at that time and whose October 1917 Revolution had inspired many Chinese liberal and leftist intellectuals. Adolf Joffe, a leading Soviet diplomat, was sent to China in 1922; he was followed a year later by Mikhail Borodin, a seasoned revolutionary. The latter proved extremely helpful in establishing the Whampoa Military Academy, organizing political agitation and propaganda, and reorganizing the KMT along Communist lines.

Sun attempted to rally the warlords to support his revolution but found them most unreceptive. He then began preparations for a Northern Expedition to neutralize the warlords' power but died in 1925, before this was achieved. Sun's death precipitated a conflict within the KMT over the line of succession, from which Chiang Kai-shek, then director of the Whampoa Academy, emerged victorious. This event marked a triumph for the right, conservative wing of the KMT over its left, liberal wing, which Sun had represented.

The May 4 Movement. In the years following the 1911 revolution, the student, intellectual, and leftist elements, imbued with the spirit of anti-imperialism, became the leaders of a full-scale nationalist movement. They espoused a series of social, political, and economic reforms under the slogan "Science and Democracy." Chinese nationalism reached a peak of intensity in 1915 as a reaction against the Twenty-one Demands presented by Japan, which included the assumption of German concessions in Shantung and the monopoly of important industries in the Yangtze valley. The decision of the Versailles peacemakers to transfer to Japan the former German rights in Shantung (as a means of inducing the former to participate in the Paris Peace Conference) triggered the May 4 Movement of 1919, generally regarded as a turning point in Chinese history. The movement began in Peking and spread rapidly to other parts of the country. Defying the authorities, Peking and Shanghai students marched into the streets and called for a general strike that lasted about a month in Shanghai. Some joined nationalist groups; others became members of leftist organizations such as the Young Socialists and the Federation of Labor Unions. As a whole, the May 4 Movement represented revolt against defeat and humiliation, reaction against warlordism and localism, protest against economic hardships and exploitation, and reaction against the privileged position of foreign merchants and investors.

Evolution of Communist Strategy. The Russian Communists and the Communist International (Comintern) watched developments in China with great interest. In 1920 the second Comintern congress formally adopted Lenin's long-standing thesis expounding a two-stage theory of revolution in backward countries, according to which a "bourgeois-democratic" revolution would be followed by a "proletarian-socialist" revolution. Since the Communists were relatively weak, Lenin argued, they could not bring about a revolution alone. As an initial step, it would be necessary to form alliances with all other classes and groups (especially the bourgeoisie and the peasantry) in a national and patriotic struggle against imperialist and feudal oppression. Having attained sufficient strength, the proletariat would then move the revolution to the next stage and establish its own dictatorship. The Comintern dispatched to China an agent—Gregory Voitinsky—to organize the Communist Party.

The formal beginning of the Communist movement in China may be dated with the founding of the Chinese Communist Party (CCP) in 1921. By this time communism had become a familiar ideology to many Chinese intellectuals and a number of communist study groups had been founded in the major cities. On or about July 1, 1921, about a dozen representatives from the various communist groups met in a girls' school in the French section of Shanghai, in what became known as the first congress of the CCP, to give the Party its formal organization and to adopt its first constitution.

Ch'en Tu-hsiu, a respected intellectual, was elected general secretary; among others who attended was Mao Tse-tung. The Comintern was represented by a Dutchman, Henricus Sneevliet (alias Maring), and the Soviet Union by Voitinsky. Chou En-lai and Chu Teh were among some fifty-five "founding members" of the CCP, although they did not attend the first congress.[1]

Mao Tse-tung represented his home province of Hunan (southeast China), where he had been active in patriotic and leftist movements since 1917, when he was twenty-four years old. He had lived in Peking in 1918–19 and had held a minor post in the Peking University library under Li Ta-chao, an important Marxist intellectual, and professor of history and chief librarian at Peking University. While in Peking, Mao met other prominent intellectuals and read widely in Western literature, Marxist as well as non-Marxist. By summer 1920 Mao considered himself a Marxist. Having attended the first congress of the CCP, he returned to Hunan to assume the post of CCP provincial secretary.

The second party congress was held in Shanghai in July 1922. Under Comintern influence, this meeting adopted a manifesto outlining the basic objectives of eliminating imperialism and warlordism and seeking national unity and independence. The CCP resolved to join the Comintern and laid the groundwork for a policy of united front and co-operation with other social classes and groups.

The third party congress was held in June 1923, at which time Mao was elected to the Central Committee. Under Comintern direction, the CCP passed a resolution commending Sun Yat-sen's stand against warlordism and imperialism. The Communists actively sought an alliance with the Nationalists, although some of the former made clear that any co-operation was a matter of expediency and would not be permitted to cloud the Communist objective of eventually seizing power. At the same time, there developed within the CCP the first in a series of internal struggles. One segment of the Party, which reportedly included Mao, criticized Ch'en Tu-hsiu and his associates for the "right" deviation of failing to stress sufficiently the leadership role of the Communist Party in any united front arrangement. Mao's group then attacked a third faction led by Chang Kuo-t'ao for committing the "left" deviationist error of stress-

[1] For a list of those who attended the first congress as well as the founding members of the CCP, see Jerome Ch'en, *Mao and the Chinese Revolution* (New York: Oxford University Press, 1967), Appendix A, pp. 361–62.

ing the purity of the Communist movement and opposing alliance with other parties and groups.

Sun Yat-sen welcomed co-operation with the Communists in the hope of destroying the warlords and attaining national unity. Thus when the KMT held its first national congress in Canton in January 1924, CCP members were admitted to membership as individuals, while the CCP continued its own life as well. Some CCP members reached responsible positions within the KMT; Mao himself was elected an alternate member of the KMT Central Executive Committee.

The first CCP-KMT alliance proved catastrophic for the Communists. Having succeeded Sun Yat-sen, Chiang Kai-shek decided to terminate relations with the Communists. In March 1926, while reiterating his faith in the united front principle, Chiang conducted a purge against Communist leaders in the Kuomintang. The CCP became apprehensive but the Comintern (now under Stalin) insisted on continuing the united front with the Nationalists. This insistence, far from being consistent with Chinese realities, was the consequence of a major struggle between Stalin and Trotsky over the question of leadership after Lenin's death in 1924. Distrustful of the bourgeoisie in general, Trotsky opposed CCP alliance with the KMT. Although by late 1927 Stalin had consolidated his position within the Soviet Party, any alteration of his views would constitute an implicit endorsement of Trotsky's argument. (Later, Stalin quietly assimilated some of Trotsky's beliefs.)

In April 1927 Chiang Kai-shek staged a massive night coup in Shanghai, killing thousands of Communists, virtually eliminating all labor leaders, and nearly finishing off the labor movement in that city. Thus ended the CCP-KMT alliance and the first united front. The incident was a blow to Stalin's position on the Chinese revolution. It also destroyed much of the proletarian base of the Chinese Communist Party.

Although this period was disastrous for the CCP, the Communists learned some important lessons. They discovered the need for military strength and for mass support, the latter to be gained through alliance with all segments of the population except the big bourgeoisie. They insisted that the CCP must lead the united front. They began to grasp the advantages of rural areas over the cities in preparing a communist revolution—an unorthodox idea by any communist standard and a departure from the teachings of Moscow.

As early as 1925, Mao turned his attention to investigating class conditions in China. His early thinking was set forth in the pamphlet *Analysis of Classes in Chinese Society* (March 1926), wherein he sought to identify the "friends" of the revolution and to isolate its "enemies." Having analyzed the conditions of the various classes, he concluded that the proletariat, the peasantry, the petty bourgeoisie, and the national bourgeoisie were among the friends of revolution while the landlords, the big bourgeoisie, and the imperialist agents were its chief enemies.

In 1926–27, Mao conducted a study of peasant conditions in his home province and summarized the results in *Report on an Investigation of the Peasant Movement in Hunan* (March 1927). This was in effect an extension of his 1926 work in which the role of the peasantry in the Communist revolution was examined and dramatized. Mao saw the peasant movement as "a mighty storm," a "hurricane" that would soon sweep before it all forces of oppression. In assessing the relative significance of various social forces in the revolutionary movement, Mao assigned a weight of 70 per cent to the peasants and 30 per cent to the workers—an appraisal that has been deleted from the current editions of this work.[2] The importance of the rural areas and the key role of the peasantry became the basis of Mao Tse-tung's revolutionary strategy. Since the proletariat was an insignificant minority in China, the "communist" revolution had to be based on some other class.

The CCP leadership, headed by Ch'en Tu-hsiu and Li Li-san, attached no particular significance to Mao's conclusions. In fact, meeting in April 1927 (immediately following Chiang's coup), the fifth congress of the CCP censured Mao for his unorthodox views and advocated a policy of insurrection in the cities. But the principal ingredients for a decisive split within the CCP had been introduced. Stressing the impracticality of directly seizing the urban, industrialized centers, Mao's group advocated a program of agitation in the countryside, peasant organization, and armed struggle. The opposing faction refused to change its strategy and went underground in Shanghai.

In September 1927, Mao Tse-tung organized a peasant uprising to coincide with the autumn harvest in Hunan. After the uprising failed, he led a contingent of armed peasants into the rugged Ching-

[2] For a detailed discussion of this point, see the exchange between Professors Benjamin I. Schwartz and Karl A. Wittfogel in *The China Quarterly*, No. 1 (January–March 1960), pp. 72–86 and No. 2 (April–June 1960), pp. 16–42, and the sources cited therein.

kang mountains on the border between Hunan and Kiangsi. There he created a revolutionary base, set up a worker-peasant government, and launched a program of land redistribution. In 1928, Chu Teh and Chou En-lai, who had been conducting uprisings in southern Hunan, joined forces with Mao and Communist armed strength gained significantly. For the next three years, in relative isolation from government troops, Mao and his associates concentrated on building the Red Army and expanding the rural base areas ("soviets"). In 1931, at the first congress of the soviets at Juichin, Kiangsi province, a Chinese Soviet Republic was proclaimed and Mao was elected chairman of the Central Soviet government.

During the same period Mao devoted a great deal of attention to the development of a host of revolutionary techniques. The early Communist experience was reviewed and summarized in *Why Is It That Red Political Power Can Exist in China?* (October 1928), *The Struggle in the Chingkang Mountains* (November 1928), *On Correcting Mistaken Ideas in the Party* (November 1929), and *A Single Spark Can Start a Prairie Fire* (January 1930). These were optimistic works stressing the ineptness of the "White" (KMT) regime and forecasting an eventual Communist victory. Special emphasis was placed on armed struggle, peasant guerrilla warfare, and the capture of cities from bases in the countryside. Mao insisted, however, that armed struggle was not the only function of the Red Army: economic, political, propaganda, and organizational tasks were equally important.

Mao quickly found that the White regime, far from being a cohesive political force, was divided by constant strife. When the ruling classes conflict with one another, he argued, the Red regime can pursue a "comparatively venturesome" policy. When there is relative stability in the ruling regime, revolutionaries must adopt a tactic of "gradual advance" and concentrate on consolidating their base areas. Realizing the relative weakness of the Communists, Mao called for patience, devotion, and hard work. Given the leadership of the Communist Party, he insisted, all difficulties would be overcome.

Mao's early successes had an important effect upon CCP leadership. At the sixth congress of the Party in July 1928, he was elected to the Central Committee although he did not even attend. The Party stressed the basic ingredients of Mao's strategy and severely criticized Ch'en Tu-hsiu for seeking premature victory in the urban centers. In 1929 Ch'en was expelled from the Party altogether; Li

Li-san was purged a year later in September 1930. The way seemed clear for Mao's assumption of leadership but another "deviation" soon developed.

From 1931 to 1935 a new "left opportunist" line expounded by Wang Ming (Ch'en Shao-yu) gained ascendancy in the Party. (In the early period of communist history, aliases were adopted frequently for security reasons.) Wang Ming was one of a group of Chinese youths who had been influenced by Trotsky while studying in the U.S.S.R. and who, upon their return, had become known as the Twenty-eight Bolsheviks. The Wang Ming group, according to official CCP history, revived the Li Li-san line by stressing quick victory in the cities, denying the importance of military activity in the countryside, and opposing united front with other parties and groups. Throughout this period, Mao was effectively barred from a position of influence within the CCP.

The Nationalists in Power. In 1926–27, Chiang Kai-shek, in addition to attacking the Communists, conducted a series of successful campaigns against the warlords and toward national unification. In 1927 his troops reached Nanking, where he consolidated his military position, set up his capital, and established the Nationalist government (1928–37). In 1928, the cause of national unity was furthered when Chiang gained control over Peking (the traditional "Northern Capital," which he renamed Peiping or "Northern Peace") and the jurisdiction of his government was recognized by many warlords.

Dominated by Chiang, the Nanking government was far from permissive or "democratic." Chiang's policies, though declared to be based on Sun Yat-sen's ideas, never actually proceeded beyond the stage of "political tutelage," that is, party dictatorship. The KMT and its Central Executive Committee exercised complete control over government and administration. Aided by German military advisers, Chiang was ambitious to build a powerful army under his personal control. Party, government, and army became indistinguishable; and Chiang simultaneously headed all three. By the early 1930s, the Nanking government was rapidly losing public support—even though it had successfully pursued a program of "rights recovery" that abolished unequal treaties, reclaimed foreign concessions, and recovered tariff autonomy for China.

In 1930, Chiang began a series of five campaigns to wipe out the Communists and destroy their strongholds. He was repelled by the

Red Army in the first (December 1930), second (spring 1931), and fourth (winter 1932–33) campaigns; and he was forced to withdraw from the third (fall 1931) after the Japanese had invaded China. The last campaign was different.

Employing overwhelming military power and a German-devised policy of multiple blockades in concentric circles, Chiang was able to overpower the Communist forces. By 1934, the Red Army faced the alternatives of being completely destroyed or crashing through Chiang's lines. Thus began, on October 15, 1934, the famous Long March from southeast China (Kiangsi) to northwest China (Shensi), covering some six thousand miles of deserts, mountains, and rivers. Committing military blunders and following a predictable course, the Red Army suffered heavy casualties. The severity of the situation compelled a meeting of the Politburo of the CCP Central Committee at Tsunyi (Kweichou province) in January 1935. Mao Tsetung succeeded in consolidating his forces, crushing the opposition, and emerging as undisputed leader—a position he was to hold for about three decades.

When the Red Army reached Shensi in October 1935, only twenty thousand of the original one hundred thousand troops remained.[3] The March had been a feat of endurance, and having participated in it remains to this day a matter of supreme honor and prestige. In 1936, the CCP established its new headquarters in Yenan, Shensi province.

The Japanese Invasion. When the Japanese launched an invasion of northeast China in September 1931, the Communists immediately stressed that national unity and resistance to the foreign aggressor took precedence over all other tasks. As early as 1933, the CCP offered a new alliance with the KMT on the condition that the latter would end its attacks on the Red Army, but the KMT refused. Chiang's initial decision was not to concentrate on resisting the Japanese invaders until he had first suppressed and defeated the Communists—a decision that was resented by some of his close associates. He changed his position and consented to a new united front only after he had been kidnapped and detained by one of his

---

[3] These figures are given by some Western scholars, including John K. Fairbank, *The United States and China,* revised edition (New York: The Viking Press, 1962), p. 234. Communist figures are thirty thousand and three hundred thousand, respectively. See Hu Chiao-mu's official CCP history, *Thirty Years of the Communist Party of China,* fourth edition (Peking: Foreign Languages Press, 1959), p. 44.

own (apparently pro-Communist) officers, Chang Hsueh-liang, in December 1936. Under the terms of the new alliance, Chiang agreed to relax his military blockade of the Communists, in return for which the CCP agreed to abandon its policy of insurrection, place the Red Army (now reorganized into the Eighth Route Army and the New Fourth Army) under KMT command, and relax its policy of land redistribution in the countryside. Not even the combined CCP-KMT strength was sufficient to withstand the Japanese armies, however. Gradually, the Communists settled down for a protracted conflict with Japan.

This gave Mao Tse-tung opportunity to develop his military thinking. In a series of major works—*On Tactics Against Japanese Imperialism* (December 1935), *Problems of Strategy in China's Revolutionary War* (December 1936), *Problems of Strategy in Guerrilla War Against Japan* (May 1938), *On Protracted War* (May 1938), and *Problems of War and Strategy* (November 1938)— Mao wrote the most exhaustive treatment by any Communist of the political, economic, and military problems of revolution and war. In particular, he argued, since the enemy is superior in power, the war would be protracted, undergoing (from the standpoint of the revolutionaries) three stages of development: "strategic defensive," "strategic stalemate," and "strategic counteroffensive." Because the revolutionaries were weak, Mao insisted, they were bound to lose ground in the initial phases of the conflict. Meanwhile, it was necessary to develop over a vast territory a war of maneuver to harass the enemy and undermine his effectiveness and morale. This required mass political mobilization, a united front of "the whole people," and the development of peasant guerrilla warfare on a national scale. Having attained sufficient strength, the revolutionaries would then launch a counteroffensive to destroy the enemy. The over-all strategy was summed up in the following terms: ". . . we should resolutely fight a decisive engagement in every campaign or battle in which we are sure of victory; we should avoid a decisive engagement in every campaign or battle in which we are not sure of victory; and we should absolutely avoid a strategically decisive engagement on which the fate of the whole nation is staked."[4]

The formation of the second CCP-KMT alliance and the resultant national unity appear to have forced Japan to intensify her invasion.

[4] "On Protracted War" (May 1938), *Selected Works,* II (Peking: Foreign Languages Press, 1965), p. 180.

Japanese armies quickly overran North China and captured the capital city of Nanking in December 1937. The national capital was moved to Hankow, which was captured a year later, and then moved to Chungking. By 1939, the Japanese forces controlled most of the major cities. Increasing corruption within the KMT and the worsening of domestic economic difficulties (particularly inflation), marked a rapid deterioration in Chiang's position, while the CCP gained in power and prestige. By 1940–41, Chiang became so fearful of the growing strength of the Communists and their ability to attract public support that he reinstituted the policy of military blockade. In January 1941, KMT troops launched a fierce assault against the New Fourth Army and thus began a semiconcealed civil war—a war within a war.

In northern and central China, the Communists were exceedingly effective in exploiting the weaknesses of the KMT. The CCP attracted widespread public support by projecting itself as the leader of a great patriotic struggle against Japan and picturing the KMT as traitor to the people's cause. It embarked on a large-scale policy of land reform in the "liberated areas." It instituted a "tripartite representative system" (the "three thirds" formula), according to which the Communists, the "progressives," and the "middle-of-the-roaders" each occupied one third of the key governmental positions. It dramatized and propagandized the autocratic and dictatorial rule of the KMT. And it capitalized on the tremendous prestige of Sun Yat-sen by formally adopting his Three People's Principles as its "minimum program."

The Communists enjoyed a number of other advantages as well: (1) they did not have to maintain a formal government; (2) they had no cities to defend, no industrial centers to protect; (3) they benefited from years of experience in guerrilla warfare; and (4) they enjoyed the superior political and military leadership of such figures as Mao Tse-tung, Chu Teh, Liu Shao-ch'i, Chou En-lai, and Lin Piao.

CCP confidence and optimism were systematically reflected in Mao's *The Chinese Revolution and the Chinese Communist Party* (December 1939)[5] and *On New Democracy* (January 1940), in

[5] According to the editors of Mao's *Selected Works,* this pamphlet "was written jointly by Comrade Mao Tse-tung and several other comrades. . . . The first chapter, 'Chinese Society,' was drafted by other comrades and revised by Comrade Mao Tse-tung. The second chapter, 'The Chinese Revolution,' was written by Comrade Mao Tse-tung himself. Another chapter, scheduled to deal with

which he envisioned the emergence of a new China out of centuries of oppression and exploitation. In this process, Mao argued, the crucial role would be played by the Communist Party, especially in determining successive united front policies and in conducting military struggle. He reiterated Lenin's argument on the two stages of revolutionary struggle in backward countries: the Communists would co-operate with bourgeois nationalists and the peasantry in a new-democratic (bourgeois-democratic) revolution to overthrow imperialism and feudalism, after which they would break off and engineer a "proletarian revolution" on their own initiative.

Having experienced a relative growth in prestige and numbers, the CCP conducted a *Cheng-feng* ("rectification campaign") in 1941–44 in order to cleanse its ranks of all "deviationist" tendencies and to establish ideological control. A large-scale program of Communist study and indoctrination was launched in the "liberated areas." In a series of works—*Reform Our Study* (May 1941), *Rectify the Party's Style of Work* (February 1942), *Oppose Stereotyped Party Writing* (February 1942), and *Talks at the Yenan Forum on Literature and Art* (May 1942)—Mao set forth the principles of ideological remolding and thought reform. He attacked "subjectivism," "sectarianism," "stereotyped party writing," and all other "bourgeois" tendencies. He stressed the importance of "culture" in the Communist revolutionary program and saw art and literature as means for propagandizing the Party's goals and raising the "revolutionary consciousness" of the masses. An extensive analysis of the various "deviationist" lines within the Party was undertaken in a *Resolution on Certain Questions in the History of Our Party,* drafted by Mao and adopted by the CCP in April 1945.

The Communist Takeover. When the Japanese surrendered in August 1945, the CCP was fully prepared to turn the anti-Japanese war into a "people's war" against the KMT. Before unleashing a full-scale civil war, Mao proposed a coalition government with the KMT in which the Communists would have an effective voice. The basis for this proposal was Mao's report *On Coalition Government,* submitted to and approved by the seventh congress of the CCP in April–June 1945. For six weeks (August 28–October 11, 1945),

'Party Building,' was left unfinished by the comrades working on it" (explanatory note on p. 305, Vol. II). Although the extent of Mao's revision is unknown, this pamphlet may be treated as his own work, since it is officially included among his writings and since he has expressed similar views elsewhere.

Mao Tse-tung met with Chiang Kai-shek at Chungking (southwest China) to negotiate the details of the coalition government and nationalization of all armed forces. But no concrete agreement was reached, partly because Chiang's real intentions appear to have been to dissolve and absorb the CCP troops. For his part, Mao insisted on maintaining sufficient Communist military and political strength eventually to overthrow the Chiang regime.

In December 1945, General George C. Marshall of the United States arrived in China with a proposal for a coalition government representing the major parties. A political consultative conference met in January 1946 and agreed on convening a national assembly formally to arrange the coalition government. But both sides violated the agreement, each confident that it would get the better of the other. In particular, General Marshall was so alarmed by Chiang's uncompromising attitude toward negotiations that in July 1946 he recommended a brief suspension of American military and economic assistance to the KMT, which by then was being administered on a massive scale. The United States did urge the Kuomintang to reform itself, but the KMT was beyond reach: leadership remained inept, dictatorship continued, corruption intensified, workers and peasants became increasingly discontented, and students and intellectuals were increasingly alienated by police tactics. Domestic economic problems, particularly inflation, became exceedingly acute. One scholar has found, for example, that "Prices rose by 40–50 per cent per annum in 1937–39, 160 per cent per annum in 1939–41, and 300 per cent per annum in 1942–45. At the end of the Resistance War [against Japan] the general price index stood at 10,075 with its December 1941 level at 100."[6]

In the civil war that ensued, KMT troops rapidly recaptured cities in south China, but the situation was different in the north, where the Red Army had long maintained powerful bases. The major area of CCP-KMT conflict was Manchuria, which the Yalta Pact of February 1945 had placed under U.S.S.R. control in return for Soviet participation in the war against Japan. While the U.S.S.R. made entry difficult for the Nationalist forces, it permitted, in violation of its pledge to the KMT, Communist military units to enter Manchuria, a prize which held a triple attraction for the CCP. Manchuria would provide the Communists with vital industrial facilities; it would put them in direct contact with the Soviet Union; and it

[6] Ch'en, op. cit., p. 245.

would provide them with a secure base from which to drive southward.

The balance of forces between the Communists and the Nationalists, although several times favoring the latter in 1945, quickly began to change and reached rough parity by mid-1948. From late 1947 on, Chiang's troops suffered consistent defeats at the hands of the Red Army, now called the People's Liberation Army (PLA). The most spectacular Nationalist success was the capture in March 1947 of the Communist capital of Yenan, which was recaptured by the PLA in April 1948. By 1949, the Communists had completed the conquest of Manchuria and had occupied Canton, Hankow, Nanking, Peking, Shanghai, and most other major cities. The victorious mood of the CCP was reflected in Mao's *On the People's Democratic Dictatorship* (June 1949), in which he stressed the need for an autocratic government led by the Communist Party and based on the alliance of workers and peasants. The Nationalists, rapidly changing capitals, finally found themselves on Taiwan. Mao Tse-tung proclaimed the Chinese People's Republic (CPR) on October 1, 1949.

The most significant reasons for the success of the Communists included: (1) the ineptness of the Chiang regime and the unpopularity of KMT dictatorship; (2) the progressive worsening of domestic conditions and the consequent alienation of large segments of the population; (3) the Japanese invasion, which helped weaken the Nationalists and render the Chiang government unable to control northern China, where the CCP became entrenched; and (4) the revolutionary strategy of Mao Tse-tung and the CCP promise to return to the Chinese people their national pride and integrity.

The Communists in Power

Having captured political power, the new Communist regime confronted a series of tasks in three principal areas: national unification, economic development, and foreign relations. Each will be considered in turn.

National Unification. The unification of the country took place in a rapid and efficient manner. It has been maintained in the face of periodic eruptions of regionalism and localism, most recently in

Canton, Shanghai, and elsewhere, arising from the cultural revolution. The Communist regime launched a massive program of reorganization and reconstruction. Three distinct but interlocking bureaucracies—the government, the army, and the Party—reached out from the center and penetrated the remotest parts of the land.

A Communist governmental machinery was put into operation immediately upon the seizure of power. Meeting in Peking in September 1949, a Chinese People's Political Consultative Conference (CPPCC) adopted three fundamental documents under which the national government operated until a CPR Constitution was proclaimed in September 1954. These documents were the Organic Law of the CPPCC, the Organic Law of the Central People's Government, and the Common Program.

The CPPCC was in effect a constituent assembly and its organic (i.e., basic) law stipulated that it would continue to function until a new constitution was adopted. Some attempt was made to render the CPPCC representative of all major parties and groups, although the Communist Party clearly dominated the scene. The Organic Law of the People's Government created a centralized bureaucracy consisting of ministries, councils, commissions, and so on. The Common Program spelled out the general ideological underpinnings of the provisional government. It specified "new democracy" as the basis of political rule and sketched the Communist position on a series of domestic and foreign issues.

The 1954 Constitution incorporated the Organic Law of the CPPCC and defined the state as "a people's democratic state" under the leadership of the proletariat. It created a National People's Congress as the sole legislative body and "the highest organ of state authority" with complete centralized control over corresponding congresses at the provincial, county, and district levels. The membership of each congress is determined by people's congresses at successively lower levels; only members of the lowest (*hsiang* or rural township) level congresses are selected by direct popular election. The Constitution created a State Council consisting of a premier and sixteen vice-premiers, a Supreme People's Court, a National Defense Council, and a variety of ministries and lesser organizations.

The army has always been a crucial component of Chinese Communism and a political and economic arm of the Party (see Chapter V). It has consisted of two main parts, the regular army (PLA) and the people's militia. The importance of the military is nowhere more apparent than in the fact that it has always been represented at the highest levels of the Communist hierarchy, including the Politburo. Lin Piao's rise to power in 1966–68 boosted further the prestige of the military.

The regular armed forces come under the control of three primary institutions: (1) the National Defense Council, a CPR committee headed by the CPR chairman and responsible for co-ordinating the country's military and defense efforts; (2) the Ministry of National Defense, a regular CPR department which exercises direct command and transmits the Council's decisions to the various agencies; and (3) the General Staff of the PLA, which enjoyed considerable autonomy in decision-making until it was placed under the National Defense Council in 1958.

The people's militia, from the revolution's earliest days in the rough countryside, has played an important role in popularizing the importance of discipline and preparedness; daily military exercises have been a routine of Chinese life since the Communist takeover. A people's militia was particularly stressed during the land reform period of 1950–52 and the commune movement of 1958 (see below). It again became prominent in connection with the Vietnam conflict and the felt need for maximum preparedness in case of a confrontation with the United States.

The governmental and military bureaucracies come under minute Party control. The Party is itself an elitist and pyramidal organization dictating policy in every office, factory, school, farm, and trade union throughout the country. Theoretically, political supremacy lies with the National Party Congress (to be distinguished from the National People's Congress of the CPR) and the corresponding Party congresses at the regional, provincial, county, and district levels. Presumably, each Party congress is supreme at its own level and controls all other organizations at that level; each elects representatives to the higher congresses. In fact, however, final authority in all instances rests with the Central Committee (of the National Party Congress), a body of about one hundred regular members and one hundred alternates, the Central Committee's Politburo of about twenty men, and the Politburo's Standing Committee of a half dozen men. A great variety of Central Committee departments—social, financial, industrial, rural, military, propaganda—carry out the day-to-day functions of control under a Secretariat elected by the Politburo. These departments are duplicated on the regional, provincial, county, and district levels. Organization literally reaches out over the entire country in a great wave of concentric rings.

The operating principle of Party organization has always been "democratic centralism," officially (and tautologically) defined as "centralism on the basis of democracy and democracy under centralized leadership." This means, in practical terms, subordination of the lower party levels to the higher levels and of the entire organization to the Standing Committee of the Politburo of the Central Committee. This enables the leadership to determine all policies ("centralism") while the rank and file is given the opportunity to "participate" in these policies and to carry them out ("democracy"). The entire enterprise aims at discipline and control. It is also effective in creating illusions of "democracy" and "equality." The unquestioned supremacy of the CCP has been formalized in the official slogan, "Politics in Command."

A massive program of ideological indoctrination instituted immediately upon the regime's founding employed every conceivable medium of force, persuasion, and propaganda. A host of mass organizations absorbed the workers and peasants. All art forms were revolutionized. New dramas, stories, songs, dances, and ballads were written to glorify the Communist revolution. Everywhere traditional values were denounced and communist virtues idealized.

"Education" became a passion and it was made compulsory, mass, and universal. The educational system was revamped several times—most recently in connection with the cultural revolution—to eliminate "bourgeois" and foreign tendencies. Great emphasis was placed on technical courses and technical training in anticipation of economic tasks ahead. The entire effort was geared, needless to say, to the Communist program of constructing a new socialist society.

By 1955, the CCP was in complete control of the situation and in close touch with the masses throughout the country. Party cadres were instructed to maintain close contact with the local population. Study groups and indoctrination meetings became life patterns of an entire country. "Thought reform," "ideological remolding," and "rectification campaigns" ("brainwashing" is not an accurate term) sought to transform the traditional Chinese personality into the "new" Communist man. The principal instruments of rectification continue to be "criticism and self-criticism," public confessions, admission of one's shortcomings and the declaration of intention to overcome them. Whether conducted inside the Communist Party or in society at large, rectification campaigns correspond, in their basic objective, to the Stalinist purges. In China, however, with the exception of the cultural revolution, they have not involved large-scale violence and bloodshed.

In 1956–57, the CCP, always intensely interested in the intellectuals, turned its attention directly toward them. A policy of encouraging the intellectuals to participate in the affairs of the state (as a means of overcoming their "bourgeois" tendencies) was adopted at a plenary session of the Central Committee in November 1956, where Mao reportedly set the "Hundred Flowers" slogan in motion. In February 1957, he delivered a speech, *On the Correct Handling of Contradictions Among the People,* stressing the policy of "Let a hundred flowers blossom, a hundred schools of thought contend."

Taking advantage of the opportunity, the intellectuals launched a fierce verbal assault against the Party, questioning its achievements and criticizing its monopoly of power and arbitrary rule. Shaken by the unexpected vehemence of the attack, the CCP immediately imposed an "anti-rightist" campaign and silenced the opposition. Mao's February speech, published in June, imposed serious constraints on the kinds of criticism that would be permitted. For practical purposes all "blossoming" and "contending" came to an end.

The cultural revolution of 1965–68 represented a wide-ranging rectification campaign that underwent distinct phases of development. The initial phase was a systematic attack on all remnants of "bourgeois" culture and marked the downfall of Party and army functionaries, government officials, professors and intellectuals. Opposition was apparently centered in the Peking Municipal Party Committee, the Propaganda Department of the CCP Central Committee, and Peking University. The purge of high-ranking officials revealed a major split in CCP ranks and the most serious challenge to Mao's leadership. It shattered the conventional belief in the homogeneity and stability of the Chinese Communist elite.

The second phase of the cultural revolution was dominated by the Red Guards—presumably Mao's youthful disciples—and involved much violence and destruction. Early in 1967 the movement spread to farms and factories and resulted in strikes and armed clashes among the factions. Although it did not massively disrupt the economy, its effect on both industry and agriculture was quickly felt. As events threatened to tear the country apart, units of the PLA, always quietly in the background, intervened to maintain stability and control.

The autumn of 1967 marked a third phase in the cultural revolution. The movement was conspicuously toned down, the Red Guards were called upon to curb their activities, and China's universities were reopened after an eighteen-month shutdown. Intent on preventing an economic breakdown, the Communist regime called on the masses to "grasp revolution and promote production." A series of "revolutionary committees" formed in 1967–68 at local and provincial levels were based on "three-in-one" alliances representing a compromise between Mao's forces, their CCP rivals, and army functionaries. The armed forces continued to occupy pivotal positions throughout the country.

The spring of 1968 signaled a fourth phase in the cultural revolution. The pervasive power of the military began to disturb Mao Tse-tung. The pre-eminence accorded the PLA was, strictly speaking, "un-Marxist" and a violation of Mao's dictum that "the Party must command the gun," not vice versa (see Chapter IV). The April 1968 purge of General Yang Ch'eng-wu, the acting chief of staff and a major figure in the cultural revolution, may have indicated dissension within the military establishment. More importantly, it began a trend toward re-establishing CCP supremacy consistent with the slogan of "Politics in Command."

The process of rebuilding the Party (and restabilizing the country as a whole) was not a smooth one, and there were eruptions of violence from time to time. Such violence is likely to be a recurring phenomenon until such time as the more moderate forces in China have succeeded in asserting their supremacy. In the process, it is of course possible that Mao's forces may be decisively defeated and overthrown. A trend toward relative stability—and a fifth phase in the cultural revolution—became noticeable through the summer and fall of 1968, when conservative Party and army forces appeared to gain significantly over the militants. The more radical elements (e.g., Red Guards) were quieted throughout China, "working-class leadership" regained prominence, worker-peasant-soldier alliance came to the fore, "production" emerged as a central concern, and order and stability were sought everywhere. In September 1968, the Mao-controlled press claimed "all-round victory" in the cultural revolution and announced the formation of revolutionary committees (in fact, coalition governments) throughout the country. Sporadic violence continued, however, as significant segments of the Red Guards resisted their subordinate position.

The cultural revolution was engineered and personally led by Mao Tse-tung. Its basic objectives appear to have been to guard against bureaucratic entrenchment through a shakeup of Party, army, and government hierarchies, to keep the leaders in close touch with the masses, and to revive the revolutionary spirit and enthusiasm (particularly in the youth) that seemed rapidly to be dissipating (see Chapter II). It is now clear that, once started, the cultural revolution gathered its own momentum, moving in directions that Mao had not anticipated and, in some cases, of which he could not have approved.

The upheaval resulted in a serious setback for China and Mao Tse-tung's leadership. Widespread domestic violence led to loss of international prestige. It adversely affected China's economic and industrial progress, as well as its once successful (apparently) nuclear development program. It fragmented and weakened the Communist Party as never before. And it led to the disaffection of the very youth that Mao had set out to "revolutionize." The military was the only group sufficiently cohesive to assume a decisive stabilizing role.

Economic Development. Communist Chinese economic policies have had two primary objectives: agricultural modernization and industrial development. The regime's attempt at agricultural reform and the transformation of peasants into modern producers underwent three stages of development: co-operativization (land reform, mutual-aid teams, and "lower" co-operatives), collectivization ("higher" co-operatives), and commune-ization.

Land reform was accomplished through the Agrarian Reform Law of June 1950, which in less than two years revolutionized social relationships in the countryside by eliminating the feudal aristocracy and redistributing the land among the peasants. The land reform program was accompanied by the creation of mutual-aid teams that pooled their land, labor, and farm implements. This was a step toward eventual collectivization of agriculture but the CCP stressed the importance of voluntary participation, incentives, and rewards.

In 1953–54 a program of Agricultural Producers Co-operatives (APCs) was launched. Initially the regime sought to develop "lower" APCs under unified management as a means of introducing the peasants to socialism. Voluntarism and the incentive principle were retained, and the peasants were to receive dividends for the shares of land which they had contributed.

Mao's speech of July 1955, *On the Question of Agricultural Co-operativization,* signaled an intensification of agricultural reform. In January 1956 the CCP announced that "lower" APCs had been fully developed and that the stage was set for the introduction of the principle of collectivization. This took the form of "higher" APCs in which the peasants would surrender their land; private ownership would not be permitted. The creation of each "higher" APC involved the amalgamation of several "lower" APCs, so that the boundaries of the former would coincide with the boundaries of a "natural village" of some one hundred households. Within two years, most Chinese peasants found themselves in "higher" APCs.

The year 1958 marked the beginning of the "Great Leap Forward" in China's economic development and the further amalgamation of "higher" APCs into thousands of communes in which "collective ownership" was replaced by "ownership by the whole people." A number of experimental communes were established quite early in the spring of 1958 but the official decision on the creation of the commune system was not announced until late August. By fall, some twenty-six thousand communes were established throughout the country.

Each commune was intended as a self-sufficient economic, social, and military unit. Special emphasis was placed on industrial development and back-yard blast furnaces studded the countryside. Communal kitchens, mess halls, nurseries, and schools were established. The basic family unit was weakened and women were placed in the center of production activity. The wage system was replaced by a combination of wages and "free supply" of food and clothing. An official slogan called for "more, better, faster, and more economical results."

The commune system involved widespread militarization and the arming of the peasantry. Each commune was considered a unit of the people's militia. Production teams, production brigades, and production battalions were set up, closely resembling military organization. Commune members were awakened at dawn and marched off to work in military formations.

The commune system was intended to make possible more efficient utilization of labor, permit dispersion of population and industry (both important in case of war), and facilitate ideological remolding and Party control. The system as a whole was presented as a step toward the creation of a future communist society.

The commune enthusiasm did not last very long; by December 1958 it was already clear that commune-ization had been premature and that the cadres had issued unwarranted and overoptimistic reports. The experiment had proved greatly wasteful of both resources and manpower; commune products were extremely poor in quality; some (e.g., back-yard steel) were not only costly but literally unusable. Limitations in capital, resources, and technical and managerial skill forced a drastic slowdown. Production targets were revised downward by 50 per cent or more, cadres were disciplined, and the regime popularized the "Red and Expert" slogan, stressing ideological commitment as well as technical proficiency. By August 1959, "higher" APCs had become fashionable once again. Two years later, the regime had turned all the way back to "lower" APCs and the peasants were allowed private plots of land. Thus began a three-year economic crisis in China, and it was exacerbated by the most serious natural disasters in many decades.

The failure of the commune system marked a personal setback for Mao Tse-tung. In December 1958, he resigned as CPR chairman (a position he had held simultaneously with his CCP chairmanship), nominally in order to devote his entire attention to Party and theoretical work. It now appears plausible that this resignation was more or less forced by Liu Shao-ch'i (among others), who was named CPR chairman in April 1959. This incident may have played a significant role in the subsequent friction between the two men.

Soviet economic assistance to China (1950–60) was administered effectively and it laid the foundation for China's emergence as a world industrial power. Soviet aid for economic development amounted to about 2.5 billion dollars (a minor sum considering the fact that U.S. assistance to Taiwan has been at about the same level). The U.S.S.R. also provided thousands of technical advisers and substantial machinery and equipment.

China's First Five-Year Plan (1953–57) emphasized industrial development, especially heavy industry (coal, steel, iron, electricity, petroleum, machine tools). The Plan was primarily designed to strengthen the military and industrial base of China, with little attention to consumer goods. Most economic assets came under direct state control; most private firms were converted into joint state-private enterprises; most small businesses were reorganized into co-operatives.

The Second Five-Year Plan (1958–62) involved little or no change from its predecessor. Industry continued to get most of the attention, although greater emphasis was placed on light industry. In the first year of the Second Plan, China sought to take a "leap forward" from agricultural backwardness into industrial modernity. The announcement was formally made that China would surpass Great Britain in fifteen years. As the failure of the great leap became apparent, greater and greater emphasis was placed on agriculture. The slogan "Walking on Two Legs" stressed the simultaneous development of agriculture and industry. Another timely slogan insisted that "The whole Party and the whole people go in for agriculture in a big way."

The early 1960s were years of economic recovery and consolidation in Communist China. Some segments of Chinese industry seem to have made a significant comeback, as shown by break-throughs in atomic and nuclear technology since 1964. The Third Five-Year Plan, which technically should have covered the 1963–67 period, was not announced until 1966. Although its text was not immediately released, the Plan appeared to stress the simultaneous development of agriculture, heavy industry, and light industry.

Foreign Relations. Communist Chinese foreign policy must be approached, for the most part, in terms of three intertwined sets of relationships: (1) those with the United States, (2) those with the Soviet Union, and (3) those with the underdeveloped countries of the "third world."

Sino-American Relations. The early Communist Chinese attitude toward the international situation was, in general terms, positive and optimistic. In 1945 Mao Tse-tung himself described Great Britain, the United States, and the U.S.S.R. as the "three great democracies" which together with China and France would help bring about an era of international stability and peace. He wrote: "The great efforts of the peoples of . . . [these countries] have made possible the defeat of the fascists, after which the peoples of these nations will build a world of stable and lasting peace. The United Nations Conference in San Francisco . . . will be the starting point of this peace."[7]

---

[7] "On Coalition Government" (April 1945), in Conrad Brandt, Benjamin

From the establishment of the CPR in October 1949 to the outbreak of the Korean conflict in June 1950, little change occurred in Peking's relatively optimistic image of the world environment. The major issue clouding Sino-American relations was Taiwan. But although the United States had sided firmly with the Chiang Kai-shek regime since the early 1940s, the Communists appeared to entertain the hope that an amicable solution would somehow be reached.

The Korean conflict decisively changed Peking's attitude not only toward the United States but toward the United Nations as well: the latter came to be viewed as an "agent of U.S. imperialism." On July 7, 1950, the Security Council established a unified command for UN forces in Korea and the next day General Douglas MacArthur was named commander. As UN forces crossed the 38th parallel on October 7, 1950, pressing toward the Chinese border at the Yalu River, the Peking regime became sufficiently concerned to intervene. On February 1, 1951, the General Assembly declared Peking an "aggressor," and on May 18 it recommended an embargo on military and strategic materials to Communist China and North Korea.

President Truman's decision to dispatch the Seventh Fleet to the Taiwan Straits in June 1950 dashed any Communist hope of capturing Formosa. Taiwan became the permanent symbol of mutual hostility in Sino-American relations, and the U.S. policy of "containment" of China was launched. Subsequently, a series of agreements with Australia, Japan, New Zealand, South Korea, and other countries completed the U.S. wall around China.

The several years that followed the Korean settlement were marked by a relative relaxation of militancy in Peking's foreign policy. From early 1954 to late 1957 China adopted a moderate attitude in world affairs by sponsoring a policy of "peaceful coexistence." Designed primarily to improve China's relations with the underdeveloped countries, this policy was also employed in an apparent desire to settle certain difficulties with the United States. At the Bandung Conference of April 1955 (see below), Chou En-lai declared that "The Chinese Government is willing to sit down and enter into negotiations with the U. S. Government to discuss the question of relaxing tension in the Far East, and especially the question of relaxing tension in the Taiwan area."[8]

Schwartz, and John K. Fairbank, *A Documentary History of Chinese Communism* (Cambridge: Harvard University Press, 1952), p. 296. This passage does not appear in the current editions of this work.

[8] New York *Times,* April 24, 1955.

When it became clear that a favorable American response would not be forthcoming, Peking reverted to its former policy of uncompromising hostility toward the United States. This attitude was aggravated by other developments, notably the failure of the great leap forward and the widening rift with the Soviet Union. Chou's Bandung initiative did lead to the beginning of talks in Geneva (1955–58) and Warsaw (since 1958) between U.S. and Chinese ambassadors; more than 140 talks have already been held.

Over the past decade, Chinese attitudes toward the United States have been exacerbated by U.S. advocacy of a "two Chinas" policy that would in effect make Taiwan a permanent, independent state. As early as January 1955, the "two Chinas" plan was known to be under "close study" by the Eisenhower Administration.[9] Writing in April 1960, Chester Bowles—soon to become Undersecretary of State under President Kennedy—called for "the creation and implementation of imaginative policies based on the reality of two Chinas."[10] On December 13, 1963, Roger Hilsman, then Assistant Secretary of State for Far Eastern Affairs, put forward the proposition that some kind of "two Chinas" policy must become the basis for accommodation with the Chinese Communists.[11]

The most insurmountable difficulty associated with the "two Chinas" theme is that it has been rejected—flatly, consistently, and in all its variations—by both the Communists and the Nationalists. The Nationalist view has always been that the mainland is a part of Taiwan; Chiang Kai-shek has repeatedly indicated his determination someday to return to the mainland, throw out the Communists, and reinstate the Kuomintang government. The Communists, for their part, have stressed the inseparability of Taiwan from the mainland. The "liberation" of Taiwan has been their most persistent foreign policy theme.

A most decisive consideration in any discussion of Sino-American relations is that everywhere the Peking regime has found itself surrounded by American military power—in Okinawa, in Taiwan, in South Korea, in Vietnam. Doubtless the Vietnam conflict has brought Sino-American relations to a new peak of hostility. United States policy-makers appear to insist on the proposition that, since China remains intent on a policy of expansion, she must be "con-

[9] New York *Times,* January 21, 1955.
[10] "The 'China Problem' Reconsidered," *Foreign Affairs,* 38:3 (April 1960), p. 486.
[11] New York *Times,* December 14, 1963.

tained." It is argued that just as the United States was able to contain Soviet Communism in Eastern Europe in the postwar period, so it should seek to limit Chinese adventurism in Southeast Asia today.

A key document frequently cited to illustrate Chinese global ambitions is Lin Piao's pamphlet on "people's wars" (see Chapter VI). In this document, the Chinese defense minister develops an analogy in which the underdeveloped countries of Africa, Asia, and Latin America constitute the "rural areas of the world" while the advanced countries of Europe and North America are the "cities." Lin argues that the same strategy of surrounding the cities from the countryside, so successfully employed within China, can be extended and applied on a global scale to defeat world imperialism.

Lin Piao's argument reflects Peking's desire to rally the underdeveloped countries to its cause. Its underlying weakness lies in the elementary fact that Peking has no control over the foreign policies of other states. In fact, Communist China has failed to convince the "third world" that the United States is the chief enemy. So far at least, the forces of nationalism in individual countries have proved far more powerful than any desire for an "international united front." Moreover, it is important to note, Lin stresses that in the making of revolution "self-reliance" may be as important as foreign assistance.

The type of argument that insists on the "containment" of China on grounds of historical analogies overlooks the point that China is not in fact the U.S.S.R., Southeast Asia is not Eastern Europe, and a policy that worked two decades ago is not necessarily applicable to the world situation today. Most importantly, this argument pays insufficient attention to the threat of mutual annihilation posed by a thermonuclear war. Nuclear technology has revolutionized world politics and has made obsolete many precepts of an earlier day. Even in the absence of nuclear weapons, however, to subscribe to a literal interpretation of Lin Piao's argument would be to confuse Chinese intentions with present capabilities. Lin's pamphlet represents an article of faith and a statement of ideological aspiration far more than any practical plan of action.

As far as the Vietnam situation is concerned, although the Chinese Communists have not thus far directly intervened, there is no guarantee that they will not do so. A U.S. land invasion of the north, or an attempt to bring down the Ho Chi Minh regime, or a threat to

Chinese territorial security may draw the Communists into military action.

Peking is probably aware of the price that she would have to pay for intervention, especially regarding her nuclear installations; in fact, this may in part explain the Chinese reluctance to get involved in Vietnam. Nevertheless, the Chinese Communists have taken a number of steps toward military preparedness in the past few years. These include: (1) extension of military service by one year, (2) some preparatory work toward evacuation of the major cities, (3) greater attention to the people's militia, and (4) reinforcement of Chinese troops on the North Vietnamese border.

Sino-Soviet Relations. Until the mid-1950s, Communist Chinese foreign policy was based on Mao Tse-tung's conception of the world as a bipolar division between the camp of socialism led by the Soviet Union and the camp of imperialism led by the United States. In this struggle, Mao insisted, every country must choose sides; there would be no neutrality, no "third road." As for China, Mao made clear in his *On the People's Democratic Dictatorship* (June 1949) that he would be "leaning to one side."

The Soviet Union recognized Communist China on October 2, 1949, barely a day after the founding of the CPR. In December of the same year Mao made an extended trip to Moscow, the most notable outcome of which was the signing in February 1950 of a thirty-year Treaty of Friendship, Alliance, and Mutual Aid between the two countries. Thus began an ambitious program of Soviet economic, technical, and military assistance to China.

Sino-Soviet relations in Stalin's time were not particularly warm or friendly. In fact, considerable friction developed as a result of Soviet insistence on their "special rights" in China, even though China was now under firm Communist rule. These rights included Soviet control over Outer Mongolia, joint management of the principal Manchurian railways, and joint exploitation of petroleum and other resources in Sinkiang.

The years immediately following Stalin's death brought considerable improvement in Sino-Soviet relations. In the fall of 1954 Khrushchev visited Peking and agreed to liquidate Soviet special rights in China. This placed the two regimes on an equal footing but Peking continued to follow Moscow's lead in foreign affairs.

Khrushchev's 1956 attack on Stalin seriously undermined Sino-Soviet relations because it was interpreted by the Chinese as, among other things, a denunciation of Mao and his "cult of personality" as well. The Chinese insisted that although Stalin had made "certain important errors," he was still a "great Marxist-Leninist" whose contributions could not be so easily dismissed. In addition, Peking charged, Khrushchev's attack had greatly weakened the unity of the international Communist movement in general.

In the fall of 1957 the Soviets launched the first sputnik and agreed to help China develop atomic capability. In November of that year Mao visited Moscow and offered a re-evaluation of the "world balance of forces" to show that the Communist bloc of nations had suddenly emerged as a vastly more powerful force in world affairs. He said metaphorically: "I am of the opinion that the international situation has now reached a new turning point. There are two winds in the world today: the East wind and the West wind. There is a Chinese saying: 'Either the East wind prevails over the West wind or the West wind over the East wind.' I think the characteristic of the situation today is the East wind prevailing over the West wind. That is to say, the socialist forces are overwhelmingly superior to the imperialist forces."

The post-Stalinist improvements in Sino-Soviet relations did not last long; an intense conflict between the two powers began to take shape. In the late 1950s, the Soviet Union appears to have suggested several times that Peking adopt an accommodating attitude toward the American policy of "two Chinas," a suggestion which understandably irritated the Chinese. In the summer of 1959 the U.S.S.R. quietly refused to honor a nuclear-sharing agreement it had signed with Peking two years earlier. In 1960 all Soviet economic assistance was terminated and Soviet technicians were withdrawn from China. At the twenty-second congress of the Communist Party of the Soviet Union in October 1961, Khrushchev made the issue of Albania an occasion to deliver another sharp attack upon Mao and his personality cult. In 1962 the U.S.S.R. refused to support Peking in its boundary conflict with India. As Soviet assistance decreased, the Chinese turned to a policy of "self-reliance" in both the economic and military fields.

In the early 1960s, the Sino-Soviet conflict broke into the open and the two Communist countries, through a series of "letters," accused one another of "deviation." The Chinese charged the Russians with collusion with the United States in signing the nuclear test-ban treaty, in the United Nations, in Vietnam, and elsewhere. They characterized the Soviet policy of "peaceful coexistence" and the developing Soviet-American *détente* as a fundamental betrayal, as "Khrushchevism," and (after Khrushchev's fall) as "Khrushchevism without Khrushchev." They criticized the Soviet Union for exaggerating the dangers of nuclear war. (In a 1965 interview with Edgar Snow, Mao did not deny that he may have advocated risking a nuclear war with the United States.[12]) Particularly during the cultural revolution, the Chinese Communists persisted in their claim to be the true inheritors of Marxism-Leninism. The center of world revolution, they maintained, had shifted from Moscow to Peking.

Relations with the Third World. The years following the Korean conflict marked a period of relative moderation in Peking's foreign policy, particularly as far as the underdeveloped countries were concerned. This appears to have been a response, at least in part, to the growing number of "new states" on the world scene and Peking's desire to attract their support. From early 1954 to late 1957 China became the principal exponent of a policy of "peaceful coexistence" in the third world. The "Five Principles of Peaceful Coexistence" were popularized throughout the Asian continent and they formed the basis for a series of treaties with Afghanistan, Burma, India (on Tibet), and Nepal. The five principles included: "(1) mutual respect for each other's territorial integrity and sovereignty, (2) mutual non-aggression, (3) mutual non-interference in each other's internal affairs, (4) equality and mutual benefit, and (5) peaceful coexistence."

The Peking regime was a major force behind the Bandung Conference of April 18–24, 1955. Attended by about thirty countries, the conference went one step beyond the five principles in explicitly introducing anti-imperialism as an integral theme. According to Peking, the "spirit of Bandung" consisted of "stressing areas of agreement rather than points of difference." Chou En-lai identified the "basis for seeking common ground among us" as the attempt to do away with "the sufferings and calamities under colonialism." The "Ten Principles of the Bandung Conference" reiterated and elaborated on the "Five Principles of Peaceful Coexistence."[13]

In the early 1960s, the Chinese Communists, in their simultaneous struggle with both the United States and the U.S.S.R., renewed their

[12] See Edgar Snow, "Interview with Mao Tse-tung," *The New Republic,* February 27, 1965, p. 19.

[13] For a review of the Bandung "tradition," see *Peking Review,* June 18, 1965, pp. 16–18.

policy of alliance and friendship with the peoples of Africa, Asia, and Latin America. They envisioned the emergence of a "third world" as an alternative to both the superpowers. Neutrality and "third road" were no longer disparaged. Indeed, Peking entertained the hope that the underdeveloped countries would form an international united front that would eventually defeat all forces of decadence and reaction, Western as well as non-Western. Chou En-lai conducted a much publicized tour of ten African states in December–January 1963–64 and concluded exuberantly that conditions for revolution were ripe throughout Africa.

China's relations with the underdeveloped countries, it has been at times suggested, have been buttressed by an appeal to racial themes. Not insignificantly, this topic was brought to the world's attention by the Soviet Union in the early 1960s.

In August 1963 *Pravda* openly accused the Chinese of racism. It reported that when the Japanese diplomat Matsumura Kenzo visited Peking in 1962, foreign minister Ch'en Yi assured him that "The East after all remains the East, and the Asians must change world history; we must unite and strengthen the ties between peoples of the same color of skin."[14] A sharp attack on alleged Chinese "racism" was delivered by the Soviet theoretician Mikhail Suslov. In his February 1964 report to the plenum of the Central Committee of the Communist Party of the Soviet Union, Suslov accused the Chinese of attempting to "impose upon the socialist countries a 'Sinified socialism,'" "foment nationalist and even racial sentiments among the peoples fighting against colonialism," "counterpoise the peoples on racial grounds," and espouse "anti-scientific doctrines." He asserted in particular that Mao's slogan "The East wind prevails over the West wind" seeks to substitute "the racial approach for the class approach."[15]

The Chinese Communists may indeed have appealed to a racial theme in their attempt to neutralize the combined American-Soviet pressures and to gain support from the non-white peoples of the world (although they have always denied this). It is unlikely, however, that the Peking regime would actually entertain a notion of racial unity with any other people. For one thing, Communism in China has not completely erased the tradition of the Middle Kingdom wherein the Chinese considered themselves politically, so-

[14] See New York *Times* (Western Edition), September 3, 1963.
[15] The report was published in *Pravda*, April 3, 1964; excerpts in *Peking Review*, May 1, 1964, pp. 15–19.

cially, culturally, and (by implication at least) racially superior to all the "barbarians" that populated the rest of the world. Indeed, some scholars speak of the emergence of a "People's Middle Kingdom" under the Communists.[16] Moreover, the Chinese Communists are fully aware of the glaring inconsistency between a racial theory and the Marxist approach. Mao himself has sought to treat the race issue in an explicitly class context. Addressing himself to the race problem in the United States (see p. 326), he said emphatically that "The contradiction between the Black masses in the United States and the U.S. ruling circles is a class contradiction." An analysis based on race, in short, is at complete variance with Chinese traditions, whether Confucian or Communist.

By the late 1960s, the Peking regime had suffered a disastrous series of setbacks in foreign relations. The policy of export of revolution had failed, particularly in Africa and Latin America. In Africa, Peking had been expelled from Ghana, Kenya, and Malawi, and there had been rightist coups in Ghana and Nigeria. The Chinese attempt to organize a second Afro-Asian conference had collapsed. The Indonesian Communist Party—once a close ally of the CCP—had been violently dispersed. With the exception of Albania, every major communist party had sided with the U.S.S.R. Everywhere the international situation seemed to turn against the Peking regime.

The more hostile Peking's perception of the world environment, the more insecure it is likely to feel. Increasing insecurity is likely to lead to greater militancy in China's attitudes, although this is not likely to be followed by military action unless Peking's immediate interests are threatened. An added difficulty is the apparent delusion under which the Peking regime continues to operate: that any global conflict is bound to establish finally the superiority of Chinese Communism.

[16] See, for example, John K. Fairbank, *China: The People's Middle Kingdom and the U.S.A.* (Cambridge: Harvard University Press, 1967).

★

CHAPTER I
Imperialism, Revolution, and War

Introductory Note

Mao Tse-tung's attempt to rewrite Chinese history in Marxist-Leninist terms begins with the division of the entire subject into six periods: primitive communism, slave society, feudalism, imperialism (as an international extension of capitalism), socialism, and communism. Primitive communism, he argues, characterized "many thousands of years of life" in prehistoric China. Feudalism and slave society applied to an independent China before the Opium War. Imperialism dominated the country for just over a century (1840–1949), turning China into a colonial, semicolonial, and semifeudal state and setting in motion China's modern revolutionary movements. The age of socialism began with the establishment of the Chinese People's Republic. The era of communism will witness the full flowering of the Chinese revolution.

The first three periods are of relatively minor importance in the over-all philosophy of Mao Tse-tung and his thoughts on them remain extremely sketchy. The age of communism, on the other hand, lies in distant history; and Marxist-Leninists, "not [being] fortune-tellers," cannot be too precise about the future. By far the most significant aspects of Mao's thought are concerned with the fourth and fifth historical periods—imperialism and socialism—which we will explore in this and the following chapter.

Mao Tse-tung explicitly identifies "imperialism" as the chief instigator of revolutionary movements in colonial and semicolonial countries. Beginning with the Opium War of 1839–42, he argues, an independent China was gradually transformed into a colonial and semicolonial China. To accomplish the aims of their aggression,

Mao holds, imperialist powers carved out spheres of influence in China. They controlled the country's trading ports, treating its markets as dumps for their own products. They granted loans to the reactionary domestic government and controlled banking and finance in China. They supplied the domestic government with the arms and matériel needed to suppress public reaction. The imperialist powers formed alliances with domestic reactionary groups (e.g., the feudal lords, the big bourgeoisie), who benefited from their policies.

As China's feudal society had developed a commodity economy, carrying within itself the "seeds of capitalism," inevitably China would have developed gradually a capitalist economic system. In other words, according to Mao, Chinese capitalism did not develop under the exclusive impetus of Western imperialism; imperialist penetration merely accelerated an already existing trend of development.[1] The development of capitalism marked, at the same time, the emergence of the two antagonistic classes, the bourgeoisie and the proletariat.

The acceleration of capitalism under imperialist penetration is an unavoidable process, for the aim of imperialism in penetrating a country, Mao holds, is not to help develop its economy along more progressive capitalist lines but precisely to arrest such development. To this end, imperialism forms alliances with all reactionary social strata that may have an interest in preserving the status quo. A chief characteristic of the imperialist penetration of China, Mao maintains, was "the collusion of imperialism with the Chinese feudal forces to arrest the development of Chinese capitalism"; feudalism became a "main prop" of imperialist rule in China. Similarly, the imperialist powers formed alliances with certain segments of the big bourgeoisie, namely, the comprador bourgeoisie and the bureaucrat-capitalists (see Prologue). Thus the imperialist forces, the feudal elements, the bureaucrat-capitalists, and the comprador bourgeoisie constitute the main enemies of revolution in colonial and semicolonial countries.

Under these conditions, according to Mao, inescapable contradictions develop between imperialism and the oppressed colony. Concurrently, competition over the same colony results in the development of international conflicts and wars involving the imperialist

---

[1] This interpretation is of recent origin, found only in the current editions of "The Chinese Revolution and the Chinese Communist Party" (p. 41, below). In the original version, Mao affirms that the traditional, stagnant China began to develop only after the impact of the West.

powers themselves. Contradictions among the imperialist powers are in turn reflected in the relationship among the pro-imperialist cliques of domestic reaction, who are divided in their allegiance to the various imperialist countries. Conflicts involving the domestic reactionary cliques lead to increased oppression of the broad masses of the people; they accelerate the contradiction between the exploiter and the exploited, between feudal lords and the peasantry, between bourgeoisie and proletariat.

The multifarious struggles of the masses arise from the multifarious contradictions found in colonial and semicolonial societies. A series of revolutionary mass movements presumably engulfs the country in a rapidly expanding "prairie fire," and eventually overruns and defeats the forces of imperialism, feudalism, and the big bourgeoisie.

Specifically, conflicts and contradictions lead to internal instability; they weaken the reactionary government and make it possible for Communist revolutionary bases to come into being. Since the country is unevenly developed, and since the power of the enemy is concentrated in the urban, industrialized centers, the revolutionaries must retreat to the countryside, relying on the local population for all their needs. There they consolidate and strengthen their position, surround the cities, gradually undermine the position of the enemy, and finally strangle him to death. The Chinese countryside, Mao insisted, provides "the indispensable, vital positions of the Chinese revolution" because "revolutionary villages can encircle the cities, but revolutionary cities cannot detach themselves from the villages."

Only after the revolutionary regime has gathered sufficient strength can a shift to the urban centers be made. In China, this shift occurred with the virtual seizure of political power throughout the country. Thus on February 8, 1949, Mao Tse-tung announced that "From now on, the formula followed in the past twenty years, 'first the rural areas, then the cities,' will be reversed and changed to the formula 'first the cities, then the rural areas.' "

It is clear that Mao envisions the emergence of three sets of contradictions in colonial and semicolonial countries: those applying to relationships among social classes and groups within the colonies, those characterizing the relationships between imperialism and the colonies, and those applying to the interactions among the imperialist powers themselves. The two latter sets of contradictions lead to global war and the eventual collapse of international capitalism. Imperialism, according to Mao, is "riddled with insuperable contradictions"; it is "sitting on a volcano"; it is its own "gravedigger." The forces of imperialism have continually declined, he argues, while those of communism have consistently grown in strength. Imperialism is doomed because it is decadent and retrogressive. Its fundamental weakness is that it is separated from its "people." The "logic" of imperialism—aggression, oppression, and exploitation—is incompatible with that of the masses.[2]

The power of imperialism, in short, is superficial and transient. Communist countries must avoid overestimating the strength of their enemy. From the long-term point of view, imperialism is feeble and destined to collapse; as such, it should be "despised." From the short-term perspective, however, imperialism is still powerful and in possession of the mechanical means of mass destruction; as such, it should be "respected." Integrating these two propositions, Mao formulates the slogan of "despising the enemy strategically, while taking full account of him tactically." This in turn provides the basis for another slogan: "Imperialism and all reactionaries are paper tigers."

War, Mao argues, is an inescapable consequence of the imperialist policy of global aggression: "The imperialists pin their hope on war."[3] He draws a sharp distinction between two types of war: "just" and "unjust." All wars waged by imperialism, he asserts, are unjust; all communist and revolutionary wars are just. The communist attitude toward war is one of avoiding unjust wars, while actively aiding and participating in just wars.

Revolutionary wars are further differentiated into those waged against imperialism (national revolutionary wars) and those waged against domestic reaction (civil or class revolutionary wars). The basic distinction between revolutionary war and counterrevolutionary war, says Mao, is that the former is rooted in, and waged by, the broad masses of the people. It is predicated upon the unity of the government and the people: "the government does not fear

[2] In studying Mao's theory of imperialism, it is essential to bear in mind the explicit distinction between imperialist governments and the peoples under their control, for it is against the former that Mao's attacks are directed. "People" are viewed as kind and peaceful everywhere; it is the reactionary rulers and the capitalist agents that lead them astray. Thus Mao's praise for the "American people" as distinct from the "American government."

[3] Quoted in *Comrade Mao Tse-tung on "Imperialism and All Reactionaries Are Paper Tigers"* (Peking: Foreign Languages Press, 1958), p. 27.

popular disapproval, because the people are most willing to wage this kind of war."

The decisive role of the people in determining the character and outcome of war, Mao asserts, stands in direct contrast to the false imperialist theory that "weapons decide everything." Even the atom bomb, he has said, cannot ensure victory in war. The outcome of a war is determined by the "spiritual atom bomb" of mass support. Mao's faith in the power of the masses appears unbounded.

Readings

IMPERIALISM AND CHINESE SOCIETY

From: "The Chinese Revolution and the Chinese Communist Party" (December 1939), *Selected Works,* II (Peking: Foreign Languages Press, 1965), pp. 306–13.

Developing along the same lines as many other nations of the world, the Chinese people (here we refer mainly to the Hans) went through many thousands of years of life in classless primitive communes. Some 4000 years have gone by since the collapse of these primitive communes and the transition to class society, which took the form first of slave and then of feudal society. Throughout the history of Chinese civilization its agriculture and handicrafts have been renowned for their high level of development; there have been many great thinkers, scientists, inventors, statesmen, soldiers, men of letters, and artists, and we have a rich store of classical works. The compass was invented in China very long ago. The art of paper-making was discovered as early as 1800 years ago. Block printing was invented 1300 years ago, and movable type 800 years ago. The use of gunpowder was known to the Chinese before the Europeans. Thus China has one of the oldest civilizations in the world; she has a recorded history of nearly 4000 years.

The Chinese nation is known throughout the world not only for its industriousness and stamina, but also for its ardent love of freedom and its rich revolutionary traditions. The history of the Han people, for instance, demonstrates that the Chinese never submit to tyrannical rule but invariably use revolutionary means to overthrow or change it. In the thousands of years of Han history, there have been hundreds of peasant uprisings, great and small, against the dark rule of the landlords and the nobility. And most dynastic changes came about as a result of such peasant uprisings. All the nationalities of China have resisted foreign oppression and have invariably resorted to rebellion to shake it off. They favor a union on the basis of equality but are against the oppression of one nationality by another. During the thousands of years of recorded history, the Chinese nation has given birth to many national heroes and revolutionary leaders. Thus the Chinese nation has a glorious revolutionary tradition and a splendid historical heritage.

The Old Feudal Society

Although China is a great nation and although she is a vast country with an immense population, a long history, a rich revolutionary tradition and a splendid historical heritage, her economic, political, and cultural development was sluggish for a long time after the transition from slave to feudal society. This feudal society, beginning with the Chou and Chin dynasties, lasted about 3000 years.

The main features of the economic and political system of China's feudal era were as follows:

(1) A self-sufficient natural economy predominated. The peasants produced for themselves not only agricultural products but most of the handicraft articles they needed. What the landlords and the nobility exacted from them in the form of land rent was also chiefly for private enjoyment and not for exchange. Although exchange developed as time went on, it did not play a decisive role in the economy as a whole.

(2) The feudal ruling class composed of landlords, the nobility, and the emperor owned most of the land, while the peasants had very little or none at all. The peasants tilled the land of the landlords, the nobility, and the royal family with their own farm implements and had to turn over to them for their private enjoyment 40, 50, 60, 70, or even 80 per cent or more of the crop. In effect the peasants were still serfs.

(3) Not only did the landlords, the nobility, and the royal family live on rent extorted from the peasants, but the landlord state also exacted tribute, taxes, and *corvée* services from them to support a horde of government officials and an army which was used mainly for their repression.

(4) The feudal landlord state was the organ of power protecting this system of feudal exploitation. While the feudal state was torn

apart into rival principalities in the period before the Chin dynasty, it became autocratic and centralized after the first Chin emperor unified China, though some feudal separatism remained. The emperor reigned supreme in the feudal state, appointing officials in charge of the armed forces, the law courts, the treasury, and state granaries in all parts of the country and relying on the landed gentry as the mainstay of the entire system of feudal rule.

It was under such feudal economic exploitation and political oppression that the Chinese peasants lived like slaves, in poverty and suffering, through the ages. Under the bondage of feudalism they had no freedom of person. The landlord had the right to beat, abuse, or even kill them at will, and they had no political rights whatsoever. The extreme poverty and backwardness of the peasants resulting from ruthless landlord exploitation and oppression is the basic reason why Chinese society remained at the same stage of socio-economic development for several thousand years.

The principal contradiction in feudal society was between the peasantry and the landlord class.

The peasants and the handicraft workers were the basic classes which created the wealth and culture of this society.

The ruthless economic exploitation and political oppression of the Chinese peasants forced them into numerous uprisings against landlord rule. There were hundreds of uprisings, great and small, all of them peasant revolts or peasant revolutionary wars. . . . The scale of peasant uprisings and peasant wars in Chinese history has no parallel anywhere else. The class struggles of the peasants, the peasant uprisings, and peasant wars constituted the real motive force of historical development in Chinese feudal society. For each of the major peasant uprisings and wars dealt a blow to the feudal regime of the time, and hence more or less furthered the growth of the social productive forces. However, since neither new productive forces, nor new relations of production, nor new class forces, nor any advanced political party existed in those days, the peasant uprisings and wars did not have correct leadership such as the proletariat and the Communist Party provide today; every peasant revolution failed, and the peasantry was invariably used by the landlords and the nobility, either during or after the revolution, as a lever for bringing about dynastic change. Therefore, although some social progress was made after each great peasant revolutionary struggle, the feudal economic relations and political system remained basically unchanged.

It is only in the last hundred years that a change of a different order has taken place.

Present-day Colonial, Semicolonial, and Semifeudal Society

As explained above, Chinese society remained feudal for 3000 years. But is it still completely feudal today? No, China has changed. After the Opium War of 1840 China gradually changed into a semi-colonial and semifeudal society. Since the Incident of September 18, 1931, when the Japanese imperialists started their armed aggression, China has changed further into a colonial, semicolonial, and semi-feudal society. We shall now describe the course of this change. . . .

As China's feudal society had developed a commodity economy, and so carried within itself the seeds of capitalism, China would of herself have developed slowly into a capitalist society even without the impact of foreign capitalism. Penetration by foreign capitalism accelerated this process. Foreign capitalism played an important part in the disintegration of China's social economy; on the one hand, it undermined the foundations of her self-sufficient natural economy and wrecked the handicraft industries both in the cities and in the peasants' homes, and on the other, it hastened the growth of a commodity economy in town and country.

Apart from its disintegrating effects on the foundations of China's feudal economy, this state of affairs gave rise to certain objective conditions and possibilities for the development of capitalist production in China. For the destruction of the natural economy created a commodity market for capitalism, while the bankruptcy of large numbers of peasants and handicraftsmen provided it with a labor market.

In fact, some merchants, landlords, and bureaucrats began investing in modern industry as far back as sixty years ago, in the latter part of the nineteenth century, under the stimulus of foreign capitalism and because of certain cracks in the feudal economic structure. About forty years ago, at the turn of the century, China's national capitalism took its first steps forward. Then about twenty years ago, during the first imperialist world war, China's national industry expanded, chiefly in textiles and flour milling, because the imperialist countries in Europe and America were preoccupied with the war and temporarily relaxed their oppression of China.

The history of the emergence and development of national capitalism is at the same time the history of the emergence and development of the Chinese bourgeoisie and proletariat. Just as a section of the merchants, landlords, and bureaucrats were precursors of the Chinese bourgeoisie, so a section of the peasants and handicraft workers were the precursors of the Chinese proletariat. As distinct social classes, the Chinese bourgeoisie and proletariat are newborn and never existed before in Chinese history. They have evolved into new social classes from the womb of feudal society. They are twins born of China's old (feudal) society, at once linked to each other and antagonistic to each other. However, the Chinese proletariat emerged and grew simultaneously not only with the Chinese national bourgeoisie but also with the enterprises directly operated by the imperialists in China. Hence, a very large section of the Chinese proletariat is older and more experienced than the Chinese bourgeoisie, and is therefore a greater and more broadly based social force.

However, the emergence and development of capitalism is only one aspect of the change that has taken place since the imperialist penetration of China. There is another concomitant and obstructive aspect, namely, the collusion of imperialism with the Chinese feudal forces to arrest the development of Chinese capitalism.

It is certainly not the purpose of the imperialist powers invading China to transform feudal China into capitalist China. On the contrary, their purpose is to transform China into their own semicolony or colony.

To this end the imperialist powers have used and continue to use military, political, economic, and cultural means of oppression, so that China has gradually become a semicolony and colony. They are as follows:

(1) The imperialist powers have waged many wars of aggression against China, for instance, the Opium War launched by Britain in 1840. . . . After defeating China in war, they not only occupied many neighboring countries formerly under her protection, but seized or "leased" parts of her territory. . . . In addition to annexing territory, they exacted huge indemnities. Thus heavy blows were struck at China's huge feudal empire.

(2) The imperialist powers have forced China to sign numerous unequal treaties by which they have acquired the right to station land and sea forces and exercise consular jurisdiction in China, and they have carved up the whole country into imperialist spheres of influence.

(3) The imperialist powers have gained control of all the important trading ports in China by these unequal treaties and have

marked off areas in many of these ports as concessions under their direct administration. They have also gained control of China's customs, foreign trade, and communications (sea, land, inland water, and air). Thus they have been able to dump their goods in China, turn her into a market for their industrial products, and at the same time subordinate her agriculture to their imperialist needs.

(4) The imperialist powers operate many enterprises in both light and heavy industry in China in order to utilize her raw materials and cheap labor on the spot, and they thereby directly exert economic pressure on China's national industry and obstruct the development of her productive forces.

(5) The imperialist powers monopolize China's banking and finance by extending loans to the Chinese government and establishing banks in China. Thus they have not only overwhelmed China's national capitalism in commodity competition, they have also secured a stranglehold on her banking and finance.

(6) The imperialist powers have established a network of comprador and merchant-usurer exploitation right across China, from the trading ports to the remote hinterland, and have created a comprador and merchant-usurer class in their service, so as to facilitate their exploitation of the masses of the Chinese peasantry and other sections of the people.

(7) The imperialist powers have made the feudal landlord class as well as the comprador class the main props of their rule in China. Imperialism [to quote the Comintern] "first allies itself with the ruling strata of the previous social structure, with the feudal lords and the trading and moneylending bourgeoisie, against the majority of the people. Everywhere imperialism attempts to preserve and to perpetuate all those precapitalist forms of exploitation (especially in the villages) which serve as the basis for the existence of its reactionary allies." [According to Stalin] "Imperialism, with all its financial and military might, is the force in China that supports, inspires, fosters, and preserves the feudal survivals, together with their entire bureaucratic-militarist superstructure."

(8) The imperialist powers supply the reactionary government with large quantities of munitions and a host of military advisers, in order to keep the warlords fighting among themselves and to suppress the Chinese people.

(9) Furthermore, the imperialist powers have never slackened their efforts to poison the minds of the Chinese people. This is their policy of cultural aggression. And it is carried out through missionary

work, through establishing hospitals and schools, publishing news-papers, and inducing Chinese students to study abroad. Their aim is to train intellectuals who will serve their interests and to dupe the people.

(10) Since September 18, 1931, the large-scale invasion of Japanese imperialism has turned a big chunk of semicolonial China into a Japanese colony.

These facts represent the other aspect of the change that has taken place since the imperialist penetration of China—the blood-stained picture of feudal China being reduced to semifeudal, semi-colonial, and colonial China.

It is thus clear that in their aggression against China the imperialist powers have on the one hand hastened the disintegration of feudal society and the growth of elements of capitalism, thereby transforming a feudal into a semifeudal society, and on the other imposed their ruthless rule on China, reducing an independent country to a semicolonial and colonial country.

Taking both these aspects together, we can see that China's colonial, semicolonial, and semifeudal society possesses the following characteristics:

(1) The foundations of the self-sufficient natural economy of feudal times have been destroyed, but the exploitation of the peasantry by the landlord class, which is the basis of the system of feudal exploitation, not only remains intact but, linked as it is with exploitation by comprador and usurer capital, clearly dominates China's social and economic life.

(2) National capitalism has developed to a certain extent and has played a considerable part in China's political and cultural life, but it has not become the principal pattern in China's social economy; it is flabby and is mostly associated with foreign imperialism and domestic feudalism in varying degrees.

(3) The autocratic rule of the emperors and nobility has been overthrown, and in its place there have arisen first the warlord-bureaucrat rule of the landlord class and then the joint dictatorship of the landlord class and the big bourgeoisie. In the occupied areas there is the rule of Japanese imperialism and its puppets.

(4) Imperialism controls not only China's vital financial and economic arteries but also her political and military power. In the occupied areas everything is in the hands of Japanese imperialism.

(5) China's economic, political, and cultural development is very uneven, because she has been under the complete or partial dom-

ination of many imperialist powers, because she has actually been in a state of disunity for a long time, and because her territory is immense.

(6) Under the twofold oppression of imperialism and feudalism, and especially as a result of the large-scale invasion of Japanese imperialism, the Chinese people, and particularly the peasants, have become more and more impoverished and have even been pauperized in large numbers, living in hunger and cold and without any political rights. The poverty and lack of freedom among the Chinese people are on a scale seldom found elsewhere.

Such are the characteristics of China's colonial, semicolonial, and semifeudal society.

This situation has in the main been determined by the Japanese and other imperialist forces; it is the result of the collusion of foreign imperialism and domestic feudalism.

The contradiction between imperialism and the Chinese nation and the contradiction between feudalism and the great masses of the people are the basic contradictions in modern Chinese society. Of course, there are others, such as the contradiction between the bourgeoisie and the proletariat and the contradictions within the reactionary ruling classes themselves. But the contradiction between imperialism and the Chinese nation is the principal one. These contradictions and their intensification must inevitably result in the incessant growth of revolutionary movements. The great revolutions in modern and contemporary China have emerged and grown on the basis of these basic contradictions.

IMPERIALISM AND CONTRADICTIONS

Internal and External Contradictions

From: "The Tasks of the Chinese Communist Party in the Period of Resistance to Japan" (May 1937), *Selected Works,* I (Peking: Foreign Languages Press, 1964), pp. 263–65.

1. As the contradiction between China and Japan has become the principal one and China's internal contradictions have dropped into a secondary and subordinate place, changes have occurred in China's international relations and internal class relations, giving rise to a new stage of development in the current situation.

2. China has long been in the grip of two acute and basic con-

tradictions, the contradiction between China and imperialism and the contradiction between feudalism and the masses of the people. In 1927 the bourgeoisie, represented by the Kuomintang, betrayed the revolution and sold China's national interests to imperialism, thus creating a situation in which the state power of the workers and peasants stood in sharp antagonism to that of the Kuomintang, and, of necessity, the task of the national and democratic revolution devolved upon the Chinese Communist Party alone.

3. Since the Incident of September 18, 1931 and especially since the Northern China Incident of 1935, the following changes have taken place in these contradictions:

(1) The contradiction between China and imperialism in general has given way to the particularly salient and sharp contradiction between China and Japanese imperialism. Japanese imperialism is carrying out a policy of total conquest of China. Consequently, the contradictions between China and certain other imperialist powers have been relegated to a secondary position, while the rift between these powers and Japan has been widened. Consequently also, the Chinese Communist Party and the Chinese people are faced with the task of linking China's anti-Japanese national united front with the world peace front. This means that China should not only unite with the Soviet Union, which has been the consistently good friend of the Chinese people, but as far as possible should work for joint opposition to Japanese imperialism with those imperialist countries which, at the present time, are willing to maintain peace and are against new wars of aggression. The aim of our united front must be resistance to Japan, and not simultaneous opposition to all the imperialist powers.

(2) The contradiction between China and Japan has changed internal class relations within China and has confronted the bourgeoisie and even the warlords with the question of survival, so that they and their political parties have been undergoing a gradual change in their political attitude. This has placed the task of establishing an anti-Japanese national united front before the Chinese Communist Party and the Chinese people. Our united front should include the bourgeoisie and all who agree to the defense of the motherland; it should represent national solidarity against the foreign foe. This task not only must, but can, be fulfilled.

(3) The contradiction between China and Japan has changed matters for the masses throughout the country (the proletariat, the peasantry, and the urban petty bourgeoisie) and for the Communist

Party, and it has changed the Party's policy. More and more people have risen to fight for national salvation. The policy proclaimed by the Communist Party after the September 18 Incident was to conclude agreements with those sections of the Kuomintang which were willing to cooperate with us for resistance, subject to three conditions (stop attacking the revolutionary base areas, guarantee the freedoms and rights of the people, arm the people), and it has developed into a policy of establishing an anti-Japanese united front of the whole nation. . . .

(4) Because of the contradiction between China and Japan, a change has also occurred in the Chinese warlord regimes and the civil wars among them, which are the product of the imperialist policy of spheres of influence and of China's semicolonial economic conditions. Japanese imperialism fosters such separate regimes and civil wars for the purpose of facilitating exclusive Japanese domination of China. Certain other imperialist powers are temporarily in favor of unity and peace in China in their own interests. The Chinese Communist Party and the Chinese people on their part are exerting their utmost efforts against civil wars and splits and for peace and unity.

(5) In terms of relative political importance the development of the national contradiction between China and Japan has demoted the domestic contradictions between classes and between political groupings to a secondary and subordinate place. But they still exist and have by no means diminished or disappeared. The same is true of the contradictions between China and the imperialist powers other than Japan. Therefore, the Chinese Communist Party and the Chinese people are faced with the following task—to make the appropriate adjustments with regard to those internal and external contradictions which can and must be adjusted at present so as to fit in with the general task of unity against Japan. This is the reason for the Chinese Communist Party's policies of peace and unity, democracy, bettering the life of the people, and negotiations with foreign countries that are opposed to Japan.

Contradiction and Revolution

From: "A Single Spark Can Start a Prairie Fire" (January 1930), *Selected Works*, I (Peking: Foreign Languages Press, 1964), pp. 120–21.

. . . The question whether there will soon be a revolutionary high tide in China can be decided only by making a detailed examination to ascertain whether the contradictions leading to a revolutionary high tide are really developing. Since contradictions are developing in the world between the imperialist countries, between the imperialist countries and their colonies, and between the imperialists and the proletariat in their own countries, there is an intensified need for the imperialists to contend for the domination of China. While the imperialist contention over China becomes more intense, both the contradiction between imperialism and the whole Chinese nation and the contradictions among the imperialists themselves develop simultaneously on Chinese soil, thereby creating the tangled warfare which is expanding and intensifying daily and giving rise to the continuous development of the contradictions among the different cliques of China's reactionary rulers. In the wake of the contradictions among the reactionary ruling cliques—the tangled warfare among the warlords—comes heavier taxation, which steadily sharpens the contradiction between the broad masses of taxpayers and the reactionary rulers. In the wake of the contradiction between imperialism and China's national industry comes the failure of the Chinese industrialists to obtain concessions from the imperialists, which sharpens the contradiction between the Chinese bourgeoisie and the Chinese working class, with the Chinese capitalists trying to find a way out by frantically exploiting the workers and with the workers resisting. In the wake of imperialist commercial aggression, Chinese merchant-capitalist extortions, heavier government taxation, etc., comes the deepening of the contradiction between the landlord class and the peasantry, that is, exploitation through rent and usury is aggravated and the hatred of the peasants for the landlords grows. Because of the pressure of foreign goods, the exhaustion of the purchasing power of the worker and peasant masses, and the increase in government taxation, more and more dealers in Chinese-made goods and independent producers are being driven into bankruptcy. Because the reactionary government, though short of provisions and funds, endlessly expands its armies and thus constantly extends the warfare, the masses of soldiers are in a constant state of privation. Because of the growth in government taxation, the rise in rent and interest demanded by the landlords, and the daily spread of the disasters of war, there are famine and banditry everywhere and the peasant masses and the urban poor can hardly keep alive. Because the schools have no money, many students fear that their education may be interrupted; because production is backward, many graduates have no hope of employment. Once we understand all these contradictions, we shall see in what a desperate situation, in what a chaotic state, China finds herself. We shall also see that the high tide of revolution against the imperialists, the warlords, and the landlords is inevitable, and will come very soon. All China is littered with dry fagots which will soon be aflame. The saying "A single spark can start a prairie fire" is an apt description of how the current situation will develop. We need only look at the strikes by the workers, the uprisings by the peasants, the mutinies of soldiers, and the strikes of students which are developing in many places to see that it cannot be long before a "spark" kindles "a prairie fire."

CONTRADICTIONS AND THE EMERGENCE OF THE RED REGIME

Contradictions in China

From: "Why Is It That Red Political Power Can Exist in China?" (October 1928), *Selected Works,* I (Peking: Foreign Languages Press, 1964), pp. 64–67.

The long-term survival inside a country of one or more small areas under Red political power completely encircled by a White regime is a phenomenon that has never occurred anywhere else in the world. There are special reasons for this unusual phenomenon. It can exist and develop only under certain conditions.

First, it cannot occur in any imperialist country or in any colony under direct imperialist rule, but can only occur in China, which is economically backward, semicolonial, and under indirect imperialist rule. For this unusual phenomenon can occur only in conjunction with another unusual phenomenon, namely, war within the White regime. It is a feature of semicolonial China that, since the first year of the Republic (1912), the various cliques of old and new warlords have waged incessant wars against one another, supported by imperialism from abroad and by the comprador and landlord classes at home. Such a phenomenon is to be found in none of the imperialist countries nor for that matter in any colony under direct imperialist rule, but only in a country like China, which is under indirect imperialist rule. Two things account for its occurrence, namely, a localized agricultural economy (not a unified capitalist economy) and the imperialist policy of marking off spheres of influence in order to divide and exploit. The prolonged splits and wars within the White regime provide a condition for the emergence and persistence of one or more small Red areas under the leadership of the Communist Party amid the encirclement of the White regime. The independent regime carved out on the borders of Hunan and Kiangsi provinces is one of many such small areas. In difficult or critical times some comrades often have doubts about the survival of Red political power and become pessimistic. The reason is that they have not found the correct explanation for its emergence and survival. If only we realize that splits and wars will never cease within the White regime in China, we shall have no doubts about the emergence, survival, and daily growth of Red political power.

Second, the regions where China's Red political power has first emerged and is able to last for a long time have not been those unaffected by the democratic revolution, such as Szechuan, Kweichow, Yunnan, and the northern provinces, but regions such as the provinces of Hunan, Kwangtung, Hupeh, and Kiangsi, where the masses of workers, peasants, and soldiers rose in great numbers in the course of the bourgeois-democratic revolution [see Chapter II] of 1926 and 1927. In many parts of these provinces trade unions and peasant associations were formed on a wide scale, and many economic and political struggles were waged by the working class and the peasantry against the landlord class and the bourgeoisie. . . . As for the present Red Army, it is a split-off from the National Revolutionary Army, which underwent democratic political training and came under the influence of the masses of workers and peasants. The elements that make up the Red Army cannot possibly come from armies . . . which have not received any democratic political training or come under the influence of the workers and peasants.

Third, whether it is possible for the people's political power in small areas to last depends on whether the nationwide revolutionary situation continues to develop. If it does, then the small Red areas will undoubtedly last for a long time, and will, moreover, inevitably become one of the many forces for winning nationwide political power. If the nationwide revolutionary situation does not continue to develop but stagnates for a fairly long time, then it will be impossible for the small Red areas to last long. Actually, the revolutionary situation in China is continuing to develop with the continuous splits and wars within the ranks of the comprador and landlord classes and of the international bourgeoisie. Therefore the small Red areas will undoubtedly last for a long time, and will also continue to expand and gradually approach the goal of seizing political power throughout the country.

Fourth, the existence of a regular Red Army of adequate strength is a necessary condition for the existence of Red political power. If we have . . . no regular Red Army, then we cannot cope with the regular White forces. . . . Therefore, even when the masses of workers and peasants are active, it is definitely impossible to create an independent regime, let alone an independent regime which is durable and grows daily, unless we have regular forces of adequate strength. It follows that the idea of "establishing independent regimes of the workers and the peasants by armed force" is an important one which must be fully grasped by the Communist Party and by the masses of workers and peasants in areas under the independent regime.

Fifth, another important condition in addition to the above is required for the prolonged existence and development of Red political power, namely, that the Communist Party organization should be strong and its policy correct.

Revolutionary Strategy

From: "The Struggle in the Chingkang Mountains" (November 1928), *Selected Works,* I (Peking: Foreign Languages Press, 1964), pp. 73–74.

China is the only country in the world today where one or more small areas under Red political power have emerged in the midst of a White regime which encircles them. We find on analysis that one reason for this phenomenon lies in the incessant splits and wars within China's comprador and landlord classes. So long as these splits and wars continue, it is possible for an armed independent regime of workers and peasants to survive and grow. In addition, its survival and growth require the following conditions: (1) a sound mass base, (2) a sound Party organization, (3) a fairly strong Red Army, (4) terrain favorable to military operations, and (5) economic resources sufficient for sustenance.

An independent regime must vary its strategy against the encircling ruling classes, adopting one strategy when the ruling class regime is temporarily stable and another when it is split up. In a period when the ruling classes are split up . . . our strategy can be comparatively adventurous and the area carved out by military operations can be comparatively large. However, we must take care to lay a solid foundation in the central districts so that we shall have something secure to rely on when the White terror strikes. In a period when the regime of the ruling classes is comparatively stable . . . our strategy must be one of gradual advance. In such a period, the worst thing in military affairs is to divide our forces for an adventurous advance, and the worst thing in local work (distributing land, establishing political power, expanding the Party, and organizing local armed forces) is to scatter our personnel and neglect to lay a solid foundation in the central districts. The defeats which many small Red areas have suffered have been due either to the absence of the requisite objective conditions or to subjective mistakes in tactics. Mistakes in tactics have been made solely because of failure to distinguish clearly between the two kinds of period, that in which the regime of the ruling classes is temporarily stable and that in which it is split up.

From the City to the Countryside

From: "The Chinese Revolution and the Chinese Communist Party" (December 1939), *Selected Works,* II (Peking: Foreign Languages Press, 1965), pp. 316–17.

It is evident . . . that the enemies of the Chinese revolution are very powerful. They include not only powerful imperialists and powerful feudal forces, but also, at times, the bourgeois reactionaries who collaborate with the imperialist and feudal forces to oppose the people. Therefore, it is wrong to underestimate the strength of the enemies of the revolutionary Chinese people. . . .

In the face of such enemies, there arises the question of revolutionary base areas. Since China's key cities have long been occupied by the powerful imperialists and their reactionary Chinese allies, it is imperative for the revolutionary ranks to turn the backward villages into advanced, consolidated base areas, into great military, political, economic, and cultural bastions of the revolution from which to fight their vicious enemies who are using the cities for attacks on the rural districts, and in this way gradually to achieve the complete victory of the revolution through protracted fighting; it is imperative for them to do so if they do not wish to compromise with imperialism and its lackeys but are determined to fight on, and if they intend to build up and temper their forces and avoid decisive battles with a powerful enemy while their own strength is inadequate. Such being the case, victory in the Chinese revolution can be won first in the rural areas, and this is possible because China's economic development is uneven (her economy not being a unified capitalist economy), because her territory is extensive (which gives the revolutionary forces room to maneuver), because the counterrevolutionary camp is disunited and full of contradictions, and because the struggle of the peasants who are the main force in the revolution is led by the Communist Party, the party of the proletariat; but on the other hand, these very circumstances make the revolution uneven and render the task of winning complete victory protracted and arduous. Clearly, then, the protracted revolutionary struggle in the revolutionary base areas consists mainly in peasant guerrilla warfare led by the Chinese Communist Party. Therefore, it is wrong to ignore the necessity of using rural districts as revolutionary base areas, to neglect painstaking work among the peasants, and to neglect guerrilla warfare.

However, stressing . . . the work in the rural base areas does not mean abandoning our work in the cities and in the other vast rural areas which are still under the enemy's rule; on the contrary, without the work in the cities and in these other rural areas, our own rural base areas would be isolated and the revolution would suffer defeat. Moreover, the final objective of the revolution is the capture of the cities, the enemy's main bases, and this objective cannot be achieved without adequate work in the cities.

It is thus clear that the revolution cannot triumph either in the rural areas or in the cities without the destruction of the enemy's army, his chief weapon against the people. Therefore, besides annihilating the enemy's troops in battle, there is the important task of disintegrating them.

From the Countryside to the City

From: "Turn the Army into a Working Force" (February 1949), *Selected Works*, IV (Peking: Foreign Languages Press, 1961), p. 337.

From now on, the formula followed in the past twenty years, "first the rural areas, then the cities," will be reversed and changed to the formula, "first the cities, then the rural areas."

From: "Report to the Second Plenary Session of the Seventh Central Committee of the Communist Party of China" (March 1949), *Selected Works,* IV (Peking: Foreign Languages Press, 1961), pp. 363–64.

From 1927 to the present the center of gravity of our work has been in the villages—gathering strength in the villages, using the villages in order to surround the cities, and then taking the cities. The period for this method of work has now ended. The period of "from the city to the village" and of the city leading the village has now begun. The center of gravity of the Party's work has shifted from the village to the city. In the south the People's Liberation Army will occupy first the cities and then the villages. Attention must be given to both city and village and it is necessary to link closely urban and rural work, workers and peasants, industry and agriculture. Under no circumstances should the village be ignored and only the city given attention; such thinking is entirely wrong. Nevertheless, the center of gravity of the work of the Party and the army must be in the cities; we must do our utmost to learn how to administer and build the cities. In the cities we must learn how to wage political, economic, and cultural struggles against the imperialists, the Kuomintang, and the bourgeoisie and also how to wage diplomatic struggles against the imperialists. We must learn how to carry on overt struggles against them, we must also learn how to carry on covert struggles against them. If we do not pay attention to these problems, if we do not learn how to wage these struggles against them and win victory in the struggles, we shall be unable to maintain our political power, we shall be unable to stand on our feet, we shall fail. After the enemies with guns have been wiped out, there will still be enemies without guns; they are bound to struggle desperately against us; we must never regard these enemies lightly. If we do not now raise and understand the problem in this way, we shall commit very grave mistakes.

IMPERIALISM AND WAR

War and Revolution

From: "Problems of War and Strategy" (November 1938), *Selected Works,* I (Peking: Foreign Languages Press, 1964), pp. 219–23.

The seizure of power by armed force, the settlement of the issue by war, is the central task and the highest form of revolution. This Marxist-Leninist principle of revolution holds good universally, for China and for all other countries.

But while the principle remains the same, its application by the party of the proletariat finds expression in varying ways according to the varying conditions. Internally, capitalist countries practice bourgeois democracy (not feudalism) when they are not fascist or not at war; in their external relations, they are not oppressed by, but themselves oppress, other nations. Because of these characteristics, it is the task of the party of the proletariat in the capitalist countries to educate the workers and build up strength through a long period of legal struggle, and thus prepare for the final overthrow of capitalism. In these countries, the question is one of a long legal struggle, of utilizing parliament as a platform, of economic and political strikes, of organizing trade unions and educating the workers. There the form of organization is legal and the form of struggle bloodless (non-military). On the issue of war, the Communist Parties in the capitalist countries oppose the imperialist wars waged by their own countries; if such wars occur, the policy of these Parties is to bring about the defeat of the reactionary governments of their own countries. The one war they want to fight is the civil war for which they are preparing. But this insurrection and war should not be launched until the bourgeoisie becomes really helpless, until the majority of the proletariat are determined to rise in arms and fight, and until the rural masses are giving willing help to the proletariat. And when the time comes to launch such an insurrection and war, the first step will be to seize the cities, and then advance into the countryside, and not the other way about. All this has been done by Communist Parties in capitalist countries, and it has been proved correct by the October Revolution in Russia.

China is different, however. The characteristics of China are that she is not independent and democratic but semicolonial and semifeudal, that internally she has no democracy but is under feudal oppression, and that in her external relations she has no national independence but is oppressed by imperialism. It follows that we have no parliament to make use of and no legal right to organize the workers to strike. Basically, the task of the Communist Party here is not to go through a long period of legal struggle before launching insurrection and war, and not to seize the big cities first and then occupy the countryside, but the reverse.

When imperialism is not making armed attacks on our country, the Chinese Communist Party either wages civil war jointly with the bourgeoisie against the warlords (lackeys of imperialism), as in . . . the Northern Expedition, or unites with the peasants and the urban petty bourgeoisie to wage civil war against the landlord class and the comprador bourgeoisie (also lackeys of imperialism), as in the War of Agrarian Revolution of 1927–36. When imperialism launches armed attacks on China, the Party unites all classes and strata in the country opposing the foreign aggressors to wage a national war against the foreign enemy, as it is doing in the present War of Resistance Against Japan.

All this shows the difference between China and the capitalist countries. In China war is the main form of struggle and the army is the main form of organization. Other forms such as mass organization and mass struggle are also extremely important and indeed indispensable and in no circumstances to be overlooked, but their purpose is to serve the war. Before the outbreak of a war all organization and struggle are in preparation for the war, as in the period from the May 4 Movement of 1919 to the May 30 Movement of 1925. After war breaks out, all organization and struggle are co-ordinated with the war either directly or indirectly, as, for instance, in the period of the Northern Expedition when all organization and struggle in the rear areas of the revolutionary army were co-ordinated with the war directly, and those in the northern warlord areas were co-ordinated with the war indirectly. Again in the period of the War of Agrarian Revolution all organization and struggle inside the Red areas were co-ordinated with the war directly, and outside the Red areas indirectly. Yet again in the present period, the War of Resistance, all organization and struggle in the rear areas of the anti-Japanese forces and in the areas occupied by the enemy are directly or indirectly co-ordinated with the war.

"In China the armed revolution is fighting the armed counter-revolution. That is one of the specific features and one of the advantages of the Chinese revolution." This thesis of Comrade Stalin's is perfectly correct and is equally valid for the Northern Expedition, the War of Agrarian Revolution, and the present War of Resistance Against Japan. They are all revolutionary wars, all directed against counterrevolutionaries, and all waged mainly by the revolutionary people, differing only in the sense that a civil war differs from a national war, and that a war conducted by the Communist Party differs from a war it conducts jointly with the Kuomintang. Of course, these differences are important. They indicate the breadth of the main forces in the war (an alliance of the workers and peas-ants, or of the workers, peasants, and bourgeoisie) and whether our antagonist in the war is internal or external (whether the war is against domestic or foreign foes, and, if domestic, whether against the northern warlords or against the Kuomintang); they also indicate that the content of China's revolutionary war differs at different stages of its history. But all these wars are instances of armed revolution fighting armed counterrevolution, they are all revolutionary wars, and all exhibit the specific features and advantages of the Chinese revolution. The thesis that revolutionary war "is one of the specific features and one of the advantages of the Chinese revolution" fits China's conditions prefectly. The main task of the party of the Chinese proletariat, a task confronting it almost from its very inception, has been to unite with as many allies as possible and, according to the circumstances, to organize armed struggles for national and social liberation against armed counterrevolution, whether internal or external. Without armed struggle the proletariat and the Communist Party would have no standing at all in China, and it would be impossible to accomplish any revolutionary task.

Our Party did not grasp this point fully during the first five or six years after it was founded, that is, from 1921 to its participation in the Northern Expedition in 1926. It did not then understand the supreme importance of armed struggle in China, or seriously prepare for war and organize armed forces, or apply itself to the study of military strategy and tactics. During the Northern Expedition it neglected to win over the army but laid one-sided stress on the mass movement, with the result that the whole mass movement collapsed the moment the Kuomintang turned reactionary. For a long time after 1927 many comrades continued to make it the Party's central task to prepare for insurrections in the cities and to work in the White areas. It was only after our victory in repelling the enemy's third "encirclement and suppression" campaign in 1931 that some comrades fundamentally changed their attitude on this question. But this was not true of the whole Party, and there were other comrades who did not think along the lines presented here.

Experience tells us that China's problems cannot be settled without armed force. An understanding of this point will help us in successfully waging the War of Resistance Against Japan from now on. The fact that the whole nation is rising in armed resistance in the war against Japan should inculcate a better understanding of the importance of this question in the whole Party, and every Party member should be prepared to take up arms and go to the front at any moment. Moreover, . . . the Party's main fields of work are in the battle zones and in the enemy's rear. This is also an excellent antidote against the tendency of some Party members to be willing only to work in Party organizations and in the mass movement but to be unwilling to study or participate in warfare, and against the failure of some schools to encourage students to go to the front, and other such phenomena. In most of China, Party organizational work and mass work are directly linked with armed struggle; there is not, and cannot be, any Party work or mass work that is isolated and stands by itself. Even in rear areas remote from the battle zones (like Yunnan, Kweichow, and Szechuan) and in enemy-occupied areas (like Peiping, Tientsin, Nanking, and Shanghai), Party organizational work and mass work are co-ordinated with the war, and should and must exclusively serve the needs of the front. In a word, the whole Party must pay great attention to war, study military matters, and prepare itself for fighting.

Just and Unjust Wars

From: "On Tactics Against Japanese Imperialism" (December 1935), *Selected Works,* I (Peking: Foreign Languages Press, 1964), pp. 170–71.

Ever since the monster of imperialism came into being, the affairs of the world have become so closely interwoven that it is impossible to separate them. We Chinese have the spirit to fight the enemy to the last drop of our blood, the determination to recover our lost territory by our own efforts, and the ability to stand on our own feet in the family of nations. . . . There is the old adage "In the Spring and Autumn Era there were no righteous wars." This is even truer of imperialism today, for it is only the oppressed nations and the oppressed classes that can wage just wars. All wars anywhere in the world in which the people rise up to fight their oppressors are just struggles. The February and October Revolutions in Russia were just wars. The revolutions of the people in various European countries after World War I were just struggles. In China, the Anti-Opium War, the War of the Taiping Heavenly Kingdom . . . , the Revolutionary War of 1911, the Northern Expedition of 1926–27, the Agrarian Revolutionary War from 1927 to the present, and the present resistance to Japan and punitive actions against traitors— these are all just wars. Now, in the mounting tide of nationwide struggle against Japan and of world-wide struggle against fascism, just wars will spread all over China and the globe. All just wars support each other, while all unjust wars should be turned into just wars—this is the Leninist line. Our war against Japan needs the support of the people of the whole world and, above all, the support of the people of the Soviet Union, which they will certainly give us because they and we are bound together in a common cause.

From: "Interview with the British Journalist James Bertram" (October 1937), *Selected Works,* II (Peking: Foreign Languages Press, 1965), pp. 57–58.

. . . All wars in history may be divided into two kinds according to their nature: just wars and unjust wars. For instance, the Great War in Europe some twenty years ago was an unjust, imperialist war. The governments of the imperialist countries forced the people to fight for the interests of imperialism and thus went against the people's interests, these circumstances necessitating a type of government such as the Lloyd George government in Britain. Lloyd George repressed the British people, forbidding them to speak against the imperialist war and banning organizations or assemblies that expressed popular opinion against the war; even though Parliament remained, it was merely the organ of a group of imperialists, a parliament which rubber-stamped the war budget. The absence of unity between the government and the people in a war gives rise to a government of absolute centralism with all centralism and no democracy [for "democratic centralism," see Introduction, Chapter V]. But historically there have also been revolutionary wars, e.g., in France, Russia, and present-day Spain. In such wars the government does not fear popular disapproval, because the people are most willing to wage this kind of war; far from fearing the people, it endeavors to arouse them and encourages them to express their views so that they will actively participate in the war, because the government rests upon the people's voluntary support. China's war of national liberation has the full approval of the people and cannot be won without their participation; therefore democratic centralism becomes a necessity. In the Northern Expedition of 1926–27, too, the victories were achieved through democratic centralism. Thus it can be seen that when the aims of a war directly reflect the interests of the people, the more democratic the government, the more effectively can the war be prosecuted. Such a government need have no fear that the people will oppose the war; rather it should be worried lest the people remain inactive or indifferent to the war. The nature of a war determines the relationship between the government and the people—this is the law of history.

From: "Interview with a *New China Daily* Correspondent on the New International Situation" (September 1939), *Selected Works,* II (Peking: Foreign Languages Press, 1965), pp. 265–66.

In Europe, a large-scale imperialist war is imminent between the German-Italian and the Anglo-French imperialist blocs which are contending for domination over the colonial peoples. In this war, each of the belligerents will brazenly declare its own cause to be just and that of its opponents unjust in order to delude people and win the support of public opinion. Actually this is a swindle. The aims of both sides are imperialist, both are fighting for the domination of colonies and semicolonies and for spheres of influence, and both are waging a predatory war. At present, they are fighting over Poland, the Balkans, and the Mediterranean litoral. This war is not at all a just war. The only just wars are non-predatory wars, wars of liberation. Communists will in no circumstances support any predatory war. They will, however, bravely step forward to support every just and non-predatory war for liberation, and they will stand in the forefront of the struggle. . . . In short, the two big imperialist blocs are feverishly preparing for war and millions of people are facing the danger of mass slaughter. Surely all this will arouse movements of resistance among the masses. Whether in Germany or in Italy, Britain or France, or anywhere else in Europe or the world at large, if the people do not want to be used as imperialist cannon fodder, they will have to rise up and oppose the imperialist war in every possible way.

Besides these two big blocs, there is a third bloc in the capitalist world, headed by the United States and including a number of Central and South American countries. In its own interests, this bloc will not enter the war for the time being. In the name of neutrality, U.S. imperialism is temporarily refraining from joining either of the belligerents, so as to be able to come on the scene later and contend for the leadership of the capitalist world. The fact that the U.S. bourgeoisie is not yet prepared to discard democracy and a peacetime economy at home is favorable to the world peace movement.

WAR AND PEACE

Abolition of War

From: "Problems of Strategy in China's Revolutionary War" (December 1936), *Selected Works*, I (Peking: Foreign Languages Press, 1964), pp. 182–83.

War, this monster of mutual slaughter among men, will be finally eliminated by the progress of human society, and in the not too distant future too. But there is only one way to eliminate it and that is to oppose war with war, to oppose counterrevolutionary war with revolutionary war, to oppose national counterrevolutionary war with national revolutionary war, and to oppose counterrevolutionary class war with revolutionary class war. History knows only two kinds of war, just and unjust. We support just wars and oppose unjust wars. All counterrevolutionary wars are unjust, all revolutionary wars are just. Mankind's era of wars will be brought to an end by our own efforts, and beyond doubt the war we wage is part of the final battle. But also beyond doubt the war we face will be part of the biggest and most ruthless of all wars. The biggest and most ruthless of unjust counterrevolutionary wars is hanging over us, and the vast majority of mankind will be ravaged unless we raise the banner of a just war. The banner of mankind's just war is the banner of mankind's salvation. The banner of China's just war is the banner of China's salvation. A war waged by the great majority of mankind and of the Chinese people is beyond doubt a just war, a most lofty and glorious undertaking for the salvation of mankind and China, and a bridge to a new era in world history. When human society advances to the point where classes and states are eliminated, there will be no more wars, counterrevolutionary or revolutionary, unjust or just; that will be the era of perpetual peace for mankind. Our study of the laws of revolutionary war springs from the desire to eliminate all wars; herein lies the distinction between us Communists and all the exploiting classes.

"Perpetual Peace"

From: "On Protracted War" (May 1938), *Selected Works,* II (Peking: Foreign Languages Press, 1965), pp. 148–50.

. . . The protracted nature of China's anti-Japanese war is inseparably connected with the fight for perpetual peace in China and the whole world. Never has there been a historical period such as the present in which war is so close to perpetual peace. For several thousand years since the emergence of classes, the life of mankind has been full of wars; each nation has fought countless wars, either internally or with other nations. In the imperialist epoch of capitalist society, wars are waged on a particularly extensive scale and with a peculiar ruthlessness. The first great imperialist war of twenty years ago was the first of its kind in history, but not the last. Only the war which has now begun comes close to being the final war, that is, comes close to the perpetual peace of mankind. . . . Why . . . do we say the present war is near to perpetual peace? The present war is the result of the development of the general crisis of world capitalism which began with World War I; this general crisis is driving the capitalist countries into a new war and, above all, driving the fascist countries into new war adventures. This war, we can foresee, will not save capitalism, but will hasten its collapse. It will be greater in scale and more ruthless than the war of twenty years ago, all nations will inevitably be drawn in, it will drag on for a very long time, and mankind will suffer greatly. But, owing to the existence of the Soviet Union and the growing political consciousness of the people of the world, great revolutionary wars will undoubtedly emerge from this war to oppose all counterrevolutionary wars, thus giving this war the character of a struggle for perpetual peace. Even if later there should be another period of war, perpetual world peace will not be far off. Once man has eliminated capitalism, he will attain the era of perpetual peace, and there will be no more need for war. Neither armies, nor warships, nor military aircraft, nor poison gas will then be needed. Thereafter and for all time, mankind will never again know war. The revolutionary wars which have already begun are part of the war for perpetual peace. The war between China and Japan, two countries which have a combined population of over five hundred million, will take an important place in this war for perpetual peace, and out of it will come the liberation of the Chinese nation. The liberated new China of the future will be inseparable from the liberated new world of the future. Hence our War of Resistance Against Japan takes on the character of a struggle for perpetual peace.

. . . History shows that wars are divided into two kinds, just and unjust. All wars that are progressive are just, and all wars that impede progress are unjust. We Communists oppose all unjust wars that impede progress, but we do not oppose progressive, just wars. Not only do we Communists not oppose just wars, we actively participate in them. As for unjust wars, World War I is an instance in which both sides fought for imperialist interests; therefore the Communists of the whole world firmly opposed that war. The way to oppose a war of this kind is to do everything possible to prevent it before it breaks out and, once it breaks out, to oppose war with war, to oppose unjust war with just war, whenever possible. Japan's war is an unjust war that impedes progress, and the peoples of the world, including the Japanese people, should oppose it and are opposing it. In our country the people and the government, the Communist Party and the Kuomintang, have all raised the banner of righteousness in the national revolutionary war against aggression. Our war is sacred and just, it is progressive and its aim is peace. The aim is peace not just in one country but throughout the world, not just temporary but perpetual peace. To achieve this aim we must wage a life-and-death struggle, be prepared for any sacrifice, persevere to the end and never stop short of the goal. However great the sacrifice and however long the time needed to attain it, a new world of perpetual peace and brightness already lies clearly before us. Our faith in waging this war is based upon the new China and the new world of perpetual peace and brightness for which we are striving. Fascism and imperialism wish to perpetuate war, but we wish to put an end to it in the not too distant future. The great majority of mankind should exert their utmost efforts for this purpose. The four hundred fifty million people of China constitute one quarter of the world's population, and if by their concerted efforts they overthrow Japanese imperialism and create a new China of freedom and equality, they will most certainly be making a tremendous contribution to the struggle for perpetual world peace. This is no vain hope, for the whole world is approaching this point in the course of its social and economic development, and provided that the majority of mankind work together, our goal will surely be attained in several decades.

THE COLLAPSE OF IMPERIALISM

"Imperialism Is Transient"

From: "The Present Situation and Our Tasks" (December 1947), *Selected Works,* IV (Peking: Foreign Languages Press, 1961), pp. 171–73.

When the reactionary Chiang Kai-shek clique launched the country-wide civil war against the people in 1946, the reason they dared take this risk was that they relied not merely on their own superior military strength but mainly on the U.S. imperialists with their atom bombs, whom they regarded as "exceptionally powerful" and "matchless in the world." On the one hand, they thought U.S. imperialism could meet their military and financial needs with a stream of supplies. On the other hand, they wildly speculated that "war between the United States and the Soviet Union is inevitable" and that "the outbreak of a third world war is inevitable." This dependence on U.S. imperialism is the common feature of the reactionary forces in all countries since World War II. It reflects the severity of the blows world capitalism received in World War II; it reflects the weakness of the reactionary forces in all countries, their panic and loss of confidence; and it reflects the might of the world revolutionary forces—all of which make reactionaries in all countries feel that there is no way out except to rely on U.S. imperialist support. But, in fact, is U.S. imperialism after World War II as powerful as Chiang Kai-shek and the reactionaries of other countries imagine? Can it really pour out a stream of supplies for them? No, that is not so. The economic power of U.S. imperialism, which grew during World War II, is confronted with unstable and daily shrinking domestic and foreign markets. The further shrinking of these markets will cause economic crises to break out. The war boom in the United States of America was only temporary. The strength of the United States of America is only superficial and transient. Irreconcilable domestic and international contradictions, like a volcano, menace U.S. imperialism every day. U.S. imperialism is sitting on this volcano. This situation has driven the U.S. imperialists to draw up a plan for enslaving the world, to run amuck like wild beasts in Europe, Asia, and other parts of the world, to muster the reactionary forces in all countries, the human dregs cast off by their peoples, to form an imperialist and anti-democratic camp against all the democratic forces headed by the Soviet Union, and to prepare for war in the hope that in the future, at a distant time, someday, they can start a third world war to defeat the democratic forces. This is a preposterous plan. The democratic forces of the world must defeat this plan and certainly can defeat it. The strength of the world anti-imperialist camp has surpassed that of the imperialist camp. It is we, not the enemy, who are in the superior position. The anti-imperialist camp headed by the Soviet Union has already been formed. The socialist Soviet Union is free from crises, on the ascendant and cherished by the world's broad masses; its strength has already surpassed that of the imperialist United States, which is seriously menaced by crises, on the decline and opposed by the world's broad masses. The People's Democracies in Europe are consolidating themselves internally and are uniting with each other. In the European capitalist countries the people's anti-imperialist forces are developing, with those in France and Italy taking the lead. Within the United States, there are people's democratic forces which are getting stronger every day. The peoples of Latin America are not slaves obedient to U.S. imperialism. In the whole of Asia a great national liberation movement has arisen. All the forces of the anti-imperialist camp are uniting and forging ahead. The Communist and Workers' Parties of nine European countries have established their Information Bureau and issued a call to the people of the world to rise against the imperialist plan of enslavement. This call to battle has inspired the oppressed people of the world, charted the course of their struggle, and strengthened their confidence in victory. It has thrown world reaction into panic and confusion. All the anti-imperialist forces in the countries of the East, too, should unite together, oppose oppression by imperialism and by their domestic reactionaries and make the goal of their struggle the emancipation of the more than one billion oppressed people of the East. We certainly should grasp our own destiny in our own hands. We should rid our ranks of all impotent thinking. All views that overestimate the strength of the enemy and underestimate the strength of the people are wrong. If everyone makes strenuous efforts, we, together with all the democratic forces of the world, can surely defeat the imperialist plan of enslavement, prevent the outbreak of a third world war, overthrow all reactionary regimes, and win lasting peace for mankind. We are soberly aware that on our way forward there will still be all kinds of obstacles and difficulties and that we should be prepared to deal with the maximum resistance and desperate struggle by all our enemies, domestic and foreign. But so long as we can grasp the science of Marxism-Leninism, have confidence in the masses, stand closely together with the masses, and lead them forward, we shall be fully able to surmount any obstacle and overcome any difficulty. Our strength will be invincible. This is the historic epoch in which world capitalism and imperialism are going down to their doom and world socialism and people's democracy are marching to victory. The dawn is ahead, we must exert ourselves.

"Imperialism Is Doomed"

From: "Cast Away Illusions, Prepare for Struggle" (August 1949), *Selected Works*, IV (Peking: Foreign Languages Press, 1961), pp. 425–31.

It is no accident that the U. S. State Department's White Paper on China-U.S. relations and Secretary of State Acheson's Letter of Transmittal to President Truman have been released at this time

[August 1949]. The publication of these documents reflects the victory of the Chinese people and the defeat of imperialism, it reflects the decline of the entire world system of imperialism. The imperialist system is riddled with insuperable internal contradictions, and therefore the imperialists are plunged into deep gloom.

Imperialism has prepared the conditions for its own doom. These conditions are the awakening of the great masses of the people in the colonies and semicolonies and in the imperialist countries themselves. Imperialism has pushed the great masses of the people throughout the world into the historical epoch of the great struggle to abolish imperialism.

Imperialism has prepared the material as well as the moral conditions for the struggle of the great masses of the people.

The material conditions are factories, railways, firearms, artillery, and the like. Most of the powerful equipment of the Chinese People's Liberation Army comes from U.S. imperialism, some comes from Japanese imperialism, and some is of our own manufacture.

The British aggression against China in 1840 was followed by the wars of aggression against China by [France, Germany, Japan, Russia, and the United States]. . . . As stated in Acheson's Letter, the United States in this last war has given the Kuomintang government material aid to the value of "more than 50 per cent" of the latter's "monetary expenditures" and "furnished the Chinese armies" (meaning the Kuomintang armies) with "military supplies." It is a war in which the United States supplies the money and guns and Chiang Kai-shek supplies the men to fight for the United States and slaughter the Chinese people. All these wars of aggression, together with political, economic, and cultural aggression and oppression, have caused the Chinese to hate imperialism, made them stop and think, "What is all this about?" and compelled them to bring their revolutionary spirit into full play and become united through struggle. They fought, failed, fought again, failed again and fought again, and accumulated 109 years of experience, accumulated the experience of hundreds of struggles, great and small, military and political, economic and cultural, with bloodshed and without bloodshed—and only then won today's basic victory. These are the moral conditions without which the revolution could not be victorious.

To serve the needs of its aggression, imperialism created the comprador system and bureaucrat-capital in China. Imperialist aggression stimulated China's social economy, brought about changes in it, and created the opposites of imperialism—the national industry and national bourgeoisie of China, and especially the Chinese proletariat working in enterprises run directly by the imperialists, those run by bureaucrat-capital, and those run by the national bourgeoisie. To serve the needs of its aggression, imperialism ruined the Chinese peasants by exploiting them through the exchange of unequal values and thereby created great masses of poor peasants, numbering hundreds of millions and comprising 70 per cent of China's rural population. To serve the needs of its aggression, imperialism created for China millions of big and small intellectuals of a new type, differing from the old type of *literatus* or scholar-bureaucrat. But imperialism and its running dogs, the reactionary governments of China, could control only a part of these intellectuals and finally only a handful. . . . Students, teachers, professors, technicians, engineers, doctors, scientists, writers, artists, and government employees, all are revolting against or parting company with the Kuomintang. The Communist Party is the party of the poor and is described in the Kuomintang's widespread, all-pervasive propaganda as a band of people who commit murder and arson, who rape and loot, who reject history and culture, renounce the motherland, have no filial piety or respect for teachers, and are impervious to all reason, who practice community of property and of women and employ the military tactics of the "human sea"—in short, a horde of fiendish monsters who perpetrate every conceivable crime and are unpardonably wicked. But strangely enough, it is this very horde that has won the support of several hundred million people, including the majority of the intellectuals, and especially the student youth.

Part of the intellectuals still want to wait and see. They think: the Kuomintang is no good and the Communist Party is not necessarily good either, so we had better wait and see. Some support the Communist Party in words, but in their hearts they are waiting to see. They are the very people who have illusions about the United States. They are unwilling to draw a distinction between the U.S. imperialists, who are in power, and the American people, who are not. They are easily duped by the honeyed words of the U.S. imperialists, as though these imperialists would deal with People's China on the basis of equality and mutual benefit without a stern, long struggle. They still have many reactionary, that is to say, antipopular, ideas in their heads, but they are not Kuomintang reactionaries. They are the middle-of-the-roaders or the right-wingers in People's China. They are the supporters of what Acheson calls "democratic individualism." The deceptive maneuvers of the Achesons still have a flimsy social base in China.

Acheson . . . admits that the U.S. imperialists are at a complete loss as to what to do about the present situation in China. The Kuomintang is so impotent that no amount of help can save it from inevitable doom; the U.S. imperialists are losing grip over things and feel helpless. Acheson says in his Letter of Transmittal:

> The unfortunate but inescapable fact is that the ominous result of the civil war in China was beyond the control of the government of the United States. Nothing that this country did or could have done within the reasonable limits of its capabilities could have changed that result; nothing that was left undone by this country has contributed to it. It was the product of internal Chinese forces, forces which this country tried to influence but could not.

According to logic, Acheson's conclusion should be, as some muddleheaded Chinese intellectuals think or say, to act like "the butcher who lays down his knife and at once becomes a Buddha" or "the robber who has a change of heart and becomes a virtuous man," that is, he should treat People's China on the basis of equality and mutual benefit and stop making trouble. But no, says Acheson, troublemaking will continue, and definitely so. Will there be any result? There will, says he. On what group of people will he rely? On the supporters of "democratic individualism." Says Acheson:

> . . . ultimately the profound civilization and the democratic individualism of China will reassert themselves and she will throw off the foreign yoke. I consider that we should encourage all developments in China which now and in the future work toward this end.

How different is the logic of the imperialists from that of the people! Make trouble, fail, make trouble again, fail again . . . till their doom; that is the logic of the imperialists and all reactionaries the world over in dealing with the people's cause, and they will never go against this logic. This is a Marxist law. When we say "imperialism is ferocious," we mean that its nature will never change, that the imperialists will never lay down their butcher knives, that they will never become Buddhas, till their doom.

Fight, fail, fight again, fail again, fight again . . . till their victory; that is the logic of the people, and they too will never go against this logic. This is another Marxist law. The Russian people's revolution followed this law, and so has the Chinese people's revolution. . . .

The slogan "Prepare for struggle" is addressed to those who still cherish certain illusions about the relations between China and the imperialist countries, especially between China and the United States. With regard to this question, they are still passive, their minds are still not made up, they are still not determined to wage a long struggle against U.S. (and British) imperialism because they still have illusions about the United States. There is still a very wide, or fairly wide, gap between these people and ourselves on this question.

The publication of the U.S. White Paper and Acheson's Letter of Transmittal is worthy of celebration, because it is a bucket of cold water and a loss of face for those who have ideas of the old type of democracy or democratic individualism, who do not approve of, or do not quite approve of, or are dissatisfied with, or are somewhat dissatisfied with, or even resent, people's democracy, or democratic collectivism, or democratic centralism, or collective heroism, or patriotism based on internationalism—but who still have patriotic feelings and are not Kuomintang reactionaries. It is a bucket of cold water particularly for those who believe that everything American is good and hope that China will model herself on the United States.

Acheson openly declares that the Chinese democratic individualists will be "encouraged" to throw off the so-called "foreign yoke." That is to say, he calls for the overthrow of Marxism-Leninism and the people's democratic dictatorship [see Chapter II] led by the Communist Party of China. For this "ism" and this system, it is alleged, are "foreign," with no roots in China, imposed on the Chinese by the German Karl Marx (who died sixty-six years ago) and the Russians Lenin (who died twenty-five years ago) and Stalin (who is still alive); this "ism" and this system, moreover, are downright bad, because they advocate the class struggle, the overthrow of imperialism, etc.; hence they must be got rid of. In this connection, it is alleged, "the democratic individualism of China will reassert itself" with the "encouragement" of President Truman, the backstage Commander in Chief [George C.] Marshall, Secretary of State Acheson (the charming foreign mandarin responsible for the publication of the White Paper), and Ambassador Leighton Stuart, who has scampered off. Acheson and his like think they are giving "encouragement," but those Chinese democratic individualists who still have patriotic feelings, even though they believe in the United States, may quite possibly feel this is a bucket of cold water thrown on them and a loss of face; for instead of dealing with the authorities of the Chinese people's democratic dictatorship in the proper way, Acheson and his like are doing this filthy work and, what is more, they have openly published it. What a loss of face! What a loss of face! To those who are patriotic, Acheson's statement is no "encouragement" but an insult.

China is in the midst of a great revolution. All China is seething with enthusiasm. The conditions are favorable for winning over and uniting with all those who do not have a bitter and deep-seated hatred for the cause of the people's revolution, even though they have mistaken ideas. Progressives should use the White Paper to persuade all these persons.

"Imperialism Is Rotten"

From: "On Some Important Problems of the Party's Present Policy" (January 1948), *Selected Works,* IV (Peking: Foreign Languages Press, 1961), pp. 181–82.

Oppose overestimation of the enemy's strength. For example: fear of U.S. imperialism; fear of carrying the battle into the Kuomintang areas; fear of wiping out the comprador-feudal system, of distributing the land of the landlords and of confiscating bureaucrat-capital; fear of a long-drawn-out war; and so on. All these are incorrect. Imperialism throughout the world and the rule of the reactionary Chiang Kai-shek clique in China are already rotten and have no future. We have reason to despise them and we are confident and certain that we shall defeat all the domestic and foreign enemies of the Chinese people. But with regard to each part, each specific struggle (military, political, economic, or ideological), we must never take the enemy lightly; on the contrary, we should take the enemy seriously and concentrate all our strength for battle in order to win victory. While we correctly point out that, strategically, with regard to the whole, we should take the enemy lightly, we must never take the enemy lightly in any part, in any specific struggle. If, with regard to the whole, we overestimate the strength of our enemy and hence do not dare to overthrow him and do not dare to win victory, we shall be committing a "right" opportunist error. If, with regard to each part, each specific problem, we are not prudent, do not carefully study and perfect the art of struggle, do not concentrate all our strength for battle and do not pay attention to winning over all the allies that should be won over (middle peasants, small independent craftsmen and traders, the middle bourgeoisie, students, teachers, professors and ordinary intellectuals, ordinary government employees, professionals, and enlightened gentry), we shall be committing a "left" opportunist error.

"Imperialism Is a Paper Tiger"

From: A speech at a meeting of the Political Bureau of the Central Committee of the Communist Party of China, Wuchang, December 1, 1958. Quoted in an explanatory footnote in "Talk with the American Correspondent Anna Louise Strong" (August 1946), *Selected Works,* IV (Peking: Foreign Languages Press, 1961), pp. 98–99.

Just as there is not a single thing in the world without a dual nature (this is the law of the unity of opposites), so imperialism and all reactionaries have a dual nature—they are real tigers and paper tigers at the same time. In past history, before they won state power and for some time afterward, the slave-owning class, the feudal land-lord class, and the bourgeoisie were vigorous, revolutionary, and progressive; they were real tigers. But with the lapse of time, because their opposites—the slave class, the peasant class, and the pro-letariat—grew in strength step by step, struggled against them and became more and more formidable, these ruling classes changed step by step into the reverse, changed into reactionaries, changed into backward people, changed into paper tigers. And eventually they were overthrown, or will be overthrown, by the people. The reactionary, backward, decaying classes retained this dual nature even in their last life-and-death struggles against the people. On the one hand, they were real tigers; they ate people, ate people by the millions and tens of millions. The cause of the people's struggle went through a period of difficulties and hardships, and along the path there were many twists and turns. To destroy the rule of im-perialism, feudalism, and bureaucrat-capitalism in China took the Chinese people more than a hundred years and cost them tens of millions of lives before the victory in 1949. Look! Were these not living tigers, iron tigers, real tigers? But in the end they changed into paper tigers, dead tigers, bean-curd tigers. These are historical facts. Have people not seen or heard about these facts? There have indeed been thousands and tens of thousands of them! Thousands and tens of thousands! Hence, imperialism and all reactionaries, looked at in essence, from a long-term point of view, from a strategic point of view, must be seen for what they are—paper tigers. On this we should build our strategic thinking. On the other hand, they are also living tigers, iron tigers, real tigers which can eat people. On this we should build our tactical thinking.

"East Wind over the West Wind"

From: A speech at the meeting of representatives of the Communist and Workers' Parties of the socialist countries, Moscow, November 18, 1957. Quoted in *Comrade Mao Tse-tung on "Imperialism and All Reactionaries are Paper Tigers,"* compiled by *Jen-min Jih-pao* (People's Daily) Editorial Department (Peking: Foreign Languages Press, 1958), pp. 24–26.

In 1946 when Chiang Kai-shek launched his attacks against us, many of our comrades and people throughout the country were very much worried: Could the war be won? I myself was also worried about this. But of one thing we were confident. At that time an American journalist named Anna Louise Strong came to Yenan. We discussed many questions in our talks, including Chiang Kai-shek, Hitler, Japan, the United States, the atom bomb, etc. I said that all the reputedly powerful reactionaries were merely paper tigers. The reason was that they were divorced from the people. You see, wasn't Hitler a paper tiger? Wasn't Hitler overthrown? I also said that the tsar was a paper tiger, the Chinese emperor was a paper tiger, Japanese imperialism was a paper tiger. You see they were all down and out. U.S. imperialism has not yet fallen and it has the atom bomb. I believe it will also fall. It is also a paper tiger. Chiang Kai-shek was very powerful. He had more than four million regular troops. At that time we were in Yenan. What was the population of Yenan? Seven thousand. How many troops did we have? We had nine hundred thousand guerrillas, all divided by Chiang Kai-shek into scores of bases. But we said Chiang Kai-shek was only a paper tiger and we would certainly defeat him. In order to struggle against the enemy, we have formed the concept over a long period, namely, that strategically we should slight all enemies, and tactically we should take full account of all enemies. That is also to say, we must slight the enemy as a whole but take full account of him so far as each and every concrete question is concerned. If we do not slight the enemy as a whole, we shall be committing the mistake of opportunism. . . . But on concrete questions and on questions concerning each and every particular enemy, if we do not take full account of the enemy, we shall be committing the mistake of adventurism. In war, battles can only be fought one by one and the enemy can only be annihilated bit by bit. . . . The same is true of eating a meal. Strategically, we slight the eating of a meal: we can finish the meal. But when actually eating, we do it a mouthful at a time. It would be impossible for you to swallow the entire feast in a single mouthful. This is called one-by-one solution. And in military literature, it is called smashing the enemy one by one. . . .

I am of the opinion that the international situation has now reached a new turning point. There are two winds in the world today: the East wind and the West wind. There is a Chinese saying: "Either the East wind prevails over the West wind or the West wind prevails over the East wind." I think the characteristic of the situation today is the East wind prevailing over the West wind. That is to say, the socialist forces are overwhelmingly superior to the imperialist forces.

★

CHAPTER II
Stages of
Revolutionary Development

Introductory Note

The recent history of mankind, according to Mao Tse-tung, has been characterized by two principal types of revolution: bourgeois and proletarian. The era of pure bourgeois revolution has passed. Modern revolutions, Mao holds, are variants of the proletarian revolution. They are divided into those occurring in advanced industrial societies with a powerful proletariat and those in colonial, semi-colonial, and semifeudal countries in which a peasantry predominates. In the first instance, the revolution goes through a single, decisive stage: the proletariat, by any means at its disposal, engineers a revolution and overthrows the bourgeoisie. Although the Communists "would always prefer" to bring about a peaceful transition to socialism, practical considerations rule such a possibility "absolutely" out of the question. This is because the basic question of revolution is that of political power, which the ruling classes never relinquish voluntarily. In short, the possibility of peaceful revolution is rejected.

In colonial and semicolonial countries, by contrast, the revolution unfolds in two successive stages: bourgeois-democratic and proletarian-socialist. The chief characteristic of the bourgeois-democratic revolution, according to Mao, is that, led by the proletariat and relying on a "united front" of all "progressive" forces in the country, it seeks to overthrow imperialism-feudalism, achieve political independence, and nationalize the main sources of public wealth (except those of national capitalism, as we shall see). Only when these aims have been attained, Mao holds, can the movement proceed to its second stage, the proletarian-socialist revolution. The distinctive feature of the second stage is that it seeks to overthrow capitalism and introduce the era of "socialist construction." The purpose of the first stage is to transform a colonial and semicolonial country into an independent one; the function of the second stage is to wipe out all remnants of domestic reaction and develop the country along fully socialist lines.

The two revolutionary stages, though distinct and clearly identifiable, constitute aspects of a single process: the complete revolutionary movement in colonial and semicolonial countries. Of the two revolutionary stages, the first provides the condition for the second. The socialist stage can be reached only after the democratic stage has been completed. Each stage is distinguished from the other mainly in terms of the classes supporting it (the "motive forces" of revolution) and the classes against which it aims (the "targets" of revolution).

The Bourgeois-Democratic Revolution. The bourgeois-democratic revolution in question is a revolution of "new" type, distinguished from the "old"-democratic revolution of former times. The most significant distinction between the two lies in whether they occur before or after the emergence of the communist party. Led by the bourgeoisie, the old-democratic revolution sought to establish a capitalist state under bourgeois dictatorship. Led by the proletariat, the new-democratic revolution seeks to establish a transitional state under the dictatorship of several revolutionary classes, mainly the proletariat, the peasantry, the petty bourgeoisie, and the national bourgeoisie.

"New democracy," Mao asserts, is a general stage in the historical development of revolution in *all* colonial and semicolonial countries. As an initial stage, neither a bourgeois nor a proletarian revolution is feasible. The new-democratic revolution is inseparable from "the whole cause of proletarian revolution."

In seeking to overthrow imperialism (externally) and feudalism (internally), the new-democratic revolution consists, in essence, of two distinct—though closely interrelated—revolutions: a national revolution to attain liberation from foreign oppression, and a democratic revolution to overthrow the domestic reactionaries and eliminate the feudal relationships in the countryside. The first is a national struggle and the second a class struggle. The national revolution is an indispensable condition for the attainment of democracy;

the democratic revolution is essential to politicizing and mobilizing the masses in the struggle against imperialism.

In seeking both political independence and rural social transformation, the democratic revolution (of the new-democratic revolution) involves an agrarian upheaval as well. The peasant question, Mao insists, is an indispensable aspect of the new-democratic revolution; without peasant support, feudalism cannot be overthrown. The bourgeois-democratic revolution is "in essence" a peasant revolution.

As a whole, then, the new-democratic revolution is characterized by the simultaneous unfolding of three revolutionary processes: a national revolution, a democratic revolution, and an agrarian revolution.

As a transitional historical phase, the new-democratic revolution involves a programmatic consideration of a series of concrete tasks in three principal spheres: politics, economics, and culture.

Politically, the unique feature of new democracy is that it is a joint dictatorship of four revolutionary classes led by the proletariat. The allies of the working class include the peasantry, the petty bourgeoisie, and the national bourgeoisie. The main enemies of the new-democratic revolution are the imperialists, the feudal lords, and the big bourgeoisie. The proletarian leadership of the revolution is due partly to the ineptness of the bourgeoisie and partly to the character of the proletariat itself as "the most advanced class" in history.

The economic policy of the new-democratic state aims at redistributing the land of the feudal aristocracy among the peasantry, nationalizing capital and enterprises of the imperialists and the big bourgeoisie, and protecting the industry and commerce of the national bourgeoisie. The objective is to clear the way for the growth of capitalism as a precondition for socialism to emerge. Since the national burgeoisie continues to be an ally, its economic interests must be protected.

The culture of new democracy, being a reflection of its politics and economics, is anti-imperialist and anti-feudal in form and content. It is a "national," "popular" culture reflecting the characteristics of the new-democratic society as a whole. It is a "scientific" culture accurately mirroring class conditions in society.

The Proletarian-Socialist Revolution. New democracy is a transitional historical phase occurring between the dictatorship of the bourgeoisie and the dictatorship of the proletariat. Another transitional phase, lying somewhere between the new-democratic republic and the socialist society, is what Mao calls the "people's democratic dictatorship." Although at times he appears to use the two formulas interchangeably, the people's democratic dictatorship has a special place in his thinking, particularly after his formal seizure of political power in October 1949.

The people's democratic dictatorship is distinguished from new democracy in some particulars. To begin with, the elements of "dictatorship" far outweigh those of "democracy": the essence of the new state form is the monopoly of all effective power in the hands of the proletariat. More importantly, the people's democratic dictatorship involves a change in the nature of class relationships within the country: although the four-class alliance of new democracy continues to persist, it is now expressed in a new formula—worker-peasant alliance—and there is already a perceptible change in the relative emphasis placed on each class. Specifically, although the national bourgeoisie continues to be included among the "people," its position has been seriously undermined. The full implications of this development will be explored presently.

At some point between 1949 and 1956, the "people's democratic dictatorship" in China was imperceptibly transformed, as it were, into the dictatorship of the proletariat. In his report to the Eighth National Party Congress on September 15, 1956, Liu Shao-ch'i announced that "the people's democratic dictatorship has in essence become one form of the dictatorship of the proletariat." On September 27 of the same year, the Eighth Party Congress adopted a resolution giving formal sanction to Liu's statement. The basic functions of the dictatorship were to ensure "democracy" for the revolutionary classes, suppress the forces of domestic reaction, defend the country against foreign aggression, and initiate the process of socialist construction.

One of the unique features of the dictatorship of the proletariat in China before the cultural revolution was the continuation of the alliance of the working class with the peasantry, the petty bourgeoisie, and (nominally) the national bourgeoisie. This practice marked a departure from the orthodox communist doctrine that the establishment of the dictatorship of the proletariat should coincide with the elimination of the national bourgeoisie.

Although the position of the national bourgeoisie was progressively undermined in China, the formal aspects of the alliance persisted. The gradual weakening of the position of this class culminated, in 1956, in the transformation of all privately owned enterprise into joint state-private enterprise in which the national bourgeoisie were paid a "fixed interest" of 5 per cent on their stocks—a practice that was discontinued in 1966. (Since most former owners were retained in managerial and professional positions, the national bourgeoisie drew additional salaries comparable to those of their counterparts in the state enterprises.) The continuation of alliance with the national bourgeoisie, the Chinese doctrine ran, was determined by the concrete utility of this class to the regime. Although the national bourgeoisie was thought feeble and vacillating, its existence was justified because it possessed modern managerial and technological skills and contributed to the economic development of the country. Accordingly, Communist Chinese policy was one of "using, restricting, and transforming" the national bourgeoisie rather than eliminating them outright. This policy underwent significant changes in the period of the great proletarian cultural revolution (see Chapter III).

From the "philosophical" point of view, the policy toward the national bourgeoisie rested on Mao's distinction between "antagonistic" and "non-antagonistic" contradictions: the former, it will be recalled, can only be resolved through violence and force; the latter, by peaceful means. Mao argued that although as a general rule the contradiction between the proletariat and the national bourgeoisie is antagonistic, in China this was not the case. He wrote: "The contradiction between the exploiter and exploited, which exists between the national bourgeoisie and the working class, is an antagonistic one. But, in the concrete conditions existing in China, such an antagonistic contradiction, if properly handled, can be transformed into a non-antagonistic one and resolved in a peaceful way."[1] Since this was presumably accomplished, the Chinese Communists did not eliminate this class by force. Rather, the aim was to "educate," "persuade," and "remold" the national bourgeoisie to accept socialism peacefully. This was nothing short of an attempt to eradicate capitalism by non-violent means, a proposition without precedent in the history of communist thought. The violence visited upon the national bourgeoisie in the cultural revolution dealt a severe blow to Mao Tse-tung's theory of non-antagonistic contradictions.

[1] *On the Correct Handling of Contradictions Among the People* (February 1957) (Peking: Foreign Languages Press, 1957), p. 10.

The Uninterrupted Revolution. Mao Tse-tung's theory of revolution is the theory of "uninterrupted revolution." As early as 1937, he wrote, "We are exponents of the theory of the transition of the revolution and we are for the transition of the democratic revolution in the direction of socialism."[2] Stated simply, the theory of uninterrupted revolution asserts that the revolutionary process unfolds ceaselessly from beginning to end. The movement of revolution, Mao argues, follows the "general law of history" and passes through a series of identifiable phases. The point is that the various stages of revolution (including the bourgeois-democratic and the proletarian-socialist) can only be divided conceptually; they form the whole of a single process. He writes: "Every Communist ought to know that, taken as a whole, the Chinese revolutionary movement . . . embraces the two stages, i.e., the democratic and the socialist revolutions, which are two essentially different revolutionary processes, and that the second process can be carried through only after the first has been completed. The democratic revolution is the necessary preparation for the socialist revolution, and the socialist revolution is the inevitable sequel to the democratic revolution. The ultimate aim for which all communists strive is to bring about a socialist and communist society."

Mao's theory of uninterrupted revolution should be distinguished from Trotsky's conception of "permanent revolution." The main differences are that Trotsky: (1) distrusted the peasantry, (2) doubted the desirability of alliance with the national bourgeoisie, (3) thought it possible to "leap over" the bourgeois-democratic revolution, (4) questioned the possibility of a joint revolutionary dictatorship, and (5) rejected the possibility of building socialism in one country in favor of a "permanent revolution" that would establish socialism at the international level.

The uninterrupted unfolding of the Chinese revolution led to the "great leap forward" of 1958 and the establishment of the commune system throughout the country (see Introduction). The Central Committee resolution of August 29, 1958, which announced the formation of the commune system, saw the communes as "the logical results of the march of events" and forecast that they would "develop into the basic social units in communist society."

As we have seen, the commune experiment proved a failure: by

[2] "Win the Masses in Their Millions for the Anti-Japanese National United Front" (May 1937), *Selected Works,* I (Peking: Foreign Languages Press, 1964), p. 290.

fall of 1958 it was already clear that its announced objectives would not materialize. It is instructive, however, that even for a year or two afterward, the communes were still being presented as "rudiments of communism." It is also significant that the Central Committee resolution of December 10, 1958, which served as a restraint on the commune-ization process, succinctly reiterated Mao Tsetung's conception of uninterrupted revolution. It said: "We are advocates of the Marxist-Leninist theory of uninterrupted revolution; we hold that no 'Great Wall' exists or can be allowed to exist between the democratic revolution and the socialist revolution and between socialism and communism."[3]

While the great leap forward represented an attempt to press the revolution to a higher stage of development, the "Great Proletarian Cultural Revolution" of 1966–68 sought to bring about a complete ideological remolding of the Chinese people and the Chinese Communist Party (see Introduction). It set out to transform the country into "a great school of Mao Tse-tung's thought," a campaign directed in part against all those who had continued to criticize the "subjective idealism" of the "great leap" experiment.

The Chinese Communists have insisted that the cultural revolution represented a new stage in the revolutionary movement. The episode, perhaps as importantly, represented an attempt to consolidate the socialist revolution and to ensure that Chinese society would move in the "right" direction after Mao is gone. This was inspired by the fear that the "true" mission of the revolution might be ignored or subverted. In particular, Mao appears to have been seriously concerned that Chinese youth increasingly lacked revolutionary enthusiasm, a fear he had conveyed to Edgar Snow as early as January 1965.[4] From this standpoint, the Red Guard movement signified Mao's attempt to mobilize the country on a mass scale, as well as his direct and personal appeal to the youth of the country to revive their ideological purity and guard against the erosion of "Mao Tse-tung's thought." It also indicated Mao's reluctance to place complete faith in the military establishment (see Introduction).

[3] "Resolution on Some Questions Concerning the People's Communes," in *Sixth Plenary Session of the Eighth Central Committee of the Communist Party of China* (Peking: Foreign Languages Press, 1958), p. 25.

[4] See Edgar Snow, "Interview with Mao Tse-tung," *The New Republic,* February 27, 1965, pp. 17–23.

Readings

OLD AND NEW REVOLUTIONS

From: "The Chinese Revolution and the Chinese Communist Party" (December 1939), *Selected Works,* II (Peking: Foreign Languages Press, 1965), pp. 326–31.

The Character of the Chinese Revolution

We have now gained an understanding of the nature of Chinese society, i.e., of the specific conditions in China; this understanding is the essential prerequisite for solving all China's revolutionary problems. We are also clear about the targets, the tasks, and the motive forces of the Chinese revolution; these are basic issues at the present stage of the revolution and arise from the special nature of Chinese society, i.e., from China's specific conditions. Understanding all this, we can now understand another basic issue of the revolution at the present stage, i.e., the character of the Chinese revolution.

What, indeed, is the character of the Chinese revolution at the present stage? Is it a bourgeois-democratic or a proletarian-socialist revolution? Obviously, it is not the latter but the former.

Since Chinese society is colonial, semicolonial, and semifeudal, since the principal enemies of the Chinese revolution are imperialism and feudalism, since the tasks of the revolution are to overthrow these two enemies by means of a national and democratic revolution in which the bourgeoisie sometimes takes part, and since the edge of the revolution is directed against imperialism and feudalism and not against capitalism and capitalist private property in general even if the big bourgeoisie betrays the revolution and becomes its enemy—since all this is true, the character of the Chinese revolution at the present stage is not proletarian-socialist but bourgeois-democratic.

However, in present-day China the bourgeois-democratic revolution is no longer of the old general type, which is now obsolete, but one of a new special type. We call this type the new-democratic revolution and it is developing in all other colonial and semicolonial countries as well as in China. The new-democratic revolution is part of the world proletarian-socialist revolution, for it resolutely opposes imperialism, i.e., international capitalism. Politically, it strives for the joint dictatorship of the revolutionary classes over the imperialists, traitors, and reactionaries, and opposes the transformation of Chinese society into a society under bourgeois dictatorship. Economically, it aims at the nationalization of all the big enterprises and capital of the imperialists, traitors, and reactionaries, and the distribution among the peasants of the land held by the landlords, while preserving private capitalist enterprise in general and not eliminating the rich-peasant economy. Thus the new type of democratic revolution clears the way for capitalism on the one hand and creates the prerequisites for socialism on the other. The present stage of the Chinese revolution is a stage of transition between the abolition of the colonial, semicolonial, and semifeudal society and the establishment of a socialist society, i.e., it is a process of new-democratic revolution. This process, begun only after the First World War and the Russian October Revolution, started in China with the May 4 Movement of 1919. A new-democratic revolution is an anti-imperialist and anti-feudal revolution of the broad masses of the people under the leadership of the proletariat. Chinese society can advance to socialism only through such a revolution; there is no other way.

The new-democratic revolution is vastly different from the democratic revolutions of Europe and America in that it results not in a dictatorship of the bourgeoisie but in a dictatorship of the united front of all the revolutionary classes under the leadership of the proletariat. In the present War of Resistance, the anti-Japanese democratic political power established in the base areas which are under the leadership of the Communist Party is the political power of the Anti-Japanese National United Front; this is neither a bourgeois nor a proletarian one-class dictatorship, but a joint dictatorship of the revolutionary classes under the leadership of the proletariat. All who stand for resistance to Japan and for democracy are entitled to share in this political power, regardless of their party affiliation.

The new-democratic revolution also differs from a socialist revolution in that it overthrows the rule of the imperialists, traitors, and reactionaries in China but does not destroy any section of capitalism which is capable of contributing to the anti-imperialist, anti-feudal struggle.

The new-democratic revolution is basically in line with the revolution envisaged in the Three People's Principles as advocated by Dr. Sun Yat-sen in 1924. . . . The Communist Party of China was referring to the . . . Three People's Principles . . . when, in its Manifesto of September 22, 1937, it declared that "the Three People's Principles being what China needs today, our Party is ready to fight for their complete realization." These Three People's Principles embody Dr. Sun Yat-sen's Three Great Policies—alliance with Russia, co-operation with the Communist Party, and assistance to the peasants and workers. In the new international and domestic conditions, any kind of Three People's Principles which departs from the Three Great Policies is not revolutionary. (Here we shall not deal with the fact that, while communism and the Three People's Principles agree on the basic political program for the democratic revolution, they differ in all other respects.)

Thus, the role of the proletariat, the peasantry, and the other sections of the petty bourgeoisie in China's bourgeois-democratic revolution cannot be ignored, either in the alignment of forces for the struggle (that is, in the united front) or in the organization of state power. Anyone who tries to bypass these classes will certainly be unable to solve the problem of the destiny of the Chinese nation or indeed any of China's problems. The Chinese revolution at the present stage must strive to create a democratic republic in which the workers, the peasants, and the other sections of the petty bourgeoisie all occupy a definite position and play a definite role. In other words, it must be a democratic republic based on a revolutionary alliance of the workers, peasants, urban petty bourgeoisie, and all others who are against imperialism and feudalism. Only under the leadership of the proletariat can such a republic be completely realized.

The Perspectives of the Chinese Revolution

Now that the basic issues—the nature of Chinese society and the targets, tasks, motive forces, and character of the Chinese revolution at the present stage—have been clarified, it is easy to see its perspectives, that is, to understand the relation between the bourgeois-democratic and the proletarian-socialist revolution, or between the present and future stages of the Chinese revolution.

There can be no doubt that the ultimate perspective of the Chinese revolution is not capitalism but socialism and communism, since China's bourgeois-democratic revolution at the present stage is not of the old general type but is a democratic revolution of a new special type—a new-democratic revolution—and since it is taking place in the new international environment of the 1930s and '40s characterized by the rise of socialism and the decline of capitalism, in the period of the Second World War and the era of revolution.

However, it is not at all surprising but entirely to be expected that a capitalist economy will develop to a certain extent within Chinese society with the sweeping away of the obstacles to the development of capitalism after the victory of the revolution, since the purpose of the Chinese revolution at the present stage is to change the existing colonial, semicolonial, and semifeudal state of society, i.e., to strive for the completion of the new-democratic revolution. A certain degree of capitalist development will be an inevitable result of the victory of the democratic revolution in economically backward China. But that will be only one aspect of the outcome of the Chinese revolution and not the whole picture. The whole picture will show the development of socialist as well as capitalist factors. What will the socialist factors be? The increasing relative importance of the proletariat and the Communist Party among the political forces in the country; leadership by the proletariat and the Communist Party which the peasantry, intelligentsia, and the urban petty bourgeoisie already accept or are likely to accept; and the state sector of the economy owned by the democratic republic, and the co-operative sector of the economy owned by the working people. All these will be socialist factors. With the addition of a favorable international environment, these factors render it highly probable that China's bourgeois-democratic revolution will ultimately avoid a capitalist future and enjoy a socialist future.

The Twofold Task of the Chinese Revolution and the Chinese Communist Party

Summing up the foregoing sections of this chapter, we can see that the Chinese revolution taken as a whole involves a twofold task. That is to say, it embraces both the bourgeois-democratic revolution (the new-democratic revolution) and the proletarian-socialist revolution, i.e., both the present and future stages of the revolution. The leadership in this twofold revolutionary task devolves on the Chinese Communist Party, the party of the proletariat, without whose leadership no revolution can succeed.

To complete China's bourgeois-democratic revolution (the new-democratic revolution) and to transform it into a socialist revolution when all the necessary conditions are ripe—such is the sum total of the great and glorious revolutionary task of the Chinese Communist Party. Every Party member must strive for its accomplishment and must under no circumstances give up halfway. Some immature Communists think that our task is confined to the present democratic revolution and does not include the future socialist revolution, or that the present revolution or the Agrarian Revolution is actually a socialist revolution. It must be emphatically pointed out that these views are wrong. Every Communist ought to know that, taken as a whole, the Chinese revolutionary movement led by the Communist Party embraces the two stages, i.e., the democratic and the socialist revolutions, which are two essentially different revolutionary processes, and that the second process can be carried through only after the first has been completed. The democratic revolution is the necessary preparation for the socialist revolution, and the socialist revolution is the inevitable sequel to the democratic revolution. The ultimate aim for which all communists strive is to bring about a socialist and communist society. A clear understanding of both the differences and the interconnections between the democratic and the socialist revolutions is indispensable to correct leadership in the Chinese revolution.

Except for the Communist Party, no political party (bourgeois or petty bourgeois) is equal to the task of leading China's two great revolutions, the democratic and the socialist revolutions, to complete fulfillment. From the very day of its birth, the Communist Party has taken this twofold task on its own shoulders and for eighteen years has fought strenuously for its accomplishment.

NEW-DEMOCRATIC REVOLUTION

From: "On New Democracy" (January 1940), *Selected Works*, II (Peking: Foreign Languages Press, 1965), pp. 342–44, 347–50, 353–54, 369–70, 380–82.

The Chinese Revolution Is Part of the World Revolution

The historical characteristic of the Chinese revolution lies in its division into the two stages, democracy and socialism, the first being no longer democracy in general, but democracy of the Chinese type, a new and special type, namely, New Democracy. How, then, has this historical characteristic come into being? Has it been in existence for the past hundred years, or is it of recent origin?

A brief study of the historical development of China and of the world shows that this characteristic did not emerge immediately after the Opium War, but took shape later, after the first imperialist world war and the October Revolution in Russia. Let us now examine the process of its formation.

Clearly, it follows from the colonial, semicolonial, and semifeudal character of present-day Chinese society that the Chinese revolution must be divided into two stages. The first step is to change the colonial, semicolonial, and semifeudal form of society into an independent, democratic society. The second is to carry the revolution forward and build a socialist society. At present the Chinese revolution is taking the first step.

The preparatory period for the first step began with the Opium War in 1840, i.e., when China's feudal society started changing into a semicolonial and semifeudal one. Then came the Movement of the Taiping Heavenly Kingdom, the Sino-French War, the Sino-Japanese War, the reform movement of 1898, the revolution of 1911, the May 4 Movement, the Northern Expedition, the War of the Agrarian Revolution, and the present War of Resistance Against Japan. Together these have taken up a whole century and in a sense they represent that first step, being struggles waged by the Chinese people, on different occasions and in varying degrees, against imperialism and the feudal forces in order to build up an independent, democratic society and complete the first revolution. The revolution of 1911 was in a fuller sense the beginning of that revolution. In its social character, this revolution is a bourgeois-democratic and not a proletarian-socialist revolution. It is still unfinished and still demands great efforts, because to this day its enemies are still very strong. When Dr. Sun Yat-sen said, "The revolution is not yet completed, all my comrades must struggle on," he was referring to the bourgeois-democratic revolution.

A change, however, occurred in China's bourgeois-democratic revolution after the outbreak of the first imperialist world war in 1914 and the founding of a socialist state on one sixth of the globe as a result of the Russian October Revolution of 1917.

Before these events, the Chinese bourgeois-democratic revolution came within the old category of the bourgeois-democratic world revolution, of which it was a part.

Since these events, the Chinese bourgeois-democratic revolution has changed; it has come within the new category of bourgeois-democratic revolutions and, as far as the alignment of revolutionary forces is concerned, forms part of the proletarian-socialist world revolution.

Why? Because the first imperialist world war and the first victorious socialist revolution, the October Revolution, have changed the whole course of world history and ushered in a new era.

It is an era in which the world capitalist front has collapsed in one part of the globe (one sixth of the world) and has fully revealed its decadence everywhere else, in which the remaining capitalist parts cannot survive without relying more than ever on the colonies and semicolonies, in which a socialist state has been established and has proclaimed its readiness to give active support to the liberation movement of all colonies and semicolonies, and in which the proletariat of the capitalist countries is steadily freeing itself from the social-imperialist influence of the social-democratic parties and has proclaimed its support for the liberation movement in the colonies and semicolonies. In this era, any revolution in a colony or semicolony that is directed against imperialism, i.e., against the international bourgeoisie or international capitalism, no longer comes within the old category of the bourgeois-democratic world revolution, but within the new category. It is no longer part of the old bourgeois, or capitalist, world revolution, but is part of the new world revolution, the proletarian-socialist world revolution. Such revolutionary colonies and semicolonies can no longer be regarded as allies of the counterrevolutionary front of world capitalism; they have become allies of the revolutionary front of world socialism.

Although such a revolution in a colonial and semicolonial country is still fundamentally bourgeois-democratic in its social character during its first stage or first step, and although its objective mission is to clear the path for the development of capitalism, it is no longer a revolution of the old type led by the bourgeoisie with the aim of establishing a capitalist society and a state under bourgeois dictatorship. It belongs to the new type of revolution led by the proletariat with the aim, in the first stage, of establishing a new-democratic society and a state under the joint dictatorship of all the revolutionary classes. Thus this revolution actually serves the purpose of clearing a still wider path for the development of socialism. In the course of its progress, there may be a number of further substages, because of changes on the enemy's side and within the ranks of our allies, but the fundamental character of the revolution remains unchanged.

Such a revolution attacks imperialism at its very roots, and is therefore not tolerated but opposed by imperialism. However, it is favored by socialism and supported by the land of socialism and the socialist international proletariat.

Therefore, such a revolution inevitably becomes part of the proletarian-socialist world revolution.

The correct thesis that "the Chinese revolution is part of the world revolution" was put forward as early as 1924–27 during the period of China's First Great Revolution. It was put forward by the Chinese Communists and endorsed by all those taking part in the anti-imperialist and anti-feudal struggle of the time. However, the significance of this thesis was not fully expounded in those days, and consequently it was only vaguely understood.

The "world revolution" no longer refers to the old world revolution, for the old bourgeois world revolution has long been a thing of the past; it refers to the new world revolution, the socialist world revolution. Similarly, to form "part of" means to form part not of the old bourgeois but of the new socialist revolution. This is a tremendous change unparalleled in the history of China and of the world. . . .

Today, the Chinese revolution has taken on still greater significance. This is a time when the economic and political crises of capitalism are dragging the world more and more deeply into the Second World War, when the Soviet Union has reached the period of transition from socialism to communism and is capable of leading and helping the proletariat and oppressed nations of the whole world in their fight against imperialist war and capitalist reaction, when the proletariat of the capitalist countries is preparing to overthrow capitalism and establish socialism, and when the proletariat, the peasantry, the intelligentsia, and other sections of the petty bourgeoisie in China have become a mighty independent political force under the leadership of the Chinese Communist Party. Situated as we are in this day and age, should we not make the appraisal that the Chinese revolution has taken on still greater world significance? I think we should. The Chinese revolution has become a very important part of the world revolution.

Although the Chinese revolution in this first stage (with its many substages) is a new type of bourgeois-democratic revolution and is not yet itself a proletarian-socialist revolution in its social character, it has long become a part of the proletarian-socialist world revolution and is now even a very important part and a great ally of this world revolution. The first step or stage in our revolution is definitely not, and cannot be, the establishment of a capitalist society under the dictatorship of the Chinese bourgeoisie, but will result in the establishment of a new-democratic society under the joint dictatorship of all the revolutionary classes of China headed by the Chinese proletariat. The revolution will then be carried forward to the second stage, in which a socialist society will be established in China.

This is the fundamental characteristic of the Chinese revolution of today, of the new revolutionary process of the past twenty years (counting from the May 4 Movement of 1919), and its concrete living essence.

The Politics of New Democracy

The new historical characteristic of the Chinese revolution is its division into two stages, the first being the new-democratic revolution. How does this manifest itself concretely in internal political and economic relations? Let us consider the question.

Before the May 4 Movement of 1919 (which occurred after the first imperialist world war of 1914 and the Russian October Revolution of 1917), the petty bourgeoisie and the bourgeoisie (through their intellectuals) were the political leaders of the bourgeois-democratic revolution. The Chinese proletariat had not yet appeared on the political scene as an awakened and independent class force, but participated in the revolution only as a follower of the petty bourgeoisie and the bourgeoisie. Such was the case with the proletariat at the time of the revolution of 1911.

After the May 4 Movement, the political leader of China's bourgeois-democratic revolution was no longer the bourgeoisie but the proletariat, although the national bourgeoisie continued to take part in the revolution. The Chinese proletariat rapidly became an awakened and independent political force as a result of its maturing and of the influence of the Russian Revolution. It was the Chinese Communist Party that put forward the slogan "Down with imperialism" and the thoroughgoing program for the whole bourgeois-democratic revolution, and it was the Chinese Communist Party alone that carried out the Agrarian Revolution.

Being a bourgeoisie in a colonial and semicolonial country and oppressed by imperialism, the Chinese national bourgeoisie retains a certain revolutionary quality at certain periods and to a certain degree—even in the era of imperialism—in its opposition to the foreign imperialists and the domestic governments of bureaucrats and warlords (instances of opposition to the latter can be found in the periods of the revolution of 1911 and the Northern Expedition), and it may ally itself with the proletariat and the petty bourgeoisie against such enemies as it is ready to oppose. In this respect the Chinese bourgeoisie differs from the bourgeoisie of old tsarist Russia. Since tsarist Russia was a military-feudal imperialism which carried on aggression against other countries, the Russian bourgeoisie was entirely lacking in revolutionary quality. There, the task of the proletariat was to oppose the bourgeoisie, not to unite with it. But China's national bourgeoisie has a revolutionary quality at certain periods and to a certain degree, because China is a colonial and semicolonial country which is a victim of aggression. Here, the task of the proletariat is to form a united front with the national bourgeoisie against imperialism and the bureaucrat and warlord governments without overlooking its revolutionary quality.

At the same time, however, being a bourgeois class in a colonial and semicolonial country and so being extremely flabby economically and politically, the Chinese national bourgeoisie also has another quality, namely, a proneness to conciliation with the enemies of the revolution. Even when it takes part in the revolution, it is unwilling to break with imperialism completely and, moreover, it is closely associated with the exploitation of the rural areas through land rent; thus it is neither willing nor able to overthrow imperialism, and much less the feudal forces, in a thorough way. So neither of the two basic problems or tasks of China's bourgeois-democratic revolution can be solved or accomplished by the national bourgeoisie. As for China's big bourgeoisie, which is represented by the Kuomintang, all through the long period from 1927 to 1937 it nestled in the arms of the imperialists and formed an alliance with the feudal forces against the revolutionary people. In 1927 and for some time afterward, the Chinese national bourgeoisie also followed the counter-revolution. During the present anti-Japanese war, the section of the big bourgeoisie represented by Wang Ching-wei has capitulated to the enemy, which constitutes a fresh betrayal on the part of the big bourgeoisie. In this respect, then, the bourgeoisie in China differs from the earlier bourgeoisie of the European and American countries, and especially of France. When the bourgeoisie in those countries, and especially in France, was still in its revolutionary era, the bourgeois revolution was comparatively thorough, whereas the bourgeoisie in China lacks even this degree of thoroughness.

Possible participation in the revolution on the one hand and proneness to conciliation with the enemies of the revolution on the other—such is the dual character of the Chinese bourgeoisie, it faces both ways. Even the bourgeoisie in European and American history had shared this dual character. When confronted by a formidable enemy, they united with the workers and peasants against him, but when the workers and peasants awakened, they turned round to unite with the enemy against the workers and peasants. This is a general rule applicable to the bourgeoisie everywhere in the world, but the trait is more pronounced in the Chinese bourgeoisie.

In China, it is perfectly clear that whoever can lead the people in overthrowing imperialism and the forces of feudalism can win the people's confidence, because these two, and especially imperialism, are the mortal enemies of the people. Today, whoever can lead the people in driving out Japanese imperialism and introducing democratic government will be the saviors of the people. History has proved that the Chinese bourgeoisie cannot fulfill this responsibility, which inevitably falls upon the shoulders of the proletariat.

Therefore, the proletariat, the peasantry, the intelligentsia, and the other sections of the petty bourgeoisie undoubtedly constitute the basic forces determining China's fate. These classes, some already awakened and others in the process of awakening, will necessarily become the basic components of the state and governmental structure in the democratic republic of China, with the proletariat as the leading force. The Chinese democratic republic which we desire to establish now must be a democratic republic under the joint dictatorship of all anti-imperialist and anti-feudal people led by the proletariat, that is, a new-democratic republic, a republic of the genuinely revolutionary new Three People's Principles with their Three Great Policies.

This new-democratic republic will be different from the old European-American form of capitalist republic under bourgeois dictatorship, which is the old democratic form and already out of date. On the other hand, it will also be different from the socialist republic of the Soviet type under the dictatorship of the proletariat which is already flourishing in the U.S.S.R., and which, moreover, will be established in all the capitalist countries and will undoubtedly become the dominant form of state and governmental structure in all the industrially advanced countries. However, for a certain historical period, this form is not suitable for the revolutions in the colonial and semicolonial countries. During this period, therefore, a third form of state must be adopted in the revolutions of all colonial and semicolonial countries, namely, the new-democratic republic. This form suits a certain historical period and is therefore transitional;

nevertheless, it is a form which is necessary and cannot be dispensed with.

Thus the numerous types of state system in the world can be reduced to three basic kinds according to the class character of their political power: (1) republics under bourgeois dictatorship, (2) republics under the dictatorship of the proletariat, and (3) republics under the joint dictatorship of several revolutionary classes. . . .

The Economy of New Democracy

If such a republic is to be established in China, it must be new-democratic not only in its politics but also in its economy.

It will own the big banks and the big industrial and commercial enterprises. . . . In the new-democratic republic under the leadership of the proletariat, the state enterprises will be of a socialist character and will constitute the leading force in the whole national economy, but the republic will neither confiscate capitalist private property in general nor forbid the development of such capitalist production as does not "dominate the livelihood of the people," for China's economy is still very backward. [The quotations in this and the following two paragraphs are from Sun Yat-sen.—Ed.]

The republic will take certain necessary steps to confiscate the land of the landlords and distribute it to those peasants having little or no land, carry out Dr. Sun Yat-sen's slogan of "land to the tiller," abolish feudal relations in the rural areas, and turn the land over to the private ownership of the peasants. A rich peasant economy will be allowed in the rural areas. Such is the policy of "equalization of landownership." "Land to the tiller" is the correct slogan for this policy. In general, socialist agriculture will not be established at this stage, though various types of co-operative enterprises developed on the basis of "land to the tiller" will contain elements of socialism.

China's economy must develop along the path of the "regulation of capital" and the "equalization of landownership," and must never be "privately owned by the few"; we must never permit the few capitalists and landlords to "dominate the livelihood of the people"; we must never establish a capitalist society of the European-American type or allow the old semifeudal society to survive. Whoever dares to go counter to this line of advance will certainly not succeed but will run into a brick wall.

Such are the internal economic relations which a revolutionary

China, a China fighting Japanese aggression, must and necessarily will establish.

Such is the economy of New Democracy.

And the politics of New Democracy are the concentrated expression of the economy of New Democracy.

The Culture of New Democracy

In the foregoing we have explained the historical characteristics of Chinese politics in the new period and the question of the new-democratic republic. We can now proceed to the question of culture.

A given culture is the ideological reflection of the politics and economics of a given society. There is in China an imperialist culture which is a reflection of imperialist rule, or partial rule, in the political and economic fields. This culture is fostered not only by the cultural organizations run directly by the imperialists in China but by a number of Chinese who have lost all sense of shame. Into this category falls all culture embodying a slave ideology. China also has a semifeudal culture which reflects her semifeudal politics and economy, and whose exponents include all those who advocate the worship of Confucius, the study of the Confucian canon, the old ethical code, and the old ideas in opposition to the new culture and new ideas. Imperialist culture and semifeudal culture are devoted brothers and have formed a reactionary cultural alliance against China's new culture. This kind of reactionary culture serves the imperialists and the feudal class and must be swept away. Unless it is swept away, no new culture of any kind can be built up. There is no construction without destruction, no flowing without damming and no motion without rest; the two are locked in a life-and-death struggle.

As for the new culture, it is the ideological reflection of the new politics and the new economy which it sets out to serve. . . .

New-democratic culture is national. It opposes imperialist oppression and upholds the dignity and independence of the Chinese nation. It belongs to our own nation and bears our own national characteristics. It links up with the socialist and new-democratic cultures of all other nations and they are related in such a way that they can absorb something from each other and help each other to develop, together forming a new world culture; but as a revolutionary national culture it can never link up with any reactionary imperialist culture of whatever nation. To nourish her own culture China needs to assimilate a good deal of foreign progressive culture, not enough of which was done in the past. We should assimilate whatever is useful to us today not only from the present-day socialist and new-democratic cultures but also from the earlier cultures of other nations; for example, from the culture of the various capitalist countries in the Age of Enlightenment. However, we should not gulp any of this foreign material down uncritically, but must treat it as we do our food—first chewing it, then submitting it to the working of the stomach and intestines with their juices and secretions, and separating it into nutriment to be absorbed and waste matter to be discarded—before it can nourish us. To advocate "wholesale Westernization" is wrong. China has suffered a great deal from the mechanical absorption of foreign material. Similarly, in applying Marxism to China, Chinese Communists must fully and properly integrate the universal truth of Marxism with the concrete practice of the Chinese revolution, or in other words, the universal truth of Marxism must be combined with specific national characteristics and acquire a definite national form if it is to be useful, and in no circumstances can it be applied subjectively as a mere formula. Marxists who make a fetish of formulas are simply playing the fool with Marxism and the Chinese revolution, and there is no room for them in the ranks of the Chinese revolution. Chinese culture should have its own form, its own national form. National in form and new-democratic in content—such is our new culture today.

New-democratic culture is scientific. Opposed as it is to all feudal and superstitious ideas, it stands for seeking truth from facts, for objective truth, and for the unity of theory and practice. On this point, the possibility exists of a united front against imperialism, feudalism, and superstition between the scientific thought of the Chinese proletariat and those Chinese bourgeois materialists and natural scientists who are progressive, but in no case is there a possibility of a united front with any reactionary idealism. In the field of political action Communists may form an anti-imperialist and anti-feudal united front with some idealists and even religious people, but we can never approve of their idealism or religious doctrines. A splendid old culture was created during the long period of Chinese feudal society. To study the development of this old culture, to reject its feudal dross and assimilate its democratic essence is a necessary condition for developing our new national culture and increasing our national self-confidence, but we should never swallow anything and everything uncritically. It is imperative to separate the fine old culture of the people, which had a more or less democratic and revolutionary character, from all the decadence of the old feudal ruling class. China's present new politics and new economy have developed out of her old politics and old economy, and her present new culture, too, has developed out of her old culture; therefore, we must respect our own history and must not lop it off. However, respect for history means giving it its proper place as a science, respecting its dialectical development, and not eulogizing the past at the expense of the present or praising every drop of feudal poison. As far as the masses and the young students are concerned, the essential thing is to guide them to look forward and not backward.

New-democratic culture belongs to the broad masses and is therefore democratic. It should serve the toiling masses of workers and peasants, who make up more than 90 per cent of the nation's population, and should gradually become their very own. There is a difference of degree, as well as a close link, between the knowledge imparted to the revolutionary cadres and the knowledge imparted to the revolutionary masses, between the raising of cultural standards and popularization. Revolutionary culture is a powerful revolutionary weapon for the broad masses of the people. It prepares the ground ideologically before the revolution comes and is an important, indeed essential, fighting front in the general revolutionary front during the revolution. People engaged in revolutionary cultural work are the commanders at various levels on this cultural front. . . . A revolutionary cultural worker who is not close to the people is a commander without an army, whose fire-power cannot bring the enemy down. To attain this objective, written Chinese must be reformed, given the requisite conditions, and our spoken language brought closer to that of the people, for the people, it must be stressed, are the inexhaustible source of our revolutionary culture.

A national, scientific, and mass culture—such is the anti-imperialist and anti-feudal culture of the people, the culture of New Democracy, the new culture of the Chinese nation.

Combine the politics, the economy and the culture of New Democracy, and you have the new-democratic republic, the Republic of China both in name and in reality, the new China we want to create.

THE PEOPLE'S DEMOCRATIC DICTATORSHIP

Nature of Dictatorship

From: "On the People's Democratic Dictatorship" (June 1949), *Selected Works,* IV (Peking: Foreign Languages Press, 1961), pp. 421, 417–19.

The people's democratic dictatorship is based on the alliance of the working class, the peasantry, and the urban petty bourgeoisie, and mainly on the alliance of the workers and the peasants, because these two classes comprise 80 to 90 per cent of China's population. These two classes are the main force in overthrowing imperialism and the Kuomintang reactionaries. The transition from New Democracy to socialism also depends mainly upon their alliance.

The people's democratic dictatorship needs the leadership of the working class. For it is only the working class that is most farsighted, most selfless, and most thoroughly revolutionary. The entire history of revolution proves that without the leadership of the working class revolution fails and that with the leadership of the working class revolution triumphs. In the epoch of imperialism, in no country can any other class lead any genuine revolution to victory. This is clearly proved by the fact that the many revolutions led by China's petty bourgeoisie and national bourgeoisie all failed.

The national bourgeoisie at the present stage is of great importance. Imperialism, a most ferocious enemy, is still standing alongside us. China's modern industry still forms a very small proportion of the national economy. No reliable statistics are available, but it is estimated, on the basis of certain data, that before the War of Resistance Against Japan the value of output of modern industry constituted only about 10 per cent of the total value of output of the national economy. To counter imperialist oppression and to raise her backward economy to a higher level, China must utilize all the factors of urban and rural capitalism that are beneficial and not harmful to the national economy and the people's livelihood, and we must unite with the national bourgeoisie in common struggle. Our present policy is to regulate capitalism, not to destroy it. But the national bourgeoisie cannot be the leader of the revolution, nor should it have the chief role in state power. The reason it cannot be the leader of the revolution and should not have the chief role in state power is that the social and economic position of the national bourgeoisie determines its weakness; it lacks foresight and sufficient courage and many of its members are afraid of the masses. . . .

"You are dictatorial." My dear sirs, you are right, that is just what we are. All the experience the Chinese people have accumulated through several decades teaches us to enforce the people's democratic dictatorship, that is, to deprive the reactionaries of the right to speak and let the people alone have that right.

Who are the people? At the present stage in China, they are the working class, the peasantry, the urban petty bourgeoisie, and the national bourgeoisie. These classes, led by the working class and the Communist Party, unite to form their own state and elect their own government; they enforce their dictatorship over the running dogs of imperialism—the landlord class and bureaucrat-bourgeoisie, as well as the representatives of those classes, the Kuomintang reactionaries and their accomplices—suppress them, allow them only to behave themselves and not to be unruly in word or deed. If they speak or act in an unruly way, they will be promptly stopped and punished. Democracy is practiced within the ranks of the people, who enjoy the rights of freedom of speech, assembly, association, and so on. The right to vote belongs only to the people, not to the reactionaries. The combination of these two aspects, democracy for the people and dictatorship over the reactionaries, is the people's democratic dictatorship.

Why must things be done this way? The reason is quite clear to everybody. If things were not done this way, the revolution would fail, the people would suffer, the country would be conquered.

"Don't you want to abolish state power?" Yes, we do, but not right now; we cannot do it yet. Why? Because imperialism still exists, because domestic reaction still exists, because classes still exist in our country. Our present task is to strengthen the people's state apparatus—mainly the people's army, the people's police, and the people's courts—in order to consolidate national defense and protect the people's interests. Given this condition, China can develop steadily, under the leadership of the working class and the Communist Party, from an agricultural into an industrial country and from a new-democratic into a socialist and communist society, can abolish classes and realize the Great Harmony. The state apparatus, including the army, the police, and the courts, is the instrument by which one class oppresses another. It is an instrument for the oppression of antagonistic classes; it is violence and not "benevolence."

"You are not benevolent!" Quite so. We definitely do not apply a policy of benevolence to the reactionaries and toward the reactionary activities of the reactionary classes. Our policy of benevolence is applied only within the ranks of the people, not beyond them to the reactionaries or to the reactionary activities of reactionary classes.

The people's state protects the people. Only when the people have such a state can they educate and remold themselves on a country-wide scale by democratic methods and, with everyone taking part, shake off the influence of domestic and foreign reactionaries (which is still very strong, will survive for a long time, and cannot be quickly destroyed), rid themselves of the bad habits and ideas acquired in the old society, not allow themselves to be led astray by the reactionaries, and continue to advance—to advance toward a socialist and communist society.

Here, the method we employ is democratic, the method of persuasion, not of compulsion. When anyone among the people breaks the law, he too should be punished, imprisoned, or even sentenced to death; but this is a matter of a few individual cases, and it differs in principle from the dictatorship exercised over the reactionaries as a class.

As for the members of the reactionary classes and individual reactionaries, so long as they do not rebel, sabotage, or create trouble after their political power has been overthrown, land and work will be given to them as well in order to allow them to live and remold themselves through labor into new people. If they are not willing to work, the people's state will compel them to work. Propaganda and educational work will be done among them too and will be done, moreover, with as much care and thoroughness as among the captured army officers in the past. This, too, may be called a "policy of benevolence" if you like, but it is imposed by us on the members of the enemy classes and cannot be mentioned in the same breath with the work of self-education which we carry on within the ranks of the revolutionary people.

Such remolding of members of the reactionary classes can be accomplished only by a state of the people's democratic dictatorship under the leadership of the Communist Party. When it is well done, China's major exploiting classes, the landlord class and the bureaucrat-bourgeoisie (the monopoly capitalist class), will be eliminated for good. There remain the national bourgeoisie; at the present stage, we can already do a good deal of suitable educational work with many of them. When the time comes to realize socialism, that is, to nationalize private enterprise, we shall carry the work of educating and remolding them a step further. The people have a powerful state apparatus in their hands—there is no need to fear rebellion by the national bourgeoisie.

Functions of Dictatorship

From: *On the Correct Handling of Contradictions Among the People* (February 1957) (Peking: Foreign Languages Press, 1957), pp. 11–13, 24–25, 38–41, 51.

Ours is a people's democratic dictatorship, led by the working class and based on the worker-peasant alliance. What is this dictatorship for? Its first function is to suppress the reactionary classes and elements and those exploiters in the country who range themselves against the socialist revolution, to suppress all those who try to wreck our socialist construction; that is to say, to solve the contradictions between ourselves and the enemy within the country. For instance, to arrest, try, and sentence certain counterrevolutionaries, and for a specified period of time to deprive landlords and bureaucrat-capitalists of their right to vote and freedom of speech—all this comes within the scope of our dictatorship. To maintain law and order and safeguard the interests of the people, it is likewise necessary to exercise dictatorship over robbers, swindlers, murderers, arsonists, hooligans, and other scoundrels who seriously disrupt social order.

The second function of this dictatorship is to protect our country from subversive activities and possible aggression by the external enemy. Should that happen, it is the task of this dictatorship to solve the external contradiction between ourselves and the enemy. The aim of this dictatorship is to protect all our people so that they can work in peace and build China into a socialist country with a modern industry, agriculture, science, and culture.

Who is to exercise this dictatorship? Naturally it must be the working class and the entire people led by it. Dictatorship does not apply in the ranks of the people. The people cannot possibly exercise dictatorship over themselves; nor should one section of them oppress another section. Lawbreaking elements among the people will be dealt with according to law, but this is different in principle from using the dictatorship to suppress enemies of the people. What applies among the people is democratic centralism [see Introduction and Chapter V]. Our Constitution lays it down that citizens of the People's Republic of China enjoy freedom of speech, of the press, of assembly, of association, of procession, of demonstration, of religious belief, and so on. Our Constitution also provides that organs of state must practice democratic centralism and must rely on the masses; that the personnel of organs of state must serve the people. Our socialist democracy is democracy in the widest sense, such as is not to be found in any capitalist country. Our dictatorship is known as the people's democratic dictatorship, led by the working class and based on the worker-peasant alliance. That is to say, democracy operates within the ranks of the people, while the working class, uniting with all those enjoying civil rights, the peasantry in the first place, enforces dictatorship over the reactionary classes and elements and all those who resist socialist transformation and oppose socialist construction. By civil rights, we mean, politically, freedom and democratic rights. . . .

But our socialist system has just been set up; it is not yet fully established, nor yet fully consolidated. In joint state-private industrial and commercial enterprises, capitalists still receive a fixed rate of interest on their capital, that is to say, exploitation still exists. So far as ownership is concerned, these enterprises are not yet completely socialist in character. Some of our agricultural and handicraft producers' co-operatives are still semisocialist, while even in the fully socialist co-operatives certain problems about ownership remain to be solved. Relationships in production and exchange are still being gradually established along socialist lines in various sectors of our economy and more and more appropriate forms are being sought. It is a complicated problem to settle on a proper ratio between accumulation and consumption within that sector of socialist economy in which the means of production are owned by the whole people and that sector in which the means of production are collectively owned, as well as between these two sectors. It is not easy to work out a perfectly rational solution to this problem all at once.

To sum up, socialist relations of production have been established; they are suited to the development of the productive forces, but they are still far from perfect, and their imperfect aspects stand in contradiction to the development of the productive forces. There is conformity as well as contradiction between the relations of production and the development of the productive forces; similarly, there is conformity as well as contradiction between the superstruc-

35182

ture and the economic base. The superstructure—our state institutions of people's democratic dictatorship and its laws, and socialist ideology under the guidance of Marxism-Leninism—has played a positive role in facilitating the victory of socialist transformation and establishment of a socialist organization of labor; it is suited to the socialist economic base, that is, socialist relations of production. . . .

The year 1956 saw the transformation of privately owned industrial and commercial enterprises into joint state-private enterprises as well as the organization of co-operatives in agriculture and handicrafts as part of the transformation of our social system. The speed and smoothness with which this was carried out are closely related to the fact that we treated the contradiction between the working class and the national bourgeoisie as a contradiction among the people. Has this class contradiction been resolved completely? No, not yet. A considerable period of time is still required to do so. However, some people say that the capitalists have been so remolded that they are now not much different from the workers, and that further remolding is unnecessary. Others go so far as to say that the capitalists are even a bit better than the workers. Still others ask, if remolding is necessary, why doesn't the working class undergo remolding? Are these opinions correct? Of course not.

In building a socialist society, all need remolding, the exploiters as well as the working people. Who says the working class doesn't need it? Of course, remolding of the exploiters and that of the working people are two different types of remolding. The two must not be confused. In the class struggle and the struggle against nature, the working class remolds the whole of society, and at the same time remolds itself. It must continue to learn in the process of its work and step by step overcome its shortcomings. It must never stop doing so. Take us who are present here, for example. Many of us make some progress each year; that is to say, we are being remolded each year. I myself had all sorts of non-Marxist ideas before. It was only later that I embraced Marxism. I learned a little Marxism from books and so made an initial remolding of my ideas, but it was mainly through taking part in the class struggle over the years that I came to be remolded. And I must continue to study if I am to make further progress, otherwise I shall lag behind. Can the capitalists be so clever as to need no more remolding?

Some contend that the Chinese bourgeoisie no longer has two sides to its character, but only one side. Is this true? No. On the one hand, members of the bourgeoisie have already become managerial personnel in joint state-private enterprises and are being transformed from exploiters into working people living by their own labor. On the other hand, they still receive a fixed rate of interest on their investments in the joint enterprises, that is, they have not yet cut themselves loose from the roots of exploitation. Between them and the working class there is still a considerable gap in ideology, sentiments, and habits of life. How can it be said that they no longer have two sides to their character? Even when they stop receiving their fixed interest payments and rid themselves of the label "bourgeoisie," they will still need ideological remolding for quite some time. If it were held that the bourgeoisie no longer has a dual character, then such study and remolding for the capitalists would no longer be needed.

But it must be said that such a view doesn't tally with the actual circumstances of our industrialists and businessmen, nor with what most of them want. During the past few years, most of them have been willing to study and have made marked progress. Our industrialists and businessmen can be thoroughly remolded only in the course of work; they should work together with the staff and workers in the enterprises, and make the enterprises the chief centers for remolding themselves. It is also important for them to change certain of their old views through study. Study for them should be optional. After they have attended study groups for some weeks, many industrialists and businessmen, on returning to their enterprises, find they speak more of a common language with the workers and the representatives of state shareholdings, and so work better together. They know from personal experience that it is good for them to keep on studying and remolding themselves. The idea just referred to that study and remolding are not necessary does not reflect the views of the majority of industrialists and businessmen. Only a small number of them think that way. . . .

It will take a considerable time to decide the issue in the ideological struggle between socialism and capitalism in our country. This is because the influence of the bourgeoisie and of the intellectuals who come from the old society will remain in our country as the ideology of a class for a long time to come. Failure to grasp this, or, still worse, failure to understand it at all, can lead to the gravest mistakes—to ignoring the necessity of waging the struggle in the ideological field. Ideological struggle is not like other forms of struggle. Crude, coercive methods should not be used in this struggle, but only the method of painstaking reasoning.

THE DICTATORSHIP OF THE PROLETARIAT

From: Liu Shao-ch'i, *The Political Report* of the Central Committee of the Communist Party of China to the Eighth National Congress of the Party (September 15, 1956) (Peking: Foreign Languages Press, 1956), pp. 9, 58.

After the establishment of the People's Republic of China, the working class has won ruling power throughout the country in conditions of a firm alliance with several hundred millions of peasants; the party of the working class—the Chinese Communist Party—has become the party that leads the state power of the whole country; therefore, the people's democratic dictatorship has in essence become one form of dictatorship of the proletariat. Thus it has become possible for the bourgeois-democratic revolution in our country to be directly transformed, by peaceful means, into a proletarian-socialist revolution. The establishment of the People's Republic of China signifies the virtual completion of the stage of bourgeois-democratic revolution in our country and the beginning of the stage of proletarian-socialist revolution: the beginning of the period of transition from capitalism to socialism. . . .

The people's democratic dictatorship in our country has gone through the period of bourgeois-democratic revolution and is passing through the period of the socialist revolution. Before the nation-wide victory of the bourgeois-democratic revolution, the people's democratic dictatorship had already been established in the revolutionary bases. This dictatorship was meant to fulfill the task of the bourgeois-democratic revolution because it only brought about changes in the feudal land system. It did not change the ownership of means of production by the national bourgeoisie, or individual ownership by the peasants. After the founding of the People's Republic of China, the people's democratic dictatorship began to shoulder the task of transition from capitalism to socialism. That is to say, it was to change the private ownership of the means of production by the bourgeoisie and the small producers into socialist, public ownership; and to eliminate in a thorough way the exploitation of man by man. Such state power, in its essence, can only be the dictatorship of the proletariat. Only when the proletariat, through its own vanguard, the Chinese Communist Party, has employed this weapon of state power without the slightest hindrance and closely rallied around itself all the working people and all other forces that are ready to accept socialism, jointly to implement the line of policy of the proletariat and, on the one hand, build the economic and cultural life along the road to socialism and, on the other, suppress the resistance of reactionary classes and cliques and guard against the intervention of foreign imperialism, will it be able to fulfill this serious and complex task.

THE GREAT LEAP FORWARD

From: "Resolution of the Central Committee of the Chinese Communist Party on the Establishment of People's Communes in the Rural Areas" (August 1958), in *People's Communes in China* (Peking: Foreign Languages Press, 1958), pp. 1–8.

1. The people's communes are the logical result of the march of events. Large, comprehensive people's communes have made their appearance, and in several places they are already widespread. They have developed very rapidly in some areas. It is highly probable that there will soon be an upsurge in setting up people's communes throughout the country and the development is irresistible. The basis for the development of the people's communes is mainly the all-round, continuous leap forward in China's agricultural production and the ever rising political consciousness of the five hundred million peasants. . . . The output of agricultural products has doubled or increased severalfold, in some cases more than ten times or scores of times. This has further stimulated emancipation of thought among the people. Large-scale agricultural capital construction and the application of more advanced agricultural technique are making their demands on labor power. The growth of rural industry also demands the transfer of some manpower from agriculture. The demand for mechanization and electrification has become increasingly urgent in China's rural areas. Capital construction in agriculture and the struggle for bumper harvests involve large-scale co-operation which cuts across the boundaries between co-operatives, townships, and counties. The people have taken to organizing themselves along military lines, working with militancy, and leading a collective life, and this has raised the political consciousness of the five hundred million peasants still further. Community dining rooms, kindergartens, nurseries, sewing groups, barbershops, public baths, happy

homes for the aged, agricultural middle schools, "Red and Expert" schools are leading the peasants toward a happier collective life and further fostering ideas of collectivism among the peasant masses. What all these things illustrate is that the agricultural co-operative with scores of families or several hundred families can no longer meet the needs of the changing situation. In the present circumstances, the establishment of people's communes with all-round management of agriculture, forestry, animal husbandry, side occupations, and fishery, where industry (the worker), agriculture (the peasant), exchange (the trader), culture and education (the student), and military affairs (the militiaman) merge into one, is the fundamental policy to guide the peasants to accelerate socialist construction, complete the building of socialism ahead of time, and carry out the gradual transition to communism.

2. Concerning the organization and size of the communes. Generally speaking, it is at present better to establish one commune to a township with the commune comprising about two thousand peassant households. Where a township embraces a vast area and is sparsely populated, more than one commune may be established, each with less than two thousand households. In some places, several townships may merge and form a single commune comprising about six or seven thousand households, according to topographical conditions and the needs for the development of production. As to the establishment of communes of more than ten thousand or even more than twenty thousand households, we need not oppose them, but for the present we should not take the initiative to encourage them.

As the people's communes grow there may be a tendency to form federations with the county as a unit. Plans should be drawn up right now on a county basis to ensure the rational distribution of people's communes. . . .

3. Concerning the methods and steps to be adopted to merge small co-operatives into bigger ones and transform them into people's communes. The merger of small co-operatives into bigger ones and their transformation into people's communes is now a common mass demand. The poor and the lower-middle peasants firmly support it; most upper-middle peasants also favor it. We must rely on the poor and the lower-middle peasants and fully encourage the masses to air their views and argue it out, unite the majority of the upper-middle peasants who favor it, overcome vacillation among the remainder, and expose and foil rumormongering and

sabotage by landlord and rich-peasant elements, so that the mass of the peasants merge the smaller co-operatives into bigger ones and transform them into communes through ideological emancipation and on a voluntary basis, without any compulsion. As to the steps to be taken, it is of course better to complete the merger into bigger co-ops and their transformation into communes at once; but where this is not feasible, it can be done in two stages, with no compulsory or rash steps. In all counties, experiments should first be made in some selected areas and the experience gained should then be popularized gradually. . . .

4. Concerning some questions of the economic policy involved in the merger of co-operatives. In the course of the merger, education should be strengthened to prevent the growth of departmentalism among a few co-operatives, which might otherwise share out too much or all of their income and leave little or no common funds before the merger. On the other hand, it must be understood that with various agricultural co-operatives established on different foundations, the amount of their public property, their indebtedness inside and outside the co-operatives, and so on will not be completely equal when they merge into bigger co-operatives. In the course of the merger, the cadres and the masses should be educated in the spirit of communism so as to recognize these differences and not resort to minute squaring of accounts, insisting on equal shares and bothering with trifles.

When a people's commune is established, it is not necessary to deal with the questions of reserved private plots of land, scattered fruit trees, share funds, and so on in a great hurry; nor is it necessary to adopt clear-cut stipulations on these questions. Generally speaking, reserved private plots of land may perhaps be turned over to collective management in the course of the merger of co-operatives; scattered fruit trees, for the time being, may remain privately owned and be dealt with sometime later. Share funds etc. can be handled after a year or two, since the funds will automatically become publicly owned with the development of production, the increase of income, and the advance in the people's consciousness.

5. Concerning the name, ownership, and system of distribution of the communes.

All the big merged co-operatives will be called people's communes. There is no need to change them into state-owned farms, for it is not proper for farms to embrace industry, agriculture, exchange, culture and education, and military affairs at the same time.

After the establishment of people's communes, there is no need immediately to transform collective [state] ownership into ownership by the people as a whole. It is better at present to maintain collective ownership to avoid unnecessary complications arising in the course of the transformation of ownership. In fact, collective ownership in people's communes already contains some elements of ownership by the people as a whole. These elements will grow constantly in the course of the continuous development of people's communes and will gradually replace collective ownership. The transition from collective ownership to ownership by the people as a whole is a process, the completion of which may take less time— three or four years—in some places, and longer—five or six years or even longer—elsewhere. Even with the completion of this transition, people's communes, like state-owned industry, are still socialist in character, where the principle of "from each according to his ability and to each according to his work" prevails. After a number of years, as the social product increases greatly, the communist consciousness and morality of the entire people are raised to a much higher degree, and universal education is instituted and developed, the differences between workers and peasants, town and country and mental and manual labor—legacies of the old society that have inevitably been carried over into the socialist period—and the remnants of unequal bourgeois rights, which are the reflection of these differences, will gradually vanish, and the function of the state will be limited to protecting the country from external aggression, but it will play no role internally. At that time Chinese society will enter the era of communism where the principle of "from each according to his ability and to each according to his needs" will be practiced.

After the establishment of people's communes it is not necessary to hurry the change from the original system of distribution, in order to avoid any unfavorable effect on production. The system of distribution should be determined according to specific conditions. Where conditions permit, the shift to a wage system may be made. But where conditions are not yet ripe, the original system of payment according to workdays may be temporarily retained (such as the system of fixed targets for output, workdays, and costs, with a part of the extra output as reward; or the system of calculating workdays on the basis of output). This can be changed when conditions permit.

Although ownership in the people's communes is still collective ownership and the system of distribution, either the wage system or payment according to workdays, is "to each according to his work" and not "to each according to his needs," the people's communes are the best form of organization for the attainment of socialism and gradual transition to communism. They will develop into the basic social units in communist society.

6. At the present stage our task is to build socialism. The primary purpose of establishing people's communes is to accelerate the speed of socialist construction and the purpose of building socialism is to prepare actively for the transition to communism. It seems that the attainment of communism in China is no longer a remote future event. We should actively use the form of the people's communes to explore the practical road of transition to communism.

THE GREAT PROLETARIAN CULTURAL REVOLUTION

A New Stage in the Socialist Revolution

From: "Decision of the Central Committee of the Chinese Communist Party Concerning the Great Proletarian Cultural Revolution" (August 8, 1966), *Peking Review*, August 12, 1966, pp. 6–11.

1. A New Stage in the Socialist Revolution

The great proletarian cultural revolution now unfolding is a great revolution that touches people to their very souls and constitutes a new stage in the development of the socialist revolution in our country, a deeper and more extensive stage.

At the Tenth Plenary Session of the Eighth Central Committee of the Party [1962], Comrade Mao Tse-tung said: To overthrow a political power, it is always necessary, first of all, to create public opinion, to do work in the ideological sphere. This is true for the revolutionary class as well as for the counterrevolutionary class. This Thesis of Comrade Mao Tse-tung's has been proved entirely correct in practice.

Although the bourgeoisie has been overthrown, it is still trying to use the old ideas, culture, customs, and habits of the exploiting classes to corrupt the masses, capture their minds, and endeavor to stage a comeback. The proletariat must do just the opposite: it must meet head on every challenge of the bourgeoisie in the ideological field and use the new ideas, culture, customs, and habits of the proletariat to change the mental outlook of the whole of society. At present, our objective is to struggle against and crush those persons in authority who are taking the capitalist road, to criticize and repudiate the reactionary bourgeois academic "authorities" and the ideology of the bourgeoisie and all other exploiting classes and to transform education, literature, and art and all other parts of the superstructure that do not correspond to the socialist economic base, so as to facilitate the consolidation and development of the socialist system.

2. The Main Current and the Zigzags

The masses of the workers, peasants, soldiers, revolutionary intellectuals, and revolutionary cadres form the main force in this great cultural revolution. Large numbers of revolutionary young people, previously unknown, have become courageous and daring pathbreakers. They are vigorous in action and intelligent. Through the media of big-character posters and great debates, they argue things out, expose and criticize thoroughly, and launch resolute attacks on the open and hidden representatives of the bourgeoisie. In such a great revolutionary movement, it is hardly avoidable that they should show shortcomings of one kind or another, but their main revolutionary orientation has been correct from the beginning. This is the main current in the great proletarian cultural revolution. It is the main direction along which the great proletarian cultural revolution continues to advance.

Since the cultural revolution is a revolution, it inevitably meets with resistance. This resistance comes chiefly from those in authority who have wormed their way into the Party and are taking the capitalist road. It also comes from the old force of habit in society. At present, this resistance is still fairly strong and stubborn. However, the great proletarian cultural revolution is, after all, an irresistible general trend. There is abundant evidence that such resistance will crumble fast once the masses become fully aroused.

Because the resistance is fairly strong, there will be reversals and even repeated reversals in this struggle. There is no harm in this. It tempers the proletariat and other working people, and especially the younger generation, teaches them lessons and gives them experience, and helps them to understand that the revolutionary road is a zigzag one, and not plain sailing.

3. Put Daring Above Everything Else and Boldly Arouse the Masses

The outcome of this great cultural revolution will be determined by whether the Party leadership does or does not dare boldly to arouse the masses.

Currently, there are four different situations with regard to the leadership being given to the movement of cultural revolution by Party organizations at various levels:

(1) There is the situation in which the persons in charge of Party organizations stand in the van of the movement and dare to arouse the masses boldly. They put daring above everything else, they are dauntless communist fighters and good pupils of Chairman Mao. They advocate the big-character posters and great debates. They encourage the masses to expose every kind of ghost and monster and also to criticize the shortcomings and errors in the work of the persons in charge. This correct kind of leadership is the result of putting proletarian politics in the forefront and Mao Tse-tung's thought in the lead.

(2) In many units, the persons in charge have a very poor understanding of the task of leadership in this great struggle, their leadership is far from being conscientious and effective, and they accordingly find themselves incompetent and in a weak position. They put fear above everything else, stick to outmoded ways and regulations, and are unwilling to break away from conventional practices and move ahead. They have been taken unawares by the new order of things, the revolutionary order of the masses, with the result that their leadership lags behind the situation, lags behind the masses.

(3) In some units, the persons in charge, who made mistakes of one kind or another in the past, are even more prone to put fear above everything else, being afraid that the masses will catch them out. Actually, if they make serious self-criticism and accept the criticism of the masses, the Party and the masses will make allowances for their mistakes. But if the persons in charge don't, they will continue to make mistakes and become obstacles to the mass movement.

(4) Some units are controlled by those who have wormed their way into the Party and are taking the capitalist road. Such persons in authority are extremely afraid of being exposed by the masses and therefore seek every possible pretext to suppress the mass movement. They resort to such tactics as shifting the targets for attack

and turning black into white in an attempt to lead the movement astray. When they find themselves very isolated and no longer able to carry on as before, they resort still more to intrigues, stabbing people in the back, spreading rumors, and blurring the distinction between revolution and counterrevolution as much as they can, all for the purpose of attacking the revolutionaries.

What the Central Committee of the Party demands of the Party committees at all levels is that they persevere in giving correct leadership, put daring above everything else, boldly arouse the masses, change the state of weakness and incompetence where it exists, encourage those comrades who have made mistakes but are willing to correct them to cast off their mental burdens and join in the struggle, and dismiss from their leading posts all those in authority who are taking the capitalist road and so make possible the recapture of the leadership for the proletarian revolutionaries.

4. Let the Masses Educate Themselves in the Movement

In the great proletarian cultural revolution, the only method is for the masses to liberate themselves, and any method of doing things on their behalf must not be used.

Trust the masses, rely on them, and respect their initiative. Cast out fear. Don't be afraid of disorder. Chairman Mao has often told us that revolution cannot be so very refined, so gentle, so temperate, kind, courteous, restrained, and magnanimous. Let the masses educate themselves in this great revolutionary movement and learn to distinguish between right and wrong and between correct and incorrect ways of doing things.

Make the fullest use of big-character posters and great debates to argue matters out, so that the masses can clarify the correct views, criticize the wrong views, and expose all the ghosts and monsters. In this way the masses will be able to raise their political consciousness in the course of the struggle, enhance their abilities and talents, distinguish right from wrong, and draw a clear line between the enemy and ourselves.

5. Firmly Apply the Class Line of the Party

Who are our enemies? Who are our friends? This is a question of the first importance for the revolution and it is likewise a question of the first importance for the great cultural revolution.

Party leadership should be good at discovering the left and developing and strengthening the ranks of the left, and should firmly rely on the revolutionary left. During the movement this is the only way to isolate thoroughly the most reactionary rightists, win over the middle, and unite with the great majority so that by the end of the movement we shall achieve the unity of more than 95 per cent of the cadres and more than 95 per cent of the masses.

Concentrate all forces to strike at the handful of ultrareactionary bourgeois rightists and counterrevolutionary revisionists, and expose and criticize to the full their crimes against the Party, against socialism, and against Mao Tse-tung's thought so as to isolate them to the maximum.

The main target of the present movement is those within the Party who are in authority and are taking the capitalist road.

Care should be taken to distinguish strictly between the anti-Party, anti-socialist rightists and those who support the Party and socialism but have said or done something wrong or have written some bad articles or other works.

Care should be taken to distinguish strictly between the reactionary bourgeois scholar despots and "authorities" on the one hand and people who have the ordinary bourgeois academic ideas on the other.

6. Correct Handling of Contradictions Among the People

A strict distinction must be made between the two different types of contradictions: those among the people and those between ourselves and the enemy. Contradictions among the people must not be made into contradictions between ourselves and the enemy; nor must contradictions between ourselves and the enemy be regarded as those among the people.

It is normal for the masses to hold different views. Contention between different views is unavoidable, necessary, and beneficial. In the course of normal and full debate, the masses will affirm what is right, correct what is wrong, and gradually reach unanimity.

The method to be used in debates is to present the facts, reason things out, and persuade through reasoning. Any method of forcing a minority holding different views to submit is impermissible. The minority should be protected, because sometimes the truth is with the minority. Even if the minority is wrong, they should still be allowed to argue their case and reserve their views.

When there is a debate, it should be conducted by reasoning, not by coercion or force.

In the course of debate, every revolutionary should be good at thinking things out for himself and should develop the communist spirit of daring to think, daring to speak, and daring to act. On the premise that they have the same main orientation, revolutionary comrades should, for the sake of strengthening unity, avoid endless debate over side issues.

7. Be on Guard Against Those Who Brand the Revolutionary Masses as "Counterrevolutionaries"

In certain schools, units, and work teams of the cultural revolution, some of the persons in charge have organized counterattacks against the masses who put up big-character posters against them. These people have even advanced such slogans as: opposition to the leaders of a unit or a work team means opposition to the Party's Central Committee, means opposition to the Party and socialism, means counterrevolution. In this way it is inevitable that their blows will fall on some really revolutionary activists. This is an error on matters of orientation, an error of line, and is absolutely impermissible.

A number of persons who suffer from serious ideological errors, and particularly some of the anti-Party and anti-socialist rightists, are taking advantage of certain shortcomings and mistakes in the mass movement to spread rumors and gossip and engage in agitation, deliberately branding some of the masses as "counterrevolutionaries." It is necessary to beware of such "pickpockets" and expose their tricks in good time.

In the course of the movement, with the exception of cases of active counterrevolutionaries where there is clear evidence of crimes such as murder, arson, poisoning, sabotage, or theft of state secrets, which should be handled in accordance with the law, no measures should be taken against students at universities, colleges, middle schools, and primary schools because of problems that arise in the movement. To prevent the struggle from being diverted from its main objective, it is not allowed, whatever the pretext, to incite the masses to struggle against each other or the students to do likewise. Even proven rightists should be dealt with on the merits of each case at a later stage of the movement.

8. The Question of Cadres

The cadres fall roughly into the following four categories:

(1) good;
(2) comparatively good;

(3) those who have made serious mistakes but have not become anti-Party, anti-socialist rightists;

(4) the small number of anti-Party, anti-socialist rightists.

In ordinary situations, the first two categories (good and comparatively good) are the great majority.

The anti-Party, anti-socialist rightists must be fully exposed, hit hard, pulled down, and completely discredited and their influence eliminated. At the same time, they should be given a way out so that they can turn over a new leaf.

9. Cultural Revolutionary Groups, Committees, and Congresses

Many new things have begun to emerge in the great proletarian cultural revolution. The cultural revolutionary groups, committees, and other organizational forms created by the masses in many schools and units are something new and of great historic importance.

These cultural revolutionary groups, committees, and congresses are excellent new forms of organization whereby under the leadership of the Communist Party the masses are educating themselves. They are an excellent bridge to keep our Party in close contact with the masses. They are organs of power of the proletarian cultural revolution.

The struggle of the proletariat against the old ideas, culture, customs, and habits left over from all the exploiting classes over thousands of years will necessarily take a very, very long time. Therefore, the cultural revolutionary groups, committees, and congresses should not be temporary organizations but permanent, standing mass organizations. They are suitable not only for colleges, schools, and government and other organizations, but generally also for factories, mines, other enterprises, urban districts, and villages.

It is necessary to institute a system of general elections, like that of the Paris Commune, for electing members to the cultural revolutionary groups and committees and delegates to the cultural revolutionary congresses. The lists of candidates should be put forward by the revolutionary masses after full discussion, and the elections should be held after the masses have discussed the lists over and over again.

The masses are entitled at any time to criticize members of the cultural revolutionary groups and committees and delegates elected to the cultural revolutionary congresses. If these members or delegates prove incompetent, they can be replaced through election or recalled by the masses after discussion.

The cultural revolutionary groups, committees, and congresses in colleges and schools should consist mainly of representatives of the revolutionary students. At the same time, they should have a certain number of representatives of the revolutionary teaching staff and workers.

10. Educational Reform

In the great proletarian cultural revolution a most important task is to transform the old educational system and the old principles and methods of teaching.

In this great cultural revolution, the phenomenon of our schools being dominated by bourgeois intellectuals must be completely changed.

In every kind of school we must apply thoroughly the policy advanced by Comrade Mao Tse-tung, of education serving proletarian politics and education being combined with productive labor, so as to enable those receiving an education to develop morally, intellectually, and physically and to become laborers with socialist consciousness and culture.

The period of schooling should be shortened. Courses should be fewer and better. The teaching material should be thoroughly transformed, in some cases beginning with simplifying complicated material. While their main task is to study, students should also learn other things. That is to say, in addition to their studies they should also learn industrial work, farming, and military affairs, and take part in the struggles of the cultural revolution as they occur to criticize the bourgeoisie.

11. The Question of Criticizing by Name in the Press

In the course of the mass movement of the cultural revolution, the criticism of bourgeois and feudal ideology should be well combined with the dissemination of the proletarian world outlook and of Marxism-Leninism, Mao Tse-tung's thought.

Criticism should be organized of typical bourgeois representatives who have wormed their way into the Party and typical reactionary bourgeois academic "authorities," and this should include criticism of various kinds of reactionary views in philosophy, history, political economy, and education, in works and theories of literature and art, in theories of natural science, and in other fields.

Criticism of anyone by name in the press should be decided after discussion by the Party committee at the same level, and in some cases submitted to the Party committee at a higher level for approval.

12. Policy Toward Scientists, Technicians, and Ordinary Members of Working Staffs

As regards scientists, technicians, and ordinary members of working staffs, as long as they are patriotic, work energetically, are not against the Party and socialism, and maintain no illicit relations with any foreign country, we should in the present movement continue to apply the policy of "unity, criticism, unity" [see Chapter V]. Special care should be taken of those scientists and scientific and technical personnel who have made contributions. Efforts should be made to help them gradually transform their world outlook and their style of work.

13. The Question of Arrangements for Integration with the Socialist Education Movement in City and Countryside

The cultural and educational units and leading organs of the Party and government in the large and medium cities are the points of concentration of the present proletarian cultural revolution.

The great cultural revolution has enriched the socialist education movement in both city and countryside and raised it to a higher level. Efforts should be made to conduct these two movements in close combination. Arrangements to this effect may be made by various regions and departments in the light of the specific conditions.

The socialist education movement now going on in the countryside and in enterprises in the cities should not be upset where the original arrangements are appropriate and the movement is going well, but should continue in accordance with the original arrangements. However, the questions that are arising in the present great proletarian cultural revolution should be put to the masses for discussion at a proper time, so as further to foster vigorously proletarian ideology and eradicate bourgeois ideology.

In some places, the great proletarian cultural revolution is being used as the focus in order to add momentum to the socialist education movement and clean things up in the fields of politics, ideology, organization, and economy. This may be done where the local Party committee thinks it appropriate.

14. Take Firm Hold of the Revolution and Stimulate Production

The aim of the great proletarian cultural revolution is to revolutionize people's ideology and as a consequence to achieve greater, faster, better, and more economical results in all fields of work. If the masses are fully aroused and proper arrangements are made, it is possible to carry on both the cultural revolution and production without one hampering the other, while guaranteeing high quality in all our work.

The great proletarian cultural revolution is a powerful motive force for the development of the social productive forces in our country. Any idea of counterposing the great cultural revolution against the development of production is incorrect.

15. The Armed Forces

In the armed forces, the cultural revolution and the socialist education movement should be carried out in accordance with the instructions of the Military Commission of the Central Committee and the General Political Department of the People's Liberation Army.

16. Mao Tse-tung's Thought Is the Guide for Action in the Great Proletarian Cultural Revolution

In the great proletarian cultural revolution, it is imperative to hold aloft the great red banner of Mao Tse-tung's thought and put proletarian politics in command. The movement for the creative study and application of Chairman Mao Tse-tung's works should be carried forward among the masses of the workers, peasants, and soldiers, the cadres and the intellectuals, and Mao Tse-tung's thought should be taken as the guide for action in the cultural revolution.

In this complex great cultural revolution, Party committees at all levels must study and apply Chairman Mao's works all the more conscientiously and in a creative way. In particular, they must study over and over again Chairman Mao's writings on the cultural revolution and on the Party's methods of leadership, such as *On New Democracy, Talks at the Yenan Forum on Literature and Art, On the Correct Handling of Contradictions Among the People, Speech at the Chinese Communist Party's National Conference on Propaganda Work, Some Questions Concerning Methods of Leadership,* and *Methods of Work of Party Committees.*

Party committees at all levels must abide by the directions given by Chairman Mao over the years, namely that they should thoroughly apply the mass line of "from the masses and to the masses" and that they should be pupils before they become teachers. They should try to avoid being one-sided or narrow. They should foster materialist dialectics and oppose metaphysics and scholasticism.

The great proletarian cultural revolution is bound to achieve brilliant victory under the leadership of the Central Committee of the Party headed by Comrade Mao Tse-tung.

"Under the Red Banner of Mao Tse-tung's Thought"

From: "An Epoch-Making Document" (An Article by the *Jen-min Jih-pao* [People's Daily], *Hung Ch'i* [Red Flag], and *Chieh-fang Jih-pao* [Liberation Daily] Editorial Departments Commemorating the Second Anniversary of the May 16, 1966, Circular of the Central Committee of the Chinese Communist Party), *Peking Review*, May 24, 1968, pp. 8–12.

The Circular, made public on May 16, 1967 (a year after its actual issuance), identified certain high-ranking officials as "rightist" and "bourgeois," with "muddled" and "hypocritical" ideas. It also announced the formation of the Mao-controlled Central Cultural Revolution Group as the supreme director of the cultural revolution.

Much of the content of the Circular is quoted or paraphrased in the document that follows. Full text in *Peking Review*, May 19, 1967, pp. 6–9.

Two years ago, the May 16, 1966, Circular of the Central Committee of the Chinese Communist Party—a brilliant, historic Marxist-Leninist document—was drawn up under the personal guidance of the great leader Chairman Mao.

This Circular is an epoch-making document for conducting the great proletarian cultural revolution; it is a militant call to the proletariat and the broad masses of revolutionary people, under the conditions of socialism, to march against the bourgeoisie and all other exploiting classes.

Two years is a short time. But what great revolutionary changes have taken place in these two years! The theory, line, principles, and policies for continuing the revolution under the dictatorship of the proletariat advanced by Chairman Mao in the Circular have smashed the resistance put up in one form after another by the bourgeois reactionary line, armed the proletarian revolutionaries and hundreds of millions of revolutionary people in our country, and displayed the mighty power of Marxism-Leninism, thus winning the decisive victory for the unprecedented, great proletarian cultural revolution during the past two years.

I

Chairman Mao points out in the Circular: The whole Party must "hold high the great banner of the proletarian cultural revolution, thoroughly expose the reactionary bourgeois stand of those so-called academic authorities who oppose the Party and socialism, thoroughly criticize and repudiate reactionary bourgeois ideas in the sphere of academic work, education, journalism, literature and art, and publishing, and seize the leadership in these cultural spheres. To achieve this, it is at the same time necessary to criticize and repudiate those representatives of the bourgeoisie who have sneaked into the Party, the government, the army, and all spheres of culture, and to clear them out or transfer some of them to other positions.

"Those representatives of the bourgeoisie who have sneaked into the Party, the government, the army, and various spheres of culture are a bunch of counterrevolutionary revisionists. Once conditions are ripe, they will seize political power and turn the dictatorship of the proletariat into a dictatorship of the bourgeoisie. Some of them we have already seen through, others we have not. Some are still trusted by us and are being trained as our successors, persons like Khrushchev, for example, who are still nestling beside us. Party committees at all levels must pay full attention to this matter."

Practice in the great proletarian cultural revolution in the past two years has fully confirmed Chairman Mao's brilliant foresight. The people have understood ever more deeply that these instructions of Chairman Mao's constitute a creative development of the Marxist-Leninist theory of the dictatorship of the proletariat, a development which will play a far-reaching historical role in consolidating the dictatorship of the proletariat and continuing the socialist revolution in our country, and in the international communist movement.

The revolutionary mass movement undertaken on an unprecedentedly large scale during the past two years, like the surging waves of the sea, has smashed the bourgeois headquarters headed by China's Khrushchev, which was hidden in our Party, brought into the open the counterrevolutionary revisionists who oppose the Communist Party, the people, and Mao Tse-tung's thought, as well as the renegades, enemy agents, and counterrevolutionary double-dealers, and crushed their criminal schemes to subvert the dictatorship of the proletariat and restore capitalism in our country.

The abundant, irrefutable evidence already brought to light has established that China's Khrushchev and the others who form the handful of top Party persons in authority taking the capitalist road are a counterrevolutionary sinister gang that represents the interests of the Kuomintang reactionaries, of imperialism, the bourgeoisie, the landlords, rich peasants, counterrevolutionaries, bad elements, and rightists. A considerable proportion of this gang are the dregs and bad eggs left by the Kuomintang reactionaries. China's Khrushchev, this top capitalist roader in the Party, is a despicable renegade who on many occasions fell on his knees before the imperialists and the Kuomintang reactionaries. . . .

These scoundrels wormed their way into our Party and usurped many important positions. They were the Khrushchevs who nestled beside us, time bombs placed in our Party and the most dangerous enemies of the proletariat under socialist conditions. Once conditions were ripe, they would seize political power, turn the dictatorship of the proletariat into a dictatorship of the bourgeoisie, and turn the socialist system into a capitalist system, into a semifeudal, semicolonial system. The historical tragedy of the restoration of capitalism in the Soviet Union and other countries controlled by revisionist renegade cliques would be repeated in China and our country would be pulled back to the dark period of Kuomintang reactionary rule.

Our struggle against these counterrevolutionaries is a sharp, complex, life-and-death struggle, a great revolution in which one class overthrows another. As Chairman Mao profoundly pointed out in one of his latest instructions: "The great proletarian cultural revolution is in essence a great political revolution under the conditions of socialism made by the proletariat against the bourgeoisie and all other exploiting classes; it is a continuation of the prolonged struggle waged by the Chinese Communist Party and the masses of revolutionary people under its leadership against the Kuomintang reactionaries, a continuation of the class struggle between the proletariat and the bourgeoisie." Victory in this struggle has greatly consolidated the dictatorship of the proletariat.

Our Party relied on the masses of revolutionary people in waging a people's war in the past and succeeded in defeating powerful domestic and foreign enemies and overthrowing the reactionary Kuomintang rule. Now, under new historical conditions, our Party again relies on the masses of revolutionary people to advance and carry out this great political revolution which has no precedent in history a revolution launched by the proletariat against the bourgeoisie and all other exploiting classes. Precisely because several hundred million revolutionary people and young Red Guard fighters have been mobilized under the guidance of Chairman Mao's proletarian revolutionary line, it has been possible to uncover and bring to light the bourgeois representatives and the dregs and bad eggs left by the Kuomintang reactionaries—persons who are most sly, insidious, and vicious, and who have hidden themselves for so long and wormed themselves in so deep.

The great victory won by the proletarian revolutionaries, by the hundreds of millions of revolutionary people and young Red Guard fighters in China in waging the soul-stirring struggle against these class enemies in this great revolution, will shine forever with unfading and militant brilliance in the history of the proletariat's revolutionary struggle.

II

The mass movement of the great proletarian cultural revolution has undertaken revolutionary mass criticism and repudiation of the handful of class enemies which in breadth and depth is without parallel in history.

Inspired by the Circular, the proletarian revolutionaries and the revolutionary masses have held high the great banner of revolutionary criticism and repudiation in line with Mao Tse-tung's thought, incisively exposed and repudiated the towering crimes against the Party, socialism, and Mao Tse-tung's thought committed by the handful of top capitalist roaders in the Party and their agents in various regions and departments, vigorously criticized and repudiated the counterrevolutionary revisionist line and the old ideas, culture, customs, and habits of the bourgeoisie and of all other exploiting classes.

The revolutionary mass criticism and repudiation has enhanced the widespread dissemination of Mao Tse-tung's thought. The enthusiasm of the masses in the creative study and application of Mao Tse-tung's thought has never been so high as today. The outlook of the people has undergone a tremendous change. Successors to the revolutionary cause of the proletariat are emerging in the course of the struggle.

The revolutionary mass criticism and repudiation has helped the proletariat attain a still more dominant position ideologically. It has helped the proletarian revolutionaries overthrow the handful of capitalist roaders in the Party not only organizationally, but also in a thoroughgoing way politically, ideologically, and theoretically, thus consolidating the dominant position of the proletariat in the political and economic spheres.

In the political and ideological spheres, either the East wind prevails over the West wind, or the West wind prevails over the East wind; either the proletariat prevails over the bourgeoisie, or the bourgeoisie prevails over the proletariat. There is no middle course.

In the great proletarian cultural revolution, the aim of the proletarian revolutionaries is precisely to fight and repudiate resolutely the bourgeois reactionaries, poisonous weeds, and those landlords, rich peasants, counterrevolutionaries, bad elements, and rightists who have not reformed themselves. The aim of the proletariat is precisely to prevail over the bourgeoisie; "equality" with the latter is out of the question. As Chairman Mao points out in the Circular: "Can equality be permitted on such basic questions as the struggle of the proletariat against the bourgeoisie, the dictatorship of the proletariat over the bourgeoisie, the dictatorship of the proletariat in the superstructure, including all the various spheres of culture, and the continued efforts of the proletariat to weed out those representatives of the bourgeoisie who have sneaked into the Communist Party and who wave 'red flags' to oppose the red flag?"

The great victories in China's great proletarian cultural revolution movement over the past two years are the mighty results won by Mao Tse-tung's thought in the revolutionary mass criticism and repudiation of the old ideology of the bourgeoisie and all other exploiting classes.

Chairman Mao often says that there is no construction without destruction. Destruction means criticism and repudiation, it means revolution. It involves reasoning things out, which is construction. Put destruction first, and in the process you have construction.

Representatives of different classes and different ideologies will continue to perform on the stage in this unprecedented, great proletarian cultural revolution, in this extremely intense class struggle. The representatives of the moribund classes will continue to put on different disguises and resort to double-faced tactics to hoodwink people. We must continue to carry out the instruction "put destruction first, and in the process you have construction," and continue to repudiate the handful of top Party persons in authority taking the capitalist road, and the reactionary world outlook of the bourgeoisie.

All comrades in the ranks of the proletarian revolutionaries must hold aloft the great red banner of Mao Tse-tung's thought, firmly act according to Mao Tse-tung's thought and adhere to the high degree of principledness of the proletariat. They must repudiate the counterrevolutionary revisionist line represented by China's Khrushchev, and repudiate right opportunism and the reactionary thinking that is left in form but right in essence. They must repudiate all reactionary factions against Marxism-Leninism, against Mao Tse-tung's thought, repudiate anarchism, the mountain stronghold mentality, sectarianism, and all manifestations of the ideology of the bourgeoisie and all other exploiting classes. They must carry revolutionary mass repudiation through to the end and clear the way ideologically for all-round victory in the great proletarian cultural revolution. This will ensure that the great red banner of Mao Tse-tung's thought will fly high on all fronts.

III

During the great proletarian cultural revolution movement, on the basis of the revolutionary great alliance formed by the proletarian revolutionaries and the broad masses of revolutionary people, there has come into existence the entirely new revolutionary committee which is based on the revolutionary "three-in-one" combination. As Chairman Mao points out: "The 'three-in-one' revolutionary committee is the creation of the working class and the masses in the current great cultural revolution."

One of Chairman Mao's latest instructions says: "There are three elements in the basic experience of the revolutionary committee: It embraces representatives of the revolutionary cadres, representatives of the armed forces, and representatives of the revolutionary masses, constituting a revolutionary 'three-in-one' combination. The revolutionary committee should exercise unified leadership, eliminate duplication in the administrative structure, follow the policy of 'better troops and simpler administration,' and organize a revolutionized leading group which links itself with the masses."

Guided by Mao Tse-tung's thought, such a revolutionary committee which has the participation of representatives of the revolutionary masses who have brought about the revolutionary great alliance, and representatives of the People's Liberation Army and revolutionary leading cadres, is the rich fruit of the struggle launched from below by the proletarian revolutionaries and the broad revolutionary masses, who have grasped Chairman Mao's theory on continuing the revolution under the dictatorship of the proletariat, to seize power from the handful of capitalist roaders in the Party.

It has greatly enriched and developed the Marxist-Leninist theory of the state.

With outstanding elements of the proletariat, who have emerged in the mass movement, taking a direct part in state administration, such an organ of power represents the basic interests of the laboring masses of workers and peasants and maintains close and extensive ties with the masses. This will be of great help to our leading bodies at all levels in revolutionizing themselves and becoming organs of power which are revolutionary, enjoy proletarian authority, maintain close ties with the masses, and are full of vitality. Such a revolutionary committee which closely unites the basic forces (representatives of the revolutionary masses), the staunch pillar (representatives of the People's Liberation Army), and the leading core (representatives of the revolutionary cadres) of the dictatorship of the proletariat has further strengthened the unity between the army and the people, between the army and the government, and between the cadres and the masses, and strengthened the dictatorship of the proletariat so that our state organs of the dictatorship of the proletariat will meet still better the needs of the socialist economic base and the need to consolidate the dictatorship of the proletariat and prevent the restoration of capitalism.

Chairman Mao long ago taught us: "Without extensive people's democracy, the dictatorship of the proletariat cannot be consolidated and political power will be unstable. Without democracy, without arousing the masses, and without supervision by the masses, it is impossible effectively to exercise dictatorship over the reactionaries and bad elements or effectively to reform them; they will continue to make trouble, and there is still the possibility of a restoration. We should be vigilant on this question, and comrades should think about it carefully." (From the speech at the 7000-strong meeting in 1962.)

The great proletarian cultural revolution has aroused the masses to the fullest extent. The broad revolutionary masses are paying attention to the major issue of consolidating proletarian political power and are taking an active part in exercising dictatorship over the class enemy. This is dictatorship by the overwhelming majority over a tiny minority, a dictatorship by the proletariat and the masses of the people over the bourgeoisie and all reactionaries, and a dictatorship by the masses of the people under the leadership of the political party of the proletariat. With the gradual winning of all-round victory in the great cultural revolution and the establishment, improvement, and growth of revolutionary committees at all levels, the dictatorship of the proletariat, in which the masses of the people are aroused to participate, will display ever greater revolutionary power.

IV

The great historic contributions of the mass movement of the great proletarian cultural revolution are magnificent and indelible.

The victory of the mass movement of the great proletarian cultural revolution is irresistible.

With inveterate class hatred, the handful of class enemies, facing their last days but unreconciled to their doom, are frantically opposing the revolutionary mass movement and trying in vain to negate the tremendous victories of the great proletarian cultural revolution. But the law of history is inexorable and operates independent of their will. No matter what criminal conspiracies and sabotage they may undertake, and no matter how much they may stir up the evil right deviationist trend of trying to reverse correct decisions, they will end up crushed by the revolutionary mass movement.

The influence of the tremendous victories in our great proletarian cultural revolution over the past two years has spread throughout the world, inspiring the militant will of the revolutionary people of all countries. We can see that the great proletarian cultural revolution has played a certain role in pushing forward the revolutionary mass movement in countries ruled by the imperialists and their lackeys and in countries ruled by the revisionist renegade cliques. The great proletarian cultural revolution which is guided by Mao Tse-tung's thought has inspired the heroism of the revolutionary people the world over in daring to struggle and to win. It has won enthusiastic support from Marxist-Leninists and the revolutionary masses throughout the world.

China's great proletarian cultural revolution has aroused extreme fear, hatred, and panic among the imperialists, the modern revisionists, and the reactionaries of all countries. These bourgeois overlords always pin their hopes on the "premature end" of China's great proletarian cultural revolution, on the "collapse" of China's proletarian political power. Like witches, they mutter vicious curses about "the gloomy prospects of the cultural revolution." But the fond dreams of these overlords have been crushed under the strides of the victorious advance of China's proletarian revolutionaries and the broad revolutionary masses.

The sweeping torrent of China's great proletarian cultural revolution is breaking through all obstacles and surging forward with powerful momentum.

We are at the key moment of winning all-round victory in the great proletarian cultural revolution. We still face arduous struggles.

In this new situation, we should follow Chairman Mao's teachings, guard against arrogance and rashness, and advance from victory to victory. We should constantly sum up our experience, pay profound attention at all times to investigation and study, be alert to new trends, new characteristics, and new problems in the class struggle, and hold firmly to the general orientation of the struggle.

We should resolutely safeguard the leadership of the proletarian headquarters headed by Chairman Mao and with Vice-Chairman Lin Piao as the deputy leader, expose and smash all conspiracies and schemes by the class enemy to undermine the proletarian headquarters. We should further purify and consolidate our class ranks, unite and win over our allies, and continue to launch offensives against the class enemy. We should strictly differentiate contradictions between the enemy and ourselves from contradictions among the people. With regard to errors within the revolutionary ranks, we should persist in Chairman Mao's traditional policy of "learning from past mistakes to avoid future ones, curing the sickness to save the patient."

We should proceed from the cardinal issue of the struggle between the two lines and deepen the revolutionary mass criticism and repudiation. We should repudiate the reactionary bourgeois ideas which come from the right and from the ultra left, resolutely oppose right opportunism, right capitulationism, and right splittism, and completely smash the evil right deviationist trend of trying to reverse correct decisions.

We should carry forward the enthusiastic mass movement for the creative study and application of Mao Tse-tung's thought on a still wider scale, continue to exert great efforts to run Mao Tse-tung's thought study classes effectively, energetically strive to consolidate and develop the revolutionary great alliance on the basis of departments, trades, and school classes and the revolutionary "three-in-one" combination, unite the great majority of the cadres and the masses, make a success of struggle-criticism-transformation in each and every unit, grasp revolution, promote production and other work and preparedness against war, and do still better in all fields.

The great Chinese People's Liberation Army has made tremendous contributions in the great proletarian cultural revolution. We should continue to develop the movement to support the army and cherish the people and strengthen the unity between the army and the people.

We should cherish and support the newborn revolutionary committees so that they are steadily consolidated and improved and become fighting headquarters which hold aloft the great red banner of Mao Tse-tung's thought and put proletarian politics to the fore. The revolutionary committees should lead the masses in their tens of millions to win new victories and carry the great proletarian cultural revolution through to the end.

Let us rally firmly around the banner of Mao Tse-tung's thought, resolutely follow Chairman Mao's proletarian revolutionary line, and fight unremittingly to fulfill in an all-round way the momentous historic task of the great proletarian cultural revolution which is the first of its kind in the history of mankind! New victories call to us, let us march forward courageously!

"All-Round Victory in the Cultural Revolution"

From: *Long Live the All-Round Victory in the Great Proletarian Cultural Revolution!* (September 7, 1968) (An Article by the *Jen-min Jih-pao* [People's Daily] and *Chieh-fang Jih-pao* [Liberation Daily] Editorial Departments "Hailing" the Establishment of Revolutionary Committees Throughout China), *Peking Review,* September 13, 1968, pp. 3–5.

Songs of triumph ring out north and south of the Tienshan Mountains, and the sun shines brightly over the Tibetan Plateau. At a time when hundreds of millions of armymen and civilians throughout the country are marching from victory to victory under the inspiration of Chairman Mao's latest instructions, revolutionary committees have been established simultaneously in the Tibet Autonomous Region and the Sinkiang Uighur Autonomous Region, China's southwestern and northwestern outposts in the battle against imperialism and revisionism!

Revolutionary committees have now been set up in all the provinces, municipalities and autonomous regions of the country with the exception of Taiwan province. This extremely magnificent spectacle—the whole country is red—is an important event in the seizing of all-round victory in the great cultural revolution. It indicates that the whole movement has entered the stage of struggle-criticism-transformation on a nationwide scale. This is a great victory for the invincible thought of Mao Tse-tung, a great victory for Chairman Mao's proletarian revolutionary line and an event of great joy in the political life of the 700 million people of our country!

We extend our hearty congratulations to the revolutionary people of all nationalities in Tibet and Sinkiang, to all the commanders and fighters of the Chinese People's Liberation Army units stationed in Tibet and Sinkiang and to the fighters working on the state farms reclaimed by the Production and Construction Corps Under the Sinkiang Military Area Command!

We extend our warm and militant salutations to the proletarian revolutionary comrades-in-arms all over the country who have closely followed Chairman Mao's revolutionary line and forged ahead courageously during the last two years!

In the great proletarian cultural revolution, the proletarian revolutionaries and the revolutionary masses of all nationalities in Tibet and Sinkiang have stood firmly on the side of Chairman Mao's revolutionary line and have conscientiously carried out Chairman Mao's latest instructions. With the firm and strong support of the People's Liberation Army, they have, after repeated trials of strength and tenacious struggles against the class enemies, finally dug out the agents of China's Khrushchev in Sinkiang . . . and . . . Tibet . . . who are a handful of renegades, U.S.-Chiang Kai-shek special agents, special agents of the Soviet revisionists and of Britain, counter-revolutionary revisionists and national splittists. Thus the daydream of these class enemies to restore capitalism and undermine the unification of the motherland has been completely smashed and a heavy blow has been dealt to the schemes of the imperialists, modern revisionists and counter-revolutionaries for carrying out subversion and sabotage in the Tibet and Sinkiang regions.

In the great struggle during the 20 months from the outburst of the storm of the "January Revolution" in Shanghai to the establishment of the two revolutionary committees in Tibet and Sinkiang, armymen and civilians throughout the country have fulfilled Chairman Mao's great call: "Proletarian revolutionaries, unite and seize power from the handful of Party persons in authority taking the capitalist road," and they have won decisive victory in the great proletarian cultural revolution across the land.

Chairman Mao has taught us: "The aim of every revolutionary struggle in the world is the seizure and consolidation of political power." The class struggle under the dictatorship of the proletariat is, in essence, still a question of political power. The bourgeoisie wants to overthrow the dictatorship of the proletariat, whereas the proletariat wants to consolidate it. The handful of capitalist roaders in the Party are representatives of the bourgeoisie in the Party. The proletariat's seizing back of that portion of power of the Party, government, finance and culture which the handful of capitalist roaders usurped is a serious struggle in which the bourgeoisie attempts to restore capitalism while the proletariat opposes its doing so. It is a continuation of the proletarian revolution and a great political revolution made by the proletariat against the bourgeoisie and all other exploiting classes.

The establishment of revolutionary committees in the provinces, municipalities and autonomous regions throughout the country proclaims the complete bankruptcy of the counterrevolutionary plot of China's Khrushchev and his agents everywhere to turn the dictatorship of the proletariat into the dictatorship of the bourgeoisie. It has completely smashed all the counterrevolutionary rumors spread by U.S. imperialism and Soviet modern revisionism and dashed to pieces the wishful thinking of imperialism and modern revisionism to bring about "peaceful evolution" in China.

The establishment of revolutionary committees in the provinces, municipalities and autonomous regions throughout the country demonstrates the unparalleled might of the invincible thought of Mao Tse-tung when it is grasped by hundreds of millions of revolutionary people. It has greatly strengthened the dictatorship of the proletariat and greatly enriched and developed Marxism-Leninism.

We heartily and warmly hail the great victory won by the revolutionary people under the leadership of the proletarian headquarters headed by Chairman Mao and with Vice-Chairman Lin Piao as its deputy leader.

We will resolutely bring into full play the proletariat's thoroughgoing revolutionary spirit, closely follow Chairman Mao's great strategic plan, and consolidate and develop this victory through consistent and untiring struggle!

Chairman Mao recently issued to the whole country the great call: "Carry out the tasks of struggle-criticism-transformation conscientiously." He pointed out: "Struggle-criticism-transformation in a factory, on the whole, goes through the following stages: establishing a three-in-one revolutionary committee; carrying out mass criticism and repudiation; purifying the class ranks; consolidating the Party organization; and simplifying the administrative structure, changing irrational rules and regulations and sending office workers to the workshops."

Chairman Mao's latest instructions reflect the objective law of the advance of the great proletarian cultural revolution to the stage of struggle-criticism-transformation. It expresses in concentrated form the pressing demands of the working class and the revolutionary masses and indicates in a clear-cut way the central tasks confronting the revolutionary committees at all levels.

Doing a good job of struggle-criticism-transformation in each unit and each department is basic to the socialist revolution and socialist construction. It is of primary and lasting importance to preventing the restoration of capitalism and consolidating and developing the dictatorship of the proletariat. This is a battle to win all-round victory in the great proletarian cultural revolution. The revolutionary committees at all levels must vigorously grasp struggle-criticism-transformation and, in fulfilling this great historic task, bring their revolutionary might into fuller play and consolidate and develop the revolutionary committees.

In order to fight the battle of struggle-criticism-transformation well, it is imperative to uphold working-class leadership and "bring into full play the leading role of the working class in the great cultural revolution and in all fields of work." And it should be seen to that every instruction of the great leader Chairman Mao and every order issued by the proletarian headquarters is carried out swiftly and smoothly; the reactionary bourgeois theory of "many centers," that is, the theory of "no center," must be resolutely opposed, and our thinking must be unified and our steps and actions must be co-ordinated at the call of the proletarian headquarters headed by Chairman Mao and with Vice-Chairman Lin Piao as its deputy leader. At the same time, it is essential to arm the workers with the invincible thought of Mao Tse-tung, make constant efforts to raise the political consciousness of the working class so that it will be able to undertake still better its great historical mission of exercising leadership in everything, in the educational revolution, in the struggle-criticism-transformation in all spheres of the superstructure and in every task for carrying out Chairman Mao's great strategic plan.

In order to fight well in the battle of struggle-criticism-transformation, it is imperative to strengthen ideological and political work, conscientiously do a good job of investigation and study and be good at seizing on typical examples. The revolutionary committees at all levels must firmly carry out all the proletarian policies put forward

. . . [by] the great leader Chairman Mao. Responsible members of the revolutionary committees must themselves select some particular points where they will gain experience and use this experience for guiding their over-all work, and report the results to the Party's Central Committee. They must forge close links with the masses, listen to the opinions of the masses and pay special attention to overcoming all tendencies to divorce themselves from the masses.

Chairman Mao has said: "Just because we have won victory, we must never relax our vigilance against the frenzied plots for revenge by the imperialists and their running dogs." We must conduct deep-going and sustained revolutionary mass criticism, take the initiative and mount fierce attacks against the class enemy, do a good job of purifying our class ranks, hit steadily, accurately and relentlessly at the handful of renegades, enemy agents, diehard capitalist roaders and the landlords, rich peasants, counterrevolutionaries, bad elements and Rightists who have not reformed themselves, and uncover all the counterrevolutionaries who are hiding in dark corners to make trouble and engage in sabotage. We must strengthen the unity between the army and the people, step up preparedness against war, strengthen our border defenses and our coastal and air defenses, and be ready at all times to liberate Taiwan and defend our country's socialist revolution and socialist construction. Should the enemy dare to touch China's sacred territory and launch an armed invasion, we will wipe him out resolutely, thoroughly, wholly and completely.

Let us closely follow the great strategic plan of the great leader Chairman Mao and march forward in giant strides to successfully accomplish the great historic tasks of struggle-criticism-transformation. Lighted by the radiance of Mao Tse-tung's thought, our great socialist motherland will surely emerge even more majestic before the people of the whole world!

Long live the victory of Chairman Mao's proletarian revolutionary line!

Long live the all-round victory in the great proletarian cultural revolution!

★

CHAPTER III
Dynamics of Revolution: United Front

Introductory Note

Revolutions, Mao believes, are irreversible historical processes developing "step by step," according to a plan whose outlines are predetermined. Although "dialectically" and historically inevitable, however, no revolution develops in an unguided, undirected, and spontaneous fashion. There is in Mao, as in all orthodox Marxist theorists, a curious fusion of revolutionary determinism and voluntarism. On the one hand, it is repeatedly asserted, the course of revolution is "independent of man's will"; on the other, it is argued, without man's active participation and direction, no revolutionary movement is likely to succeed. This means, among other things, that the revolutionary leaders must persistently seek to identify the precise points at which human intervention may be effectively introduced. They must engage in constant appraisals of the relative forces of revolution and counterrevolution, the "ebb and flow" of the revolutionary situation. The Marxian belief in the spontaneous development of revolution is rejected; submission to spontaneity is denounced as "tailism" (following rather than leading). There are certain concrete tasks to be performed, certain concrete events to be caused to happen, certain phenomena to be forced to appear, before a revolutionary movement can attain victory. Put otherwise, without systematic, conscious, and voluntary activation of a series of dynamic forces, revolutionary movements are doomed to failure, their "dialectical" character notwithstanding.

For Mao Tse-tung, the principal dynamics of revolutionary development consist of united front, the army, and the Party. These, he writes, are the three "magic weapons" of the Chinese revolution.

The relationship between them is spelled out in these terms: ". . . the united front and armed struggle are two basic weapons for defeating the enemy. The united front is a united front for carrying on armed struggle. And the Party is the heroic warrior wielding the two weapons, the united front and the armed struggle, to storm and shatter the enemy's position."

It is to a consideration of these three dynamic forces that this chapter and the following two are devoted.

To grasp the conditions under which revolutionary struggle is to be conducted at a given time, Mao insists, revolutionary leadership must undertake extensive analyses of class contradictions in society. The purpose of class analysis is to enable revolutionaries to make the necessary, crucial distinction between "friend" and "foe," between the "people" and the "enemy," at any given point in time. The interrelationships and interaction of various classes determine the nature and direction of the revolutionary movement.

The terms "people" and "enemy" have historical and developmental connotations, their content changing with the changing phases of the revolutionary movement. In general, "people" is defined as all "progressive" social forces that at any given moment support the proletariat in its quest for power; they constitute, at that point, the "motive forces" of revolution. The "enemy," by contrast, comprises all "reactionary" classes against which the revolution aims; they are, at any given point, the "targets" of revolution.

Although different societies at different times are characterized by divergences in class structure and class relationships, two relatively distinct types of class structure, corresponding to two distinct types of revolutionary environment, are identified. Advanced industrial societies are presumably characterized by a polarization of all social forces into the two antagonistic camps of the bourgeoisie and the proletariat. In colonial and semicolonial countries, by contrast, class polarization has not taken place and the situation is characterized by the coexistence of a number of precapitalist classes (e.g., the landlords, the peasantry) side by side with the capitalist classes.

In colonial and semicolonial countries the victory of the revolutionary movement is predicated upon the firm alliance of certain social forces and upon their concerted action in pursuit of specific goals. Apart from this, no revolution can expect to succeed. The problem of identifying the revolutionary social forces at various stages of revolution, mobilizing them, uniting with them, and employing their combined strength is the problem of united front and united front policy. This tactic stands in direct contrast to "individualism" and "closed-doorism," attitudes stressing the "purity" of the revolutionary movement.

The united front policy requires, among other things, a "common program" binding the participant units together and governing the relationships among them. It is a program of mutual assistance based on "principled" concession and compromise. Mao views compromise as important and necessary, provided it does not affect the basic ideological principles of the revolutionary party.

Mao Tse-tung attaches a great deal of importance to the notion of "independence and initiative" for each participating unit within the united front. This concept, however, is highly deceptive, as it does not apply uniformly to all classes and groups involved in the united front. It is in fact a slogan designed to facilitate Communist hegemony in the revolutionary movement. Without proletarian leadership, Communist doctrine runs, united front is meaningless.

To capture united front leadership, the proletariat must launch persistent struggles against all "deviationist" and "opportunist" lines throughout the revolutionary movement. It must demonstrate its "boundless activity and loyalty" and set an example in self-sacrifice, willingness to bear hardship, and dedication to the revolutionary cause. As such, Mao maintains, the united front policy is neither a policy of "all alliance and no struggle" nor one of "all struggle and no alliance." The proletariat must seek to unite with other social strata while at the same time struggling against them.

The united front policy underwent six stages of development in China, its class content fluctuating from stage to stage. These stages, the first five according to official Chinese Communist historiography, are as follows: (1) the First Revolutionary Civil War, 1924–27, (2) the Second Revolutionary Civil War, 1927–37, (3) the War of Resistance Against Japan, 1937–45, (4) the Third Revolutionary Civil War (the "War of Liberation"), 1945–49, (5) the period of socialist construction, 1949–65, and (6) the period of the cultural revolution, 1965 to the present.

The first period was characterized by co-operation between the Communists and the Nationalists in the struggle against imperialism and feudalism; it ended, as we have seen, in disaster for the Communists. The class basis of the united front comprised the proletariat, the peasantry, the petty bourgeoisie, the national bourgeoisie, and the non-comprador wing of the big bourgeoisie (for distinctions, see Prologue).

In the second stage, the contradiction between China and the foreign enemy was replaced with the antagonism between the revolutionaries and the domestic reaction. As the authoritarian policy of the Kuomintang regime continued to persist, the relationship between the forces of revolution and the bourgeoisie became one of sharp antagonism. This period saw "the big bourgeoisie going over to the counterrevolutionary camp . . . and the national bourgeoisie trailing after it." The social basis of the united front was thus limited to the proletariat, the peasantry, and the petty bourgeoisie.

During the War of Resistance Against Japan, the class basis of the united front was once again broadened to embrace the national bourgeoisie and the non-comprador wing of the big bourgeoisie. The Japanese attempt to reduce China to a colony blunted both the contradiction between China and imperialism in general and that between the proletariat and the bourgeoisie within the country. Aiming at "national salvation," Mao insisted, the united front against Japan embraced "the whole nation." It was "a united front of all parties and groups, people in all walks of life, and all armed forces, a united front of all patriots—the workers, peasants, soldiers, intellectuals, and businessmen."

During the fourth stage, the "War of Liberation," once again the big bourgeoisie were excluded from the united front; otherwise, the scope of the alliance remained unchanged. Mao wrote: "Everybody is our friend, except the imperialists, the feudalists, and the bureaucrat-capitalists, the Kuomintang reactionaries and their accomplices." The basic change, he said, was that the United States had replaced Japan in attempting to reduce China to a colony. The class basis of the united front included "the workers, peasants, urban petty bourgeoisie, national bourgeoisie, enlightened gentry, other patriotic elements, the minority nationalities, and overseas Chinese."

The united front policy of the period of socialist construction returned to the four-class alliance of the proletariat, the peasantry, the petty bourgeoisie, and the national bourgeoisie. In 1957, Mao anticipated that a policy of "long-term coexistence" would continue to characterize the relationship between the proletariat and other social strata.

The cultural revolution marked a new stage in the united front tactic, even though no formal change in policy was announced. The alliance of Communists with the national bourgeoisie was in effect ended. Members of this class were dragged into the street, attacked, abused, humiliated by the Red Guards, and the "fixed interests" allowed them in joint state-private enterprises were discontinued (see p. 78). It should be remembered, however, that this development came about nearly two decades after the Communist seizure of power and fully a decade following the official proclamation of the dictatorship of the proletariat in China.

This brief examination of the Chinese experience with the united front tactic leads to three interrelated observations: (1) the principal "enemies" of the Chinese revolution were the imperialists, the feudal lords, and the comprador bourgeoisie, (2) the firm and lasting allies of the proletariat continue to be the peasantry and the petty bourgeoisie, and (3) the temporary allies of the proletariat have included the national bourgeoisie (except during the Second Revolutionary Civil War and the cultural revolution) and the non-comprador wing of the big bourgeoisie (during the First Revolutionary Civil War and the War of Resistance Against Japan).

The united front policy does not apply to the domestic revolutionary situation alone; it is capable of addressing itself to the international struggle as well. The global significance of this policy will be examined in a subsequent chapter.

Readings

WEAPONS OF REVOLUTION

From: "Introducing *The Communist*" (October 1939), *Selected Works*, II (Peking: Foreign Languages Press, 1965), pp. 288, 295.

. . . the united front, armed struggle, and Party building are the three fundamental questions for our Party in the Chinese revolution. Having a correct grasp of these three questions and their interrelations is tantamount to giving correct leadership to the whole Chinese revolution. We are now able to draw correct conclusions concerning these three questions by virtue of our abundant experience in the eighteen years of our Party's history, our rich and profound experience of failures and successes, retreats and advances, contraction and expansion. This means that we are now able to handle the questions of the united front, of armed struggle, and of Party building in a correct way. It also means that our eighteen years of experience have taught us that the united front, armed struggle, and Party building are the Chinese Communist Party's three "magic weapons" for defeating the enemy in the Chinese revolution. This is a great achievement of the Chinese Communist Party and of the Chinese revolution. . . .

Our eighteen years of experience show that the united front and armed struggle are the two basic weapons for defeating the enemy. The united front is a united front for carrying on armed struggle. And the Party is the heroic warrior wielding the two weapons, the united front and the armed struggle, to storm and shatter the enemy's positions. That is how the three are related to each other.

From: "On Tactics Against Japanese Imperialism" (December 1935), *Selected Works,* I (Peking: Foreign Languages Press, 1964), p. 165.

. . . Like every other activity in the world, revolution always follows a tortuous road and never a straight one. The alignment of forces in the revolutionary and counterrevolutionary camps can change, just as everything else in the world changes. . . . In order to attack the forces of the counterrevolution, what the revolutionary forces need today is to organize millions upon millions of the masses and move a mighty revolutionary army into action. The plain truth is that only a force of such magnitude can crush the . . . imperialists and the traitors and collaborators. Therefore, united front tactics are the only Marxist-Leninist tactics.

CLASSES AND UNITED FRONT

The Class Shape of China

From: "Speech at the Assembly of Representatives of the Shensi-Kansu-Ningsia Border Region" (November 1941), *Selected Works,* III (Peking: Foreign Languages Press, 1965), p. 32.

. . . Chinese society is small at both ends and big in the middle, that is, the proletariat at one end and the landlord class and big bourgeoisie at the other each constitute only a small minority, while the great majority of the people consist of the peasants, the urban petty bourgeoisie, and the other intermediate classes. No political party that wants to run China's affairs properly can do so unless its policy gives consideration to the interests of these classes, unless some provision is made for the members of these classes, and unless they have the right to voice their opinions.

Friends and Enemies

From: "Analysis of the Classes in Chinese Society" (March 1926), *Selected Works*, I (Peking: Foreign Languages Press, 1964), pp. 13–19.

Who are our enemies? Who are our friends? This is a question of the first importance for the revolution. The basic reason why all previous revolutionary struggles in China achieved so little was their failure to unite with real friends in order to attack real enemies. A revolutionary party is the guide of the masses, and no revolution ever succeeds when the revolutionary party leads them astray. To ensure that we will definitely achieve success in our revolution and will not lead the masses astray, we must pay attention to uniting with our real friends in order to attack our real enemies. To distinguish real friends from real enemies, we must make a general analysis of the economic status of the various classes in Chinese society and of their respective attitudes toward the revolution.

What is the condition of each of the classes in Chinese society?

THE LANDLORD CLASS AND THE COMPRADOR CLASS. In economically backward and semicolonial China the landlord class and the comprador class are wholly appendages of the international bourgeoisie, depending upon imperialism for their survival and growth. These classes represent the most backward and most reactionary relations of production in China and hinder the development of her productive forces. Their existence is utterly incompatible with the aims of the Chinese revolution. The big landlord and big comprador classes in particular always side with imperialism and constitute an extreme counterrevolutionary group. Their political representatives are the *Etatistes* [a conservative youth group] and the right wing of the Kuomintang.

THE MIDDLE BOURGEOISIE. This class represents the capitalist relations of production in China in town and country. The middle bourgeoisie, by which is meant chiefly the national bourgeoisie, is inconsistent in its attitude toward the Chinese revolution: they feel the need for revolution and favor the revolutionary movement against imperialism and the warlords when they are smarting under the blows of foreign capital and the oppression of the warlords, but they become suspicious of the revolution when they sense that, with the militant participation of the proletariat at home and the active support of the international proletariat abroad, the revolution is threatening the hope of their class to attain the status of a big bourgeoisie. Politically, they stand for the establishment of a state under the rule of a single class, the national bourgeoisie. . . . But [this] attempt . . . is quite impracticable, because the present world situation is such that the two major forces, revolution and counter-revolution, are locked in final struggle. Each has hoisted a huge banner: one is the red banner of revolution held aloft by the Third International as the rallying point for all the oppressed classes of the world, the other is the white banner of counterrevolution held aloft by the League of Nations as the rallying point for all the counterrevolutionaries of the world. The intermediate classes are bound to disintegrate quickly, some sections turning left to join the revolution, others turning right to join the counterrevolution; there is no room for them to remain "independent." Therefore the idea cherished by China's middle bourgeoisie of an "independent" revolution in which it would play the primary role is a mere illusion.

THE PETTY BOURGEOISIE. Included in this category are the owner-peasants, the master handicraftsmen, the lower levels of the intellectuals—students, primary and secondary school teachers, lower government functionaries, office clerks, small lawyers—and the small traders. Both because of its size and class character, this class deserves very close attention. The owner-peasants and the master handicraftsmen are both engaged in small-scale production. Although all strata of this class have the same petty-bourgeois economic status, they fall into three different sections. The first section consists of those who have some surplus money or grain, that is, those who, by manual or mental labor, earn more each year than they consume for their own support. Such people very much want to get rich and are devout worshipers of Marshal Chao [god of wealth]. While they have no illusions about amassing great fortunes, they invariably desire to climb up into the middle bourgeoisie. Their mouths water copiously when they see the respect in which those small moneybags are held. People of this sort are timid, afraid of government officials, and also a little afraid of the revolution. Since they are quite close to the middle bourgeoisie in economic status, they have a lot of faith in its propaganda and are suspicious of the revolution. This section is a minority among the petty bourgeoisie and constitutes its right wing. The second section consists of those who in the main are economically self-supporting. They are quite different from the people in the first section; they also want to get rich, but Marshal Chao never lets them. In recent years, moreover, suffering from the oppression and exploitation of the imperialists, the warlords, the feudal landlords, and the big comprador-bourgeoisie, they have become aware that the world is no longer what it was. They feel they cannot earn enough to live on by just putting in as much work as before. To make both ends meet they have to work longer hours, get up earlier, leave off later, and be doubly careful at their work. They become rather abusive, denouncing the foreigners as "foreign devils," the warlords as "robber generals," and the local tyrants and evil gentry as "the heartless rich." As for the movement against the imperialists and the warlords, they merely doubt whether it can succeed (on the ground that the foreigners and the warlords seem so powerful), hesitate to join it, and prefer to be neutral, but they never oppose the revolution. This section is very numerous, making up about one half of the petty bourgeoisie. The third section consists of those whose standard of living is falling. Many in this section, who originally belonged to better-off families, are undergoing a gradual change from a position of being barely able to manage to one of living in more and more reduced circumstances. When they come to settle their accounts at the end of each year, they are shocked, exclaiming, "What? Another deficit!" As such people have seen better days and are now going downhill with every passing year, their debts mounting and their life becoming more and more miserable, they "shudder at the thought of the future." They are in great mental distress because there is such a contrast between their past and their present. Such people are quite important for the revolutionary movement; they form a mass of no small proportions and are the left wing of the petty bourgeoisie. In normal times these three sections of the petty bourgeosie differ in their attitude to the revolution. But in times of war, that is, when the tide of the revolution runs high and the dawn of victory is in sight, not only will the left wing of the petty bourgeoisie join the revolution, but the middle section too may join, and even right-wingers, swept forward by the great revolutionary tide of the proletariat and of the left wing of the petty bourgeoisie, will have to go along with the revolution. We can see from the experience of the May 30 Movement of 1925 and the peasant movement in various places that this conclusion is correct.

THE SEMIPROLETARIAT. What is here called the semiproletariat consists of five categories: (1) the overwhelming majority of the semiowner peasants, (2) the poor peasants, (3) the small handicraftsmen, (4) the shop assistants, and (5) the pedlars. The overwhelming majority of the semiowner peasants together with the poor peasants constitute a very large part of the rural masses. The peasant problem is essentially their problem. The semiowner peasants, the poor peasants, and the small handicraftsmen are engaged in production on a still smaller scale than the owner-peasants and the master handicraftsmen. Although both the overwhelming majority of the semiowner peasants and the poor peasants belong to the semiproletariat, they may be further divided into three smaller categories, upper, middle, and lower, according to their economic condition. The semiowner peasants are worse off than the owner-peasants because every year they are short of about half the food they need, and have to make up this deficit by renting land from others, selling part of their labor power, or engaging in petty trading. In late spring and early summer when the crop is still in the blade and the old stock is consumed, they borrow at exorbitant rates of interest and buy grain at high prices; their plight is naturally harder than that of the owner-peasants, who need no help from others, but they are better off than the poor peasants. For the poor peasants own no land, and receive only half the harvest or even less for their year's toil, while the semiowner peasants, though receiving only half or less than half the harvest of land rented from others, can keep the entire crop from the land they own. The semiowner peasants are therefore more revolutionary than the owner-peasants, but less revolutionary than the poor peasants. The poor peasants are tenant-peasants who are exploited by the landlords. They may again be divided into two categories according to their economic status. One category has comparatively adequate farm implements and some funds. Such peasants may retain half the product of their year's toil. To make up their deficit they cultivate side crops, catch fish or shrimps, raise poultry or pigs, or sell part of their labor power, and thus eke out a living, hoping in the midst of hardship and destitution to tide over the year. Thus their life is harder than that of the semiowner peasants, but they are better off than the other category of poor peasants. They are more revolutionary than the semiowner peasants, but less revolutionary than the other category of poor peasants. As for the latter, they have neither adequate farm implements nor funds nor enough manure, their crops are poor, and, with little left after paying rent, they have even greater need to sell part of their labor power. In hard times they piteously beg help from relatives and friends, borrowing a few *tou* or *sheng* of grain to last them a few days, and their debts pile up like loads on the backs of oxen. They are the worst off among the peasants and are highly receptive to revolutionary propaganda. The small handicraftsmen are called semiproletarians because, though they own some simple means of production and moreover are self-employed, they too are often forced to sell part of their labor power and are somewhat similar to the poor peasants in economic status. They feel the constant pinch of poverty and dread of unemployment, because of heavy family burdens and the gap between their earnings and the cost of living; in this respect too they largely resemble the poor peasants. The shop assistants are employees of shops and stores, supporting their families on meager pay and getting an increase perhaps only once in several years, while prices rise every year. If by chance you get into intimate conversation with them, they invariably pour out their endless grievances. Roughly the same in status as the poor peasants and the small handicraftsmen, they are highly receptive to revolutionary propaganda. The pedlars, whether they carry their wares around on a pole or set up stalls along the street, have tiny funds and very small earnings, and do not make enough to feed and clothe themselves. Their status is roughly the same as that of the poor peasants, and like the poor peasants they need a revolution to change the existing state of affairs.

THE PROLETARIAT. The modern industrial proletariat numbers about two million. It is not large because China is economically backward. These two million industrial workers are mainly employed in five industries—railways, mining, maritime transport, textiles, and shipbuilding—and a great number are enslaved in enterprises owned by foreign capitalists. Though not very numerous, the industrial proletariat represents China's new productive forces, is the most progressive class in modern China, and has become the leading force in the revolutionary movement. We can see the important position of the industrial proletariat in the Chinese revolution from the strength it has displayed in the strikes of the last four years, such as the seamen's strikes, the railway strike, the strikes in the Kailan and Tsiaotso coal mines, the Shameen strike, and the general strikes in Shanghai and Hong Kong after the May 30 Incident. The first reason why the industrial workers hold this position is their concentration. No other section of the people is so concentrated. The second reason is their low economic status. They have been deprived of all means of production, have nothing left but their hands, have no hope of ever becoming rich, and moreover are subjected to the most ruthless treatment by the imperialists, the warlords, and the bourgeoisie. That is why they are particularly good fighters. The coolies in the cities are also a force meriting attention. They are mostly dockers and rickshawmen, and among them, too, are sewage carters and street cleaners. Possessing nothing but their hands, they are similar in economic status to the industrial workers but are less concentrated and play a less important role in production. There is as yet little modern capitalist farming in China. By rural proletariat we mean farm laborers hired by the year, the month or the day. Having no land, farm implements, or funds, they can live only by selling their labor power. Of all the workers they work the longest hours, for the lowest wages, under the worst conditions, and with the least security of employment. They are the most hard-pressed people in the villages, and their position in the peasant movement is as important as that of the poor peasants.

Apart from all these, there is the fairly large *lumpen*-proletariat, made up of peasants who have lost their land and handicraftsmen who cannot get work. They lead the most precarious existence of all. In every part of the country they have their secret societies, which were originally their mutual-aid organizations for political and economic struggle, for instance, the Triad Society in Fukien and Kwangtung, the Society of Brothers in Hunan, Hupeh, Kweichow, and Szechuan, the Big Sword Society in Anhwei, Honan, and Shantung, the Rational Life Society in Chihli and the three northeastern provinces, and the Green Band in Shanghai and elsewhere. One of China's difficult problems is how to handle these people. Brave fighters but apt to be destructive, they can become a revolutionary force if given proper guidance.

To sum up, it can be seen that our enemies are all those in league with imperialism—the warlords, the bureaucrats, the comprador class, the big landlord class, and the reactionary section of the intelligentsia attached to them. The leading force in our revolution is the industrial proletariat. Our closest friends are the entire semi-proletariat and petty bourgeoisie. As for the vacillating middle bourgeoisie, their right wing may become our enemy and their left wing may become our friend—but we must be constantly on our guard and not let them create confusion within our ranks.

Motive Forces of Revolution

From: "The Chinese Revolution and the Chinese Communist Party" (December 1939), *Selected Works*, II (Peking: Foreign Languages Press, 1965), pp. 319–26.

Since Chinese society is colonial, semicolonial, and semifeudal, since the targets of the revolution are mainly foreign imperialist rule and domestic feudalism, and since its tasks are to overthrow these two oppressors, which of the various classes and strata in Chinese society constitute the forces capable of fighting them? This is the question of the motive forces of the Chinese revolution at the present stage. A clear understanding of this question is indispensable to a correct solution of the problem of the basic tactics of the Chinese revolution.

What classes are there in present-day Chinese society? There are the landlord class and the bourgeoisie, the landlord class and the upper stratum of the bourgeoisie constituting the ruling classes in Chinese society. And there are the proletariat, the peasantry, and the different sections of the petty bourgeoisie other than the peasantry, all of which are still the subject classes in vast areas of China.

The attitude and the stand of these classes toward the Chinese revolution are entirely determined by their economic status in society. Thus the motive forces as well as the targets and tasks of the revolution are determined by the nature of China's socioeconomic system.

Let us now analyze the different classes in Chinese society.

1. The Landlord Class

The landlord class forms the main social base for imperialist rule in China; it is a class which uses the feudal system to exploit and oppress the peasants, obstructs China's political, economic, and cultural development, and plays no progressive role whatsoever.

Therefore, the landlords, as a class, are a target and not a motive force of the revolution.

In the present War of Resistance a section of the big landlords, along with one section of the big bourgeoisie (the capitulationists) has surrendered to the Japanese aggressors and turned traitor, while another section of the big landlords, along with another section of the big bourgeoisie (the die-hards), is increasingly wavering even though it is still in the anti-Japanese camp. But a good many of the enlightened gentry who are middle and small landlords and who have some capitalist coloration display some enthusiasm for the war, and we should unite with them in the common fight against Japan.

2. The Bourgeoisie

There is a distinction between the comprador big bourgeoisie and the national bourgeoisie.

The comprador big bourgeoisie is a class which directly serves the capitalists of the imperialist countries and is nurtured by them; countless ties link it closely with the feudal forces in the countryside. Therefore, it is a target of the Chinese revolution and never in the history of the revolution has it been a motive force.

However, different sections of the comprador big bourgeoisie owe allegiance to different imperialist powers, so that when the contradictions among the latter become very acute and the revolution is directed mainly against one particular imperialist power, it becomes possible for the sections of the comprador class which serve other imperialist groupings to join the current anti-imperialist front to a certain extent and for a certain period. But they will turn against the Chinese revolution the moment their masters do.

In the present war the pro-Japanese big bourgeoisie (the capitulationists) have either surrendered or are preparing to surrender. The pro-European and pro-American big bourgeoisie (the diehards) are wavering more and more, even though they are still in the anti-Japanese camp, and they are playing the double game of simultaneously resisting Japan and opposing the Communist Party. Our policy toward the big bourgeois capitulationists is to treat them as enemies and resolutely strike them down. Toward the big bourgeois die-hards, we employ a revolutionary dual policy; on the one hand, we unite with them because they are still anti-Japanese and we should make use of their contradictions with Japanese imperialism, but on the other hand, we firmly struggle against them because they pursue a highhanded anti-Communist, reactionary policy detrimental to resistance and unity, both of which would be jeopardized without such a struggle.

The national bourgeoisie is a class with a dual character.

On the one hand, it is oppressed by imperialism and fettered by feudalism and consequently is in contradiction with both of them. In this respect it constitutes one of the revolutionary forces. In the course of the Chinese revolution it has displayed a certain enthusiasm for fighting imperialism and the governments of bureaucrats and warlords.

But on the other hand, it lacks the courage to oppose imperialism and feudalism thoroughly because it is economically and politically flabby and still has economic ties with imperialism and feudalism. This emerges very clearly when the people's revolutionary forces grow powerful.

It follows from the dual character of the national bourgeoisie that, at certain times and to a certain extent, it can take part in the revolution against imperialism and the governments of bureaucrats and warlords and can become a revolutionary force, but that at other times there is the danger of its following the comprador big bourgeoisie and acting as its accomplice in counterrevolution.

The national bourgeoisie in China, which is mainly the middle bourgeoisie, has never really held political power but has been restricted by the reactionary policies of the big landlord class and big bourgeoisie which are in power, although it followed them in opposing the revolution in the period from 1927 to 1931 (before the September 18 Incident). In the present war, it differs not only from the capitulationists of the big landlord class and big bourgeoisie but also from the big bourgeois die-hards, and so far has been a fairly good ally of ours. Therefore, it is absolutely necessary to have a prudent policy toward the national bourgeoisie.

3. The Different Sections of the Petty Bourgeoisie Other Than the Peasantry

The petty bourgeoisie, other than the peasantry, consists of the vast numbers of intellectuals, small tradesmen, handicraftsmen, and professional people.

Their status somewhat resembles that of the middle peasants. They all suffer under the oppression of imperialism, feudalism, and the big bourgeoisie, and they are being driven ever nearer to bankruptcy or destitution.

Hence these sections of the petty bourgeoisie constitute one of the motive forces of the revolution and are a reliable ally of the proletariat. Only under the leadership of the proletariat can they achieve their liberation.

Let us now analyze the different sections of the petty bourgeoisie other than the peasantry.

First, the intellectuals and student youth. They do not constitute a separate class or stratum. In present-day China most of them may be placed in the petty-bourgeois category, judging by their family origin, their living conditions, and their political outlook. Their numbers have grown considerably during the past few decades. Apart from that section of the intellectuals which has associated itself with the imperialists and the big bourgeoisie and works for them against the people, most intellectuals and students are oppressed by imperialism, feudalism, and the big bourgeoisie, and live in fear of unemployment or of having to discontinue their studies. Therefore, they tend to be quite revolutionary. They are more or less equipped with bourgeois scientific knowledge, have a keen political sense, and often play a vanguard role or serve as a link with the masses in the present stage of the revolution. . . . In particular, the large numbers of more or less impoverished intellectuals can join hands with the workers and peasants in supporting or participating in the revolution. In China, it was among the intellectuals and young students that Marxist-Leninist ideology was first widely disseminated and accepted. The revolutionary forces cannot be successfully organized and revolutionary work cannot be successfully conducted without the participation of revolutionary intellectuals. But the intellectuals often tend to be subjective and individualistic, impractical in their thinking, and irresolute in action until they have thrown themselves heart and soul into mass revolutionary struggles or made up their minds to serve the interests of the masses and become one with them. Hence although the mass of revolutionary intellectuals in China can play a vanguard role or serve as a link with the masses, not all of them will remain revolutionaries to the end. Some will drop out of the revolutionary ranks at critical moments and become passive, while a few may even become enemies of the revolution. The intellectuals can overcome their shortcomings only in mass struggles over a long period.

Second, the small tradesmen. Generally they run small shops and employ few or no assistants. They live under the threat of bankruptcy as a result of exploitation by imperialism, the big bourgeoisie, and the usurers.

Third, the handicraftsmen. They are very numerous. They possess their own means of production and hire no workers, or only one or two apprentices or helpers. Their position is similar to that of the middle peasants.

Fourth, professional people. They include doctors and men of other professions. They do not exploit other people, or do so only to a slight degree. Their position is similar to that of the handicraftsmen.

These sections of the petty bourgeoisie make up a vast multitude of people whom we must win over and whose interests we must protect because in general they can support or join the revolution and are good allies. Their weakness is that some of them are easily influenced by the bourgeoisie; consequently, we must carry on revolutionary propaganda and organizational work among them.

4. The Peasantry

The peasantry constitutes approximately 80 per cent of China's total population and is the main force in her national economy today.

A sharp process of polarization is taking place among the peasantry.

First, the rich peasants. They form about 5 per cent of the rural population (or about 10 per cent together with the landlords) and constitute the rural bourgeoisie. Most of the rich peasants in China are semifeudal in character, since they let a part of their land, practice usury, and ruthlessly exploit the farm laborers. But they generally engage in labor themselves and in this sense are part of the peasantry. The rich-peasant form of production will remain useful for a definite period. Generally speaking, they might make some contribution to the anti-imperialist struggle of the peasant masses and stay neutral in the agrarian revolutionary struggle against the landlords. Therefore we should not regard the rich peasants as belonging to the same class as the landlords and should not prematurely adopt a policy of liquidating the rich peasantry.

Second, the middle peasants. They form about 20 per cent of China's rural population. They are economically self-supporting (they may have something to lay aside when the crops are good, and occasionally hire some labor or lend small sums of money at interest); and generally they do not exploit others but are exploited by imperialism, the landlord class, and the bourgeoisie. They have no political rights. Some of them do not have enough land, and only a section (the well-to-do middle peasants) have some surplus land. Not only can the middle peasants join the anti-imperialist revolution and the Agrarian Revolution, but they can also accept socialism. Therefore the whole middle peasantry can be a reliable ally of the proletariat and is an important motive force of the revolution. The positive or negative attitude of the middle peasants is one of the factors determining victory or defeat in the revolution, and this is especially true after the Agrarian Revolution when they become the majority of the rural population.

Third, the poor peasants. The poor peasants in China, together with the farm laborers, form about 70 per cent of the rural population. They are the broad peasant masses with no land or insufficient land, the semiproletariat of the countryside, the biggest motive force of the Chinese revolution, the natural and most reliable ally of the proletariat, and the main contingent of China's revolutionary forces. Only under the leadership of the proletariat can the poor and middle peasants achieve their liberation, and only by forming a firm alliance with the poor and middle peasants can the proletariat lead the revolution to victory. Otherwise neither is possible. The term "peasantry" refers mainly to the poor and middle peasants.

5. *The Proletariat*

Among the Chinese proletariat, the modern industrial workers number from 2,500,000 to 3,000,000, the workers in small-scale industry and in handicrafts and the shop assistants in the cities total about 12,000,000, and in addition there are great numbers of rural proletarians (the farm laborers) and other propertyless people in the cities and the countryside.

In addition to the basic qualities it shares with the proletariat everywhere—its association with the most advanced form of economy, its strong sense of organization and discipline, and its lack of private means of production—the Chinese proletariat has many other outstanding qualities.

What are they?

First, the Chinese proletariat is more resolute and thoroughgoing in revolutionary struggle than any other class because it is subjected to a threefold oppression (imperialist, bourgeois, and feudal) which is marked by a severity and cruelty seldom found in other countries. Since there is no economic basis for social reformism in colonial and semicolonial China as there is in Europe, the whole proletariat, with the exception of a few scabs, is most revolutionary.

Secondly, from the moment it appeared on the revolutionary scene, the Chinese proletariat came under the leadership of its own revolutionary party—the Communist Party of China—and became the most politically conscious class in Chinese society.

Thirdly, because the Chinese proletariat by origin is largely made up of bankrupted peasants, it has natural ties with the peasant masses, which facilitates its forming a close alliance with them.

Therefore, in spite of certain unavoidable weaknesses—for instance, its smallness (as compared with the peasantry), its youth (as compared with the proletariat in the capitalist countries), and its low educational level (as compared with the bourgeoisie)—the Chinese proletariat is nonetheless the basic motive force of the Chinese revolution. Unless it is led by the proletariat, the Chinese revolution cannot possibly succeed. . . .

The Chinese proletariat should understand that although it is the class with the highest political consciousness and sense of organization, it cannot win victory by its own strength alone. In order to win, it must unite, according to varying circumstances, with all classes and strata that can take part in the revolution, and must organize a revolutionary united front. Among all the classes in Chinese society, the peasantry is a firm ally of the working class, the urban petty bourgeoisie is a reliable ally, and the national bourgeoisie is an ally in certain periods and to a certain extent. This is one of the fundamental laws established by China's modern revolutionary history.

6. The Vagrants

China's status as a colony and semicolony has given rise to a multitude of rural and urban unemployed. Denied proper means of making a living, many of them are forced to resort to illegitimate ones, hence the robbers, gangsters, beggars, and prostitutes and the numerous people who live on superstitious practices. This social stratum is unstable; while some are apt to be bought over by the reactionary forces, others may join the revolution. These people lack constructive qualities and are given to destruction rather than construction; after joining the revolution, they become a source of roving-rebel and anarchist ideology in the revolutionary ranks. Therefore, we should know how to remold them and guard against their destructiveness.

The above is our analysis of the motive forces of the Chinese revolution.

Peasants As Revolutionary Vanguards

From: "Report on an Investigation of the Peasant Movement in Hunan" (March 1927), *Selected Works,* I (Peking: Foreign Languages Press, 1964), pp. 23–24, 32–33.

. . . In a very short time, in China's central, southern, and northern provinces, several hundred million peasants will rise like a mighty storm, like a hurricane, a force so swift and violent that no power, however great, will be able to hold it back. They will smash all the trammels that bind them and rush forward along the road to liberation. They will sweep all the imperialists, warlords, corrupt officials, local tyrants, and evil gentry into their graves. Every revolutionary party and every revolutionary comrade will be put to the test, to be accepted or rejected as they decide. . . .

The poor peasants have always been the main force in the bitter fight in the countryside. They . . . are the most responsive to Communist Party leadership. They are deadly enemies of the camp of the local tyrants and evil gentry and attack it without the slightest hesitation. . . . According to the survey of Chang-sha county, the poor peasants comprise 70 per cent, the middle peasants 20 per cent, and the landlords and the rich peasants 10 per cent of the population in the rural areas. . . . This great mass of poor peasants, or altogether 70 per cent of the rural population, comprises the backbone of the peasant associations, the vanguard in the overthrow of the feudal forces, and the heroes who have performed the great revolutionary task which for long years was left undone. Without the poor peasant class . . . it would have been impossible to bring about the present revolutionary situation in the countryside, or to overthrow the local tyrants and evil gentry and complete the democratic revolution. The poor peasants, being the most revolutionary group, have gained the leadership of the peasant associations. . . . Leadership by the poor peasants is absolutely necessary. Without the poor peasants there would be no revolution. To deny their role is to deny the revolution. To attack them is to attack the revolution. They have never been wrong on the general direction of the revolution.

UNITED FRONT IN CHINA: EARLY STAGES

Lessons of History

From: "Introducing *The Communist*" (October 1939), *Selected Works,* II (Peking: Foreign Languages Press, 1965), pp. 288–91.

In the last eighteen years, the united front of the Chinese proletariat with the bourgeoisie and other classes has developed under three different sets of circumstances or through three different stages: the First Great Revolution from 1924 to 1927, the War of Agrarian Revolution from 1927 to 1937, and the present War of

Resistance Against Japan. The history of the three stages has confirmed the following laws:

(1) The Chinese national bourgeoisie will take part in the struggle against imperialism and the feudal warlords at certain times and to a certain extent, because foreign oppression is the greatest oppression to which China is subjected. Therefore, at such times, the proletariat should form a united front with the national bourgeoisie and maintain it as far as possible. (2) In other historical circumstances, the Chinese national bourgeoisie will vacillate and defect because of its economic and political flabbiness. Therefore the composition of China's revolutionary united front will not remain constant at all times, but is liable to change. At one time the national bourgeoisie may take part in it, at another it may not. (3) The Chinese big bourgeoisie, which is comprador in character, is a class which directly serves imperialism and is fostered by it. Hence the comprador Chinese big bourgeoisie has always been a target of the revolution. However, different groups within this big bourgeoisie are backed by different imperialist powers, so that when contradictions among these powers become sharper and when the edge of the revolution is mainly directed against a particular power, the big bourgeois groups dependent upon the other powers may join the struggle against that particular imperialist power to a certain extent and for a certain time. At such times, in order to weaken the enemy and add to its own reserves, the Chinese proletariat may form a united front with these groups and should maintain it as far as possible, provided it is advantageous to the revolution. (4) The comprador big bourgeoisie continues to be most reactionary even when it joins the united front alongside the proletariat in struggling against the common enemy. It stubbornly opposes any ideological, political, and organizational development of the proletariat and the proletarian party, tries to impose restrictions on them, and employs disruptive tactics such as deception, blandishments, "corrosion," and savage attacks against them; moreover, it does all this to prepare for capitulating to the enemy and splitting the united front. (5) The peasantry is the firm ally of the proletariat. (6) The urban petty bourgeoisie is a reliable ally.

The validity of these laws was confirmed during the First Great Revolution and the Agrarian Revolution, and it is being confirmed again in the present War of Resistance. Therefore, in forming a united front with the bourgeoisie (and especially with the big bourgeoisie), the party of the proletariat must carry on a stern and resolute struggle on two fronts. On the one hand, it is necessary to combat the error of neglecting the possibility that the bourgeoisie may join in the revolutionary struggle at certain times and to a certain extent. It is an error of "left" closed-doorism to regard the bourgeoisie in China as being the same as in the capitalist countries, and consequently to neglect the policy of forming a united front with the bourgeoisie and maintaining it for as long as possible. On the other hand, it is also necessary to combat the error of identifying the program, policy, ideology, practice, etc. of the proletariat with those of the bourgeoisie, and neglecting the differences in principle between them. The error here consists in neglecting the fact that the bourgeoisie (and especially the big bourgeoisie) not only exerts an influence on the petty bourgeoisie and the peasantry, but does its utmost to influence the proletariat and the Communist Party in a strenuous effort to destroy their ideological, political, and organizational independence, turn them into an appendage of the bourgeoisie and its political party, and ensure that it will reap the fruits of the revolution for itself or its political party alone; this error also consists in neglecting the fact that the bourgeoisie (and especially the big bourgeoisie) betrays the revolution whenever the revolution conflicts with its own selfish interests or with those of its own political party. To neglect all this is "right" opportunism. . . . The dual character of the Chinese bourgeoisie in the bourgeois-democratic revolution exerts a great effect on our political line and our Party building, and without grasping this dual character we cannot have a good grasp of our political line or of Party building. One important component of the political line of the Chinese Communist Party is the policy both of unity with the bourgeoisie and of struggle against it. In fact, the development and tempering of the Party through its unity and struggle with the bourgeoisie are an important component of Party building. Unity here means the united front with the bourgeoisie. Struggle here means the "peaceful" and "bloodless" struggle, ideological, political, and organizational, which goes on when we are united with the bourgeoisie and which turns into armed struggle when we are forced to break with it. If our Party does not understand that it must unite with the bourgeoisie in certain periods, it cannot advance and the revolution cannot develop; if our Party does not understand that it must wage a stern and resolute "peaceful" struggle against the bourgeoisie while uniting with it, then our Party will disintegrate ideologically, politically, and organizationally and the revolution will fail; and if our Party does not wage a stern and resolute armed struggle against the bourgeoisie when forced to break with it, our Party will likewise disintegrate and the revolution will likewise fail. The truth of all this has been confirmed by the events of the past eighteen years.

Scope and Needs

From: "Urgent Tasks Following the Establishment of Kuomintang-Communist Co-operation" (September 1937), *Selected Works,* II (Peking: Foreign Languages Press, 1965), pp. 35–40.

As far back as 1933, the Chinese Communist Party issued a declaration stating that it was ready to conclude an agreement for resisting Japan with any section of the Kuomintang army on three conditions, namely, that attacks on the Red Army be stopped, that democratic freedoms be granted to the people, and that the people be armed. This declaration was made because after the September 18 Incident in 1931, resistance to the Japanese imperialist invasion became the primary task of the Chinese people. But we did not succeed in our objective.

In August 1935, the Chinese Communist Party and the Chinese Red Army called upon all political parties and groups and the people throughout the country to organize an anti-Japanese united army and a government of national defense for a common fight against Japanese imperialism. In December of that year, the Chinese Communist Party adopted a resolution on the formation of an anti-Japanese national united front with the national bourgeoisie. In May 1936, the Red Army published an open telegram demanding that the Nanking government stop the civil war and make common cause against Japan. In August of that year, the Central Committee of the Chinese Communist Party sent a letter to the Central Executive Committee of the Kuomintang demanding that the Kuomintang stop the civil war and form a united front of the two parties to fight jointly against Japanese imperialism. In September of the same year, the Communist Party passed a resolution on the establishment of a unified democratic republic in China. Besides the declaration, the open telegram, the letter, and the resolutions, we sent representatives to hold discussions with people from the Kuomintang side on many occasions, and yet all in vain. It was only toward the end of 1936 after the Sian Incident that the plenipotentiary of the Chinese Communist Party and the responsible chief of the Kuomintang reached an agreement on a contemporary issue of vital political importance, namely, cessation of the civil war between the two parties, and brought about the peaceful settlement of the Sian Incident. This was a great event in Chinese history and provided a prerequisite for the renewal of co-operation between the two parties.

On February 10 this year, the Central Committee of the Chinese Communist Party sent a telegram to the Third Plenary Session of the Kuomintang Central Executive Committee on the eve of its meeting, making comprehensive proposals for concrete co-operation between the two parties. In that telegram we demanded that the Kuomintang give the Communist Party guarantees on the following five points: the ending of the civil war, the realization of democratic freedoms, the convening of a national assembly, speedy preparations for resisting Japan, and improvement of the people's livelihood. At the same time the Communist Party offered guarantees to the Kuomintang on the following four points: the elimination of the state of antagonism between the two regimes, the redesignation of the Red Army, the application of the new-democratic system in the revolutionary base areas, and the discontinuance of the confiscation of the land of the landlords. This was likewise an important political step, for without it the establishment of co-operation between the two parties would have been retarded, which would have been wholly detrimental to speedy preparations for resisting Japan.

Since then the two parties have moved a step closer to each other in their negotiations. The Communist Party has made more specific proposals on the question of a common political program for the two parties, on the question of lifting the ban on the mass movements and releasing political prisoners, and on the question of redesignating the Red Army. So far the common program has not yet been promulgated, nor has the ban on the mass movements been lifted, nor has the new system in the revolutionary base areas been recognized; however, about a month after the fall of Peiping and Tientsin an order was issued to the effect that the Red Army was to be redesignated as the Eighth Route Army of the National Revolutionary Army (also called the Eighteenth Group Army in the anti-Japanese battle order). The declaration of the Central Committee of our Party on the establishment of bipartisan co-operation, which had been conveyed to the Kuomintang as early as July 15, and Chiang Kai-shek's statement recognizing the legal status of the Communist Party of China, which should have been published as agreed simultaneously with the declaration, were finally released to the public (alas after a long delay) by the Kuomintang Central News Agency on September 22 and 23 respectively, when the situation at the front had become critical. The Communist Party's decla-

ration and Chiang Kai-shek's statement announced the establishment of co-operation between the two parties and laid the necessary
foundation for the great cause of alliance between the two parties to
save the nation. The declaration of the Communist Party not only
embodies the principle of unity between the two parties but also
embodies the basic principle of the great unity of the people throughout the country. It is good that Chiang Kai-shek, in his statement,
recognized the legal status of the Communist Party throughout
China and spoke of the necessity of unity to save the nation; however, he has not abandoned his Kuomintang arrogance or made any
necessary self-criticism, and we can hardly be satisfied with that.
Nevertheless, the united front between the two parties has been
proclaimed as established. This has ushered in a new epoch in the
history of the Chinese revolution. It will exert a widespread and
profound influence on the Chinese revolution and play a decisive
role in defeating Japanese imperialism.

Ever since 1924, the relationship between the Kuomintang and
the Chinese Communist Party has played a decisive role in the Chinese revolution. The revolution of 1924–27 took place as a result
of the co-operation of the two parties on the basis of a definite program. In a mere two or three years, tremendous successes were
achieved in the national revolution to which Dr. Sun Yat-sen had
devoted forty years and which he had left unaccomplished; these
successes were the establishment of the revolutionary base in
Kwangtung and the victory of the Northern Expedition. They were
the products of the formation of the united front of the two parties.
But at the very moment when the revolution was nearing its triumph, some people who failed to uphold the revolutionary cause
disrupted the two-party united front and so brought about the failure of the revolution, and the door was left open for foreign aggression. These were the products of the disruption of the united front
of the two parties. Now the newly formed united front between the
two parties has ushered in a new period in the Chinese revolution.
There are still people who do not understand the historical role of
the united front and its great future and regard it as a mere temporary makeshift devised under the pressure of circumstances; nevertheless, through this united front, the wheel of history will propel
the Chinese revolution forward to a completely new stage. Whether
China can extricate herself from the national and social crisis which
is now so grave depends on how this united front will develop. There
is already fresh evidence that the prospects are favorable. First, as

soon as the policy of the united front was put forward by the Chinese Communist Party, it won the approval of the people everywhere. This is a clear expression of the will of the people. Second, immediately after the Sian Incident was settled peacefully and the two parties ended the civil war, all political parties and groups, people in all walks of life, and all armed forces in the country achieved unprecedented unity. This unity, however, still falls far short of meeting the needs of resisting Japan, especially as the problem of unity between the government and the people remains basically unsolved. Third, and most striking of all, is the fact that the nationwide War of Resistance has started. We are not satisfied with the War of Resistance in its present state because, though national in character, it is still confined to the government and the armed forces. As we pointed out earlier, Japanese imperialism cannot be defeated through a war of resistance of this kind. Nevertheless, for the first time in a hundred years, China is definitely putting up nationwide resistance to a foreign invader, and this could never have come about without internal peace and without co-operation between the two parties. If the Japanese aggressors were able to take the four northeastern provinces without firing a single shot during the time when the two-party united front was broken up, then today, when the united front has been re-established, they will not be able to occupy more Chinese territory without paying a price in bloody battles. Fourth, there is the effect abroad. The proposal for the anti-Japanese united front put forward by the Chinese Communist Party has won the support of the workers and peasants and the Communist Parties all over the world. With the establishment of co-operation between the Kuomintang and the Communist Party, the people of various countries, and particularly of the Soviet Union, will help China more actively. China and the Soviet Union have concluded a treaty of non-aggression and the relations between the two countries can be expected to improve still further. From all this evidence we can state with certainty that the growth of the united front will carry China toward a bright and great future, namely, the defeat of Japanese imperialism and the establishment of a unified democratic republic.

However, the united front cannot accomplish this great task if it remains in its present state. The united front of the two parties must be developed further. For in its present state it is not yet broadly based or consolidated.

Should the Anti-Japanese National United Front be confined to the Kuomintang and the Communist Party? No, it should be a united front of the whole nation, with the two parties forming only a part of it. It should be a united front of all parties and groups, people in all walks of life and all armed forces, a united front of all patriots—the workers, peasants, soldiers, intellectuals, and businessmen. So far, the united front has in fact been confined to the two parties, while the masses of the workers, peasants, soldiers, and urban petty bourgeoisie and a large number of other patriots have not yet been aroused, called into action, organized, or armed. This is the most serious problem at present. It is serious because it makes victories at the front impossible. It is no longer possible to conceal the critical situation at the front both in northern China and in Kiangsu and Chekiang provinces, nor is there any need to do so; the question is how to save the situation. And the only way to save it is to put Dr. Sun Yat-sen's Testament into practice, to "arouse the masses of the people." In his deathbed Testament, Dr. Sun declared he was deeply convinced, from the experience accumulated over forty years, that only thus could the goal of revolution be achieved. What reason is there for obstinately refusing to put this testament into practice? What reason is there for failing to do so at a moment when the fate of the nation is at stake? Everybody knows that autocracy and suppression run counter to the principle of "arousing the masses of the people." Resistance by the government and the army alone can never defeat Japanese imperialism. Early in May this year we warned the ruling Kuomintang in all seriousness that unless the masses of the people were aroused to resist, China would follow the same path to disaster as Abyssinia. This point has been made not only by the Chinese Communists but by progressives throughout the country and by many intelligent members of the Kuomintang itself. Yet the policy of autocratic rule remains unchanged. As a result the government has estranged itself from the people, the army from the masses, and the military command from the rank and file. Unless the united front is reinforced by the participation of the masses, the crisis on the war fronts will inevitably be aggravated, not mitigated.

The present anti-Japanese united front still lacks a political program to replace the Kuomintang's policy of autocratic rule, a program accepted by both parties and formally promulgated. In relation to the masses the Kuomintang is continuing the same practices it has followed for the last ten years; there has been no change and on the whole everything has remained the same for the last ten years, from the government apparatus, the army system, and the policy toward civilians to financial, economic, and educational policies. . . . Resistance to Japan requires a broadly based united front, and hence all the people should be mobilized to join it. Resistance to Japan requires a consolidated united front, and this calls for a common program. The common program will be the united front's guide to action and will serve also as the tie which, like a cord, closely binds together all the organizations and individuals in the united front, all political parties and groups, people in all walks of life and all armed forces. Only in this way will we be able to speak of firm unity. We are opposed to the old binding rules, because they are unsuited to the national revolutionary war. We look forward to the introduction of new binding rules to replace the old, that is, to the promulgation of a common program and the establishment of revolutionary order. Nothing else will suit the War of Resistance.

Problems of Tactics

From: "Current Problems of Tactics in the Anti-Japanese United Front" (March 1940), *Selected Works,* II (Peking: Foreign Languages Press, 1965), pp. 422–26.

. . . The basic condition for victory in the War of Resistance is the extension and consolidation of the anti-Japanese united front. The tactics required for this purpose are to develop the progressive forces, win over the middle forces, and combat the die-hard forces; these are three inseparable links, and the means to be used to unite all the anti-Japanese forces is struggle. In the period of the anti-Japanese united front, struggle is the means to unity and unity is the aim of struggle. If unity is sought through struggle, it will live; if unity is sought through yielding, it will perish. This truth is gradually being grasped by Party comrades. However, there are still many who do not understand it; some think that struggle will split the united front or that struggle can be employed without restraint, and others use wrong tactics toward the middle forces or have mistaken notions about the die-hard forces. All this must be corrected.

. . . Developing the progressive forces means building up the forces of the proletariat, the peasantry, and the urban petty bourgeoisie, boldly expanding the Eighth Route and New Fourth Armies, establishing anti-Japanese democratic base areas on an extensive scale, building up Communist organizations throughout the country, developing national mass movements of the workers, peasants, youth, women, and children, winning over the intellectuals in all parts of the country, and spreading the movement for constitutional government among the masses as a struggle for democracy. Steady expansion of the progressive forces is the only way to prevent the situation from deteriorating, to forestall capitulation and splitting, and to lay a firm and indestructible foundation for victory in the War of Resistance. But the expansion of the progressive forces is a serious process of struggle, which must be ruthlessly waged not only against the Japanese imperialists and the traitors but also against the die-hards. For the latter are opposed to the growth of the progressive forces, while the middle section is skeptical. Unless we engage in resolute struggle against the die-hards and, moreover, get tangible results, we shall be unable to resist their pressure or dispel the doubts of the middle section. In that case the progressive forces will have no way of expanding.

. . . Winning over the middle forces means winning over the middle bourgeoisie, the enlightened gentry, and the regional power groups. They are three distinct categories, but as things are, they all belong to the middle forces. The middle bourgeoisie constitutes the national bourgeoisie as distinct from the comprador class, i.e., from the big bourgeoisie. Although it has its class contradictions with the workers and does not approve of the independence of the working class, it still wants to resist Japan and, moreover, would like to grasp political power for itself, because it is oppressed by the Japanese imperialists in the occupied areas and kept down by the big landlords and big bourgeoisie in the Kuomintang areas. When it comes to resisting Japan, it is in favor of united resistance; when it comes to winning political power, it is in favor of the movement for constitutional government and tries to exploit the contradictions between the progressives and the die-hards for its own ends. This is a stratum we must win over. Then there are the enlightened gentry who are the left wing of the landlord class, that is, the section with a bourgeois coloration, whose political attitude is roughly the same as that of the middle bourgeoisie. Although they have class contradictions with the peasants, they also have their contradictions with the big landlords and big bourgeoisie. They do not support the die-hards and they, too, want to exploit the contradictions between us and the die-hards for their own political ends. On no account should we neglect this section either, and our policy must be to win them over. As for the regional power groups, they are of two kinds—the forces which control certain regions as their own, and the troops of miscellaneous brands which do not. Although these groups are in contradiction with the progressive forces, they also have their contraditions with the Kuomintang Central Government because of the self-seeking policy it pursues at their expense; they, too, want to exploit the contradictions between us and the die-hards for their own political ends. Most of the leaders of the regional power groups belong to the big landlord class and the big bourgeoisie and, therefore, progressive as they may appear at certain times during the war, they soon turn reactionary again; nevertheless, because of their contradictions with the Kuomintang central authorities, the possibility exists of their remaining neutral in our struggle against the die-hards, provided we pursue a correct policy. Our policy toward the three categories of middle forces described above is to win them over. However, this policy differs from that of winning over the peasants and the urban petty bourgeoisie, and, moreover, it varies for each category of the middle forces. While the peasants and the urban petty bourgeoisie should be won over as basic allies, the middle forces should be won over as allies against imperialism. Among the middle forces, it is possible for the middle bourgeoisie and the enlightened gentry to join us in the common fight against Japan and also in the setting up of anti-Japanese democratic political power, but they fear agrarian revolution. In the struggle against the die-hards, some may join in to a limited degree, others may observe a benevolent neutrality, and still others a rather reluctant neutrality. But, apart from joining us in the war, the regional power groups will at most observe a temporary neutrality in our struggle against the die-hards; they are unwilling to join us in establishing democratic political power since they themselves belong to the big landlord class and the big bourgeoisie. The middle forces tend to vacillate and are bound to break up, and we should educate and criticize them appropriately, with special reference to their vacillating attitude.

The winning over of the middle forces is an extremely important task for us in the period of the anti-Japanese united front, but it can only be accomplished given certain conditions. These are: (1) that we have ample strength, (2) that we respect their interests, and (3) that we are resolute in our struggle against the die-hards and steadily win victories. If these conditions are lacking, the middle forces will vacillate or even become allies of the die-hards in the latter's attacks on us, because the die-hards are also doing their best to win over the middle forces in order to isolate us. The middle forces carry considerable weight in China and may often be the decisive factor in our struggle against the die-hards; we must therefore be prudent in dealing with them.

. . . The die-hard forces at the present time are the big landlord class and the big bourgeoisie. Divided at the moment into the group that has capitulated to Japan and the group that favors resistance, these classes will gradually become still further differentiated. Within the big bourgeoisie, the group favoring resistance is now different from the group that has already capitulated. It pursues a dual policy. It still stands for unity against Japan, but at the same time it follows the extremely reactionary policy of suppressing the progressive forces in preparation for its eventual capitulation. As it still favors unity against Japan, we can still try and keep it in the anti-Japanese united front, and the longer the better. It would be wrong to neglect our policy of winning over this group and co-operating with it and to regard it as having already capitulated and as being on the verge of launching an anti-Communist war. But at the same time, we must adopt tactics of struggle to combat its reactionary policy and carry on a determined ideological, political, and military fight against it, because all over the country it pursues the reactionary policy of suppressing the progressive forces, because instead of carrying out the common program of the revolutionary Three People's Principles it stubbornly opposes our efforts to do so, and because it works hard to prevent us from going beyond the limits it has set for us, i.e., it tries to confine us to the passive resistance it itself practices, and, moreover, it tries to assimilate us, failing which it applies ideological, political, and military pressure against us. Such is our revolutionary dual policy to meet the dual policy of the die-hards, and such is our policy of seeking unity through struggle. If in the ideological sphere we can put forward correct revolutionary theory and strike hard at their counterrevolutionary theory, if in the political sphere we adopt tactics suited to the times and strike hard at their anti-Communist and anti-progressive policies, and if in the military sphere we take appropriate measures and strike back hard at their attacks, then we shall be able to restrict the effective range of their reactionary policy and compel them to recognize the status of the progressive forces, and we shall be able to expand the progressive forces, win over the middle forces, and isolate the die-hard forces. What is more, we shall be able to induce those die-hards who are still willing to resist Japan to prolong their participation in the anti-Japanese united front, and shall thus be able to avert a large-scale civil war of the kind that broke out before. Thus the purpose of our struggle against the die-hards in the period of the anti-Japanese united front is not only to parry their attacks in order to protect the progressive forces and enable the latter to go on growing, it is also to prolong the die-hards' resistance to Japan and to preserve our co-operation with them in order to avert large-scale civil war. Without struggle, these progressive forces would be exterminated by the die-hard forces, the united front would cease to exist, there would be nothing to hinder the die-hards from capitulating to the enemy, and civil war would break out. Therefore, struggle against the die-hards is an indispensable means of uniting all the anti-Japanese forces, achieving a favorable turn in the situation and averting large-scale civil war. All our experience confirms this truth.

Independence and Initiative

From: "The Question of Independence and Initiative Within the United Front" (November 1938), *Selected Works,* II (Peking: Foreign Languages Press, 1965), pp. 215, 213–14.

To sustain a long war by long-term co-operation, or, in other words, to subordinate the class struggle to the present national struggle against Japan—such is the fundamental principle of the united front. Subject to this principle, the independent character of the parties and classes and their independence and initiative within the united front should be preserved, and their essential rights should not be sacrificed to co-operation and unity, but on the contrary must be firmly upheld within certain limits. Only thus can co-operation be promoted, indeed only thus can there be any co-operation at all. Otherwise co-operation will turn into amalgamation and the united front will inevitably be sacrificed. In a struggle that is national in character, the class struggle takes the form of national struggle, which demonstrates the identity between the two. On the one hand, for a given historical period the political and economic demands of the various classes must not be such as to disrupt co-operation; on the other hand, the demands of the national struggle (the need to resist Japan) should be the point of departure for all class struggle. Thus there is identity in the united front between unity and independence and between the national struggle and the class struggle. . . .

All political parties and groups in the united front must help each other and make mutual concessions for the sake of long-term co-operation, but such help and concessions should be positive, not negative. We must consolidate and expand our own Party and army, and at the same time should assist friendly parties and armies to consolidate and expand; the people want the government to satisfy their political and economic demands, and at the same time give the government every possible help to prosecute the War of Resistance; the factory workers demand better conditions from the owners, and at the same time work hard in the interests of resistance; for the sake of unity against foreign aggression, the landlords should reduce rent and interest, and at the same time the peasants should pay rent and interest. All these principles and policies of mutual assistance are positive, not negative or one-sided. The same should be true of mutual concessions. Each side should refrain from undermining the other and from organizing secret party branches within the other's party, government, and army. For our part we organize no secret party branches inside the Kuomintang and its government or army, and so set the Kuomintang's mind at rest, to the advantage of the War of Resistance. The saying "Refrain from doing some things in order to be able to do other things" exactly meets the case. A national War of Resistance would have been impossible without the reorganization of the Red Army, the change in the administrative system in the Red areas, and the abandonment of the policy of armed insurrection. By giving way on the latter we have achieved the former; negative measures have yielded positive results. "To fall back the better to leap forward"—that is Leninism. To regard concessions as something purely negative is contrary to Marxism-Leninism. . . . When we make concessions, fall back, turn to the defensive, or halt our advance in our relations with either allies or enemies, we should always see these actions as part of our whole revolutionary policy, as an indispensable link in the general revolutionary line, as one turn in a zigzag course. In a word, they are positive.

Alliance and Struggle

From: "Preface and Postscript to *Rural Surveys*" (March and April 1941), *Selected Works*, III (Peking: Foreign Languages Press, 1965), pp. 14–15.

The experience of the period of the ten years' civil war [1927–37] is the best and most pertinent for the present period, the War of Resistance Against Japan. This refers to the aspect of how to link ourselves with the masses and mobilize them against the enemy, but not to the aspect of the tactical line. The Party's present tactical line is different in principle from that of the past. Formerly, the Party's tactical line was to oppose the landlords and the counterrevolutionary bourgeoisie; now, it is to unite with all those landlords and members of the bourgeoisie who are not against resisting Japan. Even in the latter stage of the ten years' civil war, it was incorrect not to have adopted differing policies toward the reactionary government and political party which were launching armed attacks on us on the one hand, and toward all the social strata of a capitalist character under our own rule on the other; it was also incorrect not to have adopted differing policies toward the different groups within the reactionary government and political party. At that time, a policy of "all struggle" was pursued toward every section of society other than the peasantry and the lower strata of the urban petty bourgeoisie, and this policy was undoubtedly wrong. In agrarian policy, it was also wrong to repudiate the correct policy adopted in the early and middle periods of the ten years' civil war, whereby the landlords were given the same allotment of land as the peasants so that they could engage in farming and would not become displaced or go up into the mountains as bandits and disrupt public order. The Party's policy is now of necessity a different one; it is not "all struggle and no alliance," neither is it "all alliance and no struggle." . . . Instead, it is a policy of uniting with all social strata opposed to Japanese imperialism, of forming a united front with and yet of waging struggles against them, struggles that differ in form according to the different degrees in which their vacillating or reactionary side manifests itself in capitulation to the enemy and opposition to the Communist Party and the people. The present policy is a dual policy which synthesizes "alliance" and "struggle." In labor policy, it is the dual policy of suitably improving the workers' livelihood and of not hampering the proper development of the capitalist economy. In agrarian policy, it is the dual policy of requiring the landlords to reduce rent and interest and of stipulating that the peasants should pay this reduced rent and interest. In the sphere of political rights, it is the dual policy of allowing all the anti-Japanese landlords and capitalists the same rights of person and the same political and property rights as the workers and peasants and yet of guarding against possible counterrevolutionary activity on their part. State-owned and co-operative economy should be developed, but the main economic sector in the rural base areas today consists not of state but of private enterprises, and the sector of non-monopoly capitalism in our economy should be given the opportunity to develop and be used against Japanese imperialism and the semifeudal system. This is the most revolutionary policy for China today, and to oppose or impede its execution is undoubtedly a mistake. To preserve the communist purity of Party members scrupulously and resolutely, and to protect the useful part of the capitalist sector of the social economy and enable it to develop appropriately, are both indispensable tasks for us in the period of resisting Japan and building a democratic republic. In this period it is possible that some Communists may be corrupted by the bourgeoisie and that capitalist ideas may emerge among members of the Party, and we must fight against these decadent ideas; however, we should not mistakenly carry over the struggle against capitalist ideas within the Party to the field of social economy and oppose the capitalist sector of the economy. We must draw a clear line of demarcation between the two. The Communist Party of China is working in a complicated environment, and every Party member, and especially every cadre, must temper himself to become a fighter who understands Marxist tactics. A one-sided and oversimplified approach to problems can never lead the revolution to victory.

A Common Program

From: "On Coalition Government" (April 1945), *Selected Works*, III (Peking: Foreign Languages Press, 1965), pp. 278–79, 282–84.

An agreed common program is urgently needed by the Chinese people, the Chinese Communist Party, and all the anti-Japanese democratic parties for the purpose of mobilizing and uniting all the anti-Japanese forces of the Chinese people, completely wiping out the Japanese aggressors and building a new China that is independent, free, democratic, united, prosperous, and powerful. . . .

On the major premise that the Japanese aggressors must be completely destroyed and a new China must be built, we Communists and the overwhelming majority of the population are agreed on the following fundamental propositions at the present stage of China's development. First, China should not have a feudal, fascist, and anti-popular state system under the dictatorship of the big landlords and big bourgeoisie, because eighteen years of government by the chief ruling clique of the Kuomintang have already proved its complete bankruptcy. Second, China cannot possibly establish the old type of democratic dictatorship—a purely national-bourgeois state— and therefore should not attempt to do so, because on the one hand the Chinese national bourgeoisie has proved itself very flabby economically and politically, and on the other, for a long time now a new factor has been present, namely, the awakened Chinese proletariat with its leader, the Chinese Communist Party, which has demonstrated great capacity in the political arena and assumed leadership of the peasant masses, the urban petty bourgeoisie, the intelligentsia, and other democratic forces. Third, it is likewise impossible for the Chinese people to institute a socialist state system at the present stage when it is still their task to fight foreign and feudal oppression and the necessary social and economic conditions for a socialist state are still lacking.

What then do we propose? We propose the establishment, after the thorough defeat of the Japanese aggressors, of a state system which we call New Democracy, namely, a united front democratic alliance based on the overwhelming majority of the people, under the leadership of the working class. . . .

We Communists do not conceal our political views. Definitely and beyond all doubt, our future or maximum program is to carry China forward to socialism and communism. Both the name of our Party and our Marxist world outlook unequivocally point to this supreme ideal of the future, a future of incomparable brightness and splendor. On joining the Party, every Communist has two clearly defined objectives at heart, the new-democratic revolution now and socialism and communism in the future, and for these he will fight despite the animosity of the enemies of communism and their vulgar and ignorant calumny, abuse, and ridicule, which we must firmly combat. As for the well-meaning skeptics, we should explain things to them with good will and patience and not attack them. All this is very clear, definite, and unequivocal. . . .

There are some people who doubt whether we Communists are sincere when we declare that "the Three People's Principles being what China needs today, our Party is ready to fight for their complete realization." This is the result of their failure to understand that the basic tenets of the Three People's Principles, which Dr. Sun Yat-sen enunciated in the Manifesto of the First National Congress of the Kuomintang in 1924 and which we have accepted, coincide with certain basic tenets of our Party's program for the present stage, that is, of our minimum program. It should be pointed out that these Three People's Principles of Dr. Sun Yat-sen coincide with our Party's program for the present stage only in certain basic tenets and not in everything. Our Party's program of New Democracy is of course much more comprehensive than Dr. Sun's principles, particularly as our Party's theory, program, and practice of New Democracy have greatly developed with the development of the Chinese revolution in the twenty years since Dr. Sun's death, and will develop still further. In essence, however, these Three People's Principles are a program of New Democracy, as distinguished from the previous, old Three People's Principles; naturally they are "what China needs today" and naturally "our Party is ready to fight for their complete realization." To us Chinese Communists, the struggle for our Party's minimum program and the struggle for Dr. Sun's revolutionary, or new, Three People's Principles are basically (though not in every respect) one and the same thing. Therefore, as in the past and the present, the Chinese Communists will prove to be the most sincere and thoroughgoing executors of the revolutionary Three People's Principles in the future as well.

UNITED FRONT IN THE "WAR OF LIBERATION"

Scope

From: "Greet the New High Tide of the Chinese Revolution" (February 1947), *Selected Works*, IV (Peking: Foreign Languages Press, 1961), p. 121.

. . . [The] reactionary policies of U.S. imperialism and Chiang Kai-shek have forced all strata of the Chinese people to unite for their own salvation. These strata include the workers, peasants, urban petty bourgeoisie, national bourgeoisie, enlightened gentry, other patriotic elements, the minority nationalities, and overseas Chinese. This is a very broad united front of the whole nation. In comparison with the united front in the period of the War of Resistance Against Japan, it is not only as broad in scope but has even deeper foundations. All Party comrades must strive to consolidate and develop this united front. . . . In addition to Communists, we should continue to draw the broad ranks of progressives outside the Party and the middle elements (such as the enlightened gentry) into the organs of political power and into social undertakings.

Problems of Policy

From: "On Some Important Problems of the Party's Present Policy" (January 1948), *Selected Works,* IV (Peking: Foreign Languages Press, 1961), pp 182–86.

1. The interests of the poor peasants and farm laborers and the forward role of the poor peasant leagues must be our first concern

Our Party must launch the land reform through the poor peasants and farm laborers and must enable them to play the forward role in the peasant associations and in the government organs of the rural districts. This forward role consists in forging unity with the middle peasants for common action and not in casting aside the middle peasants and monopolizing the work. The position of the middle peasants is especially important in the old liberated areas where the middle peasants are the majority and the poor peasants and farm laborers a minority. The slogan "The poor peasants and farm laborers conquer the country and should rule the country" is wrong. In the villages, it is the farm laborers, poor peasants, middle peasants, and other working people, united together under the leadership of the Chinese Communist Party, who conquer the country and should rule the country, and it is not the poor peasants and farm laborers alone who conquer the country and should rule the country. In the country as a whole, it is the workers, peasants (including the new rich peasants), small independent craftsmen and traders, middle and small capitalists oppressed and injured by the reactionary forces, the students, teachers, professors, and ordinary intellectuals, the professionals, enlightened gentry, ordinary government employees, oppressed minority nationalities, and overseas Chinese, all united together under the leadership of the working class (through the Communist Party), who conquer the country and should rule the country, and it is not merely some of the people who conquer the country and should rule the country.

2. We must avoid adopting any adventurist policies toward the middle peasants. In the cases of middle peasants and persons of other strata whose class status has been wrongly determined, correction should be made without fail, and any of their belongings that have been distributed should be returned, as far as that is possible. The tendency to exclude middle peasants from the ranks of the peasants' representatives and from the peasants' committees and the tendency to counterpose them to the poor peasants and farm laborers in the land reform struggle must be corrected. Peasants with an income from exploitation should be classified as middle peasants if such income is less than 25 per cent of their total income, and classified as rich peasants if it is more. The land of well-to-do middle peasants must not be distributed without the owner's consent.

3. We must avoid adopting any adventurist policies toward middle and small industrialists and merchants. The policy, adopted in the

past in the liberated areas, of protecting and encouraging the development of all private industry and commerce beneficial to the national economy was correct and should be continued in the future. The policy of encouraging landlords and rich peasants to switch to industry and commerce, adopted during the period of rent and interest reduction, was also correct; it is wrong to regard such switching as a "disguise" and therefore to oppose it and confiscate and distribute the property so switched. The industrial and commercial holdings of landlords and rich peasants should in general be protected; the only industrial and commercial holdings that may be confiscated are those of bureaucrat-capitalists and of real counterrevolutionary local tyrants. Among the industrial and commercial enterprises which should be confiscated, those beneficial to the national economy must continue to operate after they have been taken over by the state and the people and must not be allowed to break up or close down. The transactions tax on the industry and commerce which are beneficial to the national economy should be levied only to the extent that it does not hamper their development. . . .

4. We must avoid adopting any adventurist policies toward students, teachers, professors, scientific workers, art workers, and ordinary intellectuals. The experience of China's student movements and revolutionary struggles has proved that the overwhelming majority of these people can take part in the revolution or remain neutral; the die-hard counterrevolutionaries are a tiny minority. Our Party should, therefore, adopt a careful attitude toward students, teachers, professors, scientific workers, art workers, and ordinary intellectuals. We should unite with them, educate them and give them posts according to the merits of each case, and only a tiny number of die-hard counterrevolutionaries among them will have to be appropriately dealt with through the mass line.

5. On the question of the enlightened gentry. Our Party's cooperation with the enlightened gentry in government bodies (consultative councils and governments) in the liberated areas during the War of Resistance Against Japan was entirely necessary and also successful. Those enlightened gentry who went through hardships and tribulations together with our Party and actually made some contribution should be given consideration according to the merits of each case, provided that this does not interfere with land reform. Those who are fairly good politically and are competent should remain in the higher government bodies and be given appropriate work. Those who are fairly good politically but are not competent

should have their livelihood assured. As for those who are of landlord or rich-peasant origin but who have not incurred the people's deep resentment, their feudal landholdings and feudal property should be distributed according to the Land Law, but it should be seen to that they do not become targets of mass struggles. Those who have sneaked into our government bodies, who have in reality always been evil, who can be of no use to the people and who have incurred the extreme hatred of the broad masses, are to be handed over to the people's courts to be tried and punished like local tyrants.

6. We must distinguish between the new rich peasants and the old rich peasants. The encouragement given to new rich peasants and well-to-do middle peasants during the period of rent and interest reduction proved effective in reassuring the middle peasants and in developing agricultural production in the liberated areas. After the equal distribution of land, we must call on the peasants to develop production so that they will be well fed and well clothed, and advise them to set up organizations for mutual aid and co-operation in agriculture, such as labor exchange teams, mutual-aid teams and work exchange groups. In the equal distribution of land the new rich peasants in the old liberated areas should be treated like well-to-do middle peasants, and their land should not be distributed without the owner's consent.

7. Among those landlords and rich peasants in the old liberated areas who changed their mode of living during the period of rent and interest reduction, the landlords who have engaged in physical labor for five years or more and the rich peasants whose condition has been reduced to that of middle or poor peasants for three years or more may now have their class status changed in accordance with their present condition, provided their behavior has been good. Those who still possess a large amount of surplus property (not a small amount) should hand over the surplus in accordance with the peasants' demands.

8. The heart of land reform is the equal distribution of the land of the feudal classes and of their property in grain, animals, and farm implements (rich peasants hand over only their surplus property); we should not overemphasize the struggle to unearth hidden wealth and in particular should not spend too much time on this matter lest it should interfere with the main work.

9. In dealing with landlords and rich peasants we should distinguish between them in accordance with the Outline Land Law.

10. Within the framework of the principle of equal distribution

of land, we should also distinguish among the big, middle, and small landlords, as well as between those landlords and rich peasants who are local tyrants and those who are not.

11. After the people's courts have given the handful of arch-criminals who are really guilty of the most heinous crimes a serious trial and sentenced them and the sentences have been approved by appropriate government organizations (committees organized by local governments at county or subregional level), it is entirely necessary for the sake of revolutionary order to shoot them and announce their execution. That is one side of the matter. The other side is that we must insist on killing less and must strictly forbid killing without discrimination. To advocate killing more or killing without discrimination is entirely wrong; this would only cause our Party to forfeit sympathy, become alienated from the masses, and fall into isolation. Trial and sentence by the people's courts, a form of struggle provided in the Outline Land Law, must be carried out in earnest; it is a powerful weapon of the peasant masses for striking at the worst elements among the landlords and rich peasants; it also avoids the mistake of beating and killing without discrimination. At the proper time (after the land struggle has reached its height), we should teach the masses to understand their own long-term interests —to regard those landlords and rich peasants who do not persist in wrecking the war effort or the land reform and who number tens of millions in the country as a whole (as many as 36 million out of a rural population of about 360 million) as a labor force for the country and to save and remold them. Our task is to abolish the feudal system, to wipe out the landlords as a class, not as individuals. In accordance with the Land Law we must give them means of production and means of livelihood, but not more than to the peasants.

12. We must criticize and struggle with certain cadres and Party members who have committed serious mistakes and certain bad elements among the masses of workers and peasants. In such criticism and struggle we should persuade the masses to adopt correct methods and forms and to refrain from rough actions. This is one side of the matter. The other side is that these cadres, Party members, and bad elements should be made to pledge that they will not retaliate against the masses. It should be announced that the masses not only have the right to criticize them freely but also have the right to dismiss them from their posts when necessary or to propose their dismissal, or to propose their expulsion from the Party

and even to hand the worst elements over to the people's courts for trial and punishment.

Policy Toward the Marginal Classes

From: "On the Question of the National Bourgeoisie and the Enlightened Gentry" (March 1948), *Selected Works,* IV (Peking: Foreign Languages Press, 1961), pp. 207–10.

The Chinese revolution at the present stage is in its character a revolution against imperialism, feudalism, and bureaucrat-capitalism waged by the broad masses of the people under the leadership of the proletariat. By the broad masses of the people is meant all those who are oppressed, injured, or fettered by imperialism, feudalism, and bureaucrat-capitalism, namely, workers, peasants, soldiers, intellectuals, businessmen, and other patriots, as clearly stated in the Manifesto of the Chinese People's Liberation Army of October 1947. In the manifesto "intellectuals" means all intellectuals who are persecuted and fettered. "Businessmen" means all the national bourgeois who are persecuted and fettered, that is, the middle and petty bourgeois. "Other patriots" refers primarily to the enlightened gentry. The Chinese revolution at the present stage is a revolution in which all these people form a united front against imperialism, feudalism, and bureaucrat-capitalism and in which the working people are the main body. By working people are meant all those engaged in manual labor (such as workers, peasants, handicraftsmen, etc.) as well as those engaged in mental labor who are close to those engaged in manual labor and are not exploiters but are exploited. The aim of the Chinese revolution at the present stage is to overthrow the rule of imperialism, feudalism, and bureaucrat-capitalism and to establish a new-democratic republic of the broad masses of the people with the working people as the main force; its aim is not to abolish capitalism in general.

We should not abandon the enlightened gentry who co-operated with us in the past and continue to co-operate with us at present, who approve of the struggle against the United States and Chiang Kai-shek and who approve of the land reform. . . . Since they gave us considerable help in the hard times during and after the War of Resistance Against Japan and did not obstruct or oppose the land reform when we were carrying it out, we should continue the policy of uniting with them. But uniting with them does not mean treating them as a force that determines the character of the Chinese revolution. The forces that determine the character of a revolution are the chief enemies on the one side and the chief revolutionaries on the other. At present our chief enemies are imperialism, feudalism, and bureaucrat-capitalism, while the main forces in our struggle against these enemies are the people engaged in manual and mental labor, who make up 90 per cent of the country's population. . . .

The few right-wingers among the national bourgeoisie who attach themselves to imperialism, feudalism, and bureaucrat-capitalism and oppose the people's democratic revolution are also enemies of the revolution, while the left-wingers among the national bourgeoisie who attach themselves to the working people and oppose the reactionaries are also revolutionaries, as are the few enlightened gentry who have broken away from the feudal class. But the former are not the main body of the enemy any more than the latter are the main body among the revolutionaries; neither is a force that determines the character of the revolution. The national bourgeoisie is a class which is politically very weak and vacillating. But the majority of its members may either join the people's democratic revolution or take a neutral stand, because they too are persecuted and fettered by imperialism, feudalism, and bureaucrat-capitalism. They are part of the broad masses of the people but not the main body, nor are they a force that determines the character of the revolution. However, because they are important economically and may either join in the struggle against the United States and Chiang Kai-shek or remain neutral in that struggle, it is possible and necessary for us to unite with them. . . . At the present stage the majority of the national bourgeoisie has a growing hatred of the United States and Chiang Kai-shek; its left-wingers attach themselves to the Communist Party and its right-wingers to the Kuomintang, while its middle elements take a hesitant, wait-and-see attitude between the two parties. These circumstances make it necessary and possible for us to win over the majority of the national bourgeoisie and isolate the minority. To achieve this aim, we should be prudent in dealing with the economic position of this class and in principle should adopt a blanket policy of protection. Otherwise we shall commit political errors.

The enlightened gentry are individual landlords and rich peasants with democratic leanings. Such people have contradictions with bureaucrat-capitalism and imperialism and to a certain extent also with the feudal landlords and rich peasants. We unite with them not because they are a political force to be reckoned with nor because they are of any economic importance (their feudal landholdings should be handed over with their consent to the peasants for distribution) but because they gave us considerable help politically during the War of Resistance and during the struggle against the United States and Chiang Kai-shek. During the period of land reform, it will help the land reform throughout the country if some of the enlightened gentry favor it. In particular, it will help win over the intellectuals (most of whom come from landlord or rich-peasant families), the national bourgeoisie (most of whom have ties with the land), and the enlightened gentry throughout the country (who number several hundred thousand) and help isolate the chief enemy of the Chinese revolution, the Chiang Kai-shek reactionaries. It is precisely because they have this role that the enlightened gentry also constitute an element in the revolutionary united front against imperialism, feudalism, and bureaucrat-capitalism; therefore, attention must also be paid to the question of uniting with them. During the period of the War of Resistance, what we required of the enlightened gentry was that they should favor resistance against Japan, favor democracy (not be anti-Communist), and favor reduction of rent and interest; at the present stage, what we require of them is that they favor the struggle against the United States and Chiang Kai-shek, favor democracy (not be anti-Communist), and favor the land reform. If they can meet these requirements, we should unite with them without exception and while uniting with them educate them.

UNITED FRONT IN THE STAGE OF SOCIALISM

From: *On the Correct Handling of Contradictions Among the People* (February 1957) (Peking: Foreign Languages Press, 1957), pp. 8–11, 18–19.

The term "the people" has different meanings in different countries, and in different historical periods in each country. Take our country, for example. During the War of Resistance to Japanese aggression, all those classes, strata, and social groups which opposed Japanese aggression belonged to the category of the people, while the Japanese imperialists, Chinese traitors, and the pro-Japanese elements belonged to the category of enemies of the people. During the War of Liberation, the United States imperialists and their henchmen—the bureaucrat-capitalists and landlord class—and the Kuomintang reactionaries, who represented these two classes, were the enemies of the people, while all other classes, strata, and social groups which opposd these enemies belonged to the category of the people. At this stage of building socialism, all classes, strata, and social groups which approve, support, and work for the cause of socialist construction belong to the category of the people, while those social forces and groups which resist the socialist revolution, and are hostile to and try to wreck socialist construction, are enemies of the people.

The contradictions between ourselves and our enemies are antagonistic ones. Within the ranks of the people, contradictions among the working people are non-antagonistic, while those between the exploiters and the exploited classes have, apart from their antagonistic aspect, a non-antagonistic aspect. Contradictions among the people have always existed. But their content differs in each period of the revolution and during the building of socialism. In the conditions existing in China today what we call contradictions among the people include the following: contradictions within the working class, contradictions within the peasantry, contradictions within the intelligentsia, contradictions between the working class and the peasantry, contradictions between the working class and peasantry on the one hand and the intelligentsia on the other, contradictions between the working class and other sections of the working people on the one hand and the national bourgeoisie on the other, contradictions within the national bourgeoisie, and so forth. Our people's government is a government that truly represents the interests of the people and serves the people, yet certain contradictions do exist between the government and the masses. These include contradictions between the interests of the state, collective interests, and individual interests; between democracy and centralism; between those in positions of leadership and the led, and contradictions arising from the bureaucratic practices of certain state functionaries in their relations with the masses. All these are contradictions among the people. Generally speaking, underlying the contradictions among the people is the basic identity of the interests of the people.

In our country, the contradiction between the working class and the national bourgeoisie is a contradiction among the people. The class struggle waged between the two is, by and large, a class struggle within the ranks of the people. This is because of the dual character of the national bourgeoisie in our country. In the years of the bourgeois-democratic revolution, there was a revolutionary side to their character; there was also a tendency to compromise with the enemy, this was the other side. In the period of the socialist revolution, exploitation of the working class to make profits is one side, while support of the Constitution and willingness to accept socialist transformation is the other. The national bourgeoisie differs from the imperialists, the landlords, and the bureaucrat-capitalists. The contradiction between exploiter and exploited, which exists between the national bourgeoisie and the working class, is an antagonistic one. But, in the concrete conditions existing in China, such an antagonistic contradiction, if properly handled, can be transformed into a non-antagonistic one and resolved in a peaceful way. But if it is not properly handled, if, say, we do not follow a policy of uniting, criticizing, and educating the national bourgeoisie, or if the national bourgeoisie does not accept this policy, then the contradiction between the working class and the national bourgeoisie can turn into an antagonistic contradiction as between ourselves and the enemy.

Since the contradictions between ourselves and the enemy and those among the people differ in nature, they must be solved in different ways. To put it briefly, the former is a matter of drawing a line between us and our enemies, while the latter is a matter of distinguishing between right and wrong. It is, of course, true that drawing a line between ourselves and our enemies is also a question of distinguishing between right and wrong. For example, the question as to who is right, we or the reactionaries at home and abroad—that is, the imperialists, the feudalists, and bureaucrat-capitalists—is also a question of distinguishing between right and wrong, but it is different in nature from questions of right and wrong among the people. . . .

Under ordinary circumstances, contradictions among the people are not antagonistic. But if they are not dealt with properly, or if we relax vigilance and lower our guard, antagonism may arise. In a socialist country, such a development is usually only of a localized and temporary nature. This is because there the exploitation of man by man has been abolished and the interests of the people are basically the same.

★
CHAPTER IV
Dynamics of Revolution:
The Army

Introductory Note

In Mao Tse-tung's voluntaristic interpretation of Marxism-Leninism, the military plays a crucial role. As we have seen in the previous chapter, Mao views the army, the Party, and the united front as the three essential weapons of the Chinese revolution.

"Political power," Mao writes after Lenin, "grows out of the barrel of a gun." But he adds immediately: "Our principle is that the Party commands the gun, and the gun must never be allowed to command the Party." A "Marxist military line," in other words, must be integrated with and subordinated to a "Marxist political line." War is more than a series of military operations; it has economic, "cultural," and "educational" components. A revolutionary army is more than a mere fighting force. As an "army of labor," it performs economic functions and engages in production activity. As a "cultural army," it performs propaganda tasks. The function of "education" is to imbue the masses with proletarian ideology and to fan their revolutionary enthusiasm. Military activity is not a substitute for, and does not pre-empt, other forms of activity: ". . . to emphasize armed struggle does not mean giving up other forms of struggle; on the contrary, armed struggle will not succeed unless co-ordinated with other forms of struggle." All forms of activity, however, must be judged by political criteria. Military operations must have concrete political aims.

The political, economic, "cultural," and "educational" tasks of the army are designed to promote "democracy" within the military as well as in the army's relationships with the masses. Internal "democracy" is epitomized in the slogan "Unity between officers and men"; external "democracy," in "Unity between the army and the people."

"Democracy" and "equality" as means for achieving internal cohesion and control were stressed by Mao Tse-tung as early as 1928. He wrote then that in the Red Army everybody "from the commander to the cook" receives absolutely equal treatment, which is why "the soldiers have no complaints against anyone."[1] Just a year later, however, Mao looked upon equalitarianism as "a mere illusion of peasants and small proprietors."[2] By 1936, "military equalitarianism" was viewed as a companion of "military adventurism."[3]

The principal objective of the army's external political work, according to Mao, is to achieve "Unity between the army and the people." This task derives from the premise that military struggle is not an isolated struggle, that without mass mobilization armed activity cannot succeed: "The richest source of power to wage war lies in the masses of the people." Apart from mobilizing the masses, arming them, and preparing them for revolutionary action, fighting loses its significance. Mao repeatedly points out that although militarily strong, the basic political weakness of the Kuomintang and the Japanese armies was that they were isolated from the masses. He said in a 1936 interview with Edgar Snow: "The Red Army won its many victories—beginning with only a few dozen rifles in the hands of determined revolutionaries—because its solid base in the people attracted friends even among the White troops and among the civilian populace. . . . The enemy was infinitely our superior militarily, but politically it was immobilized."[4] Mao's untiring emphasis on maintaining the closest possible ties with the masses culminated in the formation of the "Three Main Rules of Discipline" and the "Eight Points for Attention," first stated in 1928 and reissued with minor changes in 1947 (see p. 198).

The question of "Unity between the army and the people" is a question of "mass line" (see Chapter V) in military work. This and similar slogans are intended to create the illusion of participation and equality and to maintain Communist morale. They are neces-

[1] "The Struggle in the Chingkang Mountains" (November 1928), *Selected Works,* I (Peking: Foreign Languages Press, 1964), p. 83.
[2] "On Correcting Mistaken Ideas in the Party" (December 1929), ibid., p. 111.
[3] "Problems of Strategy in China's Revolutionary War" (December 1936), ibid., p. 236.
[4] Edgar Snow, *Red Star over China* (New York: Grove Press, 1961), p. 94.

sary, according to Mao, for transforming the Communist army into a "people's army" and the Communist war into a "people's war."

The operational principles of Mao Tse-tung's military thinking were derived from the practical necessity of staging a revolution in a colonial and semicolonial country. They were developed over a long period of time, reflecting the gradual maturing of the Red Army (later People's Liberation Army or PLA), and were crystallized in 1947 in its "Ten Operational Principles" (see p. 225–26).

Mao identified several characteristics, which together distinguished China from other countries and determined the form and content of the military policy that was adopted. First, China was a colonial, semicolonial, and semifeudal country, internally under feudal oppression and externally under the pressure of several imperialist countries. Second, China was a country vast in territory, enormous in (a largely peasant) population, and huge in potential military power. Third, armed "counterrevolution" was the main form of struggle utilized by both the domestic and foreign reactionaries. Fourth, China had remained uneven in its development—politically, militarily, and economically—and was inferior to its foreign enemies in all these respects. Finally, despite all its weaknesses, China had entered an "era of progress," symbolized in the emergence of the Communist Party and the Red Army.

These conditions led to the following conclusions: (1) the Chinese revolution would have to involve a protracted, armed struggle; (2) the revolutionary party and the revolutionary army would have to retreat to the countryside, establish revolutionary bases there, and rely on the rural population for foodstuff, material resources, and manpower; and (3) the principal form of armed struggle would have to be peasant guerrilla warfare.

On several occasions, Mao Tse-tung approvingly cites Stalin's observation that "In China, it is armed revolution against armed counterrevolution. This is one of the characteristics and one of the advantages of the Chinese revolution." Faced with a fully armed enemy in a protracted conflict, no revolutionary movement can expect to survive unless it, too, adopts armed struggle as the principal form of revolutionary activity. A protracted war, according to Mao, undergoes three principal stages of development: "strategic defensive," "strategic stalemate," and "strategic counteroffensive." In the first phase, the revolutionaries being weak, the major function is to retreat and protect themselves. In the next stage, the forces of revolution gradually grow in strength while the enemy increasingly weakens. In the final stage, the revolutionaries attain decisive military superiority over their opponents. Given the necessary time, in other words, a transformation in the balance of forces between revolution and reaction is bound to take place.

Since the power of imperialism-feudalism is concentrated in the urban centers, Mao argues, to carry the protracted war to victory, the Red regime must turn to the rural areas, gradually expand and consolidate itself, encircle the cities, and choke the enemy to death. A "good" revolutionary base must meet a number of criteria: a first-rate party organization, a solid mass base, adequate military strength, a terrain favorable to guerrilla operations, economic self-sufficiency, and isolation from the main enemy forces.

Mao Tse-tung distinguishes between the two basic types of warfare: (1) regular warfare, consisting of positional and mobile warfare, and (2) irregular warfare, consisting of guerrilla warfare. Positional warfare is territory-oriented; it involves extensive trench-work and heavy fortifications. It is used in both strategic defensive (when the revolutionary army seeks to defend a key position) and strategic offensive (when it is confronted with an isolated and helpless enemy force). On the whole, however, for the revolutionary army in a colonial and semicolonial country, positional warfare takes a subordinate place to mobile and guerrilla warfare.

Mobile warfare is warfare "over an extended, shifting, and indefinite front: a strategy depending for success on a high degree of mobility in difficult terrain, and featured by swift attack and withdrawal, swift concentration and dispersal."[5] It stresses the fluidity of operational fronts and is consonant with the policy of "Fight when you can win, move away when you can't win."

The most important form of armed struggle in a colonial and semicolonial country is guerrilla warfare—so much so that it must be considered from a strategic point of view. The main operational requirement of a protracted war is to develop popular, mass guerrilla warfare to preserve and consolidate one's own strength and undermine that of the enemy. The operational principles of guerrilla warfare have been summarized by Mao Tse-tung on a number of occasions. The most important set of tenets takes the shape of a well-known formula: "The enemy advances, we retreat; the enemy

[5] Quoted in ibid., p. 98.

camps, we harass; the enemy tires, we attack; the enemy retreats, we pursue."[6]

Guerrilla warfare is the weapon of the militarily weak; it is fought vis-à-vis a superior enemy. The major task is the preservation of one's effective strength, not the holding of the cities. The important consideration is time, not space. Thus Mao argues that since guerrilla warfare requires space for maneuvering, it would not be feasible in a small country such as Belgium. Geographic limitations, however, may be overcome by a variety of conditions, among them, inept domestic government or foreign support of the guerrillas.

The principal use of guerrilla warfare is not in destroying the enemy but in harassing him, confusing him, disrupting his lines of communication, forcing him to disperse his strength, and, most importantly perhaps, undermining his morale. Destruction of the enemy takes place mainly through regular warfare. Guerrilla warfare, in other words, is not a substitute for conventional forces. Unconventional warfare becomes conventional as the guerrillas gain military superiority over the enemy.

The general relationship between the various forms of warfare in the three stages of protracted war is as follows: guerrilla warfare plays the central role in the middle (often the longest) stage and a secondary role in the first and the last stages. Mobile warfare is particularly important in the first and the third stages. In a revolutionary war, positional warfare plays a supplementary role from beginning to end. Only after the revolution has triumphed does positional warfare come to assume a superior status vis-à-vis guerrilla and mobile warfare. "Premature regularization," however, is strictly prohibited.

[6] "A Single Spark Can Start a Prairie Fire" (January 1930), *Selected Works,* I (Peking: Foreign Languages Press, 1964), p. 124.

Readings

CHARACTER AND DIMENSIONS
OF MILITARY ACTIVITY

Party Leadership

From: "Resolution on Certain Questions in the History of Our Party" (adopted by the CCP Central Committee on April 20, 1945), *Selected Works,* III (Peking: Foreign Languages Press, 1965), pp. 197–98, 205–6. (Although this document is in the third person singular, it was actually written by Mao Tse-tung himself. See Introduction.)

. . . Comrade Stalin said, "In China the armed revolution is fighting the armed counterrevolution. That is one of the specific features and one of the advantages of the Chinese revolution." Like Comrade Stalin, Comrade Mao Tse-tung had correctly pointed out as far back as the early period of the Agrarian Revolutionary War [1927–37] that, in the Chinese revolution, armed struggle is the main form of struggle and an army composed chiefly of peasants is the main form of organization, for the reason that semicolonial and semifeudal China is a large, non-uniform country which lacks democracy and industry. Comrade Mao Tse-tung also pointed out that the vast rural areas inhabited by the broad masses of the peasantry are the indispensable, vital positions of the Chinese revolution (revolutionary villages can encircle the cities, but revolutionary cities cannot detach themselves from the villages), and that China can and must establish armed revolutionary base areas as the starting point for country-wide victory (democratic unification of the whole country). In the period of the 1924–27 revolution, when a coalition government had been formed through Kuomintang-Communist cooperation, the base areas had certain big cities as their centers, but even then, in order to consolidate the foundations of the base areas, it was necessary, under the leadership of the proletariat, to build a people's army with the peasants as the main body and solve the land problem in the rural areas. But in the period of the Agrarian Revolutionary War, since the cities were all occupied by powerful counterrevolutionary forces, base areas had to be set up, expanded, and consolidated mainly by relying on peasant guerrilla warfare (not on positional warfare) and first of all in the countryside where counterrevolutionary rule was weak (and not in the key cities).

At the present stage of the Chinese revolution, military struggle is the main form of political struggle. During the Agrarian Revolutionary War it became the most urgent question in the Party line. Comrade Mao Tse-tung has applied Marxism-Leninism and formulated not only the correct political line for the Chinese revolution, but also, beginning with the period of the Agrarian Revolutionary War, the correct military line subordinate to this political line. Comrade Mao Tse-tung's military line proceeds from two fundamental points. First, our army is and can be an army of only one kind; it must be an instrument subordinate to the ideological leadership of the proletariat and serving the struggle of the people and the building of revolutionary base areas. Second, our war is and can be a war of only one kind; it must be a war in which we recognize that the enemy is strong and we are weak, that the enemy is big and we are small, and in which therefore we fully utilize the enemy's weaknesses and our strong points and fully rely on the strength of the masses for survival, victory, and expansion. From the first point, it follows that the Red Army (now the Eighth Route Army, the New Fourth Army, and the other armed forces of the people) must fight wholeheartedly for the line, program, and policies of the Party, that is, for all the manifold interests of the whole people, and must combat the tendencies toward warlordism which run counter to this. Therefore, the Red Army must oppose the purely military point of view and the roving-rebel ideology, according to which the military does not obey the political, or even commands the political. The Red Army must simultaneously shoulder the threefold task of fighting, doing mass work, and raising funds (which at present means production); doing mass work means becoming a propagandist and organizer for the Party and for the people's political power and means helping the local people in land distribution (at present, the reduction of rent and interest) and in establishing armed forces, organs of political power, and Party organizations. Hence, in its relations with the government and the people, it is required that the Red Army scrupulously respect the organs of the people's political power and the mass organizations, strengthen their prestige, and strictly observe the Three Main Rules of Discipline and the Eight Points for Attention [see p. 198]. Within the army it is necessary to establish a correct relationship between officers and men and to have both an appropriate democratic life and an authoritative military discipline based on political consciousness.

The Party and the Gun

From: "Problems of War and Strategy" (November 1938), *Selected Works*, II (Peking: Foreign Languages Press, 1965), pp. 224–25.

. . . Every Communist must grasp the truth, "Political power grows out of the barrel of a gun." Our principle is that the Party commands the gun, and the gun must never be allowed to command the Party. Yet, having guns, we can create Party organizations. . . . We can also create cadres, create schools, create culture, create mass movements. Everything in Yenan has been created by having guns. All things grow out of the barrel of a gun. According to the Marxist theory of the state, the army is the chief component of state power. Whoever wants to seize and retain state power must have a strong army. . . . The guns of the Russian Communist Party created socialism. We shall create a democratic republic. Experience in the class struggle in the era of imperialism teaches us that it is only by the power of the gun that the working class and the laboring masses can defeat the armed bourgeoisie and landlords; in this sense we may say that only with guns can the whole world be transformed. We are advocates of the abolition of war, we do not want war; but war can only be abolished through war, and in order to get rid of the gun it is necessary to take up the gun.

War and Politics

From: "On Protracted War" (May 1938), *Selected Works*, II (Peking: Foreign Languages Press, 1965), pp. 152–55.

. . . "War is the continuation of politics." In this sense war is politics and war itself is a political action; since ancient times there has never been a war that did not have a political character. The anti-Japanese war is a revolutionary war waged by the whole nation, and victory is inseparable from the political aim of the war—to drive out Japanese imperialism and build a new China of freedom and equality —inseparable from the general policy of persevering in the War of Resistance and in the united front, from the mobilization of the entire people, and from the political principles of the unity between officers and men, the unity between army and people, and the disintegration of the enemy forces, and inseparable from the effective application of united front policy, from mobilization on the cultural front, and from the efforts to win international support and the support of the people inside Japan. In a word, war cannot for a single moment be separated from politics. Any tendency among the anti-Japanese armed forces to belittle politics by isolating war from it and advocating the idea of war as an absolute is wrong and should be corrected.

. . . But war has its own particular characteristics and in this sense it cannot be equated with politics in general. "War is the continuation of politics by other . . . means." When politics develops to a certain stage beyond which it cannot proceed by the usual means, war breaks out to sweep the obstacles from the way. For instance, the semi-independent status of China is an obstacle to the political growth of Japanese imperialism, hence Japan has unleashed a war of aggression to sweep away that obstacle. What about China? Imperialist oppression has long been an obstacle to China's bourgeois-democratic revolution, hence many wars of liberation have been waged in the effort to sweep it away. Japan is now using war for the purpose of oppressing China and completely blocking the advance of the Chinese revolution, and therefore China is compelled to wage the War of Resistance in her determination to sweep away this obstacle. When the obstacle is removed, our political aim will be attained and the war concluded. But if the obstacle is not completely swept away, the war will have to continue till the aim is fully accomplished. Thus anyone who seeks a compromise before the task of the anti-Japanese war is fulfilled is bound to fail, because even if a compromise were to occur for one reason or another, the war would break out again, since the broad masses of the people would certainly not submit but would continue the war until its political objective was achieved. It can therefore be said that politics is war without bloodshed while war is politics with bloodshed. . . .

. . . A national revolutionary war as great as ours cannot be won without extensive and thoroughgoing political mobilization. Before the anti-Japanese war there was no political mobilization for resistance to Japan, and this was a great drawback, as a result of which China has already lost a move to the enemy. After the war began, political mobilization was very far from extensive, let alone thoroughgoing. It was the enemy's gunfire and the bombs dropped by enemy airplanes that brought news of the war to the great majority of the people. That was also a kind of mobilization, but it was done for us by the enemy, we did not do it ourselves. Even now the people in the remoter regions beyond the noise of the guns are carrying on quietly as usual. This situation must change, or otherwise we cannot win in our life-and-death struggle. We must never lose another move to the enemy; on the contrary, we must make full use of this move, political mobilization, to get the better of him. This move is crucial; it is indeed of primary importance, while our inferiority in weapons and other things is only secondary. The mobilization of the common people throughout the country will create a vast sea in which to drown the enemy, create the conditions that will make up for our inferiority in arms and other things, and create the prerequisites for overcoming every difficulty in the war. To win victory, we must persevere in the War of Resistance, in the united front, and in the protracted war. But all these are inseparable from the mobilization of the common people. To wish for victory and yet neglect political mobilization is like wishing to "go south by driving the chariot north," and the result would inevitably be to forfeit victory.

. . . What does political mobilization mean? First, it means telling the army and the people about the political aim of the war. It is necessary for every soldier and civilian to see why the war must be fought and how it concerns him. The political aim of the war is "to drive out Japanese imperialism and build a new China of freedom and equality"; we must proclaim this aim to everybody, to all soldiers and civilians, before we can create an anti-Japanese upsurge and unite hundreds of millions as one man to contribute their all to the war. Secondly, it is not enough merely to explain the aim to them; the steps and policies for its attainment must also be given, that is, there must be a political program. . . . Without a clear-cut, concrete political program it is impossible to mobilize all the armed forces and the whole people to carry the war against Japan through to the end. Thirdly, how should we mobilize them? By word of mouth, by leaflets and bulletins, by newspapers, books, and pamphlets, through plays and films, through schools, through the mass organizations, and through our cadres. What has been done so far in the Kuomintang areas is only a drop in the ocean, and moreover it has been done in a manner ill-suited to the people's tastes and in a spirit uncongenial to them; this must be drastically changed. Fourthly, to mobilize once is not enough; political mobilization for the War of Resistance must be continuous. Our job is not to recite our political program to the people, for nobody will listen to such recitations; we must link the political mobilization for the war with developments in the war and with the life of the soldiers and the people, and make it a continuous movement. This is a matter of immense importance on which our victory in the war primarily depends.

"The Purely Military Viewpoint"

From: "On Correcting Mistaken Ideas in the Party" (December 1929), *Selected Works*, I (Peking: Foreign Languages Press, 1964), pp. 105–8.

The purely military viewpoint is very highly developed among a number of comrades in the Red Army. It manifests itself as follows:

1. These comrades regard military affairs and politics as opposed to each other and refuse to recognize that military affairs are only one means of accomplishing political tasks. Some even say, "If you are good militarily, naturally you are good politically; if you are not good militarily, you cannot be any good politically"—this is to go a step further and give military affairs a leading position over politics.

2. They think that the task of the Red Army, like that of the White army, is merely to fight. They do not understand that the Chinese Red Army is an armed body for carrying out the political tasks of the revolution. Especially at present, the Red Army should certainly not confine itself to fighting; besides fighting to destroy the enemy's military strength, it should shoulder such important tasks as doing propaganda among the masses, organizing the masses, arming them, helping them to establish revolutionary political power, and setting up Party organizations. . . . Without these objectives, fighting loses its meaning and the Red Army loses the reason for its existence.

3. Hence, organizationally, these comrades subordinate the departments of the Red Army doing political work to those doing military work, and put forward the slogan "Let Army Headquarters handle outside matters." If allowed to develop, this idea would involve the danger of estrangement from the masses, control of the government by the army, and departure from proletarian leadership —it would be to take the path of warlordism like the Kuomintang army.

4. At the same time, in propaganda work they overlook the importance of propaganda teams. On the question of mass organization, they neglect the organizing of soldiers' committees in the army

and the organizing of the local workers and peasants. As a result, both propaganda and organizational work are abandoned.

5. They become conceited when a battle is won and dispirited when a battle is lost.

6. Selfish departmentalism—they think only of the Fourth Army and do not realize that it is an important task of the Red Army to arm the local masses. This is cliquism in a magnified form.

7. Unable to see beyond their limited environment in the Fourth Army, a few comrades believe that no other revolutionary forces exist. Hence their extreme addiction to the idea of conserving strength and avoiding action. This is a remnant of opportunism.

8. Some comrades, disregarding the subjective and objective conditions, suffer from the malady of revolutionary impetuosity; they will not take pains to do minute and detailed work among the masses, but, riddled with illusions, want only to do big things. This is a remnant of putschism [i.e., tendency toward premature revolutionary activity].

The sources of the purely military viewpoint are:

1. A low political level. From this flows the failure to recognize the role of political leadership in the army and to recognize that the Red Army and the White army are fundamentally different.

2. The mentality of mercenaries. Many prisoners captured in past battles have joined the Red Army, and such elements bring with them a markedly mercenary outlook, thereby providing a basis in the lower ranks for the purely military viewpoint.

3. From the two preceding causes there arises a third, overconfidence in military strength and absence of confidence in the strength of the masses of the people.

4. The Party's failure actively to attend to and discuss military work is also a reason for the emergence of the purely military viewpoint among a number of comrades.

The methods of correction are as follows:

1. Raise the political level in the Party by means of education, destroy the theoretical roots of the purely military viewpoint, and be clear on the fundamental difference between the Red Army and the White army. At the same time, eliminate the remnants of opportunism and putschism and break down the selfish departmentalism of the Fourth Army.

2. Intensify the political training of officers and men and especially the education of ex-prisoners. At the same time, as far as

possible let the local governments select workers and peasants experienced in struggle to join the Red Army, thus organizationally weakening or even eradicating the purely military viewpoint.

3. Arouse the local Party organizations to criticize the Party organizations in the Red Army and the organs of mass political power to criticize the Red Army itself, in order to influence the Party organizations and the officers and men of the Red Army.

4. The Party must actively attend to and discuss military work. All the work must be discussed and decided upon by the Party before being carried out by the rank and file.

5. Draw up Red Army rules and regulations which clearly define its tasks, the relationship between its military and its political apparatus, the relationship between the Red Army and the masses of the people, and the powers and functions of the soldiers' committees and their relationship with the military and political organizations.

"An Army of Labor"

From: "Get Organized!" (November 1943), *Selected Works*, III (Peking: Foreign Languages Press, 1965), p. 153.

. . . This year the peasant masses and the people in the army, the government and other organizations, the schools and the factories of the [Shensi-Kansu-Ningsia] Border Region have been conducting a production campaign in accordance with the resolutions of the meeting of senior cadres convened last winter by the Northwest Bureau of the Central Committee. Great achievements and advances have been scored in every field of production this year and the Border Region has taken on a new look. Facts have fully borne out the correctness of the policy adopted by the conference of senior cadres. The gist of this policy is to organize the masses, to mobilize and organize into a great army of labor all the available forces without exception—the people, the army, the government and other organizations, and the schools—all men and women, young and old, who can contribute their labor power on a part-time or full-time basis. We have an army for fighting as well as an army for labor. For fighting we have the Eighth Route and New Fourth Armies; but even they do a dual job, warfare and production. With these two kinds of armies, and with a fighting army skilled in these two tasks and in mass work, we can overcome our difficulties and defeat Japanese imperialism.

From: "We Must Learn to Do Economic Work" (January 1945), *Selected Works,* III (Peking: Foreign Languages Press, 1965), pp. 243–44.

Some people say that if the army units go in for production, they will be unable to train or fight, and that if the government and other organizations do so, they will be unable to do their own work. This is a false argument. In recent years our army units in the Border Region have undertaken production on a big scale to provide themselves with ample food and clothing and have simultaneously done their training and conducted their political studies and literacy and other courses much more successfully than before, and there is greater unity than ever within the army and between the army and the people. While there was a large-scale production campaign at the front last year, great successes were gained in the fighting and in addition an extensive training campaign was started. And thanks to production, the personnel of the government and other organizations live a better life and work with greater devotion and efficiency; this is the case both in the Border Region and at the front.

From: "Turn the Army into a Working Force" (February 1949), *Selected Works,* IV (Peking: Foreign Languages Press, 1961), pp. 337–38.

. . . The army is not only a fighting force, it is mainly a working force. All army cadres should learn how to take over and administer cities. In urban work they should learn how to be good at dealing with the imperialists and Kuomintang reactionaries, good at dealing with the bourgeoisie, good at leading the workers and organizing trade unions, good at mobilizing and organizing the youth, good at uniting with and training cadres in the new liberated areas, good at managing industry and commerce, good at running schools, newspapers, news agencies, and broadcasting stations, good at handling foreign affairs, good at handling problems relating to the democratic parties and people's organizations, good at adjusting the relations between the cities and the rural areas and solving the problems of food, coal, and other daily necessities, and good at handling monetary and financial problems. In short, all urban problems, with which in the past our army cadres and fighters were unfamiliar, should from now on be shouldered by them. . . . The army is still a fighting force, and in this respect there must be absolutely no relaxing; to relax would be a mistake. Nevertheless, the time has come for us to set ourselves the task of turning the army into a working force. If we do not now set ourselves this task and resolve to perform it, we shall be making an extremely big mistake. We are preparing to send 53,000 cadres south with the army, but this is a very small number. The occupation of eight or nine provinces and scores of big cities will require a huge number of working cadres, and to solve this problem the army must rely chiefly on itself. The army is a school.

From: "On Production by the Army for Its Own Support and on the Importance of the Great Movements for Rectification and for Production" (April 1945), *Selected Works,* III (Peking: Foreign Languages Press, 1965), pp. 327–28.

Production by the army for its own support has not only improved the army's living conditions and lightened the burden on the people, thereby making it possible further to expand the army. In addition, it has had many immediate effects. They are as follows:

(1) Improved relations between officers and men. Officers and men work together in production and become like brothers.

(2) Better attitude to labor. What we now have is neither the old mercenary system nor universal military service, but a third system, the system of mobilizing volunteers. It is better than the mercenary system since it does not produce so many loafers, but it is not so good as universal military service. Nevertheless, our present conditions only allow us to adopt the system of mobilizing volunteers, and not that of universal military service. The mobilized soldiers have to lead an army life for a long time, which may impair their attitude to labor and so turn some of them into loafers or taint them with certain bad habits characteristic of the warlord armies. But since the army began to produce for its own support, the attitude to labor has improved and loafer ways have been overcome.

(3) Strengthened discipline. Far from weakening discipline in battle and in army life, labor discipline in production actually strengthens it.

(4) Improved relations between the army and the people. Once an armed force begins to "keep house" for itself, encroachments upon the property of the people seldom or never occur. As the army and the people exchange labor and help each other in production, the friendship between them is strengthened.

(5) Less grumbling in the army about the government and improved relations between the two.

(6) An impetus to the great production campaign of the people. Once the army engages in production, the need for government and

other organizations to do likewise becomes more obvious, and they do so more energetically; also, the need for a universal campaign of the whole people to increase production naturally becomes more obvious, and this too is carried on more energetically.

"A Cultural Army"

From: "The United Front in Cultural Work" (October 1944), *Selected Works,* III (Peking: Foreign Languages Press, 1965), p. 235.

. . . In our work the war comes first, then production, then cultural work. An army without culture is a dull-witted army, and a dull-witted army cannot defeat the enemy.

From: "Talks at the Yenan Forum on Literature and Art" (May 1942), *Selected Works,* III (Peking: Foreign Languages Press, 1965), pp. 69–70.

In our struggle for the liberation of the Chinese people there are various fronts, among which there are the fronts of the pen and of the gun, the cultural and the military fronts. To defeat the enemy we must rely primarily on the army with guns. But this army alone is not enough; we must also have a cultural army, which is absolutely indispensable for uniting our own ranks and defeating the enemy. Since the May 4 Movement such a cultural army has taken shape in China, and it has helped the Chinese revolution, gradually reduced the domain of China's feudal culture and of the comprador culture which serves imperialist aggression, and weakened their influence. To oppose the new culture the Chinese reactionaries can now only "pit quantity against quality." In other words, reactionaries have money, and though they can produce nothing good, they can go all out and produce in quantity. Literature and art have been an important and successful part of the cultural front since the May 4 Movement. During the ten years' civil war, the revolutionary literature and art movement grew greatly. That movement and the revolutionary war both headed in the same general direction, but these two fraternal armies were not linked together in their practical work because the reactionaries had cut them off from each other. It is very good that since the outbreak of the War of Resistance Against Japan, more and more revolutionary writers and artists have been coming to Yenan and our other anti-Japanese base areas. But it does not necessarily follow that, having come to the base areas, they have already integrated themselves completely with the masses of the people here. The two must be completely integrated if we are to push ahead with our revolutionary work.

THE ARMY AND THE PEOPLE

Man over Weapons

From: "On Protracted War" (May 1938), *Selected Works,* II (Peking: Foreign Languages Press, 1965), p. 143.

. . . the so-called theory that "weapons decide everything" . . . constitutes a mechanical approach to the question of war and a subjective and one-sided view. Our view is opposed to this; we see not only weapons but also people. Weapons are an important factor in war, but not the decisive factor; it is people, not things, that are decisive. The contest of strength is not only a contest of military and economic power, but also a contest of human power and morale. Military and economic power is necessarily wielded by people.

The Army and "Democracy"

From: "On Protracted War" (May 1938), *Selected Works,* II (Peking: Foreign Languages Press, 1965), pp. 186–87.

. . . The richest source of power to wage war lies in the masses of the people. It is mainly because of the unorganized state of the Chinese masses that Japan dares to bully us. When this defect is remedied, then the Japanese aggressor, like a mad bull crashing into a ring of flames, will be surrounded by hundreds of millions of our people standing upright, the mere sound of their voices will strike terror into him, and he will be burned to death. China's armies must have an uninterrupted flow of reinforcements, and the abuses of press-ganging and of buying substitutes, which now exist at the lower levels, must immediately be banned and replaced by widespread and enthusiastic political mobilization, which will make it easy to enlist millions of men. We now have great difficulties in raising money for the war, but once the people are mobilized, finances too will cease to be a problem. Why should a country as large and populous as China suffer from lack of funds? The army must become one with the people so that they see it as their own army. Such an army will be invincible, and an imperialist power like Japan will be no match for it.

. . . Many people think that it is wrong methods that make for strained relations between officers and men and between the army and the people, but I always tell them that it is a question of basic attitude (or basic principle), of having respect for the soldiers and the people. It is from this attitude that the various policies, methods, and forms ensue. If we depart from this attitude, then the policies, methods, and forms will certainly be wrong, and the relations between officers and men and between the army and the people are bound to be unsatisfactory. Our three major principles for the army's political work are, first, unity between officers and men; second, unity between the army and the people; and third, the disintegration of the enemy forces. To apply these principles effectively, we must start with this basic attitude of respect for the soldiers and the people, and of respect for the human dignity of prisoners of war once they have laid down their arms. Those who take all this as a technical matter and not one of basic attitude are indeed wrong, and they should correct their view.

Rejection of Warlordism

From: "Get Organized!" (November 1943), *Selected Works,* III (Peking: Foreign Languages Press, 1965), pp. 158–59.

. . . Our troops must observe the correct principles that govern relations between the army and the people, between the army and the government, between the army and the Party, between officers and men, and between military work and political work, and relations among the cadres, and must never commit the errors of warlordism. Officers must cherish their men and must not be indifferent to their well-being or resort to corporal punishment; the army must cherish the people and never encroach upon their interests; the army must respect the government and the Party and never "assert independence." Our Eighth Route and New Fourth Armies are the armed forces of the people; they have always been very good, and are indeed the best in the country. But it is true that in recent years errors of warlordism of a certain kind have arisen, and some comrades in the army have become arrogant and highhanded in their behavior toward the soldiers, the people, the government, and the Party, always blaming the comrades doing local work but never themselves, always seeing their own achievements but never their own shortcomings, and always welcoming flattery but never criticism. Such phenomena are to be found, for example, in the Shensi-Kansu-

Ningsia border region. The tendency has been basically overcome as a result of the conference of senior cadres and the meeting of military and political cadres last year and of the campaigns to "support the government and cherish the people" and "support the army" during the Spring Festival this year, but there is still a residue which we must make further efforts to eradicate. These faults are also to be found in the base areas in northern and central China, and the Party organizations and the army there must endeavor to eradicate them.

The Army's Overriding Purpose

From: "On Coalition Government" (April 1945), *Selected Works,* III (Peking: Foreign Languages Press, 1965), pp. 264–67.

This army is powerful because all its members have a discipline based on political consciousness; they have come together and they fight not for the private interests of a few individuals or a narrow clique, but for the interests of the broad masses and of the whole nation. The sole purpose of this army is to stand firmly with the Chinese people and to serve them wholeheartedly.

Guided by this purpose, this army has an indomitable spirit and is determined to vanquish all enemies and never to yield. No matter what the difficulties and hardships, so long as a single man remains, he will fight on.

Guided by this purpose, this army has achieved remarkable unity in its own ranks and with those outside its ranks. Internally, there is unity between officers and men, between the higher and lower ranks, and between military work, political work, and rear service work; and externally, there is unity between the army and the people, between the army and government organizations, and between our army and the friendly armies. It is imperative to overcome anything that impairs this unity.

Guided by this purpose, this army has a correct policy for winning over enemy officers and men and for dealing with prisoners of war. Without exception all members of the enemy forces who surrender, who come over to our side, or who, after laying down their arms, wish to join in fighting the common foe, are welcomed and given proper education. It is forbidden to kill, maltreat, or insult any prisoner of war.

Guided by this purpose, this army has built up a system of strategy and tactics which is essential for the people's war. It is skilled in flexible guerrilla warfare conducted in accordance with the changing concrete conditions and is also skilled in mobile warfare.

Guided by this purpose, this army has built up a system of political work which is essential for the people's war and is aimed at promoting unity in its own ranks, unity with the friendly armies and unity with the people, and at disintegrating the enemy forces and ensuring victory in battle.

Guided by this purpose, the entire army, operating under conditions of guerrilla warfare, is able to utilize, and has in fact utilized, the intervals between battles and between training periods to produce grain and other necessities, thus becoming wholly, half, or at least partly self-supporting, so that economic difficulties are overcome, living conditions improved, and the burden on the people lightened. Every possibility has been exploited to establish a number of small-scale armament works in various military base areas.

Furthermore, this army is powerful because it has the people's self-defense corps and the militia—the vast armed organizations of the masses—fighting in co-ordination with it. In the liberated areas of China all men and women, from youth to middle age, are organized in the people's anti-Japanese self-defense corps on a voluntary and democratic basis and without giving up their work in production. The cream of the self-defense corps, except for those who join the army or the guerrilla units, is brought into the militia. Without the co-operation of these armed forces of the masses it would be impossible to defeat the enemy.

Finally, this army is powerful because of its division into two parts, the main forces and the regional forces, with the former available for operations in any region whenever necessary and the latter concentrating on defending their own localities and attacking the enemy there in co-operation with the local militia and the self-defense corps. This division of labor has won the wholehearted support of the people. Without this correct division of labor—if, for example, attention were paid only to the role of the main forces while that of the regional forces were neglected—it would likewise be impossible to defeat the enemy in the conditions obtaining in China's liberated areas. Under the regional forces, numerous armed working teams have been organized, which are well trained and hence better qualified for military, political, and mass work; they penetrate into the rearmost areas behind the enemy lines, strike at the enemy, and arouse the masses to anti-Japanese struggle, thus giving support to the frontal military operations of the various liberated areas. In all this they have achieved great success. . . .

Such is a real people's war. Only by waging such a people's war can we defeat the national enemy. The Kuomintang has failed precisely because of its desperate opposition to a people's war.

The Three Rules and the Eight Points

From: "On the Reissue of the Three Main Rules of Discipline and the Eight Points for Attention—Instruction of the General Headquarters of the Chinese People's Liberation Army" (October 1947), *Selected Works*, IV (Peking: Foreign Languages Press, 1961), p. 155.

1. Our Army's Three Main Rules of Discipline and Eight Points for Attention have been practiced for many years, but their contents vary slightly in army units in different areas. They have now been unified and are hereby reissued. It is expected that you will take this version as the standard one for thorough education and strict enforcement. As to other matters needing attention, the high command of the armed forces in different areas may lay down additional points in accordance with specific conditions and order their enforcement.

2. The Three Main Rules of Discipline are as follows:

    (1) Obey orders in all your actions.

    (2) Don't take a single needle or piece of thread from the masses.

    (3) Turn in everything captured.

3. The Eight Points for Attention are as follows:

    (1) Speak politely.

    (2) Pay fairly for what you buy.

    (3) Return everything you borrow.

    (4) Pay for anything you damage.

    (5) Don't hit or swear at people.

    (6) Don't damage crops.

    (7) Don't take liberties with women.

    (8) Don't ill-treat captives.

"DEMOCRACY" WITHIN THE ARMY

Political, Economic, and Military "Democracy"

From: "The Struggle in the Chingkang Mountains" (November 1928), *Selected Works*, I (Peking: Foreign Languages Press, 1964), p. 83.

Apart from the role played by the Party, the reason why the Red Army has been able to carry on in spite of such poor material conditions and such frequent engagements is its practice of democracy. The officers do not beat the men; officers and men receive equal treatment; soldiers are free to hold meetings and to speak out; trivial formalities have been done away with; and the accounts are open for all to inspect. The soldiers handle the mess arrangements and, out of the daily five cents for cooking oil, salt, firewood, and vegetables, they can even save a little for pocket money, amounting to roughly six or seven coppers per person per day, which is called "mess savings." All this gives great satisfaction to the soldiers. The newly captured soldiers in particular feel that our army and the Kuomintang army are worlds apart. They feel spiritually liberated, even though material conditions in the Red Army are not equal to those in the White army. The very soldiers who had no courage in the White army yesterday are very brave in the Red Army today; such is the effect of democracy. The Red Army is like a furnace in which all captured soldiers are transmuted the moment they come over. In China the army needs democracy as much as the people do. Democracy in our army is an important weapon for undermining the feudal mercenary army.

From: "On the Great Victory in the Northwest and on the New Type of Ideological Education Movement in the Liberation Army" (March 1948), *Selected Works*, IV (Peking: Foreign Languages Press, 1961), pp. 214–15.

. . . What is most noteworthy . . . is the new type of ideological education movement in the army, which was carried out for more than two months last winter by the methods of pouring out grievances and the three checkups. The correct unfolding of the movement for pouring out grievances (the wrongs done to the laboring people by the old society and by the reactionaries) and the three checkups (on class origin, performance of duty, and will to fight) greatly heightened the political consciousness of commanders and fighters throughout the army in the fight for the emancipation of the exploited working masses, for nationwide land reform, and for the destruction of the common enemy of the people, the Chiang Kai-shek bandit gang. It also greatly strengthened the firm unity of all commanders and fighters under the leadership of the Communist Party. On this basis, the army achieved greater purity in its ranks, strengthened discipline, unfolded a mass movement for training, and further developed its political, economic, and military democracy in a completely well-led and orderly way. Thus the army has become united as one man, with everybody contributing his ideas and his strength, fearless of sacrifice and capable of overcoming material difficulties, an army which displays mass heroism and daring in destroying the enemy. Such an army will be invincible.

From: "The Democratic Movement in the Army" (January 1948), *Selected Works,* IV (Peking: Foreign Languages Press, 1961), pp. 191–92.

The policy for political work in our army units is fully to arouse the masses of soldiers, the commanders, and all working personnel in order to achieve, through a democratic movement under centralized leadership, three major objectives, namely, a high degree of political unity, an improvement in living conditions, and a higher level of military technique and tactics. The Three Checkups and Three Improvements ["organizational consolidation, ideological education, and rectification of style of work"] now being enthusiastically carried out in our army units are intended to attain the first two of these objectives through the methods of political and economic democracy.

With regard to economic democracy, the representatives elected by the soldiers must be ensured the right to assist (but not to bypass) the company leadership in managing the company's supplies and mess.

With regard to military democracy, in periods of training there must be mutual instruction as between officers and soldiers and among the soldiers themselves; and in periods of fighting the companies at the front must hold big and small meetings of various kinds. Under the direction of the company leadership, the masses of soldiers should be roused to discuss how to attack and capture enemy positions and how to fulfill other combat tasks. When the fighting lasts several days, several such meetings should be held. This kind of military democracy was practiced with great success in the battle of Panlung in northern Shensi and in the battle of Shihchia-chuang in the Shansi-Chahar-Hopei area. It has been proved that the practice can only do good and can do no harm whatsoever.

The masses of soldiers should have the right to expose the errors and misdeeds of bad elements among the cadres. We should be confident that the soldiers will cherish all the good and comparatively good cadres. Moreover, the soldiers should have the right, when necessary, to nominate those whom they trust from their own ranks for lower-level cadre posts, subject to appointment by the higher level. When there is an acute shortage of lower-level cadres, this kind of nomination is very useful. It is not to be the rule, however, but is to be done only when necessary.

"Democracy" and "Ultrademocracy"

From: "On Correcting Mistaken Ideas in the Party" (December 1929), *Selected Works,* I (Peking: Foreign Languages Press, 1964), pp. 108–11.

. . . ultrademocracy is still deep-rooted in the minds of many comrades. Witness the various expressions of reluctance to carry out Party decisions.

The methods of correction are as follows:

1. In the sphere of theory, destroy the roots of ultrademocracy. First it should be pointed out that the danger of ultrademocracy lies in the fact that it damages or even completely wrecks the Party organization and weakens or even completely undermines the Party's fighting capacity, rendering the Party incapable of fulfilling its fighting tasks and thereby causing the defeat of the revolution. Next, it should be pointed out that the source of ultrademocracy consists in the petty bourgeoisie's individualistic aversion to discipline. When this characteristic is brought into the Party, it develops into ultra-democratic ideas politically and organizationally. These ideas are utterly incompatible with the fighting tasks of the proletariat.

2. In the sphere of organization, ensure democracy under centralized guidance. It should be done on the following lines:

(1) The leading bodies of the Party must give a correct line of guidance and find solutions when problems arise, in order to establish themselves as centers of leadership.

(2) The higher bodies must be familiar with the life of the masses and with the situation in the lower bodies so as to have an objective basis for correct guidance.

(3) No Party organization at any level should make casual de-

cisions in solving problems. Once a decision is reached, it must be firmly carried out.

(4) All decisions of any importance made by the Party's higher bodies must be promptly transmitted to the lower bodies and the Party rank and file. The method is to call meetings of activists or general membership meetings of the Party branches or even of the columns (when circumstances permit) and to assign people to make reports at such meetings.

(5) The lower bodies of the Party and the Party rank and file must discuss the higher bodies' directives in detail in order to understand their meaning thoroughly and decide on the methods of carrying them out. . . .

Absolute equalitarianism became quite serious in the Red Army at one time. Here are some examples. On the matter of allowances to wounded soldiers, there were objections to differentiating between light and serious cases, and the demand was raised for equal allowances for all. When officers rode on horseback, it was regarded not as something necessary for performing their duties but as a sign of inequality. Absolutely equal distribution of supplies was demanded, and there was objection to somewhat larger allotments in special cases. In the hauling of rice, the demand was made that all should carry the same load on their backs, irrespective of age or physical condition. Equality was demanded in the allotment of billets, and the Headquarters would be abused for occupying larger rooms. Equality was demanded in the assignment of fatigue duties, and there was unwillingness to do a little more than the next man. It even went so far that when there were two wounded men but only one stretcher, neither could be carried away because each refused to yield priority to the other. Absolute equalitarianism, as shown in these examples, is still very serious among officers and soldiers of the Red Army.

Absolute equalitarianism, like ultrademocracy in political matters, is the product of a handicraft and small peasant economy— the only difference being that the one manifests itself in material affairs, while the other manifests itself in political affairs.

The method of correction: we should point out that, before the abolition of capitalism, absolute equalitarianism is a mere illusion of peasants and small proprietors, and that even under socialism there can be no absolute equality, for material things will then be distributed on the principle of "from each according to his ability, to each according to his work" as well as on that of meeting the needs of the work. The distribution of material things in the Red Army must be more or less equal, as in the case of equal pay for officers and men, because this is required by the present circumstances of the struggle. But absolute equalitarianism beyond reason must be opposed because it is not required by the struggle; on the contrary, it hinders the struggle.

THE ARMY AND REVOLUTIONARY WAR

From: "Problems of Strategy in China's Revolutionary War" (December 1936), *Selected Works,* I (Peking: Foreign Languages Press, 1964), pp. 179–82, 186–91, 196–200.

The Laws of War Are Developmental

The laws of war are a problem which anyone directing a war must study and solve.

The laws of revolutionary war are a problem which anyone directing a revolutionary war must study and solve.

The laws of China's revolutionary war are a problem which anyone directing China's revolutionary war must study and solve.

We are now engaged in a war; our war is a revolutionary war; and our revolutionary war is being waged in this semicolonial and semifeudal country of China. Therefore, we must study not only the laws of war in general, but the specific laws of revolutionary war, and the even more specific laws of revolutionary war in China.

It is well known that when you do anything, unless you understand its actual circumstances, its nature, and its relations to other things, you will not know the laws governing it, or know how to do it, or be able to do it well.

War is the highest form of struggle for resolving contradictions, when they have developed to a certain stage, between classes, nations, states, or political groups, and it has existed ever since the emergence of private property and of classes. Unless you understand the actual circumstances of war, its nature and its relations to other things, you will not know the laws of war, or know how to direct war, or be able to win victory.

Revolutionary war, whether a revolutionary class war or a revolutionary national war, has its own specific circumstances and nature, in addition to the circumstances and nature of war in general. Therefore, besides the general laws of war, it has specific laws of its own.

Unless you understand its specific circumstances and nature, unless you understand its specific laws, you will not be able to direct a revolutionary war and wage it successfully.

China's revolutionary war, whether civil war or national war, is waged in the specific environment of China and so has its own specific circumstances and nature distinguishing it both from war in general and from revolutionary war in general. Therefore, besides the laws of war in general and of revolutionary war in general, it has specific laws of its own. Unless you understand them, you will not be able to win in China's revolutionary war.

Therefore, we must study the laws of war in general, we must also study the laws of revolutionary war, and, finally, we must study the laws of China's revolutionary war. . . .

. . . the different laws for directing different wars are determined by the different circumstances of those wars—differences in their time, place, and nature. As regards the time factor, both war and its laws develop; each historical stage has its special characteristics, and hence the laws of war in each historical stage have their special characteristics and cannot be mechanically applied in another stage. As for the nature of war, since revolutionary war and counterrevolutionary war both have their special characteristics, the laws governing them also have their own characteristics, and those applying to one cannot be mechanically transferred to the other. As for the factor of place, since each country or nation, especially a large country or nation, has its own characteristics, the laws of war for each country or nation also have their own characteristics, and here, too, those applying to one cannot be mechanically transferred to the other. In studying the laws for directing wars that occur at different historical stages, that differ in nature and that are waged in different places and by different nations, we must fix our attention on the characteristics and development of each, and must oppose a mechanical approach to the problem of war. . . .

The Important Thing Is to Be Good at Learning

Why have we organized the Red Army? For the purpose of defeating the enemy. Why do we study the laws of war? For the purpose of applying them in war.

To learn is no easy matter and to apply what one has learned is even harder. Many people appear impressive when discoursing on military science in classrooms or in books, but when it comes to actual fighting, some win battles and others lose them. Both the history of war and our own experience in war have proved this point. Where then does the crux lie?

In real life, we cannot ask for "ever victorious generals," who are few and far between in history. What we can ask for is generals who are brave and sagacious and who normally win their battles in the course of a war, generals who combine wisdom with courage. To become both wise and courageous one must acquire a method, a method to be employed in learning as well as in applying what has been learned.

What method? The method is to familiarize ourselves with all aspects of the enemy situation and our own, to discover the laws governing the actions of both sides, and to make use of these laws in our own operations.

The military manuals issued in many countries point both to the necessity of a "flexible application of principles according to circumstances" and to the measures to be taken in case of defeat. They point to the former in order to warn a commander against subjectively committing mistakes through too rigid an application of principles, and to the latter in order to enable him to cope with the situation after he has committed subjective mistakes or after unexpected and irresistible changes have occurred in the objective circumstances.

Why are subjective mistakes made? Because the way the forces in a war or a battle are disposed or directed does not fit the conditions of the given time and place, because subjective direction does not correspond to, or is at variance with, the objective conditions, in other words, because the contradiction between the subjective and the objective has not been resolved. People can hardly avoid such situations whatever they are doing, but some people prove themselves more competent than others. As in any job we demand a comparatively high degree of competence, so in war we demand more victories or, conversely, fewer defeats. Here the crux is to bring the subjective and the objective into proper correspondence with each other.

Take an example in tactics. If the point chosen for attack is on one of the enemy's flanks and is located precisely where his weak spot happens to be, and in consequence the assault succeeds, then the subjective corresponds with the objective, that is, the commander's reconnaissance, judgment, and decision have corresponded with the enemy's actual situation and dispositions. If the point chosen for attack is on another flank or in the center and the attack hits a snag and makes no headway, then such correspondence is lacking. If the attack is properly timed, if the reserves are used neither too late nor too early, and if all the other dispositions and operations in the battle are such as to favor us and not the enemy, then the subjective direction throughout the battle completely corresponds with the objective situation. Such complete correspondence is extremely rare in a war or a battle, in which the belligerents are groups of live human beings bearing arms and keeping their secrets from each other; this is quite unlike handling inanimate objects or routine matters. But if the direction given by the commander corresponds in the main with the actual situation, that is, if the decisive elements in the direction correspond with the actual situation, then there is a basis for victory.

A commander's correct dispositions stem from his correct decisions, his correct decisions stem from his correct judgments, and his correct judgments stem from a thorough and necessary reconnaissance and from pondering on and piecing together the data of various kinds gathered through reconnaissance. He applies all possible and necessary methods of reconnaissance, and ponders on the information gathered about the enemy's situation, discarding the dross and selecting the essential, eliminating the false and retaining the true, proceeding from the one to the other and from the outside to the inside; then, he takes the conditions on his own side into account, and makes a study of both sides and their interrelations, thereby forming his judgments, making up his mind, and working out his plans. Such is the complete process of knowing a situation which a military man goes through before he formulates a strategic plan, a campaign plan, or a battle plan. But instead of doing this, a careless military man bases his military plans on his own wishful thinking, and hence his plans are fanciful and do not correspond with reality. A rash military man relying solely upon enthusiasm is bound to be tricked by the enemy, or lured on by some superficial or partial aspect of the enemy's situation, or swayed by irresponsible suggestions from subordinates that are not based on real knowledge or deep insight, and so he runs his head against a brick wall, because he does not know or does not want to know that every military plan must be based on the necessary reconnaissance and on careful consideration of the enemy's situation, his own situation, and their interrelations.

The process of knowing a situation goes on not only before the formulation of a military plan but also after. In carrying out the plan from the moment it is put into effect to the end of the operation, there is another process of knowing the situation, namely, the process of practice. In the course of this process, it is necessary to examine anew whether the plan worked out in the preceding process corresponds with reality. If it does not correspond with reality, or if it does not fully do so, then in the light of our new knowledge, it becomes necessary to form new judgments, make new decisions, and change the original plan so as to meet the new situation. The plan is partially changed in almost every operation, and sometimes it is even changed completely. A rash man who does not understand the need for such alterations or is unwilling to make them, but who acts blindly, will inevitably run his head against a brick wall.

The above applies to a strategic action, a campaign, or a battle. Provided he is modest and willing to learn, an experienced military man will be able to familiarize himself with the character of his own forces (commanders, men, arms, supplies, etc., and their sum total), with the character of the enemy forces (likewise, commanders, men, arms, supplies, etc., and their sum total), and with all other conditions related to the war, such as politics, economics, geography, and weather; such a military man will have a better grasp in directing a war or an operation and will be more likely to win victories. He will achieve this because, over a long period of time, he has come to know the situation on the enemy side and his own, discovered the laws of action, and resolved the contradictions between the subjective and the objective. This process of knowing is extremely important; without such a long period of experience, it would be difficult to understand and grasp the laws of an entire war. Neither a beginner nor a person who fights only on paper can become a really able high-ranking commander; only one who has learned through actual fighting in war can do so.

All military laws and military theories which are in the nature of principles are the experience of past wars summed up by people in former days or in our own times. We should seriously study these lessons, paid for in blood, which are a heritage of past wars. That is one point. But there is another. We should put these conclusions to the test of our own experience, assimilating what is useful, rejecting what is useless, and adding what is specifically our own. The latter is very important, for otherwise we cannot direct a war.

Reading is learning, but applying is also learning and the more important kind of learning at that. Our chief method is to learn warfare through warfare. A person who has had no opportunity to go to school can also learn warfare—he can learn through fighting in war. A revolutionary war is a mass undertaking; it is often not a matter of first learning and then doing, but of doing and then learning, for doing is itself learning. There is a gap between the ordinary civilian and the soldier, but it is no Great Wall, and it can be quickly closed, and the way to close it is to take part in revolution, in war. By saying that it is not easy to learn and to apply, we mean that it is hard to learn thoroughly and to apply skillfully. By saying that civilians can very quickly become soldiers, we mean that it is not difficult to cross the threshold. To put the two statements together, we may cite the Chinese adage "Nothing in the world is difficult for one who sets his mind to it." To cross the threshold is not difficult, and mastery, too, is possible provided one sets one's mind to the task and is good at learning.

The laws of war, like the laws governing all other things, are reflections in our minds of objective realities; everything outside of the mind is objective reality. Consequently what has to be learned and known includes the state of affairs on the enemy side and that on our side, both of which should be regarded as the object of study, while the mind (the capacity to think) alone is the subject performing the study. Some people are good at knowing themselves and poor at knowing their enemy, and some are the other way round; neither can solve the problem of learning and applying the laws of war. There is a saying in the book of Sun Wu Tzu, the great military scientist of ancient China, "Know the enemy and know yourself, and you can fight a hundred battles with no danger of defeat," which refers both to the stage of learning and to the stage of application, both to knowing the laws of the development of objective reality and to deciding on our own action in accordance with these laws in order to overcome the enemy facing us. We should not take this saying lightly.

War is the highest form of struggle between nations, states, classes, or political groups, and all the laws of war are applied by warring nations, states, classes, or political groups for the purpose of achieving victory for themselves. Unquestionably, victory or defeat in war is determined mainly by the military, political, economic, and natural conditions on both sides. But not by these alone. It is also determined by each side's subjective ability in directing the war. In his endeavor to win a war, a military man cannot overstep the limitations imposed by the material conditions; within these limitations, however, he can and must strive for victory. The stage of action for a military man is built upon objective material conditions, but on that stage he can direct the performance of many a drama, full of sound and color, power and grandeur. Therefore, given the objective material foundations, i.e., the military, political, economic, and natural conditions, our Red Army commanders must display their prowess and marshal all their forces to crush the national and class enemies and to transform this evil world. Here is where our subjective ability in directing war can and must be exercised. We do not permit any of our Red Army commanders to become a blundering hothead; we decidedly want every Red Army commander to become a hero who is both brave and sagacious, who possesses both all-conquering courage and the ability to remain master of the situation throughout the changes and vicissitudes of the entire war. Swimming in the ocean of war, he not only must not flounder but must make sure of reaching the opposite shore with measured strokes. The laws for directing war constitute the art of swimming in the ocean of war.

So much for our methods.

What Are the Characteristics of China's Revolutionary War?

What then are the characteristics of China's revolutionary war? I think there are four principal ones.

The first is that China is a vast, semicolonial country which is unevenly developed politically and economically and which has gone through the revolution of 1924–27. . . .

China's political and economic development is uneven—a weak capitalist economy coexists with a preponderant semifeudal economy; a few modern industrial and commercial cities coexist with a vast stagnant countryside; several million industrial workers coexist with several hundred millions of peasants and handicraftsmen laboring under the old system; big warlords controlling the central government coexist with small warlords controlling the provinces; two kinds of reactionary armies, the so-called Central Army under Chiang Kai-shek and "miscellaneous troops" under the warlords in the provinces, exist side by side; a few railways, steamship lines, and motor roads exist side by side with a vast number of wheelbarrow paths and footpaths, many of which are difficult to negotiate even on foot.

China is a semicolonial country—disunity among the imperialist powers makes for disunity among the ruling groups in China. There is a difference between a semicolonial country controlled by several countries and a colony controlled by a single country.

China is a vast country—"When it is dark in the east, it is light in the west; when things are dark in the south, there is still light in the north." Hence one need not worry about lack of room for maneuver.

China has gone through a great revolution—this has provided the seeds from which the Red Army has grown, provided the leader of the Red Army, namely, the Chinese Communist Party, and provided the masses with experience of participation in a revolution.

We say, therefore, that the first characteristic of China's revolutionary war is that it is waged in a vast semicolonial country which is unevenly developed politically and economically and which has gone through a revolution. This characteristic basically determines our military strategy and tactics as well as our political strategy and tactics.

The second characteristic is that our enemy is big and powerful.

How do matters stand with the Kuomintang, the enemy of the Red Army? It is a party that has seized political power and has more or less stabilized its power. It has gained the support of the world's principal counterrevolutionary states. It has remodeled its army, which has thus become different from any other army in Chinese history and on the whole similar to the armies of modern states; this army is much better supplied with weapons and matériel than the Red Army, and is larger than any army in Chinese history, or for that matter than the standing army of any other country. There is a world of difference between the Kuomintang army and the Red Army. The Kuomintang controls the key positions or life lines in the politics, economy, communications, and culture of China; its political power is nationwide.

The Chinese Red Army is thus confronted with a big and powerful enemy. This is the second characteristic of China's revolutionary war. It necessarily makes the military operations of the Red Army different in many ways from those of wars in general and from those of the civil war in the Soviet Union or of the Northern Expedition.

The third characteristic is that the Red Army is small and weak.

The Chinese Red Army, starting as guerrilla units, came into being after the defeat of the first great revolution. This occurred in a period of relative political and economic stability in the reactionary capitalist countries of the world as well as in a period of reaction in China.

Our political power exists in scattered and isolated mountainous or remote regions and receives no outside help whatsoever. Economic and cultural conditions in the revolutionary base areas are backward compared with those in the Kuomintang areas. The revolutionary base areas embrace only rural districts and small towns. These areas were extremely small in the beginning and have not grown much larger since. Moreover, they are fluid and not stationary, and the Red Army has no really consolidated bases.

The Red Army is numerically small, its arms are poor, and it has great difficulty in obtaining supplies such as food, bedding, and clothing.

This characteristic presents a sharp contrast to the preceding one. From this sharp contrast have arisen the strategy and tactics of the Red Army.

The fourth characteristic is Communist Party leadership and the Agrarian Revolution.

This characteristic is the inevitable consequence of the first one. It has given rise to two features. On the one hand, despite the fact that China's revolutionary war is taking place in a period of reaction in China and throughout the capitalist world, victory is possible because it is under the leadership of the Communist Party and has the support of the peasantry. Thanks to this support, our base areas, small as they are, are politically very powerful and stand firmly opposed to the enormous Kuomintang regime, while militarily they place great difficulties in the way of the Kuomintang attacks. Small as it is, the Red Army has great fighting capacity, because its members, led by the Communist Party, are born of the Agrarian Revolution and are fighting for their own interests, and because its commanders and fighters are politically united.

The Kuomintang, on the other hand, presents a sharp contrast. It opposes the Agrarian Revolution and therefore has no support from the peasantry. Though it has a large army, the Kuomintang cannot make its soldiers and the many lower-ranking officers, who were originally small producers, risk their lives willingly for it. Its officers and men are politically divided, which reduces its fighting capacity.

Our Strategy and Tactics Ensuing from These Characteristics

Thus the four principal characteristics of China's revolutionary war are: a vast semicolonial country which is unevenly developed politically and economically and which has gone through a great revolution; a big and powerful enemy; a small and weak Red Army; and the Agrarian Revolution. These characteristics determine the line for guiding China's revolutionary war as well as many of its strategic and tactical principles. It follows from the first and fourth characteristics that it is possible for the Chinese Red Army to grow and defeat its enemy. It follows from the second and third characteristics that it is impossible for the Chinese Red Army to grow very rapidly or defeat its enemy quickly; in other words, the war will be protracted and may even be lost if it is mishandled.

These are the two aspects of China's revolutionary war. They exist simultaneously, that is, there are favorable factors and there are difficulties. This is the fundamental law of China's revolutionary war, from which many other laws ensue. The history of our ten years of war has proved the validity of this law. He who has eyes but fails to see this fundamental law cannot direct China's revolutionary war, cannot lead the Red Army to victories.

It is clear that we must correctly settle all the following matters of principle:

Determine our strategic orientation correctly, oppose adventurism when on the offensive, oppose conservatism when on the defensive, and oppose flightism when shifting from one place to another.

Oppose guerrilla-ism in the Red Army, while recognizing the guerrilla character of its operations.

Oppose protracted campaigns and a strategy of quick decision, and uphold the strategy of protracted war and campaigns of quick decision.

Oppose fixed battle lines and positional warfare, and favor fluid battle lines and mobile warfare.

Oppose fighting merely to rout the enemy, and uphold fighting to annihilate the enemy.

Oppose the strategy of striking with two "fists" in two directions at the same time [i.e., dispersing one's forces], and uphold the strategy of striking with one "fist" in one direction at one time.

Oppose the principle of maintaining one large rear area, and uphold the principle of small rear areas.

Oppose an absolutely centralized command, and favor a relatively centralized command.

Oppose the purely military viewpoint and the ways of roving rebels, and recognize that the Red Army is a propagandist and organizer of the Chinese revolution.

Oppose bandit ways, and uphold strict political discipline.

Oppose warlord ways, and favor both democracy within proper limits and an authoritative discipline in the army.

Oppose an incorrect, sectarian policy on cadres, and uphold the correct policy on cadres.

Oppose the policy of isolation, and affirm the policy of winning over all possible allies.

Oppose keeping the Red Army at its old stage, and strive to develop it to a new stage.

STRATEGY IN PROTRACTED WAR

Stages of Protracted War

From: "On Protracted War" (May 1938), *Selected Works,* II (Peking: Foreign Languages Press, 1965), pp. 121–24, 136–41, 143.

. . . Why is the War of Resistance Against Japan a protracted war? Why will the final victory be China's? What is the basis for these statements?

The war between China and Japan is not just any war, it is specifically a war of life and death between semicolonial and semifeudal China and imperialist Japan, fought in the 1930s. Herein lies the basis of the whole problem. The two sides in the war have many contrasting features, which will be considered in turn below.

. . . THE JAPANESE SIDE. First, Japan is a powerful imperialist country, which ranks first in the East in military, economic, and political-organizational power, and is one of the five or six foremost imperialist countries of the world. These are the basic factors in Japan's war of aggression. The inevitability of the war and the impossibility of quick victory for China are due to Japan's imperialist system and her great military, economic, and political-organizational power. Secondly, however, the imperialist character of Japan's social economy determines the imperialist character of her war, a war that is retrogressive and barbarous. In the 1930s, the internal and external contradictions of Japanese imperialism have driven her not only to embark on an adventurist war unparalleled in scale but also to approach her final collapse. In terms of social development, Japan is no longer a thriving country; the war will not lead to the pros-

perity sought by her ruling classes but to the very reverse, the doom
of Japanese imperialism. This is what we mean by the retrogressive
nature of Japan's war. It is this reactionary quality, coupled with
the military-feudal character of Japanese imperialism, that gives rise
to the peculiar barbarity of Japan's war. All of which will arouse to
the utmost the class antagonisms within Japan, the antagonism between the Japanese and the Chinese nations, and the antagonism
between Japan and most other countries of the world. The reactionary and barbarous character of Japan's war constitutes the primary
reason for her inevitable defeat. Thirdly, Japan's war is conducted
on the basis of her great military, economic, and political-
organizational power, but at the same time it rests on an inadequate
natural endowment. Japan's military, economic, and political-
organizational power is great but quantitatively inadequate. Japan is
a comparatively small country, deficient in manpower and in military,
financial, and material resources, and she cannot stand a long war.
Japan's rulers are endeavoring to resolve this difficulty through
war, but again they will get the very reverse of what they desire;
that is to say, the war they have launched to resolve this difficulty
will eventually aggravate it and even exhaust Japan's original resources. Fourthly and lastly, while Japan can get international support from the fascist countries, the international opposition she is
bound to encounter will be greater than her international support.
This opposition will gradually grow and eventually not only can-
cel out the support but even bear down upon Japan herself. Such is
the law that an unjust cause finds meager support, and such is the
consequence of the very nature of Japan's war. To sum up, Japan's
advantage lies in her great capacity to wage war, and her disadvantages lie in the reactionary and barbarous nature of her war, in the
inadequacy of her manpower and material resources, and in her
meager international support. These are the characteristics on the
Japanese side.

. . . THE CHINESE SIDE. First, we are a semicolonial and semifeudal country. The Opium War, the Taiping Revolution, the reform movement of 1898, the revolution of 1911, and the Northern
Expedition—the revolutionary or reform movements which aimed at
extricating China from her semicolonial and semifeudal state—all
met with serious setbacks, and China remains a semicolonial and
semifeudal country. We are still a weak country and manifestly inferior to the enemy in military, economic, and political-organizational
power. Here again one can find the basis for the inevitability of the

war and the impossibility of quick victory for China. Secondly, however, China's liberation movement, with its cumulative development over the last hundred years, is now different from that of any previous period. Although the domestic and foreign forces opposing it have caused it serious setbacks, at the same time they have tempered the Chinese people. Although China today is not so strong as Japan militarily, economically, politically, and culturally, yet there are factors in China more progressive than in any other period of her history. The Communist Party of China and the army under its leadership represent these progressive factors. It is on the basis of this progress that China's present war of liberation can be protracted and can achieve final victory. By contrast with Japanese imperialism, which is declining, China is a country rising like the morning sun. China's war is progressive, hence its just character. Because it is a just war, it is capable of arousing the nation to unity, of evoking the sympathy of the people in Japan, and of winning the support of most countries in the world. Thirdly, and again by contrast with Japan, China is a very big country with vast territory, rich resources, a large population, and plenty of soldiers, and is capable of sustaining a long war. Fourthly and lastly, there is broad international support for China stemming from the progressive and just character of her war, which is again exactly the reverse of the meager support for Japan's unjust cause. To sum up, China's disadvantage lies in her military weakness, and her advantages lie in the progressive and just character of her war, her great size, and her abundant international support. These are China's characteristics.

. . . Thus it can be seen that Japan has great military, economic, and political-organizational power, but that her war is reactionary and barbarous, her manpower and material resources are inadequate, and she is in an unfavorable position internationally. China, on the contrary, has less military, economic, and political-organizational power, but she is in her era of progress, her war is progressive and just, she is moreover a big country, a factor which enables her to sustain a protracted war, and she will be supported by most countries. The above are the basic, mutually contradictory characteristics of the Sino-Japanese war. They have determined and are determining all the political policies and military strategies and tactics of the two sides; they have determined and are determining the protracted character of the war and its outcome, namely, that the final victory will go to China and not to Japan. The war is a contest between these characteristics. They will change in the course of the war, each according to its own nature; and from this everything else will follow. These characteristics exist objectively and are not invented to deceive people; they constitute all the basic elements of the war, and are not incomplete fragments; they permeate all major and minor problems on both sides and all stages of the war, and they are not matters of no consequence. If anyone forgets these characteristics in studying the Sino-Japanese war, he will surely go wrong; and even though some of his ideas win credence for a time and may seem right, they will inevitably be proved wrong by the course of the war. . . .

. . . Since the Sino-Japanese war is a protracted one and final victory will belong to China, it can reasonably be assumed that this protracted war will pass through three stages. The first stage covers the period of the enemy's strategic offensive and our strategic defensive. The second stage will be the period of the enemy's strategic consolidation and our preparation for the counteroffensive. The third stage will be the period of our strategic counteroffensive and the enemy's strategic retreat. It is impossible to predict the concrete situation in the three stages, but certain main trends in the war may be pointed out in the light of present conditions. The objective course of events will be exceedingly rich and varied, with many twists and turns, and nobody can cast a horoscope for the Sino-Japanese war; nevertheless it is necessary for the strategic direction of the war to make a rough sketch of its trends. Although our sketch may not be in full accord with the subsequent facts and will be amended by them, it is still necessary to make it in order to give firm and purposeful strategic direction to the protracted war.

. . . The first stage has not yet ended. The enemy's design is to occupy Canton, Wuhan, and Lanchow and link up these three points. To accomplish this aim the enemy will have to use at least fifty divisions, or about one and a half million men, spend from one and a half to two years, and expend more than ten thousand million yen. In penetrating so deeply, he will encounter immense difficulties, with consequences disastrous beyond imagination. As for attempting to occupy the entire length of the Canton-Hankow Railway and the Sian-Lanchow Highway, he will have to fight perilous battles and even so may not fully accomplish his design. But in drawing up our operational plan we should base ourselves on the assumption that the enemy may occupy the three points and even certain additional areas, as well as link them up, and we should make dispositions for a protracted war, so that even if he does so, we shall be able to cope with him. In this stage the form of fighting we should adopt is primarily mobile warfare, supplemented by guerrilla and positional warfare [see below]. Through the subjective errors of the Kuomintang military authorities, positional warfare was assigned the primary role in the first phase of this stage, but it is nevertheless supplementary from the point of view of the stage as a whole. In this stage, China has already built up a broad united front and achieved unprecedented unity. Although the enemy has used and will continue to use base and shameless means to induce China to capitulate in the attempt to realize his plan for a quick decision and to conquer the whole country without much effort, he has failed so far, nor is he likely to succeed in the future. In this stage, in spite of considerable losses, China will make considerable progress, which will become the main basis for her continued resistance in the second stage. In the present stage the Soviet Union has already given substantial aid to China. On the enemy side, there are already signs of flagging morale, and his army's momentum of attack is less in the middle phase of this stage than it was in the initial phase, and it will diminish still further in the concluding phase. Signs of exhaustion are beginning to appear in his finances and economy; war-weariness is beginning to set in among his people and troops; and within the clique at the helm of the war, "war frustrations" are beginning to manifest themselves and pessimism about the prospects of the war is growing.

. . . The second stage may be termed one of strategic stalemate. At the tail end of the first stage, the enemy will be forced to fix certain terminal points to his strategic offensive owing to his shortage of troops and our firm resistance, and upon reaching them he will stop his strategic offensive and enter the stage of safeguarding his occupied areas. In the second stage, the enemy will attempt to safeguard the occupied areas and to make them his own by the fraudulent method of setting up puppet governments, while plundering the Chinese people to the limit; but again he will be confronted with stubborn guerrilla warfare. Taking advantage of the fact that the enemy's rear is unguarded, our guerrilla warfare will develop extensively in the first stage, and many base areas will be established, seriously threatening the enemy's consolidation of the occupied areas, and so in the second stage there will still be widespread fighting. In this stage, our form of fighting will be primarily guerrilla warfare, supplemented by mobile warfare. China will still retain a large regular army, but she will find it difficult to launch the strategic counteroffensive immediately because, on the one hand, the enemy will adopt a strategically defensive position in the big cities and along the main lines of communication under his occupation and, on the other hand, China will not yet be adequately equipped technically. Except for the troops engaged in frontal defense against the enemy, our forces will be switched in large numbers to the enemy's rear in comparatively dispersed dispositions, and, basing themselves on all the areas not actually occupied by the enemy and coordinating with the people's local armed forces, they will launch extensive, fierce guerrilla warfare against enemy-occupied areas, keeping the enemy on the move as far as possible in order to destroy him in mobile warfare, as is now being done in Shansi province. The fighting in the second stage will be ruthless, and the country will suffer serious devastation. But the guerrilla warfare will be successful, and if it is well conducted the enemy may be able to retain only about one third of his occupied territory, with the remaining two thirds in our hands, and this will constitute a great defeat for the enemy and a great victory for China. By then the enemy-occupied territory as a whole will fall into three categories: first, the enemy base areas; second, our base areas for guerrilla warfare; and third, the guerrilla areas contested by both sides. The duration of this stage will depend on the degree of change in the balance of forces between us and the enemy and on the changes in the international situation; generally speaking, we should be prepared to see this stage last a comparatively long time and to weather its hardships. It will be a very painful period for China; the two big problems will be economic difficulties and the disruptive activities of the traitors. The enemy will go all out to wreck China's united front, and the traitor organizations in all the occupied areas will merge into a so-called "unified government." Owing to the loss of big cities and the hardships of war, vacillating elements within our ranks will clamor for compromise, and pessimism will grow to a serious extent. Our tasks will then be to mobilize the whole people to unite as one man and carry on the war with unflinching perseverance, to broaden and consolidate the united front, sweep away all pessimism and ideas of compromise, promote the will to hard struggle, and apply new wartime policies, and so to weather the hardships. In the second stage, we will have to call upon the whole country resolutely to maintain a united government, we will have to oppose splits and systematically improve fighting techniques, reform the armed forces, mobilize the entire people, and prepare for the counteroffensive. The international situation will become still more unfavorable to Japan and the main international forces will incline toward giving more help to China. . . . Japan's threat to Southeast Asia and Siberia will become greater, and there may even be another war. As regards Japan, scores of her divisions will be inextricably bogged down in China. Widespread guerrilla warfare and the people's anti-Japanese movement will wear down this big Japanese force, greatly reducing it and also disintegrating its morale by stimulating the growth of homesickness, war-weariness and even anti-war sentiment. Though it would be wrong to say that Japan will achieve no results at all in her plunder of China, yet, being short of capital and harassed by guerrilla warfare, she cannot possibly achieve rapid or substantial results. This second stage will be the transitional stage of the entire war; it will be the most trying period but also the pivotal one. Whether China becomes an independent country or is reduced to a colony will be determined not by the retention or loss of the big cities in the first stage but by the extent to which the whole nation exerts itself in the second. If we can persevere in the War of Resistance, in the united front, and in the protracted war, China will in that stage gain the power to change from weakness to strength. It will be the second act in the three-act drama of China's War of Resistance. And through the efforts of the entire cast it will become possible to perform a most brilliant last act.

. . . The third stage will be the stage of the counteroffensive to recover our lost territories. Their recovery will depend mainly upon the strength which China has built up in the preceding stage and which will continue to grow in the third stage. But China's strength alone will not be sufficient, and we shall also have to rely on the support of international forces and on the changes that will take place inside Japan, or otherwise we shall not be able to win; this adds to China's tasks in international propaganda and diplomacy. In the third stage, our war will no longer be one of strategic defensive, but will turn into a strategic counteroffensive manifesting itself in strategic offensives; and it will no longer be fought on strategically interior lines, but will shift gradually to strategically exterior lines [see below]. Not until we fight our way to the Yalu River can this war be considered over. The third stage will be the last in the protracted war, and when we talk of persevering in the war to the end, we mean going all the way through this stage. Our primary form of fighting will still be mobile warfare, but positional warfare will rise to importance. While positional defense cannot be regarded as important in the first stage because of the prevailing circumstances, positional attack will become quite important in the third stage because of the changed conditions and the requirements of the task. In the third stage guerrilla warfare will again provide strategic support by supplementing mobile and positional warfare, but it will not be the primary form as in the second stage.

. . . It is thus obvious that the war is protracted and consequently ruthless in nature. The enemy will not be able to gobble up the whole of China but will be able to occupy many places for a considerable time. China will not be able to oust the Japanese quickly, but the greater part of her territory will remain in her hands. Ultimately the enemy will lose and we will win, but we shall have a hard stretch of road to travel.

. . . The Chinese people will become tempered in the course of this long and ruthless war. The political parties taking part in the war will also be steeled and tested. The united front must be persevered in; only by persevering in the united front can we persevere in the war; and only by persevering in the united front and in the war can we win final victory. Only thus can all difficulties be overcome. After traveling the hard stretch of road we shall reach the highway to victory. This is the natural logic of the war. . . .

. . . China moving from inferiority to parity and then to superiority, Japan moving from superiority to parity and then to inferiority; China moving from the defensive to stalemate and then to the counteroffensive, Japan moving from the offensive to the safeguarding of her gains and then to retreat—such will be the course of the Sino-Japanese war and its inevitable trend.

. . . Hence the questions and the conclusions are as follows: Will China be subjugated? The answer is, No, she will not be subjugated, but will win final victory. Can China win quickly? The answer is, No, she cannot win quickly, and the war must be a protracted one. Are these conclusions correct? I think they are.

Strategic Retreat and Strategic Counteroffensive

From: "Problems of Strategy in China's Revolutionary War" (December 1936), *Selected Works,* I (Peking: Foreign Languages Press, 1964), pp. 215–18, 223–25.

The objective of strategic retreat is to conserve military strength and prepare for the counteroffensive. Retreat is necessary because not to retreat a step before the onset of a strong enemy inevitably means to jeopardize the preservation of one's own forces. In the past, however, many people were stubbornly opposed to retreat, considering it to be an "opportunist line of pure defense." Our history has proved that their opposition was entirely wrong.

To prepare for a counteroffensive, we must select or create conditions favorable to ourselves but unfavorable to the enemy, so as to bring about a change in the balance of forces, before we go on to the stage of the counteroffensive.

In the light of our past experience, during the stage of retreat we should in general secure at least two of the following conditions before we can consider the situation as being favorable to us and unfavorable to the enemy and before we can go over to the counteroffensive. These conditions are:

(1) The population actively supports the Red Army.
(2) The terrain is favorable for operations.
(3) All the main forces of the Red Army are concentrated.
(4) The enemy's weak spots have been discovered.
(5) The enemy has been reduced to a tired and demoralized state.
(6) The enemy has been induced to make mistakes.

The first condition, active support of the population, is the most important one for the Red Army. It means having a base area. Moreover, given this condition, it is easy to achieve conditions 4, 5, and 6. Therefore, when the enemy launches a full-scale offensive, the Red Army generally withdraws from the White area into the base area, because that is where the population is most active in supporting the Red Army against the White army. Also, there is a difference between the borders and the central district of a base area; in the latter the people are better at blocking the passage of information to the enemy, better at reconnaissance, transportation, joining in the fighting, and so on. Thus when we were combating the first, second, and third "encirclement and suppression" campaigns in Kiangsi, all the places selected as "terminal points for the retreat" were situated where the first condition, popular support, was excellent or quite good. This characteristic of our base areas made the Red Army's operations very different from ordinary operations and was the main reason why the enemy subsequently had to resort to the policy of blockhouse warfare.

One advantage of operating on interior lines is that it makes it possible for the retreating army to choose terrain favorable to itself and force the attacking army to fight on its terms. In order to defeat a strong army, a weak army must carefully choose favorable terrain as a battleground. But this condition alone is not enough and must be accompanied by others. The first of these is popular support. The next is a vulnerable enemy, for instance, an enemy who is tired or has made mistakes, or an advancing enemy column that is comparatively poor in fighting capacity. In the absence of these conditions, even if we have found excellent terrain, we have to disregard it and continue to retreat in order to secure them. In the White areas there is no lack of good terrain, but we do not have the favorable condition of active popular support. If other conditions are not yet fulfilled, the Red Army has no alternative but to retreat toward its base area. Distinctions such as those between the White areas and the Red areas also usually exist between the borders and the central district of a base area.

Except for local units and containing forces, all our assault troops should, on principle, be concentrated. When attacking an enemy who is on the defensive strategically, the Red Army usually disperses its own forces. Once the enemy launches a full-scale offensive, the Red Army effects a "retreat toward the center." The terminal point chosen for the retreat is usually in the central section of the base area, but sometimes it is in the frontal or rear sections, as circumstances require. By such a retreat toward the center all the main forces of the Red Army can be concentrated.

Another essential condition for a weak army fighting a strong one is to pick out the enemy's weaker units for attack. But at the beginning of the enemy's offensive we usually do not know which of his advancing columns is the strongest and which the second strongest, which is the weakest and which the second weakest, and so a process of reconnaissance is required. This often takes a considerable time. That is another reason why strategic retreat is necessary.

If the attacking enemy is far more numerous and much stronger than we are, we can accomplish a change in the balance of forces only when the enemy has penetrated deeply into our base area and tasted all the bitterness it holds for him. As the chief of staff of one of Chiang Kai-shek's brigades remarked during the third "encirclement and suppression" campaign, "Our stout men have worn themselves thin and our thin men have worn themselves to death." Or, in the words of Chen Ming-shu, Commander in Chief of the Western Route of the Kuomintang's "Encirclement and Suppression" Army, "Everywhere the National Army gropes in the dark, while the Red Army walks in broad daylight." By then the enemy army, although still strong, is much weakened, its soldiers are tired, its morale is sagging, and many of its weak spots are revealed. But the Red Army, though weak, has conserved its strength and stored up its energy, and is waiting at its ease for the fatigued enemy. At such a time it is generally possible to attain a certain parity between the two sides, or to change the enemy's absolute superiority to relative superiority and our absolute inferiority to relative inferiority, and occasionally even to become superior to the enemy. When fighting against the third "encirclement and suppression" campaign in Kiangsi, the Red Army executed a retreat to the extreme limit (to concentrate in the rear section of the base area); if it had not done so, it could not have defeated the enemy, because the enemy's "encirclement and suppression" forces were then over ten times the size of the Red Army. When Sun Wu Tzu said, "Avoid the enemy when he is full of vigor, strike when he is fatigued and withdraws," he was referring to tiring and demoralizing the enemy so as to reduce his superiority.

Finally, the object of retreat is to induce the enemy to make mistakes or to detect his mistakes. One must realize that an enemy commander, however wise, cannot avoid making some mistakes over a relatively long period of time, and hence it is always possible for us to exploit the openings he leaves us. The enemy is liable to make mistakes, just as we ourselves sometimes miscalculate and give him openings to exploit. In addition, we can induce the enemy to make mistakes by our own actions, for instance, by "counterfeiting an appearance," as Sun Wu Tzu called it, that is, by making a feint to the east but attacking in the west. If we are to do this, the terminal point for the retreat cannot be rigidly limited to a definite area. Sometimes when we have retreated to the predetermined area and not yet found openings to exploit, we have to retreat farther and wait for the enemy to give us an opening.

The favorable conditions which we seek by retreating are in general those stated above. But this does not mean that a counter-offensive cannot be launched until all these conditions are present. The presence of all of them at the same time is neither possible nor necessary. But a weak force operating on interior lines against a strong enemy should strive to secure such conditions as are necessary in the light of the enemy's actual situation. All views to the contrary are incorrect. . . .

To defeat the offensive of an enemy who enjoys absolute superiority we rely on the situation created during the stage of our strategic retreat, a situation which is favorable to ourselves, unfavorable to the enemy, and different from that at the beginning of his offensive. It takes many elements to make up such a situation. All this has been dealt with above.

However, the presence of these conditions and of a situation favorable to ourselves and unfavorable to the enemy does not mean that we have already defeated him. Such conditions and such a situation provide the possibility for our victory and his defeat, but do not constitute the reality of victory or defeat; they have not yet brought actual victory or defeat to either army. To bring about victory or defeat a decisive battle between the two armies is necessary. Only a decisive battle can settle the question as to which army is the victor and which the vanquished. This is the sole task in the stage of strategic counteroffensive. The counteroffensive is a long process, the most fascinating, the most dynamic, and also the final stage of a defensive campaign. What is called active defense refers chiefly to this strategic counteroffensive, which is in the nature of a decisive engagement.

Conditions and situations are created not only in the stage of the strategic retreat, but continue to be created in that of the counteroffensive. Whether in form or in nature, they are not exactly the same in the latter stage as in the former.

What might remain the same in form and in nature, for example, is the fact that the enemy troops will be even more fatigued and depleted, which is simply a continuation of their fatigue and depletion in the previous stage.

But wholly new conditions and a wholly new situation are bound to emerge. Thus, when the enemy has suffered one or more defeats, the conditions advantageous to us and disadvantageous to him will not be confined to his fatigue, etc., but a new factor will have been added, namely, that he has suffered defeats. New changes will take place in the situation, too. When the enemy begins to maneuver his troops in a disorderly way and to make false moves, the relative strengths of the two opposing armies will naturally no longer be the same as before.

But if it is not the enemy's forces but ours that have suffered one or more defeats, then both the conditions and the situation will change in the opposite direction. That is to say, the enemy's disadvantages will be reduced, while on our side disadvantages will emerge and even grow. That again will be something entirely new and different.

A defeat for either side will lead directly and speedily to a new effort by the defeated side to avert disaster, to extricate itself from the new conditions and the new situation unfavorable to it and favorable to the enemy and to re-create such conditions and such a situation as are favorable to it and unfavorable to its opponent, in order to bring pressure to bear on the latter.

The effort of the winning side will be exactly the opposite. It will strive to exploit its victory and inflict still greater damage on the enemy, add to the conditions that are in its favor and further improve its situation, and prevent the enemy from succeeding in extricating himself from his unfavorable conditions and unfavorable situation and averting disaster.

Thus, for either side, the struggle at the stage of the decisive battle is the most intense, the most complicated, and the most changeful as well as the most difficult and trying in the whole war or the whole campaign; it is the most exacting time of all from the point of view of command.

In the stage of counteroffensive, there are many problems, the chief of which are the starting of the counteroffensive, the concentration of troops, mobile warfare, war of quick decision, and war of annihilation.

Whether in a counteroffensive or in an offensive, the principles with regard to these problems do not differ in their basic character. In this sense we may say that a counteroffensive is an offensive.

Still, it is not exactly an offensive. The principles of the counteroffensive are applied when the enemy is on the offensive. The principles of the offensive are applied when the enemy is on the defensive. In this sense, there are certain differences between a counteroffensive and an offensive.

Principles of Operation Summarized

From: "The Present Situation and Our Tasks" (December 1947), *Selected Works,* IV (Peking: Foreign Languages Press, 1961), pp. 161–62.

. . . Our principles of operation are:

1. Attack dispersed, isolated enemy forces first; attack concentrated, strong enemy forces later.

2. Take small and medium cities and extensive rural areas first; take big cities later.

3. Make wiping out the enemy's effective strength our main objective; do not make holding or seizing a city or place our main ob-

jective. Holding or seizing a city or place is the outcome of wiping out the enemy's effective strength, and often a city or place can be held or seized for good only after it has changed hands a number of times.

4. In every battle, concentrate an absolutely superior force (two, three, four, and sometimes even five or six times the enemy's strength), encircle the enemy forces completely, strive to wipe them out thoroughly, and do not let any escape from the net. In special circumstances, use the method of dealing crushing blows to the enemy, that is, concentrate all our strength to make a frontal attack and also to attack one or both of his flanks, with the aim of wiping out one part and routing another so that our army can swiftly move its troops to smash other enemy forces. Strive to avoid battles of attrition in which we lose more than we gain or only break even. In this way, although we are inferior as a whole (in terms of numbers), we are absolutely superior in every part and every specific campaign, and this ensures victory in the campaign. As times goes on, we shall become superior as a whole and eventually wipe out all the enemy.

5. Fight no battle unprepared, fight no battle you are not sure of winning; make every effort to be well prepared for each battle, make every effort to ensure victory in the given set of conditions as between the enemy and ourselves.

6. Give full play to our style of fighting—courage in battle, no fear of sacrifice, no fear of fatigue, and continuous fighting (that is, fighting successive battles in a short time without rest).

7. Strive to wipe out the enemy through mobile warfare. At the same time, pay attention to the tactics of positional attack and capture enemy fortified points and cities.

8. With regard to attacking cities, resolutely seize all enemy fortified points and cities which are weakly defended. Seize at opportune moments all enemy fortified points and cities defended with moderate strength, provided circumstances permit. As for strongly defended enemy fortified points and cities, wait till conditions are ripe and then take them.

9. Replenish our strength with all the arms and most of the personnel captured from the enemy. Our army's main sources of manpower and material are at the front.

10. Make good use of the intervals between campaigns to rest, train, and consolidate our troops. Periods of rest, training, and con-

solidation should in general not be very long, and the enemy should so far as possible be permitted no breathing space.

TYPES OF WARFARE

Positional, Mobile, and Guerrilla Warfare

From: "On Protracted War" (May 1938), *Selected Works,* II (Peking: Foreign Languages Press, 1965), pp. 119–20, 172–74.

. . . Our strategy should be to employ our main forces to operate over an extended and fluid front. To achieve success, the Chinese troops must conduct their warfare with a high degree of mobility on extensive battlefields, making swift advances and withdrawals, swift concentrations and dispersals. This means large-scale mobile warfare, and not positional warfare depending exclusively on defense works with deep trenches, high fortresses, and successive rows of defensive positions. It does not mean the abandonment of all the vital strategic points, which should be defended by positional warfare as long as profitable. But the pivotal strategy must be mobile warfare. Positional warfare is also necessary, but strategically it is auxiliary and secondary. Geographically the theater of the war is so vast that it is possible for us to conduct mobile warfare most effectively. In the face of the vigorous actions of our forces, the Japanese army will have to be cautious. Its war machine is ponderous and slow-moving, with limited efficiency. If we concentrate our forces on a narrow front for a defensive war of attrition, we would be throwing away the advantages of our geography and economic organization. . . . In the early periods of the war, we must avoid any major decisive battles, and must first employ mobile warfare gradually to break the morale and combat effectiveness of the enemy troops.

Besides employing trained armies to carry on mobile warfare, we must organize great numbers of guerrilla units among the peasants. One should know that the anti-Japanese volunteer units in the three northeastern provinces are only a minor demonstration of the latent power of resistance that can be mobilized from the peasants of the whole country. The Chinese peasants have very great latent power; properly organized and directed, they can keep the Japanese army busy twenty-four hours a day and worry it to death. It must be remembered that the war will be fought in China, that is to say, the

Japanese army will be entirely surrounded by the hostile Chinese people, it will be forced to move in all its provisions and guard them, it must use large numbers of troops to protect its lines of communications and constantly guard against attacks, and it needs large forces to garrison Manchuria and Japan as well.

In the course of the war, China will be able to capture many Japanese soldiers and seize many weapons and munitions with which to arm herself; at the same time China will win foreign aid to reinforce the equipment of her troops gradually. Therefore China will be able to conduct positional warfare in the latter period of the war and make positional attacks on the Japanese-occupied areas. Thus Japan's economy will crack under the strain of China's long resistance and the morale of the Japanese forces will break under the trial of innumerable battles. On the Chinese side, however, the growing latent power of resistance will be constantly brought into play and large numbers of revolutionary people will be pouring into the front lines to fight for their freedom. The combination of all these and other factors will enable us to make the final and decisive attacks on the fortifications and bases in the Japanese-occupied areas and drive the Japanese forces of aggression out of China. . . .

. . . Among the forms of warfare in the anti-Japanese war mobile warfare comes first and guerrilla warfare second. When we say that in the entire war mobile warfare is primary and guerrilla warfare supplementary, we mean that the outcome of the war depends mainly on regular warfare, especially in its mobile form, and that guerrilla warfare cannot shoulder the main responsibility in deciding the outcome. It does not follow, however, that the role of guerrilla warfare is unimportant in the strategy of the war. Its role in the strategy of the war as a whole is second only to that of mobile warfare, for without its support we cannot defeat the enemy. In saying this we also have in mind the strategic task of developing guerrilla warfare into mobile warfare. Guerrilla warfare will not remain the same throughout this long and cruel war, but will rise to a higher level and develop into mobile warfare. Thus the strategic role of guerrilla warfare is twofold, to support regular warfare and to transform itself into regular warfare. Considering the unprecedented extent and duration of guerrilla warfare in China's War of Resistance, it is all the more important not to underestimate its strategic role. Guerrilla warfare in China, therefore, has not only its tactical but also its peculiar strategic problems. . . . the forms of warfare in the three strategic stages of the War of Resistance are as follows.

In the first stage mobile warfare is primary, while guerrilla and positional warfare are supplementary. In the second stage guerrilla warfare will advance to the first place and will be supplemented by mobile and positional warfare. In the third stage mobile warfare will again become the primary form and will be supplemented by positional and guerrilla warfare. But the mobile warfare of the third stage will no longer be undertaken solely by the original regular forces; part, possibly quite an important part, will be undertaken by forces which were originally guerrillas but which will have progressed from guerrilla to mobile warfare. From the viewpoint of all three stages in China's War of Resistance Against Japan, guerrilla warfare is definitely indispensable. Our guerrilla war will present a great drama unparalleled in the annals of war. For this reason, out of the millions of China's regular troops, it is absolutely necessary to assign at least several hundred thousand to disperse through all enemy-occupied areas, arouse the masses to arm themselves, and wage guerrilla warfare in co-ordination with the masses. The regular forces so assigned should shoulder this sacred task conscientiously, and they should not think their status lowered because they fight fewer big battles and for the time being do not appear as national heroes. Any such thinking is wrong. Guerrilla warfare does not bring as quick results or as great renown as regular warfare, but "a long road tests a horse's strength and a long task proves a man's heart," and in the course of this long and cruel war guerrilla warfare will demonstrate its immense power; it is indeed no ordinary undertaking. Moreover, such regular forces can conduct guerrilla warfare when dispersed and mobile warfare when concentrated, as the Eighth Route Army has been doing. The principle of the Eighth Route Army is "Guerrilla warfare is basic, but lose no chance for mobile warfare under favorable conditions." This principle is perfectly correct; the views of its opponents are wrong.

. . . At China's present technical level, positional warfare, defensive or offensive, is generally impracticable, and this is where our weakness manifests itself. Moreover, the enemy is also exploiting the vastness of our territory to bypass our fortified positions. Hence positional warfare cannot be an important, still less the principal, means for us. But in the first and second stages of the war, it is possible and essential, within the scope of mobile warfare, to employ localized positional warfare in a supplementary role in campaigns. Semipositional "mobile defense" is a still more essential part of mobile warfare undertaken for the purpose of resisting the enemy at every step, thereby depleting his forces and gaining extra time. China must strive to increase her supplies of modern weapons so that she can fully carry out the tasks of positional attack in the stage of the strategic counteroffensive. In this third stage positional warfare will undoubtedly play a greater role, for then the enemy will be holding fast to his positions, and we shall not be able to recover our lost territory unless we launch powerful positional attacks in support of mobile warfare. Nevertheless, in the third stage too, we must exert our every effort to make mobile warfare the primary form of warfare. For the art of directing war and the active role of man are largely nullified in positional warfare such as that fought in Western Europe in the second half of World War I. It is only natural that the war should be taken "out of the trenches," since the war is being fought in the vast expanses of China and since our side will remain poorly equipped technically for quite a long time. Even during the third stage, when China's technical position will be better, she will hardly surpass her enemy in that respect, and so will have to concentrate on highly mobile warfare, without which she cannot achieve final victory. Hence, throughout the War of Resistance China will not adopt positional warfare as primary; the primary or important forms are mobile warfare and guerrilla warfare. These two forms of warfare will afford full play to the art of directing war and to the active role of man—what a piece of good fortune out of our misfortune!

Mobile Warfare

From: "Problems of Strategy in China's Revolutionary War" (December 1936), *Selected Works,* I (Peking: Foreign Languages Press, 1964), pp. 239–42.

Mobile warfare or positional warfare? Our answer is mobile warfare. So long as we lack a large army or reserves of ammunition, and so long as there is only a single Red Army force to do the fighting in each base area, positional warfare is generally useless to us. For us, positional warfare is generally inapplicable in attack as well as in defense.

One of the outstanding characteristics of the Red Army's operations, which follows from the fact that the enemy is powerful while the Red Army is deficient in technical equipment, is the absence of fixed battle lines.

The Red Army's battle lines are determined by the direction in which it is operating. As its operational direction often shifts, its battle lines are fluid. Though the main direction does not change in a given period of time, within its ambit the secondary directions may shift at any moment; when we find ourselves checked in one direction, we must turn to another. If, after a time, we also find ourselves checked in the main direction, then we must change it too.

In a revolutionary civil war, there cannot be fixed battle lines, which was also the case in the Soviet Union. The difference between the Soviet Army and ours is that its battle lines were not so fluid as ours. There cannot be absolutely fixed battle lines in any war, because the vicissitudes of victory and defeat, advance and retreat, preclude it. But relatively fixed battle lines are often to be found in the general run of wars. Exceptions occur only where an army faces a much stronger enemy, as is the case with the Chinese Red Army in its present stage.

Fluidity of battle lines leads to fluidity in the size of our base areas. Our base areas are constantly expanding and contracting, and often as one base area falls another rises. This fluidity of territory is entirely a result of the fluidity of the war.

Fluidity in the war and in our territory produces fluidity in all fields of construction in our base areas. Construction plans covering several years are out of the question. Frequent changes of plan are all in the day's work.

It is to our advantage to recognize this characteristic. We must base our planning on it and must not have illusions about a war of advance without any retreats, take alarm at any temporary fluidity of our territory or of the rear areas of our army, or endeavor to draw up detailed long-term plans. We must adapt our thinking and our work to the circumstances, be ready to sit down as well as to march on, and always have our marching rations handy. It is only by exerting ourselves in today's fluid way of life that tomorow we can secure relative stability, and eventually full stability.

The exponents of the strategy of "regular warfare" which dominated our fifth countercampaign denied this fluidity and opposed what they called "guerrilla-ism." Those comrades who opposed fluidity managed affairs as though they were the rulers of a big state, and the result was an extraordinary and immense fluidity—the 25,000-*li* Long March. . . .

"Fight when you can win, move away when you can't win"—this is the popular way of describing our mobile warfare today. There is no military expert anywhere in the world who approves only of fighting and never of moving, though few people do as much moving as we do. We generally spend more time in moving than in fighting and would be doing well if we fought an average of one sizable battle a month. All our "moving" is for the purpose of "fighting," and all our strategy and tactics are built on "fighting." Nevertheless, there are times when it is inadvisable for us to fight. In the first place, it is inadvisable to fight when the force confronting us is too large; second, it is sometimes inadvisable to fight when the force confronting us, though not so large, is very close to other enemy forces; third, it is generally inadvisable to fight an enemy force that is not isolated and is strongly entrenched; fourth, it is inadvisable to continue an engagement in which there is no prospect of victory. In any one of these situations we are prepared to move away. Such moving away is both permissible and necessary. For our recognition of the necessity of moving away is based on our recognition of the necessity of fighting. Herein lies the fundamental characteristic of the Red Army's mobile warfare.

Mobile warfare is primary, but we do not reject positional warfare where it is possible and necessary. It should be admitted that positional warfare should be employed for the tenacious defense of particular key points in a containing action during the strategic defensive, and when, during the strategic offensive, we encounter an enemy force that is isolated and cut off from help. We have had considerable experience in defeating the enemy by such positional warfare; we have cracked open many enemy cities, blockhouses, and forts and broken through fairly well-fortified enemy field positions. In future we shall increase our efforts and remedy our inadequacies in this respect. We should be all means advocate positional attack or defense when circumstances require and permit it. At the present time, what we are opposed to is the general use of positional warfare or putting it on an equal footing with mobile warfare; that is impermissible.

Guerrilla Warfare

From: "Problems of Strategy in Guerrilla War Against Japan" (May 1938), *Selected Works,* II (Peking: Foreign Languages Press, 1965), pp. 81–94, 102–11.

The Basic Principle of War Is to Preserve Oneself and Destroy the Enemy

Before discussing the question of strategy in guerrilla warfare in concrete terms, a few words are needed on the fundamental problem of war.

All the guiding principles of military operations grow out of the one basic principle: to strive to the utmost to preserve one's own strength and destroy that of the enemy. In a revolutionary war, this principle is directly linked with basic political principles. For instance, the basic political principle of China's War of Resistance Against Japan, i.e., its political aim, is to drive out Japanese imperialism and build an independent, free, and happy new China. In terms of military action this principle means the use of armed force to defend our motherland and to drive out the Japanese invaders. To attain this end, the operations of the armed units take the form of doing their utmost to preserve their own strength on the one hand and destroy the enemy's on the other. How then do we justify the encouragement of heroic sacrifice in war? Every war exacts a price, sometimes an extremely high one. Is this not in contradiction with "preserving oneself"? In fact, there is no contradiction at all; to put it more exactly, sacrifice and self-preservation are both opposite and complementary to each other. For such sacrifice is essential not only for destroying the enemy but also for preserving oneself—partial and temporary "non-preservation" (sacrifice, or paying the price) is necessary for the sake of general and permanent preservation. From this basic principle stems the series of principles guiding military operations, all of which—from the principles of shooting (taking cover to preserve oneself, and making full use of fire-power to destroy the enemy) to the principles of strategy—are permeated with the spirit of this basic principle. All technical, tactical, and strategic principles represent applications of this basic principle. The principle of preserving oneself and destroying the enemy is the basis of all military principles.

Six Specific Problems of Strategy in Guerrilla War Against Japan

Now let us see what policies or principles have to be adopted in guerrilla operations against Japan before we can attain the object of preserving ourselves and destroying the enemy. Since the guerrilla units in the War of Resistance (and in all other revolutionary wars) generally grow out of nothing and expand from a small to a large force, they must preserve themselves and, moreover, they must expand. Hence the question is, what policies or principles have to be adopted before we can attain the object of preserving and expanding ourselves and destroying the enemy?

Generally speaking, the main principles are as follows: (1) the use of initiative, flexibility, and planning in conducting offensives within the defensive, battles of quick decision within protracted war, and exterior-line operations within interior-line operations, (2) coordination with regular warfare, (3) establishment of base areas, (4) the strategic defensive and the strategic offensive, (5) the development of guerrilla warfare into mobile warfare, and (6) correct relationship of command. These six items constitute the whole of the strategic program for guerrilla war against Japan and are the means necessary for the preservation and expansion of our forces, for the destruction and expulsion of the enemy, for co-ordination with regular warfare and the winning of final victory.

Initiative, Flexibility, and Planning in Conducting Offensives Within the Defensive, Battles of Quick Decision Within Protracted War, and Exterior-line Operations Within Interior-line Operations

Here the subject may be dealt with under four headings: (1) the relationship between the defensive and the offensive, between protractedness and quick decision, and between the interior and exterior lines, (2) the initiative in all operations, (3) flexible employment of forces, and (4) planning in all operations.

To start with the first.

If we take the War of Resistance as a whole, the fact that Japan is a strong country and is attacking while China is a weak country and is defending herself makes our war strategically a defensive and protracted war. As far as the operational lines are concerned, the Japanese are operating on exterior and we on interior lines. This is one aspect of the situation. But there is another aspect which is just the reverse. The enemy forces, though strong (in arms, in certain qualities of their men, and certain other factors), are numerically small, whereas our forces, though weak (likewise, in arms, in certain qualities of our men, and certain other factors), are numerically very large. Added to the fact that the enemy is an alien nation invading our country while we are resisting his invasion on our own soil, this determines the following strategy. It is possible and necessary to use tactical offensives within the strategic defensive, to fight campaigns and battles of quick decision within a strategically protracted war and to fight campaigns and battles on exterior lines within strategically interior lines. Such is the strategy to be adopted in the War of Resistance as a whole. It holds true both for regular and for guerrilla warfare. Guerrilla warfare is different only in degree and form. Offensives in guerrilla warfare generally take the form of surprise attacks. Although surprise attacks can and should be employed in regular warfare too, the degree of surprise is less. In guerrilla warfare, the need to bring operations to a quick decision is very great, and our exterior-line ring of encirclement of the enemy in campaigns and battles is very small. All these distinguish it from regular warfare.

Thus it can be seen that in their operations guerrilla units have to concentrate the maximum forces, act secretly and swiftly, attack the enemy by surprise, and bring battles to a quick decision, and that they must strictly avoid passive defense, procrastination, and the dispersal of forces before engagements. Of course, guerrilla warfare includes not only the strategic but also the tactical defensive. The latter embraces, among other things, containing and outpost actions during battles; the disposition of forces for resistance at narrow passes, strategic points, rivers, or villages in order to deplete and exhaust the enemy; and action to cover withdrawal. But the basic principle of guerrilla warfare must be the offensive, and guerrilla warfare is more offensive in its character than regular warfare. The offensive, moreover, must take the form of surprise attacks, and to expose ourselves by ostentatiously parading our forces is even less permissible in guerrilla warfare than in regular warfare. From the fact that the enemy is strong and we are weak it necessarily follows that, in guerrilla operations in general even more than in regular warfare, battles must be decided quickly, though on some occasions guerrilla fighting may be kept up for several days, as in an assault on a small and isolated enemy force cut off from help. Because of its dispersed character, guerrilla warfare can spread everywhere, and in many of its tasks, as in harassing, containing, and disrupting the enemy and in mass work, its principle is dispersal of forces; but a guerrilla unit, or a guerrilla formation, must concentrate its main forces when it is engaged in destroying the enemy, and especially when it is striving to smash an enemy attack. "Concentrate a big force to strike at a small section of the enemy force" remains a principle of field operations in guerrilla warfare.

Thus it can also be seen that, if we take the War of Resistance as a whole, we can attain the aim of our strategic defensive and finally defeat Japanese imperialism only through the cumulative effect of many offensive campaigns and battles in both regular and guerrilla warfare, namely, through the cumulative effect of many victories in offensive actions. Only through the cumulative effect of many campaigns and battles of quick decision, namely, the cumulative effect of many victories achieved through quick decision in offensive campaigns and battles, can we attain our goal of strategic protractedness, which means gaining time to increase our capacity to resist while hastening or awaiting changes in the international situation and the internal collapse of the enemy, in order to be able to launch a strategic counteroffensive and drive the Japanese invaders out of China. We must concentrate superior forces and fight exterior-line operations in every campaign or battle, whether in the stage of strategic defensive or in that of strategic counteroffensive, in order to encircle and destroy the enemy forces, encircling part if not all of them, destroying part if not all of the forces we have encircled, and inflicting heavy casualties on the encircled forces if we cannot capture them in large numbers. Only through the cumulative effect of many such battles of annihilation can we change the relative position as between the enemy and ourselves, thoroughly smash his strategic encirclement—that is, his scheme of exterior-line operations—and finally, in co-ordination with international forces and the revolutionary struggles of the Japanese people, surround the Japanese imperialists and deal them the *coup de grâce*. These results are to be achieved mainly through regular warfare, with guerrilla warfare making a secondary contribution. What is common to both, however, is the accumulation of many minor victories to make a major victory. Herein lies the great strategic role of guerrilla warfare in the War of Resistance.

Now let us discuss initiative, flexibility, and planning in guerrilla warfare.

What is initiative in guerrilla warfare?

In any war, the opponents contend for the initiative, whether on a battlefield, in a battle area, in a war zone, or in the whole war, for the initiative means freedom of action for an army. Any army which, losing the initiative, is forced into a passive position and ceases to have freedom of action faces the danger of defeat or extermination. Naturally, gaining the initiative is harder in strategic defensive and interior-line operations and easier in offensive exterior-line operations. However, Japanese imperialism has two basic weaknesses, namely, its shortage of troops and the fact that it is fighting on foreign soil. Moreover, its underestimation of China's strength and the internal contradictions among the Japanese militarists have given rise to many mistakes in command, such as piecemeal reinforcement, lack of strategic co-ordination, occasional absence of a main direction for attack, failure to grasp opportunities in some operations, and failure to wipe out encircled forces, all of which may be considered the third weakness of Japanese imperialism. Thus, despite the advantage of being on the offensive and operating on exterior lines, the Japanese militarists are gradually losing the initiative, because of their shortage of troops (their small territory, small population, inadequate resources, feudalistic imperialism, etc.), because of the fact that they are fighting on foreign soil (their war is imperialist and barbarous), and because of their stupidities in command. Japan is neither willing nor able to conclude the war at present, nor has her strategic offensive yet come to an end, but, as the general trend shows, her offensive is confined within certain limits, which is the inevitable consequence of her three weaknesses; she cannot go on indefinitely till she swallows the whole of China. Already there are signs that Japan will one day find herself in an utterly passive position. China, on the other hand, was in a rather passive position at the beginning of the war, but, having gained experience, she is now turning to the new policy of mobile warfare, the policy of taking the offensive, seeking quick decisions and operating on exterior lines in campaigns and battles, which, together with the policy of developing widespread guerrilla warfare, is helping China to build up a position of initiative day by day.

The question of the initiative is even more vital in guerrilla warfare. For most guerrilla units operate in very difficult circumstances, fighting without a rear, with their own weak forces facing the enemy's strong forces, lacking experience (when the units are newly organized), being separated, etc. Nevertheless, it is possible to build up the initiative in guerrilla warfare, the essential condition being to seize on the enemy's three weaknesses. Taking advantage of the enemy's shortage of troops (from the viewpoint of the war as a whole), the guerrilla units can boldly use vast areas as their fields of operation; taking advantage of the fact that the enemy is an alien invader and is pursuing a most barbarous policy, the guerrilla units can boldly enlist the support of millions upon millions of people; and taking advantage of the stupidities in the enemy's command, the guerrilla units can give full scope to their resourcefulness. While the regular army must seize on all these weaknesses of the enemy and turn them to good account in order to defeat him, it is even more important for the guerrilla units to do so. As for the guerrilla units' own weaknesses, they can be gradually reduced in the course of the struggle. Moreover, these weaknesses sometimes constitute the very condition for gaining the initiative. For example, it is precisely because the guerrilla units are small that they can mysteriously appear and disappear in their operations behind enemy lines, without the enemy's being able to do anything about them, and thus enjoy a freedom of action such as massive regular armies never can.

When the enemy is making a converging attack from several directions, a guerrilla unit can exercise initiative only with difficulty and can lose it all too easily. In such a case, if its appraisals and dispositions are wrong, it is liable to get into a passive position and consequently fail to smash the converging enemy attack. This may occur even when the enemy is on the defensive and we are on the offensive. For the initiative results from making a correct appraisal of the situation (both our own and that of the enemy) and from making the correct military and political dispositions. A pessimistic appraisal out of accord with the objective conditions and the passive dispositions ensuing from it will undoubtedly result in the loss of the initiative and throw one into a passive position. On the other hand, an overoptimistic appraisal out of accord with the objective conditions and the risky (unjustifiably risky) dispositions ensuing from it will also result in the loss of the initiative and eventually land one in a position similar to that of the pessimists. The initiative is not an innate attribute of genius, but is something an intelligent leader attains through openminded study and correct appraisal of the objective conditions and through correct military and political dispositions. It follows that the initiative is not ready-made but is something that requires conscious effort.

When forced into a passive position through some incorrect appraisal and disposition or through overwhelming pressure, a guerrilla unit must strive to extricate itself. How this can be done depends on the circumstances. In many cases it is necessary to "move away." The ability to move is the distinctive feature of a guerrilla unit. To move away is the principal method for getting out of a passive position and regaining the initiative. But it is not the sole method. The moment when the enemy is most energetic and we are in the greatest difficulties is often the very moment when things begin to turn against him and in our favor. Frequently a favorable situation recurs and the initiative is regained as a result of "holding out a little longer."

Next, let us deal with flexibility.

Flexibility is a concrete expression of the initiative. The flexible employment of forces is more essential in guerrilla warfare than in regular warfare.

A guerrilla commander must understand that the flexible employment of his forces is the most important means of changing the situation as between the enemy and ourselves and of gaining the initiative. The nature of guerrilla warfare is such that guerrilla forces must be employed flexibly in accordance with the task in hand and with such circumstances as the state of the enemy, the terrain, and the local population, and the chief ways of employing the forces are dispersal, concentration, and shifting of position. In employing his forces, a guerrilla commander is like a fisherman casting his net, which he should be able to spread wide as well as draw in tight. When casting his net, the fisherman has to ascertain the depth of the water, the speed of the current, and the presence or absence of obstructions; similarly, when dispersing his units, a guerrilla commander must take care not to incur losses through ignorance of the situation or through miscalculated action. Just as the fisherman must keep a grip on the cord in order to draw his net in tight, so the guerrilla commander must maintain liaison and communication with all his forces and keep enough of his main forces at hand. Just as a frequent change of position is necessary in fishing, so a frequent shift of position is necessary for a guerrilla unit. Dispersal, concentration, and shifting of position are the three ways of flexibly employing forces in guerrilla warfare.

Generally speaking, the dispersal of guerrilla units, or "breaking up the whole into parts," is employed chiefly: (1) when we want to threaten the enemy with a wide frontal attack because he is on the defensive, and there is temporarily no chance to mass our forces for action, (2) when we want to harass and disrupt the enemy throughout an area where his forces are weak, (3) when we are unable to break through the enemy's encirclement and try to slip away by making ourselves less conspicuous, (4) when we are restricted by terrain or supplies, or (5) when we are carrying on mass work over a wide area. But whatever the circumstances, when dispersing for action we should pay attention to the following: (1) we should never make an absolutely even dispersal of forces, but should keep a fairly large part in an area convenient for maneuver, so that any possible exigency can be met and there is a center of gravity for the task being carried out in dispersion; and (2) we should assign to the dispersed units clearly defined tasks, fields of operation, time limits for actions, places for reassembly, and ways and means of liaison.

Concentration of forces, or "assembling the parts into a whole," is the method usually applied to destroy an enemy when he is on the offensive and sometimes to destroy some of his stationary forces when he is on the defensive. Concentration of forces does not mean absolute concentration, but the massing of the main forces for use in one important direction while retaining or dispatching part of the forces for use in other directions to contain, harass, or disrupt the enemy, or to carry on mass work.

Although the flexible dispersal or concentration of forces according to circumstances is the principal method in guerrilla warfare, we must also know how to shift (or transfer) our forces flexibly. When the enemy feels seriously threatened by guerrillas, he will send troops to attack or suppress them. Hence the guerrilla units will have to take stock of the situation. If advisable, they should fight where they are; if not, they should lose no time in shifting elsewhere. Sometimes, in order to crush the enemy units one by one, guerrilla units which have destroyed an enemy force in one place may immediately shift to another so as to wipe out a second enemy force; sometimes, finding it inadvisable to fight in one place, they may have to disengage quickly and fight the enemy elsewhere. If the enemy's forces in a certain place present a particularly serious threat, the guerrilla units should not linger, but should move off with lightning speed. In general, shifts of position should be made with secrecy and speed. In order to mislead, decoy, and confuse the enemy, they should constantly use stratagems, such as making a feint to the east but attacking in the west, appearing now in the south and now in the north, hit-and-run attacks, and night actions.

Flexibility in dispersal, concentration, and shifts of position is a concrete expression of the initiative in guerrilla warfare, whereas rigidity and inertia inevitably lead to passivity and cause unnecessary losses. But a commander proves himself wise not just by recognition of the importance of employing his forces flexibly but by skill in dispersing, concentrating, or shifting them in good time according to the specific circumstances. This wisdom in sensing changes and choosing the right moment to act is not easily acquired; it can be gained only by those who study with a receptive mind and investigate and ponder diligently. Prudent consideration of the circumstances is essential to prevent flexibility from turning into impulsive action.

Lastly, we come to planning.

Without planning, victories in guerrilla warfare are impossible. Any idea that guerrilla warfare can be conducted in haphazard fashion indicates either a flippant attitude or ignorance of guerrilla warfare. The operations in a guerrilla zone as a whole, or those of a guerrilla unit or formation, must be preceded by as thorough planning as possible, by preparation in advance for every action. Grasping the situation, setting the tasks, disposing the forces, giving military and political training, securing supplies, putting the equipment in good order, making proper use of the people's help, etc.—all these are part of the work of the guerrilla commanders, which they must carefully consider and conscientiously perform and check up on. There can be no initiative, no flexibility, and no offensive unless they do so. True, guerrilla conditions do not allow as high a degree of planning as do those of regular warfare, and it would be a mistake to attempt very thorough planning in guerrilla warfare. But it is necessary to plan as thoroughly as the objective conditions permit, for it should be understood that fighting the enemy is no joke.

The above points serve to explain the first of the strategic principles of guerrilla warfare, the principle of using initiative, flexibility, and planning in conducting offensives within the defensive, battles of quick decision within protracted war, and exterior-line operations within interior-line operations. It is the key problem in the strategy of guerrilla warfare. The solution of this problem provides the major guarantee of victory in guerrilla warfare so far as military command is concerned.

Although a variety of matters have been dealt with here, they all revolve around the offensive in campaigns and battles. The initiative can be decisively grasped only after victory in an offensive. Every offensive operation must be organized on our initiative and not launched under compulsion. Flexibility in the employment of forces revolves around the effort to take the offensive, and planning likewise is necessary chiefly in order to ensure success in offensive operations. Measures of tactical defense are meaningless if they are divorced from their role of giving either direct or indirect support to an offensive. Quick decision refers to the tempo of an offensive, and exterior lines refer to its scope. The offensive is the only means of destroying the enemy and is also the principal means of self-preservation, while pure defense and retreat can play only a temporary and partial role in self-preservation and are quite useless for destroying the enemy.

The principle stated above is basically the same for both regular and guerrilla war; it differs to some degree only in its form of expression. But in guerrilla war it is both important and necessary to note this difference. It is precisely this difference in form which distinguishes the operational methods of guerrilla war from those of regular war. If we confuse the two different forms in which the principle is expressed, victory in guerrilla war will be impossible.

Co-ordination with Regular Warfare

The second problem of strategy in guerrilla warfare is its co-ordination with regular warfare. It is a matter of clarifying the relation between guerrilla and regular warfare on the operational level, in the light of the nature of actual guerrilla operations. An understanding of this relation is very important for effectiveness in defeating the enemy.

There are three kinds of co-ordination between guerrilla and regular warfare, co-ordination in strategy, in campaigns, and in battles.

Taken as a whole, guerrilla warfare behind the enemy lines, which cripples the enemy, pins him down, disrupts his supply lines, and inspires the regular forces and the people throughout the country, is co-ordinated with regular warfare in strategy. Take the case of the guerrilla warfare in the three northeastern provinces. Of course, the question of co-ordination did not arise before the nationwide War of Resistance, but since the war began the significance of such co-ordination has become obvious. Every enemy soldier the guerrillas kill there, every bullet they make the enemy expend, every enemy soldier they stop from advancing south of the Great Wall can be reckoned a contribution to the total strength of the resistance. It is, moreover, clear that they are having a demoralizing effect on the whole enemy army and all Japan and a heartening effect on our whole army and people. Still clearer is the role in strategic co-ordination played by the guerrilla warfare along the Peiping-Suiyuan, Peiping-Hankow, Tientsin-Pukow, Tatung-Puchow, Chengting-Taiyuan, and Shanghai-Hangchow Railways. Not only are the guerrilla units performing the function of co-ordination with the regular forces in our present strategic defensive, when the enemy is on the strategic offensive; not only will they co-ordinate with the regular forces in disrupting the enemy's hold on the occupied territory, after he concludes his strategic offensive and switches to the safeguarding of his gains; they will also co-ordinate with the regular forces in driving out the enemy forces and recovering all the lost territories, when the regular forces launch the strategic counteroffensive. The great role of guerrilla warfare in strategic co-ordination must not be overlooked. The commanders both of the guerrilla units and of the regular forces must clearly understand this role.

In addition, guerrilla warfare performs the function of co-ordination with regular warfare in campaigns. For instance, in the campaign at Hsinkou, north of Taiyuan, the guerrillas played a remarkable role in co-ordination both north and south of Yenmenkuan by wrecking the Tatung-Puchow Railway and the motor roads running through Pinghsingkuan and Yangfangkou. Or take another instance. After the enemy occupied Fenglingtu, guerrilla warfare, which was already widespread throughout Shansi province and was conducted mainly by the regular forces, played an even greater role through co-ordination with the defensive campaigns west of the Yellow River in Shensi province and south of the Yellow River in Honan province. Again, when the enemy attacked southern Shantung, the guerrilla warfare in the five provinces of northern China contributed a great deal through co-ordination with the campaigns of our army. In performing a task of this sort, the leaders of each guerrilla base behind the enemy lines, or the commanders of a guerrilla formation temporarily dispatched there, must dispose their forces well and, by adopting different tactics suited to the time and place, move energetically against the enemy's most vital and vulnerable spots in order to cripple him, pin him down, disrupt his supply lines, inspire our armies campaigning on the interior lines, and so fulfill their duty of co-ordinating with the campaign. If each guerrilla zone or unit goes it alone without giving any attention to co-ordinating with the campaigns of the regular forces, its role in strategic co-ordination will lose a great deal of its significance, although it will still play some such role in the general strategy. All guerrilla commanders should give this point serious attention. To achieve co-ordination in campaigns, it is absolutely necessary for all larger guerrilla units and guerrilla formations to have radio equipment.

Finally, co-ordination with the regular forces in battles, in actual fighting on the battlefield, is the task of all guerrilla units in the vicinity of an interior-line battlefield. Of course, this applies only to guerrilla units operating close to the regular forces or to units of regulars dispatched on temporary guerrilla missions. In such cases, a guerrilla unit has to perform whatever task it is assigned by the commander of the regular forces, which is usually to pin down some of the enemy's forces, disrupt his supply lines, conduct reconnaissance, or act as guides for the regular forces. Even without such an assignment, the guerrilla unit should carry out these tasks on its own initiative. To sit by idly, neither moving nor fighting, or to move about without fighting, would be an intolerable attitude for a guerrilla unit.

The Establishment of Base Areas

The third problem of strategy in anti-Japanese guerrilla warfare is the establishment of base areas, which is important and essential because of the protracted nature and ruthlessness of the war. The recovery of our lost territories will have to await the nationwide strategic counteroffensive; by then the enemy's front will have extended deep into central China and cut it in two from north to south, and a part or even a greater part of our territory will have fallen into the hands of the enemy and become his rear. We shall have to extend guerrilla warfare all over this vast enemy-occupied area, make a front out of the enemy's rear, and force him to fight ceaselessly throughout the territory he occupies. Until such time as our strategic counteroffensive is launched and so long as our lost territories are not recovered, it will be necessary to persist in guerrilla warfare in the enemy's rear, certainly for a fairly long time, though one cannot say definitely for how long. This is why the war will be a protracted one. And in order to safeguard his gains in the occupied areas, the enemy is bound to step up his anti-guerrilla measures and, especially after the halting of his strategic offensive, to embark on relentless suppression of the guerrillas. With ruthlessness thus added to protractedness, it will be impossible to sustain guerrilla warfare behind the enemy lines without base areas.

What, then, are these base areas? They are the strategic bases on which the guerrilla forces rely in performing their strategic tasks and achieving the object of preserving and expanding themselves and destroying and driving out the enemy. Without such strategic bases, there will be nothing to depend on in carrying out any of our strategic tasks or achieving the aim of the war. It is a characteristic of guerrilla warfare behind the enemy lines that it is fought without a rear, for the guerrilla forces are severed from the country's general rear. But guerrilla warfare could not last long or grow without base areas. The base areas, indeed, are its rear.

History knows many peasant wars of the "roving rebel" type, but none of them ever succeeded. In the present age of advanced communications and technology, it would be all the more groundless to imagine that one can win victory by fighting in the manner of roving rebels. However, this roving-rebel idea still exists among impoverished peasants, and in the minds of guerrilla commanders it becomes the view that base areas are neither necessary nor important. Therefore, ridding the minds of guerrilla commanders of this idea is a prerequisite for deciding on a policy of establishing base areas. The question of whether or not to have base areas and of whether or not to regard them as important, in other words, the conflict between the idea of establishing base areas and that of fighting like roving rebels, arises in all guerrilla warfare, and, to a certain extent, our anti-Japanese guerrilla warfare is no exception. Therefore the struggle against the roving-rebel ideology is an inevitable process. Only when this ideology is thoroughly overcome and the policy of establishing base areas is initiated and applied will there be conditions favorable for the maintenance of guerrilla warfare over a long period. . . .

The Strategic Defensive and the Strategic Offensive in Guerrilla War

The fourth problem of strategy in guerrilla war concerns the strategic defensive and the strategic offensive. This is the problem of how the policy of offensive warfare, which we mentioned in our discussion of the first problem, is to be carried out in practice, when we are on the defensive and when we are on the offensive in our guerrilla warfare against Japan.

Within the nationwide strategic defensive or strategic offensive (to be more exact, the strategic counteroffensive), small-scale strategic defensives and offensives take place in and around each guerrilla base area. By strategic defensive we mean our strategic situation and policy when the enemy is on the offensive and we are on the defensive; by strategic offensive we mean our strategic situation and policy when the enemy is on the defensive and we are on the offensive.

1. THE STRATEGIC DEFENSIVE IN GUERRILLA WAR. After guerrilla warfare has broken out and grown to a considerable extent, the enemy will inevitably attack the guerrilla base areas, especially in the period when his strategic offensive against the country as a whole is brought to an end and he adopts the policy of safeguarding his occupied areas. It is essential to recognize the inevitability of such attacks, for otherwise the guerrilla commanders will be caught wholly unprepared, and in the face of heavy enemy attacks they will undoubtedly become alarmed and confused and their forces will be routed.

To wipe out the guerrillas and their base areas, the enemy frequently resorts to converging attacks. For instance, in each of the four or five "punitive expeditions" directed against the Wutai mountain region, the enemy made a planned advance in three, four, or even six or seven columns simultaneously. The larger the scale of the guerrilla fighting, the more important the position of the base areas, and the greater the threat to the enemy's strategic centers and vital communication lines, the fiercer will be the enemy's attacks. Therefore, the fiercer the enemy's attacks on a guerrilla area, the greater the indication that the guerrilla warfare there is successful and is being effectively co-ordinated with the regular fighting.

When the enemy launches a converging attack in several columns, the guerrilla policy should be to smash it by counterattack. It can be easily smashed if each advancing enemy column consists of only one unit, whether big or small, has no follow-up units, and is unable to station troops along the route of advance, construct blockhouses, or build motor roads. When the enemy launches a converging attack, he is on the offensive and operating on exterior lines, while we are on the defensive and operating on interior lines. As for our dispositions, we should use our secondary forces to pin down several enemy columns, while our main force should launch surprise attacks (chiefly in the form of ambushes) in a campaign or battle against a single enemy column, striking it when it is on the move. The enemy, though strong, will be weakened by repeated surprise attacks and will often withdraw when he is halfway; the guerrilla units can then make more surprise attacks during the pursuit and weaken him still further. The enemy generally occupies the county towns or other towns in our base areas before he stops his offensive or begins to withdraw, and we should encircle these towns, cutting off his grain supply and severing his communications, so that when he cannot hold out and begins to retreat, we can seize the opportunity to pursue and attack him. After smashing one column, we should shift our forces to smash another, and, by smashing them one by one, shatter the converging attack.

A big base area like the Wutai mountain region forms a military area, which is divided into four or five, or even more, military subareas, each with its own armed forces operating independently. By employing the tactics described above, these forces have often smashed the enemy's attacks simultaneously or successively.

In our plan of operations against a converging attack by the enemy, we generally place our main force on interior lines. But when we have the strength to spare, we should use our secondary forces (such as the county or the district guerrilla units, or even detachments of the main force) on exterior lines to disrupt the enemy's communications and pin down his reinforcements. Should the enemy stay put in our base area, we may reverse the tactics, namely, leave some of our forces in the base area to invest the enemy while employing the main force to attack the region whence he has come and to step up our activities there, in order to induce him to withdraw and attack our main force. . . .

In the course of operations against a converging attack, the local anti-Japanese self-defense corps and all the mass organizations should mobilize for action and in every way help our troops to fight the enemy. In fighting the enemy, it is important both to enforce local martial law and, as far as possible, to "strengthen our defense works and clear the fields." The purpose of the former is to suppress traitors and prevent the enemy from getting information, and of the latter to assist our own operations (by strengthening our defense works) and prevent the enemy from getting food (by clearing the fields). "Clearing the fields" means harvesting the crops as soon as they are ripe.

When the enemy retreats, he often burns down the houses in the cities and towns he has occupied and razes the villages along his route, with the purpose of destroying the guerrilla base areas; but in so doing he deprives himself of shelter and food in his next offensive, and the damage recoils upon his own head. This is a concrete illustration of what we mean by one and the same thing having two contradictory aspects.

A guerrilla commander should not think of abandoning his base area and shifting to another, unless it proves impossible, after repeated operations, to smash the enemy's heavy converging attacks. In these circumstances he must guard against pessimism. So long as the leaders do not blunder in matters of principle, it is generally possible to smash the converging attacks and hold on to the base areas in the mountainous regions. It is only in the plains that, when confronted by a heavy converging attack, the guerrilla commander should consider other measures in the light of the specific circumstances, namely, leaving many small units for scattered operations, while temporarily shifting large guerrilla formations to some mountainous region, so that they can return and resume their activities in the plains once the main forces of the enemy move away.

Generally speaking, the Japanese cannot adopt the principle of blockhouse warfare, which the Kuomintang employed in the days of the civil war, because their forces are inadequate in relation to China's vast territory. However, we should reckon with the possibility that they may use it to some extent against those guerrilla base areas which pose a particular threat to their vital positions, but even in such circumstances we should be prepared to keep up guerrilla warfare in those areas. Since we have had the experience of being able to maintain guerrilla warfare during the civil war, there is not the slightest doubt of our greater capacity to do so in a national war. Though, in point of relative military strength, the enemy can throw forces that are vastly superior in quantity as well as in quality against some of our base areas, there remain the insoluble national contradiction between us and the enemy and the unavoidable weaknesses of his command. Our victories are based on thorough work among the masses and flexible tactics in our operations.

2. THE STRATEGIC OFFENSIVE IN GUERRILLA WAR. After we have smashed an enemy offensive and before the enemy starts a new offensive, he is on the strategic defensive and we are on the strategic offensive.

At such times our operational policy is not to attack enemy forces which are entrenched in defensive positions and which we are not sure of defeating, but systematically to destroy or drive out the small enemy units and puppet forces in certain areas, which our guerrilla units are strong enough to deal with, and to expand our areas, arouse the masses for struggle against Japan, replenish and train our troops, and organize new guerrilla units. If the enemy still remains on the defensive when these tasks are under way, we can expand our new areas still further and attack weakly garrisoned cities and communication lines and hold them for as long as circumstances permit. These are all tasks of the strategic offensive, and the purpose is to take advantage of the fact that the enemy is on the defensive so that we may effectively build up our own military and mass strength, effectively reduce the enemy's strength, and prepare to smash the enemy methodically and vigorously when he mounts an offensive again.

It is essential to rest and train our troops, and the best time for doing so is when the enemy is on the defensive. It is not a question of shutting ourselves off from everything else for rest and training, but of finding time for rest and training while expanding our areas, mopping up small enemy units, and arousing the people. This is usually also the time for tackling the difficult problem of getting food supplies, bedding, clothing, etc.

It is also the time for destroying the enemy's communication lines on a large scale, hampering his transport, and giving direct support to the regular forces in their campaigns.

At such times the guerrilla base areas, guerrilla zones, and guerrilla units are in high spirits, and the areas devastated by the enemy are gradually rehabilitated and revived. The people in the enemy-occupied territories are also delighted, and the fame of the guerrillas resounds everywhere. On the other hand, in the camp of the enemy and his running dogs, the traitors, panic and disintegration are mounting, while there is growing hatred of the guerrillas and their base areas and preparations to deal with them are intensified. During the strategic offensive, therefore, it is impermissible for the guerrilla commanders to become so elated as to underrate the enemy and forget to strengthen unity in their own ranks and to consolidate their base areas and their forces. At such times, they must skillfully watch the enemy's every move for signs of any new offensive against us, so that the moment it comes they can wind up their strategic offensive in good order, turn to the strategic defensive, and thereby smash the enemy's offensive.

Development of Guerrilla War into Mobile War

The fifth problem of strategy in guerrilla war against Japan is its development into mobile war, a development which is necessary and possible because the war is protracted and ruthless. If China could speedily defeat the Japanese invaders and recover her lost territories, and if the war were neither protracted nor ruthless, this would not be necessary. But as, on the contrary, the war is protracted and ruthless, guerrilla warfare cannot adapt itself to such a war except by developing into mobile warfare. Since the war is protracted and ruthless, it is possible for the guerrilla units to undergo the necessary steeling and gradually to transform themselves into regular forces, so that their mode of operations is gradually regularized and guerrilla warfare develops into mobile warfare. The necessity and possibility of this development must be clearly recognized by the guerrilla commanders if they are to persist in, and systematically carry out, the policy of turning guerrilla warfare into mobile warfare.

In many places, such as the Wutai mountain region, the present guerrilla warfare owes its growth to the strong detachments sent there by the regular forces. The operations there, though generally of a guerrilla character, have contained an element of mobile warfare from the very beginning. This element will gradually increase as the war goes on. Herein lies the advantage which makes possible the swift expansion of the present anti-Japanese guerrilla warfare and its rapid development to a higher level; thus the conditions for guerrilla warfare are far superior to what they were in the three north-eastern provinces.

To transform guerrilla units waging guerrilla warfare into regular forces waging mobile warfare, two conditions are necessary—an increase in numbers, and an improvement in quality. Apart from directly mobilizing the people to join the forces, increased numbers can be attained by amalgamating small units, while better quality depends on steeling the fighters and improving their weapons in the course of the war.

In amalgamating small units, we must, on the one hand, guard against localism, whereby attention is concentrated exclusively on local interests and centralization is impeded, and, on the other, guard against the purely military approach, whereby local interests are brushed aside.

Localism exists among the local guerrilla units and local governments, which are frequently preoccupied with local considerations to the neglect of the general interest, or which prefer to act each on its own because they are unaccustomed to acting in larger groups. The commanders of the main guerrilla units or of the guerrilla formations must take this into account and adopt the method of gradual amalgamation of part of the local units, allowing the localities to keep some of their forces and expand their guerrilla warfare; the commanders should draw these units into joint operations and then bring about their amalgamation without breaking up their original organization or reshuffling their cadres, so that the small groups may integrate smoothly into the larger group.

As against localism, the purely military approach represents the wrong viewpoint held in the main forces by those who are bent on expanding their own strength and who neglect to assist the local armed units. They do not realize that the development of guerrilla warfare into mobile warfare means not the abandonment of guerrilla warfare, but the gradual formation, in the midst of widespread guerrilla warfare, of a main force capable of conducting mobile warfare, a force around which there must still be numerous guerrilla units carrying on extensive guerrilla operations. These guerrilla units are powerful auxiliaries to the main force and serve as inexhaustible reserves for its continuous growth. Therefore, if a commander of a main force has made the mistake of neglecting the interests of the local population and the local government as a result of a purely military approach, he must correct it in order that the expansion of the main force and the multiplication of the local armed units may both receive due attention.

To raise the quality of the guerrilla units it is imperative to raise their political and organizational level and improve their equipment, military technique, tactics, and discipline, so that they gradually pattern themselves on the regular forces and shed their guerrilla ways. Politically, it is imperative to get both the commanders and the fighters to realize the necessity of raising the guerrilla units to the level of the regular forces, to encourage them to strive toward this end, and to guarantee its attainment by means of political work. Organizationally, it is imperative gradually to fulfill all the requirements of a regular formation in the following respects—military and political organs, staff and working methods, a regular supply system, a medical service, etc. In the matter of equipment, it is imperative to acquire better and more varied weapons and increase the supply of the necessary communications equipment. In the matter of military technique and tactics, it is imperative to raise the guerrilla units to the level required of a regular formation. In the matter of discipline, it is imperative to raise the level so that uniform standards are observed, every order is executed without fail, and all slackness is eliminated. To accomplish all these tasks requires a prolonged effort, and it cannot be done overnight; but that is the direction in which we must develop. Only thus can a main force be built up in each guerrilla base area and mobile warfare emerge for more effective attacks on the enemy. Where detachments or cadres have been sent in by the regular forces, the goal can be achieved more easily. Hence all the regular forces have the responsibility of helping the guerrilla units to develop into regular units.

The Relationship of Command

The last problem of strategy in guerrilla war against Japan concerns the relationship of command. A correct solution of this problem is one of the prerequisites for the unhampered development of guerrilla warfare.

Since guerrilla units are a lower level of armed organization characterized by dispersed operations, the methods of command in guerrilla warfare do not allow as high a degree of centralization as in regular warfare. If any attempt is made to apply the methods of command in regular warfare to guerrilla warfare, its great flexibility will inevitably be restricted and its vitality sapped. A highly centralized command is in direct contradiction to the great flexibility of guerrilla warfare and must not and cannot be applied to it.

However, guerrilla warfare cannot be successfully developed without some centralized command. When extensive regular warfare and extensive guerrilla warfare are going on at the same time, their operations must be properly co-ordinated; hence the need for a command co-ordinating the two, i.e., for a unified strategic command by the national general staff and the war-zone commanders. In a guerrilla zone or guerrilla base area with many guerrilla units, there are usually one or more guerrilla formations (sometimes together with regular formations) which constitute the main force, a number of other guerrilla units, big and small, which represent the supplementary force, and many armed units composed of people not withdrawn from production; the enemy forces there usually form a unified complex to concert their operations against the guerrillas. Consequently, the problem arises of setting up a unified or centralized command in such guerrilla zones or base areas.

Hence, as opposed both to absolute centralization and to absolute decentralization, the principle of command in guerrilla war should be centralized strategic command and decentralized command in campaigns and battles.

Centralized strategic command includes the planning and direction of guerrilla warfare as a whole by the state, the co-ordination of guerrilla warfare with regular warfare in each war zone, and the unified direction of all the anti-Japanese armed forces in each guerrilla zone or base area. Here lack of harmony, unity, and centralization is harmful, and every effort must be made to ensure all three. In general matters, that is, matters of strategy, the lower levels should report to the higher and follow their instructions so as to ensure concerted action. Centralization, however, stops at this point, and it would likewise be harmful to go beyond it and interfere with the lower levels in matters of detail like the specific dispositions for a campaign or battle. For such details must be settled in the light of specific conditions, which change from time to time and from place to place and are quite beyond the knowledge of the distant higher levels of command. This is what is meant by the principle of decentralized command in campaigns and battles. The same principle generally applies in regular operations, especially when communications are inadequate. In a word, it means guerrilla warfare waged independently and with the initiative in our hands within the framework of a unified strategy.

Where a guerrilla base area constitutes a military area divided into subareas, each comprising several counties, each of which is again divided into districts, the relationship between the various levels, from the headquarters of the military area and subareas down to the county and district governments, is one of consecutive subordination, and every armed force must, according to its nature, be under the direct command of one of these. On the principle that has been enunciated, in the relationship of command at these levels, matters of general policy should be centralized in the higher levels, while actual operations should be carried out in the light of the specific circumstances by the lower levels, which should have the right of independent action. If a higher level has something to say about the actual operations undertaken at a lower level, it can and should advance its views as "instructions" but must not issue hard and fast "commands." The more extensive the area, the more complex the situation, and the greater the distance between the higher and the lower levels, the more advisable it becomes to allow greater independence to the lower levels in their actual operations and thus give those operations a character conforming more closely to the local requirements, so that the lower levels and the local personnel may develop the ability to work independently, cope with complicated situations, and successfully expand guerrilla warfare. For an armed unit or bigger formation which is engaged in a concentrated operation, the principle to be applied is one of centralization in its internal relationship of command, since the situation is clear to the higher command; but the moment this unit or formation breaks up for dispersed action, the principle of centralization in general matters and of decentralization in details should be applied, for then the specific situation cannot be clear to the higher command.

Absence of centralization where it is needed means negligence by the higher levels or usurpation of authority by the lower levels, neither of which can be tolerated in the relationship between higher and lower levels, especially in the military sphere. If decentralization is not effected where it should be, that means monopolization of power by the higher levels and lack of initiative on the part of the lower levels, neither of which can be tolerated in the relationship between higher and lower levels, especially in the command of guerrilla warfare. The above principles constitute the only correct policy for solving the problem of the relationship of command.

★

CHAPTER V
Dynamics of Revolution:
The Communist Party

Introductory Note

The communist party is the most crucial variable in the entire course of revolutionary development. From beginning to end, the strategy of "revolutionary war" is conceived and operationalized by the party. The fate of the revolution depends upon it.

Mao Tse-tung's conception of the party follows closely those of Lenin and Stalin. "The Communist Party of China," he writes, "is a party built and developed on the model of the Communist Party of the Soviet Union." Indeed, Lenin's conception of the party, and the rigid criteria associated with his view, have become more or less standard in communist thought. Specifically, Lenin insisted, the party of the proletariat must be a small, highly disciplined, and elitist organization imbued with Marxist revolutionary theory. The political struggle "requires special qualities; it requires professional revolutionaries." In effect, Lenin called not for a proletarian party but for "a committee of professional revolutionaries" characterized by "democratic centralism" and by "truly iron discipline."[1] Though elitist, the party must remain in close touch with the masses and create a "revolutionary mood" among them.

The party is a quasi-military organization in pursuit of revolutionary goals: "Socialist parties are not debating clubs, but organizations of the fighting proletariat."[2] This does not mean, however, that the party should restrict its activities to armed struggle alone. On the contrary, it is necessary to combine all forms of struggle—

[1] "What Is to Be Done?" (1901–2), *Selected Works,* II (New York: International Publishers, 1943), pp. 124, 136.
[2] "The Collapse of the Second International" (Summer 1915), ibid., V, p. 172.

political, legal, military—and to develop the capacity to switch from one form to the other in the shortest possible time and under the most demanding conditions.

The party of the proletariat, Lenin insists, is the only agency capable of bringing that class to political consciousness. On its own the working class develops "only trade union consciousness," a limited and inferior form of awareness. In other words, Lenin's attitude toward the working class is ambivalent: the proletariat, while the most advanced class, is incapable of attaining political awareness on its own initiative.

The Leninist theory of the party was summarized by Stalin in terms of six principal features. The party, he said, is the "vanguard" and the "general staff" of the proletariat (note military terminology); it is the "highest class organization" of the proletariat; it is the "embodiment of discipline and organization" of the proletariat; it is an instrument of the dictatorship of the proletariat; it is the "embodiment of unity of will" of the proletariat; it "becomes strong by purging itself of opportunist elements."[3] Stalin's conception of the party may be said to have gone beyond Lenin's in one respect: whereas Lenin consistently viewed the party as a class phenomenon, Stalin tended to attribute an independent existence to the party. The party, he insisted in 1923, is "an organism living its own separate life."[4] And elsewhere: the party "crowns the whole edifice" of revolutionary organization.[5] These statements have the effect of removing the class basis of the communist party—strictly speaking a heretical view. Stalin recapitulated his own ideas on the party (as well as those of Lenin) by identifying the twelve "fundamental conditions" for the "bolshevization" of a revolutionary party,[6] a statement which was adopted by Mao Tse-tung as one of "the most basic documents of our Party's rectification movement."[7]

The foremost requirement of a communist revolutionary party, Mao Tse-tung believes, is to arm itself with Marxist-Leninist revo-

[3] "The Foundations of Leninism" (April–May 1924), *Works*, VI (Moscow: Foreign Languages Publishing House, 1953), pp. 177–91.

[4] "The Twelfth Congress of the R.C.P.(B.)" (April 1923), ibid., V, p. 199.

[5] "The Fourteenth Congress of the C.P.S.U.(B.)" (December 1925), ibid., VIII, p. 351.

[6] See "The Prospects of the Communist Party of Germany and the Question of Bolshevization" (February 1925), ibid., VII, pp. 38–41.

[7] Ch'en Po-ta, *Stalin on the Chinese Revolution* (Peking: Foreign Languages Press, 1953), p. 27.

lutionary theory. In particular, the party of the proletariat must demonstrate creativity and flexibility in adapting Marxism-Leninism to the actual circumstances in which it finds itself. Once this integration takes place, revolution enters a new, more "progressive" phase.

The party of the proletariat, Mao Tse-tung states, is the "highest form" of class organization. Mao's attitude toward the proletariat itself is ambivalent, however. He sees the working class as incapable of developing political consciousness on its own. To achieve consciousness, it must rely on the infallible elite of the communist party. The communist intelligentsia is viewed as belonging to a social stratum quite distinct from the proletariat. The elitist strand in communism, first introduced by Lenin, is perpetuated by Mao Tse-tung.

The party of the proletariat, Mao believes, is an organization of dedicated revolutionaries. A communist, he writes, must show "absolute devotion to the cause." He "should be frank, faithful, and active, looking upon the interests of the revolution as his very life and subordinating his personal interests to those of the revolution; he should . . . be more concerned about the Party and the masses than about the individual, and more concerned about others than about himself."

The party, in short, absorbs and represents the most conscious and the most progressive elements of the proletariat. At the same time, however, it will be unable to make a revolution on its own strength alone. To do so, it must unite with the non-proletarian masses of the people. Put otherwise, although there is elitism, the era of elite revolution is past.

Internally, Mao maintains, the most distinctive feature of the communist party is its reliance on democratic centralism and rectification campaigns (see Introduction). The chief principle of party organization—democratic centralism—is widely popularized as a means for maximizing "liberty" and "equality." In fact, however, it is designed to enable the leadership to call forth the initiative and enthusiasm of the masses while at the same time maintaining complete control.

Rectification campaigns have been the basic tools for maintaining party unity as well as for eliminating challenges to party leadership, whether internal or external. Under Mao's direction, such campaigns have been conducted by the Chinese Communist Party since the 1930s, their most recent and most far-reaching manifestation being the cultural revolution.

The principal instrument for rectification is the party's practice of "criticism and self-criticism." This presumably indicates the party's willingness to open its doors to criticism from outside as well as to permit expression of divergent views in its own ranks. The policy of external criticism rests on the argument that, being "science," Marxism-Leninism has no fear of subjecting itself to scrutiny. This was precisely the attitude underscoring the "Hundred Flowers" incident of 1956–57, in which the Party actively invited outside criticism. Mao said: "As a scientific truth, Marxism fears no criticism. If it did, and could be defeated in argument, it would be worthless. . . . Carrying out the policy of letting a hundred flowers blossom and a hundred schools of thought contend will not weaken but strengthen the leading position of Marxism in the ideological field."

The "Hundred Flowers" policy, of course, met with decisive defeat. As "blossoming" and "contending" mounted, the regime clamped down on adverse opinion. In a revised version of his speech, Mao Tse-tung drew a sharp distinction between "fragrant flowers" and "poisonous weeds" and proposed a number of criteria for determining the correctness of external criticism.

Mao Tse-tung's rectification campaigns correspond, in their basic objective, to Stalinist purges. They constitute a means through which party leadership periodically frees itself of internal and external competition, clears its ranks of various "deviations," and puts forth the ideological oneness that a revolutionary party is expected to exhibit.

The most significant concept in the Communist Party's external relations is undoubtedly the "mass line." The revolutionary party brings political enlightenment not only to the proletariat but to the masses of the people as a whole (including the peasantry and "enlightened" segments of the bourgeoisie). Mao's attitude toward the masses—as his attitude toward the working class—is ambivalent. On the one hand, the masses are viewed as the "real heroes" and the "makers of history"; on the other, they are considered to have extremely low political awareness and rationality. "Our comrades," warns Mao, "must not assume that everything they themselves understand is understood by the masses." The revolutionary party guides the masses and is the most decisive factor in fanning their revolutionary enthusiasm.

The importance attached to the mass line directly depends on the realization that, although the masses lack political consciousness, without their support the party cannot lead the revolution to victory. The heart of the mass line concept lies in the attempt to convert party policy into the action of the masses and to leave the masses with the illusion that the party line is really a reflection of their own desires and views. The greater the party's skill in mobilizing and politicizing the masses and the greater its ability to create an atmosphere of popular commitment, the better its chances to consolidate its position and implement its program. The persistent identification of the party with the "people" is one of the main features of Mao Tse-tung's revolutionary strategy. Indeed, it is the basic component of Mao's definition of "revolutionary war."

Readings

THE PARTY AND REVOLUTION

A Marxist-Leninist Party

From: "Revolutionary Forces of the World Unite, Fight Against Imperialist Aggression!" (November 1948), *Selected Works,* IV (Peking: Foreign Languages Press, 1961), p. 284.

If there is to be revolution, there must be a revolutionary party. Without a revolutionary party, without a party built on the Marxist-Leninist revolutionary theory and in the Marxist-Leninist revolutionary style, it is impossible to lead the working class and the broad masses of the people to defeat imperialism and its running dogs. In the more than one hundred years since the birth of Marxism, it was only through the example of the Russian Bolsheviks in leading the October Revolution, in leading socialist construction, and in defeating fascist aggression that revolutionary parties of a new type were formed and developed in the world. With the birth of revolutionary parties of this type, the face of the world revolution has changed. The change has been so great that transformations utterly inconceivable to people of the older generation have come into being amid fire and thunder. The Communist Party of China is a party built and developed on the model of the Communist Party of the Soviet Union. With the birth of the Communist Party of China, the face of the Chinese revolution took on an altogether new aspect. Is this fact not clear enough?

Revolutionary Theory and Revolutionary Practice

From: "The Role of the Chinese Communist Party in the National War" (October 1938), *Selected Works,* II (Peking: Foreign Languages Press, 1965), pp. 208–10.

Generally speaking, all Communist Party members who can do so should study the theory of Marx, Engels, Lenin, and Stalin, study our national history, and study current movements and trends; moreover, they should help to educate members with less schooling. The cadres in particular should study these subjects carefully, while members of the Central Committee and senior cadres should give them even more attention. No political party can possibly lead a great revolutionary movement to victory unless it possesses revolutionary theory and a knowledge of history and has a profound grasp of the practical movement.

The theory of Marx, Engels, Lenin, and Stalin is universally applicable. We should regard it not as a dogma, but as a guide to action. Studying it is not merely a matter of learning terms and phrases but of learning Marxism-Leninism as the science of revolution. It is not just a matter of understanding the general laws derived by Marx, Engels, Lenin, and Stalin from their extensive study of real life and revolutionary experience, but of studying their standpoint and method in examining and solving problems. Our Party's mastery of Marxism-Leninism is now rather better than it used to be, but is still far from being extensive or deep. Ours is the task of leading a great nation of several hundred million in a great and unprecedented struggle. For us, therefore, the spreading and deepening of the study of Marxism-Leninism present a big problem demanding an early solution which is possible only through concentrated effort. . . . I hope to see an all-Party emulation in study which will show who has really learned something, and who has learned more and learned better. So far as shouldering the main responsibility of leadership is concerned, our Party's fighting capacity will be much greater and our task of defeating Japanese imperialism will be more quickly accomplished if there are one or two hundred comrades with a grasp of Marxism-Leninism which is systematic and not fragmentary, genuine and not hollow.

Another of our tasks is to study our historical heritage and use the Marxist method to sum it up critically. Our national history goes back several thousand years and has its own characteristics and innumerable treasures. But in these matters we are mere schoolboys. Contemporary China has grown out of the China of the past; we are Marxist in our historical approach and must not lop off our history. We should sum up our history from Confucius to Sun Yat-sen and take over this valuable legacy. This is important for guiding the great movement of today. Being Marxists, Communists are internationalists, but we can put Marxism into practice only when it is integrated with the specific characteristics of our country and acquires a definite national form. The great strength of Marxism-Leninism lies precisely in its integration with the concrete revolutionary practice of all countries. For the Chinese Communist Party, it is a matter of learning to apply the theory of Marxism-Leninism to the specific circumstances of China. For the Chinese Communists who are part of the great Chinese nation, flesh of its flesh and blood of its blood, any talk about Marxism in isolation from China's characteristics is merely Marxism in the abstract, Marxism in a vacuum. Hence to apply Marxism concretely in China so that its every manifestation has an undubitably Chinese character, i.e., to apply Marxism in the light of China's specific characteristics, becomes a problem which it is urgent for the whole Party to understand and solve. Foreign stereotypes must be abolished, there must be less singing of empty, abstract tunes, and dogmatism must be laid to rest; they must be replaced by the fresh, lively Chinese style and spirit which the common people of China love. To separate internationalist content from national form is the practice of those who do not understand the first thing about internationalism. We, on the contrary, must link the two closely. In this matter there are serious errors in our ranks which should be conscientiously overcome.

The Example of Mao Tse-tung

From: "Resolution on Certain Questions in the History of Our Party" (adopted by the CCP Central Committee on April 20, 1945), *Selected Works,* III (Peking: Foreign Languages Press, 1965), pp. 177–78, 210–11. (Although this document is in the third person singular, it was actually written by Mao Tse-tung himself. See Introduction.)

Ever since its birth in 1921, the Communist Party of China has made the integration of the universal truth of Marxism-Leninism with the concrete practice of the Chinese revolution the guiding prin-

ciple in all its work, and Comrade Mao Tse-tung's theory and practice of the Chinese revolution represent this integration. With the
founding of our Party a new stage of the Chinese revolution was immediately unfolded, the stage of the new-democratic revolution, as
pointed out by Comrade Mao Tse-tung. Throughout the twenty-four
years of struggle for New Democracy (from 1921 to 1945), throughout the three historical periods—the First Great Revolution, the
Agrarian Revolution, and the War of Resistance Against Japan—our
Party has consistently led the broad masses of the Chinese people in
extremely arduous and bitter revolutionary struggles against their
enemies, imperialism and feudalism, and has gained great successes
and rich experience. In the course of its struggle the Party has produced its own leader, Comrade Mao Tse-tung. Representing the
Chinese proletariat and the Chinese people, Comrade Mao Tse-tung
has creatively applied the scientific theory of Marxism-Leninism, the
acme of human wisdom, to China, a large semifeudal and semicolonial country in which the peasantry constitutes the bulk of the
masses and the immediate task is to fight against imperialism and
feudalism, a country with a vast area and a huge population, where
the situation is extremely complicated and the struggle extremely
hard, and he has brilliantly developed the theories of Lenin and
Stalin on the colonial and semicolonial question as well as Stalin's
theory concerning the Chinese revolution. It is only because the
Party has firmly adhered to the correct Marxist-Leninist line and
waged a victorious struggle against all erroneous ideas opposed to
this line that it has scored great achievements in these three periods,
has arrived at today's unprecedented ideological, political, and organizational solidarity and unity, has developed into the powerful
revolutionary force of today, having over 1,200,000 members and
leading China's liberated areas with their population of nearly
100,000,000 and an army of nearly 1,000,000, and has become the
center of gravity for the whole nation in the War of Resistance
Against Japan and in the cause of liberation. . . .

The correctness or incorrectness of any political, military, or organizational line has ideological roots—it depends on whether or not
the line starts from Marxist-Leninist dialectical materialism and historical materialism and whether or not the line starts from the objective realities of the Chinese revolution and the objective needs of
the Chinese people. From the very day he embraced the cause of the
Chinese revolution, Comrade Mao Tse-tung has devoted himself to
applying the universal truth of Marxism-Leninism to the investiga-

tion and study of the actual conditions of Chinese society; time and again during the period of the Agrarian Revolutionary War, he laid great stress on the principle "No investigation, no right to speak," and time and again fought against the dangers of dogmatism and subjectivism. Indeed, the political, military, and organizational lines then laid down by Comrade Mao Tse-tung were brilliant achievements which he made on the basis of the universal truth of Marxism-Leninism, of dialectical and historical materialism, by his concrete analysis of the actual situation and its characteristics inside and outside the country and inside and outside the Party and by his concrete summing up of the historical experience of the Chinese revolution, and especially of the 1924–27 revolution. For Chinese Communists, living and fighting in China, the purpose of studying dialectical materialism and historical materialism should be to apply them to the study and solution of the practical problems of the Chinese revolution, as Comrade Mao Tse-tung has done.

The Future of the Party

From: "On the People's Democratic Dictatorship" (June 1949), *Selected Works,* IV (Peking: Foreign Languages Press, 1961), p. 411.

The first of July 1949 marks the fact that the Communist Party of China has already lived through twenty-eight years. Like a man, a political party has its childhood, youth, manhood, and old age. The Communist Party of China is no longer a child or a lad in his teens but has become an adult. When a man reaches old age, he will die; the same is true of a party. When classes disappear, all instruments of class struggle—parties and the state machinery—will lose their function, cease to be necessary, therefore gradually wither away and end their historical mission; and human society will move to a higher stage. We are the opposite of the political parties of the bourgeoisie. They are afraid to speak of the extinction of classes, state power, and parties. We, on the contrary, declare openly that we are striving hard to create the very conditions which will bring about their extinction. The leadership of the Communist Party and the state power of the people's dictatorship are such conditions. Anyone who does not recognize this truth is no communist. Young comrades who have not studied Marxism-Leninism and have only recently joined the Party may not yet understand this truth. They must understand it—only then can they have a correct world outlook. They must understand that the road to the abolition of classes, to the abolition of state power, and to the abolition of parties is the road all mankind must take; it is only a question of time and conditions.

BUILDING THE PARTY

From: "Introducing *The Communist*" (October 1939), *Selected Works*, II (Peking: Foreign Languages Press, 1965), pp. 285–86, 292–96.

The Central Committee has long planned to publish an internal Party journal, and now at last the plan has materialized. Such a journal is necessary for building up a bolshevized Chinese Communist Party, a party which is national in scale and has a broad mass character, a party which is fully consolidated ideologically, politically, and organizationally. This necessity is all the more obvious in the present situation, which has special features: on the one hand, the danger of capitulation, of a split, and of retrogression within the anti-Japanese national united front is increasing daily, while on the other, our Party has stepped out of its narrow confines and become a major national party. The duty of the Party is to mobilize the masses to overcome the dangers of capitulation, a split, and retrogression and prepare against all possible eventualities so that in case they occur, the Party and the revolution will not suffer unexpected losses. An internal Party journal is indeed most necessary at a time like this.

This internal Party journal is called *The Communist*. What is its purpose? What will it deal with? In what way will it differ from other Party publications?

Its purpose is to help build a bolshevized Chinese Communist Party which is national in scale, has a broad mass character, and is fully consolidated ideologically, politically, and organizationally. The building of such a party is imperative for the victory of the Chinese revolution and on the whole the subjective and objective conditions for it are present; indeed this great undertaking is now in progress. A special Party periodical is needed to help achieve this great task, which is beyond the capability of an ordinary Party publication, and this is why *The Communist* is now being published.

To a certain extent our Party is already national in scale and has a broad mass character; and it is already a bolshevized party, consolidated ideologically, politically, and organizationally, so far as its core of leadership, a part of its membership, and its general line and revolutionary work are concerned.

That being so, why set a new task?

The reason is that we now have many new branches, which have a great many new members but which cannot yet be considered as having a broad mass character, as being ideologically, politically, and organizationally consolidated, or as being bolshevized. At the same time, there is the problem of raising the political level of the older Party members and of making further progress in bolshevizing the older branches and consolidating them ideologically, politically, and organizationally. The circumstances in which the Party now finds itself and the responsibilities it is shouldering are quite unlike those in the revolutionary civil war period; the circumstances are much more complex and the responsibilities much heavier. . . .

. . . there have been three distinct stages in the building up of the Party, its development, consolidation, and bolshevization.

The first stage was the Party's infancy. In the early and middle phases of this stage the Party's line was correct and the revolutionary zeal both of the rank and file and of the cadres was exceedingly high; hence the victories in the First Great Revolution. But after all, ours was then still an infant Party, it lacked experience concerning the three basic problems of the united front, armed struggle, and Party building, it did not have much knowledge of Chinese history and Chinese society or of the specific features and laws of the Chinese revolution, and it lacked a comprehensive understanding of the unity between the theory of Marxism-Leninism and the practice of the Chinese revolution. Hence in the last phase of this stage, or at the critical juncture of this stage, those occupying a dominant position in the Party's leading body failed to lead the Party in consolidating the victories of the revolution and, as a result, they were deceived by the bourgeoisie and brought the revolution to defeat. The Party organizations expanded in this stage but they were not consolidated, and they failed to help Party members and cadres become firm and stable ideologically and politically. There were plenty of new members, but they were not given the necessary Marxist-Leninist education. There was also abundant experience in work, but it was not summed up properly. Many careerists sneaked into the Party, but they were not combed out. The Party was caught in a maze of schemes and intrigues both of enemies and of allies, but it lacked vigilance. Within the Party, activists came forward in great numbers, but they were not turned into the mainstay of the Party in good time. The Party had some revolutionary armed units under its command, but it was unable to keep a tight grip on them. The reasons for all this were inexperience, insufficient depth of revolutionary understanding, and ineptitude in integrating the theory of Marxism-Leninism with the practice of the Chinese revolution. Such was the first stage of Party building.

The second stage was the War of the Agrarian Revolution. Our Party was able to wage a successful agrarian revolutionary struggle for ten years because of the experience it had gained in the first stage, because of its better understanding of Chinese history and society and of the specific features and laws of the Chinese revolution, and because its cadres had a better grasp of the theory of Marxism-Leninism and were better able to integrate it with the practice of the Chinese revolution. Although the bourgeoisie had turned traitor, our Party was able to rely firmly on the peasantry. The Party organization not only grew afresh but also became consolidated. Day in, day out the enemy tried to sabotage our Party, but the Party drove out the saboteurs. Once again large numbers of cadres came forward in the Party, and this time they became its mainstay. The Party blazed the trail of people's political power and thus learned the art of government. The Party created strong armed forces and thus learned the art of war. These were momentous advances and achievements. Nevertheless, in the course of these great struggles some of our comrades sank into the quagmire of opportunism, or did so at least for a time, and again the reasons were that they did not learn modestly from the experience of the past, did not acquire an understanding of Chinese history and society and of the specific features and laws of the Chinese revolution, and did not have an understanding of the unity between the theory of Marxism-Leninism and the practice of the Chinese revolution. Hence throughout this stage certain people who held leading positions in the Party failed to adhere to correct political and organizational lines. . . . Not until the Tsunyi meeting (the meeting of the Political Bureau at Tsunyi, Kweichow, in January 1935) did the Party definitively take the road of bolshevization and lay the foundations for its subsequent victory. . . .

The third stage is that of the anti-Japanese national united front. We have been in this stage for three years now and these years of struggle are extremely important. Drawing on its experience in the two preceding revolutionary stages, on its organizational strength and the strength of its armed forces, on its high political prestige among the people of the whole country, and on its deeper understanding of the unity between the theory of Marxism-Leninism and the practice of the Chinese revolution, our Party has not only established the anti-Japanese national united front but has also been conducting the great War of Resistance Against Japan. Organizationally, it has stepped out of its narrow confines and become a major national party. Its armed forces are again growing and are becoming still stronger in the struggle against the Japanese aggressors. Its influence among the whole people is becoming more extensive. These are all great achievements. However, many of our new Party members have not yet been given education, many of the new organizations have not yet been consolidated, and there is still a vast difference between them and the older members and organizations. Many of the new Party members and cadres have not yet had sufficient revolutionary experience. They still know little or nothing about Chinese history and society or about the specific features and laws of the Chinese revolution. Their understanding of the unity between the theory of Marxism-Leninism and the practice of the Chinese revolution is far from being comprehensive. During the expansion of the Party's organizations, a good many careerists and enemy saboteurs did succeed in sneaking in despite the fact that the Central Committee stressed the slogan "Expand the Party boldly, but do not let a single undesirable in." Although the united front was formed and has been maintained for three years now, the bourgeoisie, and especially the big bourgeoisie, has constantly been trying to destroy our Party, the big bourgeois capitulators and die-hards have been instigating serious friction throughout the country, and the anti-Communist clamor is incessant. All this is being used by the big bourgeois capitulators and die-hards to prepare the way for capitulating to Japanese imperialism, breaking up the united front, and dragging China backward. Ideologically, the big bourgeoisie is trying to "corrode" communism, while politically and organizationally it is trying to liquidate the Communist Party, the border region, and the Party's armed forces. In these circumstances it is undoubtedly our task to overcome the dangers of capitulation, a split, and retrogression, to maintain the national united front and Kuomintang-Communist co-operation as far as possible, to work for continued resistance to Japan and continued unity and progress, and at the same time to prepare against all possible eventualities so that in case they occur, the Party and the revolution will not suffer unexpected losses. To this end, we must strengthen the Party's organization and its armed forces, and mobilize the whole people for resolute struggle against capitulation, a split, and retrogression. The accomplishment of this task depends upon the efforts of the whole Party, upon the unrelenting and persistent struggle of all Party members, cadres, and organizations everywhere and at every level. We are confident that the Chinese Communist Party with its eighteen years of experience will be able to achieve these objectives by the joint efforts of its experienced older members and cadres and its vigorous and youthful newer members and cadres, by the joint efforts of its well-tried bolshevized Central Committee and its local organizations, and by the joint efforts of its powerful armed forces and the progressive masses.

We have set out the principal experiences and principal problems of our Party in its eighteen years of history. . . .

How are we to build up our Party today? How can we build up "a bolshevized Chinese Communist Party, a party which is national in scale and has a broad mass character, a party which is fully consolidated ideologically, politically, and organizationally"? The answer can be found by studying the Party's history, by studying Party building in connection with the united front and armed struggle, in connection with the problem of both uniting and struggling with the bourgeoisie, and with that of persistence in guerrilla warfare against Japan by the Eighth Route and the New Fourth Armies and the establishment of anti-Japanese base areas.

To sum up our eighteen years of experience and our current new experience on the basis of our understanding of the unity between the theory of Marxism-Leninism and the practice of the Chinese revolution, and to spread this experience throughout the Party, so that our Party becomes as solid as steel and avoids repeating past mistakes—such is our task.

PARTY LEADERSHIP

"The Proletariat Must Lead"

From: "The Tasks of the Chinese Communist Party in the Period of Resistance to Japan" (May 1937), *Selected Works,* I (Peking: Foreign Languages Press, 1964), pp. 273–74.

. . . It is a law confirmed by Chinese history that the Chinese bourgeoisie, which may participate in fighting imperialism and feudalism in certain historical circumstances, vacillates and turns traitor in others because of its economic and political flabbiness. Thus it is history's verdict that China's bourgeois-democratic revolution against imperialism and feudalism is a task that can be completed, not under the leadership of the bourgeoisie, but only under that of the proletariat. What is more, it is possible to overcome the bourgeoisie's inherent vacillation and lack of thoroughness and to prevent the miscarriage of the revolution only by bringing the perseverance and thoroughness of the proletariat in the democratic revolution into full play. Is the proletariat to follow the bourgeoisie, or is the bourgeoisie to follow the proletariat? This question of responsibility for leadership in the Chinese revolution is the linchpin upon which the success or failure of the revolution depends. The experience of 1924–27 shows how the revolution forged ahead when the bourgeoisie followed the political leadership of the proletariat and met defeat when the proletariat became the political tail of the bourgeoisie through the fault of the Communist Party. This piece of history should not be allowed to repeat itself. In the present circumstances, without the political leadership of the proletariat and its party it is impossible to establish an anti-Japanese national united front, to attain the objectives of peace, democracy, and armed resistance, and to defend the motherland, and impossible to set up a unified democratic republic. Today the bourgeoisie, represented by the Kuomintang, is still very passive and conservative, and the proof of this is its long hesitation about accepting the anti-Japanese national united front initiated by the Communist Party. This situation increases the responsibility of the proletariat and its party for giving political leadership. To function as the general staff in resisting Japan and saving the nation is a responsibility the Communist Party cannot relinquish, an obligation it cannot decline.

. . . How does the proletariat give political leadership through its party to all the revolutionary classes in the country? First, by putting forward basic political slogans that accord with the course of historical development and by putting forward slogans of action for each stage of development and each major turn of events in order to translate these political slogans into reality. For instance, we have put forward the basic slogans for "an anti-Japanese national united front" and for "a unified democratic republic," but we have also put forward the slogans "End the civil war," "Fight for democracy," and "Carry out armed resistance" as specific objectives for concerted action by the entire nation; without such specific objectives political leadership is out of the question. Second, the proletariat, and especially its vanguard the Communist Party, should set an example through its boundless enthusiasm and loyalty in achieving the specific objectives when the whole country goes into action for them. In the fight to fulfill all the tasks of the anti-Japanese national united front and the democratic republic, Communists should be the most farsighted, the most self-sacrificing, the most resolute, and the least prejudiced in sizing up situations, and should rely on the majority of the masses and win their support. Third, the Communist Party should establish proper relations with its allies and develop and consolidate its alliance with them, while adhering to the principle of never relinquishing its defined political objectives. Fourth, it should expand the ranks of the Communist Party and maintain its ideological unity and strict discipline. It is by doing all these things that the Communist Party gives effect to its political leadership of the people throughout China. They constitute the foundation for guaranteeing our political leadership and for ensuring that the revolution will win complete victory and not be disrupted by the vacillations of our allies.

"Arduous Struggles"

From: "Problems of Strategy in China's Revolutionary War" (December 1936), *Selected Works,* I (Peking: Foreign Languages Press, 1964), pp. 192–94.

. . . Of all the social strata and political groupings in semicolonial China, the proletariat and the Communist Party are the ones most free from narrow-mindedness and selfishness, are politically the most farsighted, the best organized, and the readiest to learn with an open mind from the experience of the vanguard class, the proletariat, and its political party throughout the world and to make use of this experience in their own cause. Hence only the proletariat and the Communist Party can lead the peasantry, the urban petty bourgeoisie and bourgeoisie, can overcome the narrow-mindedness of the peasantry and the petty bourgeoisie, the destructiveness of the unemployed masses, and also (provided the Communist Party does not err in its policy) the vacillation and lack of thoroughness of the bourgeoisie—and can lead the revolution and the war on to the road of victory. . . .

The Chinese Communist Party has led China's revolutionary war courageously and resolutely, and for fifteen long years has demonstrated to the whole nation that it is the people's friend, fighting at all times in the forefront of the revolutionary war in defense of the people's interests and for their freedom and liberation.

By its arduous struggles and by the martyrdom of hundreds of thousands of its heroic members and tens of thousands of its heroic cadres, the Communist Party of China has played a great educative role among hundreds of millions of people throughout the country. The Party's great historic achievements in its revolutionary struggles have provided the prerequisite for the survival and salvation of China at this critical juncture when she is being invaded by a national enemy; and this prerequisite is the existence of a political leadership enjoying the confidence of the vast majority of the people and chosen by them after long years of testing. Today, the people accept what the Communist Party says more readily than what any other political party says. Were it not for the arduous struggles of the Chinese Communist Party in the last fifteen years, it would be impossible to save China in the face of the new menace of subjugation. . . .

The Chinese Communist Party has led and continues to lead the stirring, magnificent, and victorious revolutionary war. This war is not only the banner of China's liberation, but has international revolutionary significance as well. The eyes of the revolutionary people the world over are upon us. In the new stage, the stage of the anti-Japanese national revolutionary war, we shall lead the Chinese revolution to its completion and exert a profound influence on the revolution in the East and in the whole world. Our revolutionary war has proved that we need a correct Marxist military line as well as a correct Marxist political line. Fifteen years of revolution and war have hammered out such political and military lines. We believe that from now on, in the new stage of the war, these lines will be further developed, filled out, and enriched in new circumstances, so that we can attain our aim of defeating the national enemy. History tells us that correct political and military lines do not emerge and develop spontaneously and tranquilly, but only in the course of struggle. These lines must combat "left" opportunism on the one hand and "right" opportunism on the other. Without combating and thoroughly overcoming these harmful tendencies which damage the revolution and the revolutionary war, it would be impossible to establish a correct line and win victory in this war.

"Communists Should Set Examples"

From: "The Role of the Chinese Communist Party in the National War" (October 1938), *Selected Works*, II (Peking: Foreign Languages Press, 1965), pp. 197–98.

. . . Communists should show a high degree of initiative in the national war, and show it concretely, that is, they should play an exemplary vanguard role in every sphere. Our war is being waged under adverse circumstances. National consciousness, national self-respect, and national self-confidence are not sufficiently developed among the broad masses, the majority of the people are unorganized, China's military power is weak, the economy is backward, the political system is undemocratic, corruption and pessimism exist, and a lack of unity and solidarity is to be found within the united front; these are among the adverse circumstances. Therefore, Communists must consciously shoulder the great responsibility of uniting the entire nation so as to put an end to all such undesirable phenomena. Here the exemplary vanguard role of the Communists is of vital importance. Communists in the Eighth Route and New Fourth Armies should set an example in fighting bravely, carrying out orders, observing discipline, doing political work, and fostering internal unity and solidarity. In their relations with friendly parties and armies, Communists should take a firm stand of unity for resistance to Japan, uphold the program of the united front, and set an example in carrying out the tasks of resistance; they should be true in word and resolute in deed, free from arrogance and sincere in consulting and co-operating with the friendly parties and armies, and they should be models in interparty relations within the united front. Every Communist engaged in government work should set an example of absolute integrity, of freedom from favoritism in making appointments, and of hard work for little remuneration. Every Communist working among the masses should be their friend and not a boss over them, an indefatigable teacher and not a bureaucratic politician. At no time and in no circumstances should a Communist place his personal interests first; he should subordinate them to the interests of the nation and of the masses. Hence selfishness, slacking, corruption, seeking the limelight, and so on, are most contemptible, while selflessness, working with all one's energy, wholehearted devotion to public duty, and quiet hard work will command respect. Communists should work in harmony with all progressives outside the Party and endeavor to unite the entire people to do away with whatever is undesirable. It must be realized that Communists form only a small section of the nation, and that there are large numbers of progressives and activists outside the Party with whom we must work. It is entirely wrong to think that we alone are good and no one else is any good. As for people who are politically backward, Communists should not slight or despise them, but should befriend them, unite with them, convince them, and encourage them to go forward. The attitude of Communists toward any person who has made mistakes in his work should be one of persuasion in order to help him change and start afresh and not one of exclusion, unless he is incorrigible. Communists should set an example in being practical as well as farsighted. For only by being practical can they fulfill the appointed tasks, and only farsightedness can prevent them from losing their bearings in the march forward. Communists should therefore set an example in study; at all times they should learn from the masses as well as teach them. Only by learning from the people, from actual circumstances and from the friendly parties and armies, and by knowing them well, can we be practical in our work and farsighted as to the future. In a long war and in adverse circumstances, the dynamic energy of the whole nation can be mobilized in the struggle to overcome difficulties, defeat the enemy, and build a new China only if the Communists play an exemplary vanguard role to the best of their ability together with all the advanced elements among the friendly parties and armies and among the masses.

Discipline and "Democracy"

From: "The Role of the Chinese Communist Party in the National War" (October 1938), *Selected Works,* II (Peking: Foreign Languages Press, 1965), pp. 203–5.

In view of . . . serious violations of discipline, we must affirm anew the discipline of the Party, namely:

(1) the individual is subordinate to the organization;
(2) the minority is subordinate to the majority;
(3) the lower level is subordinate to the higher level; and
(4) the entire membership is subordinate to the Central Committee.

Whoever violates these articles of discipline disrupts Party unity. Experience proves that some people violate Party discipline through not knowing what it is, while others . . . violate it knowingly and take advantage of many Party members' ignorance to achieve their treacherous purposes. Hence it is necessary to educate members in Party discipline so that the rank and file will not only observe discipline themselves but will exercise supervision over the leaders so that they, too, observe it. . . . If we are to ensure the development of inner-Party relations along the right lines, besides the four most important articles of discipline mentioned above we must work out a set of fairly detailed Party rules which will serve to unify the actions of the leading bodies at all levels. . . .

In the present great struggle, the Chinese Communist Party demands that all its leading bodies and all its members and cadres should give the fullest expression to their initiative, which alone can ensure victory. This initiative must be demonstrated concretely in the ability of the leading bodies, the cadres, and the Party rank and file to work creatively, in their readiness to assume responsibility, in the exuberant vigor they show in their work, in their courage and ability to raise questions, voice opinions, and criticize defects, and in the comradely supervision that is maintained over the leading bodies and the leading cadres. Otherwise, "initiative" will be an empty thing. But the exercise of such initiative depends on the spread of democracy in Party life. It cannot be brought into play if there is not enough democracy in Party life. Only in an atmosphere of democracy can large numbers of able people be brought forward. Ours is a country in which small-scale production and the patriarchal system prevail, and taking the country as a whole there is as yet no democratic life; consequently, this state of affairs is reflected in our Party by insufficient democracy in Party life. This phenomenon hinders the entire Party from exercising its initiative to the full. Similarly, it has led to insufficient democracy in the united front and in the mass movements. For these reasons, education in democracy must be carried on within the Party so that members can understand the meaning of democratic life, the meaning of the relationship between democracy and centralism, and the way in which democratic centralism should be put into practice. Only in this way can we really extend democracy within the Party and at the same time avoid ultra-democracy and the *laissez faire* which destroys discipline.

It is also essential to extend democracy in our Party organizations in the army to the degree necessary to stimulate the initiative of the Party members and increase the combat effectiveness of the troops. However, there cannot be as much democracy in the Party organizations in the army as in the local Party organizations. Both in the army and in the local organizations, inner-Party democracy is meant to strengthen discipline and increase combat effectiveness, not to weaken them.

The extension of democracy in the Party should be seen as an essential step in its consolidation and development, and as an important weapon enabling it to be most active in the great struggle, to prove equal to its tasks, create fresh strength, and surmount the difficulties of the war.

"Democracy" and "Centralism"

From: "Interview with the British Journalist James Bertram" (October 1937), *Selected Works,* II (Peking: Foreign Languages Press, 1965), p. 57.

QUESTION: Is not "democratic centralism" a self-contradictory term?

ANSWER: We must look not only at the term but at the reality. There is no impassable gulf between democracy and centralism, both of which are essential for China. On the one hand, the government we want must be truly representative of the popular will; it must have the support of the broad masses throughout the country and the people must be free to support it and have every opportunity of influencing its policies. This is the meaning of democracy. On the other hand, the centralization of administrative power is also necessary, and once the policy measures demanded by the people are transmitted to their own elected government through their representative body, the government will carry them out and will certainly be able to do so smoothly, so long as it does not go against the policy adopted in accordance with the people's will. This is the meaning of centralism. Only by adopting democratic centralism can a government be really strong, and this system must be adopted by China's government of national defense in the anti-Japanese war.

Role of Cadres

From: "Win the Masses in Their Millions for the Anti-Japanese National United Front" (May 1937), *Selected Works,* I (Peking: Foreign Languages Press, 1964), p. 291.

A great revolution requires a great party and many first-rate cadres to guide it. In China, with a population of 450 million, it is impossible to carry through our great revolution, which is unprecedented in history, if the leadership consists of a small, narrow group and if the Party leaders and cadres are petty-minded, shortsighted, and incompetent. The Chinese Communist Party has been a large party for a long time and it is still large despite the losses during the period of reaction; it has many good leaders and cadres, but still not enough. Our Party organizations must be extended all over the country and we must purposefully train tens of thousands of cadres and hundreds of first-rate leaders. They must be cadres and leaders versed in Marxism-Leninism, politically farsighted, competent in work, full of the spirit of self-sacrifice, capable of tackling problems on their own, steadfast in the midst of difficulties, and loyal and devoted in serving the nation, the class, and the Party. It is on these cadres and leaders that the Party relies for its links with the membership and the masses, and it is by relying on their firm leadership of the masses that the Party can succeed in defeating the enemy. Such cadres and leaders must be free from selfishness, from individualistic heroism, ostentation, sloth, passivity, and sectarian arrogance, and they must be selfless national and class heroes; such are the qualities and the style of work demanded of the members, cadres, and leaders of our Party. Such is the spiritual legacy handed down to us by the tens of thousands of members, the thousands of cadres, and the scores of first-rate leaders who have laid down their lives for the cause. Beyond any doubt, we ought to acquire these qualities, do still better in remolding ourselves, and raise ourselves to a higher revolutionary level. But even this is not enough; we must also regard it as our duty to discover many more new cadres and leaders in the Party and the country. Our revolution depends on cadres. As Stalin said, "Cadres decide everything."

Party Committees

From: "On Strengthening the Party Committee System" (September 1948), *Selected Works*, IV (Peking: Foreign Languages Press, 1961), pp. 267–68.

The Party committee system is an important Party institution for ensuring collective leadership and preventing any individual from monopolizing the conduct of affairs. It has recently been found that in some (of course not all) leading bodies it is the habitual practice for one individual to monopolize the conduct of affairs and decide important problems. Solutions to important problems are decided not by Party committee meetings but by one individual, and membership in the Party committees has become nominal. Differences of opinion among committee members cannot be resolved and are left unresolved for a long time. Members of the Party committees maintain only formal, not real, unity among themselves. This situation must be changed. From now on, a sound system of Party committee meetings must be instituted in all leading bodies, from the bureaus of the Central Committee to the prefectural Party committees; from the Party committees of the fronts to the Party committees of brigades and military areas (subcommissions of the Revolutionary Military Commission or leading groups); and the leading Party members' groups in government bodies, people's organizations, the news agency, and the newspaper offices. All important problems (of course, not the unimportant, trivial problems, or problems whose solutions have already been decided after discussion at meetings and need only be carried out) must be submitted to the committee for discussion, and the committee members present should express their views fully and reach definite decisions which should then be carried out by the members concerned. The same procedure should be followed by Party committees below the prefectural and brigade levels. In the higher leading bodies there should also be meetings of the leading cadres in the departments (for example, the propaganda department and the organizational department), commissions (for example, the labor, women's, and youth commissions), schools (for example, Party schools), and offices (for example, the research offices). Of course, we must see to it that the meetings are not too long or too frequent and they must not get bogged down in discussion of petty matters lest the work be hindered. On important problems which are complicated and on which opinions differ, there must, in addition, be personal consultations before the meeting to enable the members to think things over, lest decisions by the meeting become a mere formality or no decision can be reached. Party committee meetings must be divided into two categories, standing committee meetings and plenary sessions, and the two should not be confused. Furthermore, we must take care that neither collective leadership nor personal responsibility is overemphasized to the neglect of the other. In the army, the person in command has the right to make emergency decisions during battle and when circumstances require.

Methods of Work of Party Committees

From: "Methods of Work of Party Committees" (March 1949), *Selected Works*, IV (Peking: Foreign Languages Press, 1961), pp. 377–81.

1. The secretary of a Party committee must be good at being a "squad leader." A Party committee has ten to twenty members; it

is like a squad in the army, and the secretary is like the "squad leader." It is indeed not easy to lead this squad well. Each bureau or subbureau of the Central Committee now leads a vast area and shoulders very heavy responsibilities. To lead means not only to decide general and specific policies but also to devise correct methods of work. Even with correct general and specific policies, troubles may still arise if methods of work are neglected. To fulfill its task of exercising leadership, a Party committee must rely on its "squad members" and enable them to play their parts to the full. To be a good "squad leader," the secretary should study hard and investigate thoroughly. A secretary or deputy secretary will find it difficult to direct his "squad" well if he does not take care to do propaganda and organizational work among his own "squad members," is not good at handling his relations with committee members, or does not study how to run meetings successfully. If the "squad members" do not march in step, they can never expect to lead tens of millions of people in fighting and construction. Of course, the relation between the secretary and the committee members is one in which the minority must obey the majority, so it is different from the relation between a squad leader and his men. Here we speak only by way of analogy.

2. Place problems on the table. This should be done not only by the "squad leader" but by the committee members too. Do not talk behind people's backs. Whenever problems arise, call a meeting, place the problems on the table for discussion, take some decisions, and the problems will be solved. If problems exist and are not placed on the table, they will remain unsolved for a long time and even drag on for years. The "squad leader" and the committee members should be tolerant and understanding in their relations with each other. Nothing is more important than mutual tolerance, understanding, support, and friendship between the secretary and the committee members, between the Central Committee and its bureaus, and between the bureaus and the area Party committees. In the past this point received little attention, but since the Seventh Party Congress much progress has been made in this respect and the ties of friendship and unity have been greatly strengthened. We should continue to pay constant attention to this point in the future.

3. "Exchange information." This means that members of a Party committee should keep each other informed and exchange views on matters that have come to their attention. This is of great importance in achieving a common language. Some fail to do so. . . . In the past some of our high-ranking cadres did not have a common lan-

guage even on basic theoretical problems of Marxism-Leninism, because they had not studied enough. There is more of a common language in the Party today, but the problem has not yet been fully solved. For instance, in the land reform there is still some difference in the understanding of what is meant by "middle peasants" and "rich peasants."

4. Ask your subordinates about matters you don't understand or don't know, and do not lightly express your approval or disapproval. Some documents, after having been drafted, are withheld from circulation for a time because certain questions in them need to be clarified and it is necessary to consult the lower levels first. We should never pretend to know what we don't know, we should [as Confucius said] "not feel ashamed to ask and learn from people below," and we should listen carefully to the views of the cadres at the lower levels. Be a pupil before you become a teacher; learn from the cadres at the lower levels before you issue orders. In handling problems, this should be the practice of all bureaus of the Central Committee and Party committees of the fronts, except in military emergencies or when the facts of the matter are already clear. To do this will not lower one's prestige, but can only raise it. Since our decisions incorporate the correct views of the cadres at the lower levels, the latter will naturally support them. What the cadres at the lower levels say may or may not be correct; we must analyze it. We must heed the correct views and act upon them. The reason why the leadership of the Central Committee is correct is chiefly that it synthesizes the material, reports, and correct views coming from different localities. It would be difficult for the Central Committee to issue correct orders if the localities did not provide material and put forward opinions. Listen also to the mistaken views from below; it is wrong not to listen to them at all. Such views, however, are not to be acted upon but to be criticized.

5. Learn to "play the piano." In playing the piano all ten fingers are in motion; it won't do to move some fingers only and not others. But if all ten fingers press down at once, there is no melody. To produce good music, the ten fingers should move rhythmically and in co-ordination. A Party committee should keep a firm grasp on its central task and at the same time, around the central task, it should unfold the work in other fields. At present, we have to take care of many fields; we must look after the work in all the areas, armed units, and departments, and not give all our attention to a few problems, to the exclusion of others. Wherever there is a problem, we

must put our finger on it, and this is a method we must master. Some play the piano well and some badly, and there is a great difference in the melodies they produce. Members of Party committees must learn to "play the piano" well.

6. "Grasp firmly." That is to say, the Party committee must not merely "grasp" but must "grasp firmly" its main tasks. One can get a grip on something only when it is grasped firmly, without the slightest slackening. Not to grasp firmly is not to grasp at all. Naturally, one cannot get a grip on something with an open hand. When the hand is clenched as if grasping something but is not clenched tightly, there is still no grip. Some of our comrades do grasp the main tasks, but their grasp is not firm and so they cannot make a success of their work. It will not do to have no grasp at all, nor will it do if the grasp is not firm.

7. "Have a head for figures." That is to say, we must attend to the quantitative aspect of a situation or problem and make a basic quantitative analysis. Every quality manifests itself in a certain quantity, and without quantity there can be no quality. To this day many of our comrades still do not understand that they must attend to the quantitative aspect of things—the basic statistics, the main percentages, and the quantitative limits that determine the qualities of things. They have no "figures" in their heads and as a result cannot help making mistakes. For instance, in carrying out the land reform it is essential to have such figures as the percentages of landlords, rich peasants, middle peasants, and poor peasants among the population and the amount of land owned by each group, because only on this basis can we formulate correct policies. Whom to call a rich peasant, whom a well-to-do middle peasant, and how much income derived from exploitation makes a person a rich peasant as distinct from a well-to-do middle peasant—in all these cases, too, the quantitative limits must be ascertained. In all mass movements we must make a basic investigation and analysis of the number of active supporters, opponents, and neutrals and must not decide problems subjectively and without basis.

8. "Notice to Reassure the Public." Notice of meetings should be given beforehand; this is like issuing a "Notice to Reassure the Public," so that everybody will know what is going to be discussed and what problems are to be solved and can make timely preparations. In some places, meetings of cadres are called without first preparing reports and draft resolutions, and only when people have arrived for the meeting are makeshifts improvised; this is just like

the saying "Troops and horses have arrived, but food and fodder are not ready," and that is no good. Don't call a meeting in a hurry if the preparations are not completed.

9. "Fewer and better troops and simpler administration." Talks, speeches, articles, and resolutions should all be concise and to the point. Meetings also should not go on too long.

10. Pay attention to uniting and working with comrades who differ with you. This should be borne in mind both in the localities and in the army. It also applies to relations with people outside the Party. We have come together from every corner of the country and should be good at uniting in our work not only with comrades who hold the same views as we but also with those who hold different views. There are some among us who have made very serious mistakes; we should not be prejudiced against them but should be ready to work with them.

11. Guard against arrogance. For anyone in a leading position, this is a matter of principle and an important condition for maintaining unity. Even those who have made no serious mistakes and have achieved very great success in their work should not be arrogant. Celebration of the birthdays of Party leaders is forbidden. Naming places, streets, and enterprises after Party leaders is likewise forbidden. We must keep to our style of plain living and hard work and put a stop to flattery and exaggerated praise.

12. Draw two lines of distinction. First, between revolution and counterrevolution. . . . Secondly, within the revolutionary ranks, it is necessary to make a clear distinction between right and wrong, between achievements and shortcomings, and to make clear which of the two is primary and which secondary. For instance, do the achievements amount to 30 per cent or to 70 per cent of the whole? It will not do either to understate or to overstate. We must have a fundamental evaluation of a person's work and establish whether his achievements amount to 30 per cent and his mistakes to 70 per cent, or vice versa. If his achievements amount to 70 per cent of the whole, then his work should in the main be approved. It would be entirely wrong to describe work in which the achievements are primary as work in which the mistakes are primary. In our approach to problems we must not forget to draw these two lines of distinction, between revolution and counterrevolution and between achievements and shortcomings. We shall be able to handle things well if we bear these two distinctions in mind; otherwise we shall confuse the nature of the problems. To draw these distinctions well, careful

study and analysis are of course necessary. Our attitude toward every person and every matter should be one of analysis and study.

The members of the Political Bureau and I personally feel that only by using the above methods can Party committees do their work well. In addition to conducting Party congresses well, it is most important for the Party committees at all levels to perform their work of leadership well. We must make efforts to study and perfect the methods of work so as to raise further the Party committees' level of leadership.

THE PARTY AND THE MASSES

The Mass Line

From: "Some Questions Concerning Methods of Leadership" (June 1943), *Selected Works,* III (Peking: Foreign Languages Press, 1965), pp. 117–20.

1. There are two methods which we Communists must employ in whatever work we do. One is to combine the general with the particular; the other is to combine the leadership with the masses.

2. In any task, if no general and widespread call is issued, the broad masses cannot be mobilized for action. But if persons in leading positions confine themselves to a general call—if they do not personally, in some of the organizations, go deeply and concretely into the work called for, make a break-through at some single point, gain experience and use this experience for guiding other units—then they will have no way of testing the correctness or of enriching the content of their general call, and there is the danger that nothing may come of it. . . . Select two or three units (but not too many) from the organization itself and from other organizations, schools, or army units in the vicinity. Make a thorough study of those units, acquire a detailed knowledge of the development of the rectification movement in them and a detailed knowledge of the political history, the ideological characteristics, the zeal in study, and the strong and weak points in the work of some (again not too many) representative members of their personnel. Furthermore, give personal guidance to those in charge to find concrete solutions for the practical problems facing those units. The leaders in every organization, school, or army unit must do likewise, as each of these has a number of subordinate units. Moreover, this is the method by which the leaders combine leading and learning. No one in a leading position

is competent to give general guidance to all the units unless he derives concrete experience from particular individuals and events in particular subordinate units. This method must be promoted everywhere so that leading cadres at all levels learn to apply it.

3. Experience . . . proves it is essential for the success of the rectification that a leading group should be formed in each unit in the course of the movement, made up of a small number of activists and with the heads of the given unit as its nucleus, and that this leading group should link itself closely with the masses taking part in the movement. However active the leading group may be, its activity will amount to fruitless effort by a handful of people unless combined with the activity of the masses. On the other hand, if the masses alone are active without a strong leading group to organize their activity properly, such activity cannot be sustained for long, or carried forward in the right direction, or raised to a high level. The masses in any given place are generally composed of three parts, the relatively active, the intermediate, and the relatively backward. The leaders must therefore be skilled in uniting the small number of active elements around the leadership and must rely on them to raise the level of the intermediate elements and to win over the backward elements. A leading group that is genuinely united and linked with the masses can be formed only gradually in the process of mass struggle, and not in isolation from it. In the process of a great struggle, the composition of the leading group in most cases should not and cannot remain entirely unchanged throughout the initial, middle, and final stages; the activists who come forward in the course of the struggle must constantly be promoted to replace those original members of the leading group who are inferior by comparison or who have degenerated. One fundamental reason why the work in many places and many organizations cannot be pushed ahead is the lack of a leading group which is united, linked with the masses, and kept constantly healthy. . . .

4. In all the practical work of our Party, all correct leadership is necessarily "from the masses, to the masses." This means: take the ideas of the masses (scattered and unsystematic ideas) and concentrate them (through study turn them into concentrated and systematic ideas), then go to the masses and propagate and explain these ideas until the masses embrace them as their own, hold fast to them and translate them into action, and test the correctness of these ideas in such action. Then once again concentrate ideas from the masses and once again go to the masses so that the ideas are

persevered in and carried through. And so on, over and over again in an endless spiral, with the ideas becoming more correct, more vital, and richer each time. Such is the Marxist theory of knowledge.

5. The concept of a correct relationship between the leading group and the masses in an organization or in a struggle, the concept that correct ideas on the part of the leadership can only be "from the masses, to the masses," and the concept that the general call must be combined with particular guidance when the leadership's ideas are being put into practice—these concepts must be propagated everywhere during the present rectification movement in order to correct the mistaken viewpoints among our cadres on these questions. Many comrades do not see the importance of, or are not good at, drawing together the activists to form a nucleus of leadership, and they do not see the importance of, or are not good at, linking this nucleus of leadership closely with the masses, and so their leadership becomes bureaucratic and divorced from the masses. Many comrades do not see the importance of, or are not good at, summing up the experience of mass struggles, but fancying themselves clever, are fond of voicing their subjectivist ideas, and so their ideas become empty and impractical. Many comrades rest content with making a general call with regard to a task and do not see the importance of, or are not good at, following it up immediately with particular and concrete guidance, and so their call remains on their lips, or on paper or in the conference room, and their leadership becomes bureaucratic.

Rejection of "Bureaucracy"

From: "Get Organized!" (November 1943), *Selected Works,* III (Peking: Foreign Languages Press, 1965), p. 158.

We Communists must be able to integrate ourselves with the masses in all things. If our Party members spend their whole lives sitting indoors and never go out to face the world and brave the storm, what good will they be to the Chinese people? None at all, and we do not need such people as Party members. We Communists ought to face the world and brave the storm, the great world of mass struggle and the mighty storm of mass struggle. "Three cobblers with their wits combined equal Chukeh Liang, the mastermind." In other words, the masses have great creative power. In fact there are thousands upon thousands of Chukeh Liangs among the Chinese people; every village, every town has its own. We should go to the masses and learn from them, synthesize their experience into better, articulated principles and methods, then do propaganda among the masses and call upon them to put these principles and methods into practice so as to solve their problems and help them achieve liberation and happiness. If our comrades doing local work are isolated from the masses, fail to understand their feelings and to help them organize their production and improve their livelihood, and if they confine themselves to collecting "public grain for national salvation" without realizing that 10 per cent of their energy is quite enough for this purpose provided they first devote 90 per cent to helping the masses solve the problem of "private grain for the people's own salvation," then these comrades are contaminated with the Kuomintang style of work and covered with the dust of bureaucracy. The Kuomintang only demands things from the people and gives them nothing in return. If a member of our Party acts in this way, his style of work is that of the Kuomintang, and his face, caked with the dust of bureaucracy, needs a good wash in a basin of hot water. In my opinion, this bureaucratic style is to be found in local work in all our anti-Japanese base areas, and there are comrades who are isolated from the masses because they lack the mass viewpoint. We must firmly do away with this style of work before we can have close ties with the masses.

Rejection of "Closed-doorism"

From: "Speech at the Assembly of Representatives of the Shensi-Kansu-Ningsia Border Region" (November 1941), *Selected Works,* III (Peking: Foreign Languages Press, 1965), pp. 33–34.

Communists must listen attentively to the views of people outside the Party and let them have their say. If what they say is right, we ought to welcome it, and we should learn from their strong points; if it is wrong, we should let them finish what they are saying and then patiently explain things to them. A Communist must never be opinionated or domineering, or think that he is good in everything while others are good in nothing; he must never shut himself up in his little room, or brag and boast and lord it over others. Apart from the die-hard reactionaries who are in league with the Japanese aggressors and with the traitors and are sabotaging resistance and unity, and who of course have no right to speak, everyone is entitled to freedom of speech, and it does not matter even if what he says is wrong. Affairs of state are the public affairs of the whole nation and not the private affairs of a single party or group. Hence Communists have the duty to co-operate democratically with non-Party people and have no right to exclude them and monopolize everything. The Communist Party is a political party which works in the interests of the nation and people and which has absolutely no private ends to pursue. It should be supervised by the people and must never go against their will. Its members should be among the people and with them and must not set themselves above them. Members of the Assembly and comrades, this Communist Party principle of democratic co-operation with non-Party people is fixed and unalterable. So long as parties exist, people who join them will always be a minority while those outside them will always be the majority; hence our Party members must always co-operate with non-Party people, and they should make a good start right here in the Assembly. With this policy of ours, I believe that Communist members of the Assembly will get very good training here and overcome their "closed-doorism" and sectarianism. We are not a small, opinionated sect and we must learn how to open our doors and co-operate democratically with non-Party people, and how to consult with others. Perhaps even now there are Communists who may say, "If it is necessary to co-operate with others, then leave me out." But I am sure there are very few. I can assure you that the overwhelming majority of our members will certainly be able to carry out the line of the Central Committee of our Party. At the same time I wish to ask all non-Party comrades to realize what we stand for, to understand that the Communist Party is not a small sect or clique pursuing private ends. No! The Communist Party sincerely and honestly wishes to set the affairs of state to rights. But we still have many failings. We are not afraid to admit them and are determined to get rid of them. We shall do so by strengthening education within the Party and by co-operating democratically with non-Party people. It is only by subjecting our failings to such a cross fire, both from within and from without, that we can remedy them and really set the affairs of state to rights.

PURGE AND RECTIFICATION

Marxism and Subjectivism

From: "Reform Our Study" (May 1941), *Selected Works*, III (Peking: Foreign Languages Press, 1965), pp. 17–24.

I propose that we should reform the method and the system of study throughout the Party. The reasons are as follows:

I

The twenty years of the Communist Party of China have been twenty years in which the universal truth of Marxism-Leninism has become more and more integrated with the concrete practice of the Chinese revolution. If we recall how superficial and meager our understanding of Marxism-Leninism and of the Chinese revolution was during our Party's infancy, we can see how much deeper and richer it is now. For a hundred years, the finest sons and daughters of the disaster-ridden Chinese nation fought and sacrificed their lives, one stepping into the breach as another fell, in quest of the truth that would save the country and the people. This moves us to song and tears. But it was only after World War I and the October Revolution in Russia that we found Marxism-Leninism, the best of truths, the best of weapons for liberating our nation. And the Communist Party of China has been the initiator, propagandist, and organizer in the wielding of this weapon. As soon as it was linked with the concrete practice of the Chinese revolution, the universal truth of Marxism-Leninism gave an entirely new complexion to the Chinese revolution. Since the outbreak of the War of Resistance Against Japan, our Party, basing itself on the universal truth of Marxism-Leninism, has taken a further step in its study of the concrete practice of this war and in its study of China and the world today, and has also made a beginning in the study of Chinese history. These are all very good signs.

II

However, we still have shortcomings, and very big ones too. Unless we correct these shortcomings, we shall not, in my opinion, be able to take another step forward in our work and in our great cause of integrating the universal truth of Marxism-Leninism with the concrete practice of the Chinese revolution.

First, take the study of current conditions. We have achieved some success in our study of present domestic and international conditions, but for such a large political party as ours, the material we have collected is fragmentary and our research work unsystematic on each and every aspect of these subjects, whether it be the political, military, economic, or cultural aspect. Generally speaking, in the last twenty years we have not done systematic and thorough work in collecting and studying material on these aspects, and we are lacking in a climate of investigation and study of objective reality. To behave like "a blindfolded man catching sparrows," or "a blind man groping for fish," to be crude and careless, to indulge in verbiage, to rest content with a smattering of knowledge—such is the extremely bad style of work that still exists among many comrades in our Party, a style utterly opposed to the fundamental spirit of Marxism-Leninism. Marx, Engels, Lenin, and Stalin have taught us that it is necessary to study conditions conscientiously and to proceed from objective reality and not from subjective wishes; but many of our comrades act in direct violation of this truth.

Second, take the study of history. Although a few Party members and sympathizers have undertaken this work, it has not been done in an organized way. Many Party members are still in a fog about Chinese history, whether of the last hundred years or of ancient times. There are many Marxist-Leninist scholars who cannot open their mouths without citing ancient Greece; but as for their own ancestors—sorry, they have been forgotten. There is no climate of serious study either of current conditions or of past history.

Third, take the study of international revolutionary experience, the study of the universal truth of Marxism-Leninism. Many comrades seem to study Marxism-Leninism not to meet the needs of revolutionary practice, but purely for the sake of study. Consequently, though they read, they cannot digest. They can only cite odd quotations from Marx, Engels, Lenin, and Stalin in a one-sided manner, but are unable to apply the stand, viewpoint, and method of Marx, Engels, Lenin, and Stalin to the concrete study of China's present conditions and her history or to the concrete analysis and solution of the problems of the Chinese revolution. Such an attitude toward Marxism-Leninism does a great deal of harm, particularly among cadres of the middle and higher ranks.

The three aspects I have just mentioned, neglect of the study of current conditions, neglect of the study of history, and neglect of the application of Marxism-Leninism, all constitute an extremely bad style of work. Its spread has harmed many of our comrades. . . .

Although we are studying Marxism, the way many of our people study it runs directly counter to Marxism. That is to say, they violate the fundamental principle earnestly enjoined on us by Marx, Engels, Lenin, and Stalin, the unity of theory and practice. Having violated this principle, they invent an opposite principle of their own, the separation of theory from practice. In the schools and in the education of cadres at work, teachers of philosophy do not guide students to study the logic of the Chinese revolution; teachers of economics do not guide them to study the characteristics of the Chinese economy; teachers of political science do not guide them to study the tactics of the Chinese revolution; teachers of military science do not guide them to study the strategy and tactics adapted to China's special features; and so on and so forth. . . . Thus a perverse mentality has been created among many students; instead of showing an interest in China's problems and taking the Party's directives seriously, they give all their hearts to the supposedly eternal and immutable dogmas learned from their teachers.

Of course, what I have just said refers to the worst type in our Party, and I am not saying that it is the general case. However, people of this type do exist; what is more, there are quite a few of them and they cause a great deal of harm. This matter should not be treated lightly.

III

In order to explain this idea further, I should like to contrast two opposite attitudes.

First, there is the subjectivist attitude.

With this attitude, a person does not make a systematic and thorough study of the environment, but works by sheer subjective enthusiasm and has a blurred picture of the face of China today. With this attitude, he chops up history, knows only ancient Greece but not China, and is in a fog about the China of yesterday and the day before yesterday. With this attitude, a person studies Marxist-Leninist theory in the abstract and without any aim. He goes to Marx, Engels, Lenin, and Stalin not to seek the stand, viewpoint, and method with which to solve the theoretical and tactical problems of the Chinese revolution but to study theory purely for theory's sake. He does not shoot the arrow at the target but shoots at random. Marx, Engels, Lenin, and Stalin have taught us that we should proceed from objective realities and that we should derive laws from them to serve as our guide to action. For this purpose, we should, as Marx has said, appropriate the material in detail and subject it to scientific analysis and synthesis. Many of our people do not act in this way but do the opposite. A good number of them are doing research work but have no interest in studying either the China of today or the China of yesterday and confine their interest to the study of empty "theories" divorced from reality. Many others are doing practical work, but they too pay no attention to the study of objective conditions, often rely on sheer enthusiasm, and substitute their personal feelings for policy. Both kinds of people, relying on the subjective, ignore the existence of objective realities. When making speeches, they indulge in a long string of headings, A, B, C, D, 1, 2, 3, 4, and when writing articles, they turn out a lot of verbiage. They have no intention of seeking truth from facts, but only a desire to curry favor by claptrap. They are flashy without substance, brittle without solidity. They are always right, they are the number one authority under heaven, "imperial envoys" who rush everywhere. Such is the style of work of some comrades in our ranks. To govern one's own conduct by this style is to harm oneself, to teach it to others is to harm others, and to use it to direct the revolution is to harm the revolution. To sum up, this subjectivist method which is contrary to science and Marxism-Leninism is a formidable enemy of the Communist Party, the working class, the people, and the nation; it is a manifestation of impurity in Party spirit. A formidable enemy stands before us, and we must overthrow him. Only when subjectivism is overthrown can the truth of Marxism-Leninism prevail, can Party spirit be strengthened, can the revolution be victorious. We must assert that the absence of a scientific attitude, that is, the absence of the Marxist-Leninist approach of uniting theory and practice, means that Party spirit is either absent or deficient. . . .

Secondly, there is the Marxist-Leninist attitude.

With this attitude, a person applies the theory and method of Marxism-Leninism to the systematic and thorough investigation and study of the environment. He does not work by enthusiasm alone but, as Stalin says, combines revolutionary sweep with practicalness. With this attitude he will not chop up history. It is not enough for him to know ancient Greece, he must know China; he must know the revolutionary history not only of foreign countries but also of China, not only the China of today but also the China of yesterday and of the day before yesterday. With this attitude, one studies the theory of Marxism-Leninism with a purpose, that is, to integrate Marxist-Leninist theory with the actual movement of the Chinese revolution and to seek from this theory the stand, viewpoint, and method with which to solve the theoretical and tactical problems of the Chinese revolution. Such an attitude is one of shooting the arrow at the target. The "target" is the Chinese revolution, the "arrow" is Marxism-Leninism. We Chinese Communists have been seeking this arrow because we want to hit the target of the Chinese revolution and of the revolution of the East. To take such an attitude is to seek truth from facts. "Facts" are all the things that exist objectively, "truth" means their internal relations, that is, the laws governing them, and "to seek" means to study. We should proceed from the actual conditions inside and outside the country, the province, county, or district, and derive from them, as our guide to action, laws which are inherent in them and not imaginary, that is, we should find the internal relations of the events occurring around us. And in order to do that we must rely not on subjective imagination, not on momentary enthusiasm, not on lifeless books, but on facts that exist objectively; we must appropriate the material in detail and, guided by the general principles of Marxism-Leninism, draw correct conclusions from it. Such conclusions are not mere lists of phenomena in A, B, C, D order or writings full of platitudes, but are scientific conclusions. Such an attitude is one of seeking truth from facts and not of currying favor by claptrap. It is the manifestation of Party spirit, the Marxist-Leninist style of uniting theory and practice. It is the attitude every Communist Party member should have at the very least. He who adopts this attitude will be neither "top-heavy, thin-stemmed, and shallow of root" nor "sharp-tongued, thick-skinned, and hollow inside."

IV

In accordance with the above views, I would like to make the following proposals:

1. We should place before the whole Party the task of making a systematic and thorough study of the situation around us. On the basis of the theory and method of Marxism-Leninism, we should make a detailed investigation and study of developments in the economic, financial, political, military, cultural, and party activities

of our enemies, our friends, and ourselves, and then draw the proper and necessary conclusions. To this end, we should direct our comrades' attention to the investigation and study of these practical matters. We should get our comrades to understand that the twofold basic task of the leading bodies of the Communist Party is to know conditions and to master policy; the former means knowing the world and the latter changing the world. We should get our comrades to understand that without investigation there is no right to speak, and that bombastic twaddle and a mere list of phenomena in 1, 2, 3, 4 order are of no use. Take propaganda work, for instance; if we do not know the situation with regard to the propaganda of our enemies, our friends, and ourselves, we shall be unable to decide on a correct propaganda policy. In the work of any department, it is necessary to know the situation first and only then can the work be well handled. The fundamental link in changing the Party's style of work is to carry out plans for investigation and study throughout the Party.

2. As for China's history in the last hundred years, we should assemble qualified persons to study it, in co-operation and with a proper division of labor, and so overcome the present disorganized state of affairs. First it is necessary to make analytical studies in the several fields of economic history, political history, military history, and cultural history, and only then will it be possible to make synthetical studies.

3. As for education for cadres whether at work or in schools for cadres, a policy should be established of focusing such education on the study of the practical problems of the Chinese revolution and using the basic principles of Marxism-Leninism as the guide, and the method of studying Marxism-Leninism statically and in isolation should be discarded. Moreover, in studying Marxism-Leninism, we should use the *History of the Communist Party of the Soviet Union (Bolsheviks), Short Course* as the principal material. It is the best synthesis and summing up of the world communist movement of the past hundred years, a model of the integration of theory and practice, and so far the only comprehensive model in the whole world. When we see how Lenin and Stalin integrated the universal truth of Marxism with the concrete practice of the Soviet revolution and thereby developed Marxism, we shall know how we should work in China.

We have made many detours. But error is often the precursor of what is correct. I am confident that in the context of the Chinese revolution and the world revolution, which is so intensely alive and so richly varied, this reform of our study will certainly yield good results.

Marxism and "Liberalism"

From: "Combat Liberalism" (September 7, 1937), *Selected Works*, II (Peking: Foreign Languages Press, 1965), pp. 31–33.

We stand for active ideological struggle because it is the weapon for ensuring unity within the Party and the revolutionary organizations in the interest of our fight. Every Communist and revolutionary should take up this weapon.

But liberalism rejects ideological struggle and stands for unprincipled peace, thus giving rise to a decadent, Philistine attitude and bringing about political degeneration in certain units and individuals in the Party and the revolutionary organizations.

Liberalism manifests itself in various ways.

To let things slide for the sake of peace and friendship when a person has clearly gone wrong, and refrain from principled argument because he is an old acquaintance, a fellow townsman, a schoolmate, a close friend, a loved one, an old colleague, or an old subordinate. Or to touch on the matter lightly instead of going into it thoroughly, so as to keep on good terms. The result is that both the organization and the individual are harmed. This is one type of liberalism.

To indulge in irresponsible criticism in private instead of actively putting forward one's suggestions to the organization. To say nothing to people to their faces but to gossip behind their backs, or to say nothing at a meeting but to gossip afterward. To show no regard at all for the principles of collective life but to follow one's own inclination. This is a second type.

To let things drift if they do not affect one personally; to say as little as possible while knowing perfectly well what is wrong, to be worldly-wise and play safe and seek only to avoid blame. This is a third type.

Not to obey orders but to give pride of place to one's own opinions. To demand special consideration from the organization but to reject its discipline. This is a fourth type.

To indulge in personal attacks, pick quarrels, vent personal spite, or seek revenge instead of entering into an argument and struggling against incorrect views for the sake of unity or progress or getting the work done properly. This is a fifth type.

To hear incorrect views without rebutting them and even to hear counterrevolutionary remarks without reporting them, but instead to take them calmly as if nothing had happened. This is a sixth type.

To be among the masses and fail to conduct propaganda and agitation or speak at meetings or conduct investigations and inquiries among them, and instead to be indifferent to them and show no concern for their well-being, forgetting that one is a Communist and behaving as if one were an ordinary non-Communist. This is a seventh type.

To see someone harming the interests of the masses and yet not feel indignant, or dissuade or stop him or reason with him, but to allow him to continue. This is an eighth type.

To work halfheartedly without a definite plan or direction; to work perfunctorily and muddle along—"So long as one remains a monk, one goes on tolling the bell." This is a ninth type.

To regard oneself as having rendered great service to the revolution, to pride oneself on being a veteran, to disdain minor assignments while being quite unequal to major tasks, to be slipshod in work and slack in study. This is a tenth type.

To be aware of one's own mistakes and yet make no attempt to correct them, taking a liberal attitude toward oneself. This is an eleventh type.

We could name more. But these eleven are the principal types. They are all manifestations of liberalism.

Liberalism is extremely harmful in a revolutionary collective. It is a corrosive which eats away unity, undermines cohesion, causes apathy, and creates dissension. It robs the revolutionary ranks of compact organization and strict discipline, prevents policies from being carried through, and alienates the Party organizations from the masses which the Party leads. It is an extremely bad tendency.

Liberalism stems from petty-bourgeois selfishness, it places personal interests first and the interests of the revolution second, and this gives rise to ideological, political, and organizational liberalism.

People who are liberals look upon the principles of Marxism as abstract dogma. They approve of Marxism, but are not prepared to practice it or to practice it in full; they are not prepared to replace their liberalism by Marxism. These people have their Marxism, but they have their liberalism as well—they talk Marxism but practice liberalism; they apply Marxism to others but liberalism to themselves. They keep both kinds of goods in stock and find a use for each. This is how the minds of certain people work.

Liberalism is a manifestation of opportunism and conflicts fundamentally with Marxism. It is negative and objectively has the effect of helping the enemy; that is why the enemy welcomes its preservation in our midst. Such being its nature, there should be no place for it in the ranks of the revolution.

We must use Marxism, which is positive in spirit, to overcome liberalism, which is negative. A Communist should have largeness of mind and he should be staunch and active, looking upon the interests of the revolution as his very life and subordinating his personal interests to those of the revolution; always and everywhere he should adhere to principle and wage a tireless struggle against all incorrect ideas and actions, so as to consolidate the collective life of the Party and strengthen the ties between the Party and the masses; he should be more concerned about the Party and the masses than about any private person, and more concerned about others than about himself. Only thus can he be considered a Communist.

All loyal, honest, active, and upright Communists must unite to oppose the liberal tendencies shown by certain people among us, and set them on the right path. This is one of the tasks on our ideological front.

Subjectivism and Sectarianism

From: "Rectify the Party's Style of Work" (February 1942), *Selected Works,* III (Peking: Foreign Languages Press, 1965), pp. 35–36, 40–41, 43, 48–50.

What is the problem now facing our Party? The general line of the Party is correct and presents no problem, and the Party's work has been fruitful. The Party has several hundred thousand members who are leading the people in extremely hard and bitter struggles against the enemy. This is plain to everybody and beyond all doubt.

Then is there or is there not any problem still facing our Party? I say there is and, in a certain sense, the problem is quite serious.

What is the problem? It is the fact that there is something in the minds of a number of our comrades which strikes one as not quite right, not quite proper.

In other words, there is still something wrong with our style of study, with our style in the Party's internal and external relations, and with our style of writing. By something wrong with the style of study we mean the malady of subjectivism. By something wrong with our style in Party relations we mean the malady of sectarianism. By something wrong with the style of writing we mean the malady of stereotyped Party writing. All these are wrong, they are ill winds. . . .

To accomplish the task of overthrowing the enemy, we must accomplish the task of rectifying these styles within the Party. The style of study and the style of writing are also the Party's style of work. Once our Party's style of work is put completely right, the people all over the country will learn from our example. Those outside the Party who have the same kind of bad style will, if they are good and honest people, learn from our example and correct their mistakes, and thus the whole nation will be influenced. So long as our Communist ranks are in good order and march in step, so long as our troops are picked troops and our weapons are good weapons, any enemy, however powerful, can be overthrown.

Let me speak now about subjectivism.

Subjectivism is an improper style of study; it is opposed to Marxism-Leninism and is incompatible with the Communist Party. What we want is the Marxist-Leninist style of study. What we call style of study means not just style of study in the schools but in the whole Party. It is a question of the method of thinking of comrades in our leading bodies, of all cadres and Party members, a question of our attitude toward Marxism-Leninism, of the attitude of all Party comrades in their work. As such, it is a question of extraordinary, indeed of primary, importance. . . .

There is only one kind of true theory in this world, theory that is drawn from objective reality and then verified by objective reality; nothing else is worthy of the name of theory in our sense. Stalin said that theory becomes aimless when it is not connected with practice. Aimless theory is useless and false and should be discarded. We should point the finger of scorn at those who are fond of aimless theorizing. Marxism-Leninism is the most correct, scientific, and revolutionary truth, born out of and verified by objective reality, but many who study Marxism-Leninism take it as lifeless dogma, thus impeding the development of theory and harming themselves as well as other comrades. . . .

Let me now speak about the question of sectarianism.

Having been steeled for twenty years, our Party is no longer dominated by sectarianism. Remnants of sectarianism, however, are still found both in the Party's internal relations and in its external relations. Sectarian tendencies in internal relations lead to exclusiveness toward comrades inside the Party and hinder inner-

Party unity and solidarity, while sectarian tendencies in external relations lead to exclusiveness toward people outside the Party and hinder the Party in its task of uniting the whole people. Only by uprooting this evil in both its aspects can the Party advance unimpeded in its great task of achieving unity among all Party comrades and among all the people of our country. . . .

The remnants of sectarianism must be eliminated from the Party's external as well as its internal relations. The reason is this: we cannot defeat the enemy by merely uniting the comrades throughout the Party, we can defeat the enemy only by uniting the people throughout the country. For twenty years the Communist Party of China has done great and arduous work in the cause of uniting the people of the whole country, and the achievements in this work since the outbreak of the War of Resistance are even greater than in the past. This does not mean, however, that all our comrades already have a correct style in dealing with the masses and are free from sectarian tendencies. No. In fact, sectarian tendencies still exist among a number of comrades, and in some cases to a very serious degree. Many of our comrades tend to be overbearing in their relations with non-Party people, look down upon them, despise or refuse to respect them or appreciate their strong points. This is indeed a sectarian tendency. After reading a few Marxist books, such comrades become more arrogant instead of more modest, and invariably dismiss others as no good without realizing that in fact their own knowledge is only half-baked. Our comrades must realize the truth that Communist Party members are at all times a minority as compared with non-Party people. Supposing one out of every hundred persons were a Communist, then there would be 4,500,000 Communists among China's population of 450,000,000. Yet, even if our membership reached this huge figure, Communists would still form only 1 per cent of the whole population, while 99 per cent would be non-Party people. What reason can we then have for not co-operating with non-Party people? As regards all those who wish to co-operate with us or might co-operate with us, we have only the duty of co-operating and absolutely no right to shut them out. But some Party members do not understand this and look down upon, or even shut out, those who wish to co-operate with us. There are no grounds whatsoever for doing so. Have Marx, Engels, Lenin, and Stalin given us any grounds? They have not. On the contrary, they have always earnestly enjoined us to form close ties with the masses and not divorce ourselves from them. Or has the Central

Committee of the Communist Party of China given us any grounds? No. Among all its resolutions there is not a single one that says we may divorce ourselves from the masses and so isolate ourselves. On the contrary, the Central Committee has always told us to form close ties with the masses and not to divorce ourselves from them. Thus any action divorcing us from the masses has no justification at all and is simply the mischievous result of the sectarian ideas some of our comrades have themselves concocted. As such sectarianism remains very serious among some of our comrades and still obstructs the application of the Party line, we should carry out extensive education within the Party to meet this problem. Above all, we should make our cadres really understand how serious the problem is and how utterly impossible it is to overthrow the enemy and attain the goal of the revolution unless Party members unite with the non-Party cadres and with non-Party people.

All sectarian ideas are subjectivist and are incompatible with the real needs of the revolution; hence the struggle against sectarianism and the struggle against subjectivism should go on simultaneously.

There is no time today to talk about the question of stereotyped Party writing; I shall discuss it at another meeting. Stereotyped Party writing is a vehicle for filth, a form of expression for subjectivism and sectarianism. It does people harm and damages the revolution, and we must get rid of it completely.

To combat subjectivism we must propagate materialism and dialectics. However, there are many comrades in our Party who lay no stress on the propaganda either of materialism or of dialectics. Some tolerate subjectivist propaganda and regard it with equanimity. They think they believe in Marxism, but make no effort to propagate materialism and do not give it a thought or express any opinion when they hear or read subjectivist stuff. This is not the attitude of a Communist. It allows many of our comrades to be poisoned by subjectivist ideas, which numb their sensitivity. We should therefore launch a campaign of enlightenment within the Party to free the minds of our comrades from the fog of subjectivism and dogmatism and should call upon them to boycott subjectivism, sectarianism, and stereotyped Party writing. . . . Our comrades must develop a good nose for this purpose; they should take a sniff at everything and distinguish the good from the bad before they decide whether to welcome it or boycott it. Communists must always go into the whys and wherefores of anything, use their own heads, and carefully think over whether or not it corresponds to reality and is really well founded; on no account should they follow blindly and encourage slavishness.

Finally, in opposing subjectivism, sectarianism, and stereotyped Party writing we must have in mind two purposes: first, "learn from past mistakes to avoid future ones," and second, "cure the sickness to save the patient." The mistakes of the past must be exposed without sparing anyone's sensibilities; it is necessary to analyze and criticize what was bad in the past with a scientific attitude so that work in the future will be done more carefully and done better. This is what is meant by "learn from past mistakes to avoid future ones." But our aim in exposing errors and criticizing shortcomings, like that of a doctor curing a sickness, is solely to save the patient and not to doctor him to death. A person with appendicitis is saved when the surgeon removes his appendix. So long as a person who has made mistakes does not hide his sickness for fear of treatment or persist in his mistakes until he is beyond cure, so long as he honestly and sincerely wishes to be cured and to mend his ways, we should welcome him and cure his sickness so that he can become a good comrade. We can never succeed if we just let ourselves go, and lash out at him. In treating an ideological or a political malady, one must never be rough and rash but must adopt the approach of "curing the sickness to save the patient," which is the only correct and effective method.

The "Eight-legged Essay"

From: "Oppose Stereotyped Party Writing" (February 1942), *Selected Works*, III (Peking: Foreign Languages Press, 1965), pp. 56–63.

Let us now analyze stereotyped Party writing and see where its evils lie. Using poison as an antidote to poison, we shall imitate the form of the stereotyped eight-section essay and set forth the following "eight legs," which might be called the eight major indictments. [The eight-legged essay refers to the ancient Chinese genre stressing form rather than substance.—Ed.]

The first indictment against stereotyped Party writing is that it fills endless pages with empty verbiage. Some of our comrades love to write long articles with no substance, very much like the "footbindings of a slattern, long as well as smelly." Why must they write such long and empty articles? There can be only one explanation; they are determined the masses shall not read them. Because the articles are long and empty, the masses shake their heads at the very sight of them. How can they be expected to read them? Such writings are good for nothing except to bluff the naïve, among whom they spread bad influences and foster bad habits. . . .

The second indictment against stereotyped Party writing is that it strikes a pose in order to intimidate people. Some stereotyped Party writing is not only long and empty, but also pretentious with the deliberate intention of intimidating people; it carries the worst kind of poison. Writing long-winded and empty articles may be set down to immaturity, but striking a pose to overawe people is not merely immature but downright knavish. . . . What is scientific never fears criticism, for science is truth and fears no refutation. But those who write subjectivist and sectarian articles and speeches in the form of Party stereotypes fear refutation, are very cowardly, and therefore rely on pretentiousness to overawe others, believing that they can thereby silence people and "win the day." Such pretentiousness cannot reflect truth but is an obstacle to truth. Truth does not strike a pose to overawe people but talks and acts honestly and sincerely. . . . For the proletariat the sharpest and most effective weapon is a serious and militant scientific attitude. The Communist Party lives by the truth of Marxism-Leninism, by seeking truth from facts, by science, and not by intimidating people. Needless to say, the idea of attaining fame and position for oneself by pretentiousness is even more contemptible. In short, when organizations make decisions and issue instructions and when comrades write articles and make speeches, they must without exception depend on Marxist-Leninist truth and seek to serve a useful purpose. This is the only basis on which victory in the revolution can be achieved; all else is of no avail.

The third indictment against stereotyped Party writing is that it shoots at random, without considering the audience. . . . Communists who really want to do propaganda must consider their audience and bear in mind those who will read their articles and slogans or listen to their speeches and their talk; otherwise they are in effect resolving not to be read or listened to by anyone. Many people often take it for granted that what they write and say can be easily understood by everybody, when it is not so at all. How can people understand them when they write and speak in Party stereotypes? The saying "to play the lute to a cow" implies a gibe at the audience. If we substitute the idea of respect for the audience, the gibe is turned against the player. Why should he strum away without considering his audience? What is worse, he is producing a Party stereotype as raucous as a crow, and yet he insists on cawing at the masses. When shooting an arrow, one must aim at the target; when playing the lute, one must consider the listener; how, then, can one write articles or make speeches without taking the reader or the audience into account? Suppose we want to make friends with a person, whoever he may be, can we become bosom friends if we do not understand each other's hearts, do not know each other's thoughts? It simply will not do for our propaganda workers to rattle on without investigating, studying, and analyzing their audience.

The fourth indictment against stereotyped Party writing is its drab language that reminds one of a *piehsan*. Like our stereotyped Party writing, the creatures known in Shanghai as "little *piehsan*" are wizened and ugly. If an article or a speech merely rings the changes on a few terms in a classroom tone without a shred of vigor or spirit, is it not rather like a *piehsan,* drab of speech and repulsive in appearance? If someone enters primary school at seven, goes to middle school in his teens, graduates from college in his twenties, and never has contact with the masses of the people, he is not to blame if his language is poor and monotonous. But we are revolutionaries working for the masses, and if we do not learn the language of the masses, we cannot work well. At present many of our comrades doing propaganda work make no study of language. Their propaganda is very dull, and few people care to read their articles or listen to their talk. . . .

The fifth indictment against stereotyped Party writing is that it arranges items under a complicated set of headings, as if starting a Chinese pharmacy. Go and take a look at any Chinese pharmacy, and you will see cabinets with numerous drawers, each bearing the name of a drug—toncal, foxglove, rhubarb, saltpeter . . . indeed, everything that should be there. This method has been picked up by our comrades. In their articles and speeches, their books and reports, they use first the big Chinese numerals, second the small Chinese numerals, third the characters for the ten celestial stems, fourth the characters for the twelve earthly branches, and then capital A, B, C, D, then small a, b, c, d, followed by the Arabic numerals and what not! How fortunate that the ancients and the foreigners created all these symbols for us so that we can start a Chinese pharmacy without the slightest effort. For all its verbiage, an article that bristles with such symbols, that does not pose, analyze or solve problems and that does not take a stand for or against anything is devoid of real content and nothing but a Chinese pharmacy. . . .

If an article or speech is important and meant to give guidance, it ought to pose a particular problem, then analyze it and then make a synthesis pointing to the nature of the problem and providing the method for solving it; in all this, formalist methods are useless. Since infantile, crude, Philistine and lazy-minded formalist methods are prevalent in our Party, we must expose them; only thus can everybody learn to use the Marxist method to observe, pose, analyze and solve problems; only thus can we do our work well and only thus can our revolutionary cause triumph.

The sixth indictment against stereotyped Party writing is that it is irresponsible and harms people wherever it appears. All the offenses mentioned above are due partly to immaturity and partly to an insufficient sense of responsibility. . . . Many people write articles and make speeches without prior study or preparation, and after writing an article, they do not bother to go over it several times . . . but instead offhandedly send it to be published. Often the result is "A thousand words from the pen in a stream, but ten thousand li away from the theme." Talented though these writers may appear, they actually harm people. This bad habit, this weak sense of responsibility, must be corrected.

The seventh indictment against stereotyped Party writing is that it poisons the whole Party and jeopardizes the revolution. The eighth indictment is that its spread would wreck the country and ruin the people. These two indictments are self-evident and require no elaboration. In other words, if stereotyped Party writing is not transformed but is allowed to develop unchecked, the consequences will be very serious indeed. The poison of subjectivism and sectarianism is hidden in stereotyped Party writing, and if this poison spreads it will endanger both the Party and the country.

Inner-Party Criticism

From: "On Correcting Mistaken Ideas in the Party" (December 1929), *Selected Works,* I (Peking: Foreign Languages Press, 1964), pp. 109–12.

Disregard of organizational discipline in the Party organization in the Fourth Army manifests itself as follows:

(a) Failure of the minority to submit to the majority. For example, when a minority finds its motion voted down, it does not sincerely carry out the Party decisions. . . .

(b) Criticism made without regard to organizational discipline:

1. Inner-Party criticism is a weapon for strengthening the Party

organization and increasing its fighting capacity. In the Party organization of the Red Army, however, criticism is not always of this character, and sometimes turns into personal attack. As a result, it damages the Party organization as well as individuals. This is a manifestation of petty-bourgeois individualism. The method of correction is to help Party members understand that the purpose of criticism is to increase the Party's fighting capacity in order to achieve victory in the class struggle and that it should not be used as a means of personal attack.

2. Many Party members make their criticisms not inside, but outside, the Party. The reason is that the general membership has not yet grasped the importance of the Party organization (its meetings and so forth), and sees no difference between criticism inside and outside the organization. The method of correction is to educate Party members so that they understand the importance of Party organization and make their criticisms of Party committees or comrades at Party meetings. . . .

Another point that should be mentioned in connection with inner-Party criticism is that some comrades ignore the major issues and confine their attention to minor points when they make their criticism. They do not understand that the main task of criticism is to point out political and organizational mistakes. As to personal shortcomings, unless they are related to political and organizational mistakes, there is no need to be overcritical and to embarrass the comrades concerned. Moreover, once such criticism develops, there is the great danger that the Party members will concentrate entirely on minor faults, and everyone will become timid and overcautious and forget the Party's political tasks.

The main method of correction is to educate Party members so that a political and scientific spirit pervades their thinking and their Party life. To this end we must: (1) teach Party members to apply the Marxist-Leninist method in analyzing a political situation and appraising the class forces, instead of making a subjective analysis and appraisal; (2) direct the attention of Party members to social and economic investigation and study, so as to determine the tactics of struggle and methods of work, and help comrades to understand that without investigation of actual conditions they will fall into the pit of fantasy and putschism [see p. 189]; (3) in inner-Party criticism, guard against subjectivism, arbitrariness and the vulgarization of criticism; statements should be based on facts and criticism should center on politics.

The Meaning of "Rectification"

From: *Speech at the Chinese Communist Party's National Conference on Propaganda Work* (March 1957) (Peking: Foreign Languages Press, 1966), pp. 12–14.

. . . Rectification means correcting one's way of thinking and style of work. Rectification movements were conducted within the Communist Party during the anti-Japanese war, during the War of Liberation and in the early days after the founding of the People's Republic of China. Now the Central Committee of the Communist Party has decided on another rectification within the Party to be started this year. Non-Party people may take part in it, or they need not if they do not wish to. The main thing in this rectification movement is to criticize the following three errors in one's way of thinking and style of work—subjectivism, bureaucracy and sectarianism. As in the rectification movement in the anti-Japanese war, the method this time will be first to study a number of documents, and then, on the basis of such study, to examine one's own thinking and work and unfold criticism and self-criticism to expose shortcomings and mistakes and promote what is right and good. On the one hand, we must be strict and conduct criticism and self-criticism of mistakes and shortcomings seriously, and not perfunctorily, and correct them; on the other hand, we must not be rough but must follow the principle of "learning from past mistakes to avoid future ones and curing the sickness to save the patient," and we must oppose the method of "finishing people off with a single blow."

Ours is a great Party, a glorious Party, a correct Party. This must be affirmed as a fact. But we still have shortcomings, and this, too, must be affirmed as a fact. We should not affirm everything, but only what is correct; at the same time, we should not negate everything, but only what is wrong. Our achievements are the main thing in our work, and yet there are not a few shortcomings and mistakes. That is why we need a rectification movement. Will it undermine our Party's prestige if we criticize our own subjectivism, bureaucracy and sectarianism? I think not. On the contrary, it will serve to enhance our Party's prestige. The rectification movement during the anti-Japanese war proved this. It enhanced the prestige of our Party, of our Party comrades and our veteran cadres, and it also enabled the new cadres to make great progress. . . . The Communist Party does not fear criticism because we are Marxists, the truth is on our side. . . . Rectification means the whole Party studying Marxism through criticism and self-criticism. We can certainly learn more about Marxism in the course of the rectification movement.

"Fragrant Flowers" and "Poisonous Weeds"

From: *On the Correct Handling of Contradictions Among the People* (February 1957) (Peking: Foreign Languages Press, 1957), pp. 15–18, 50–56.

While we stand for freedom with leadership and democracy under centralized guidance, in no sense do we mean that coercive measures should be taken to settle ideological matters and questions involving the distinction between right and wrong among the people. Any attempt to deal with ideological matters or questions involving right and wrong by administrative orders or coercive measures will not only be ineffective but harmful. We cannot abolish religion by administrative orders; nor can we force people not to believe in it. We cannot compel people to give up idealism, any more than we can force them to believe in Marxism. In settling matters of an ideological nature or controversial issues among the people, we can only use democratic methods, methods of discussion, of criticism, of persuasion and education, not coercive, highhanded methods. In order to carry on their production and studies effectively and to order their lives properly, the people want their government, the leaders of productive work and of educational and cultural bodies to issue suitable orders of an obligatory nature. It is common sense that the maintenance of law and order would be impossible without administrative orders. Administrative orders and the method of persuasion and education complement each other in solving contradictions among the people. Administrative orders issued for the maintenance of social order must be accompanied by persuasion and education, for in many cases administrative orders alone will not work.

In 1942 we worked out the formula "unity—criticism—unity" to describe this democratic method of resolving contradictions among the people. To elaborate, this means to start off with a desire for unity and resolve contradictions through criticism or struggle so as to achieve a new unity on a new basis. Our experience shows that this is a proper method of resolving contradictions among the people. In 1942 we used this method to resolve contradictions inside the Communist Party, namely, contradictions between the doctrinaires and the rank-and-file membership, between doctrinairism and Marxism. At one time in waging inner-Party struggle, the "left" doctrinaires used the method of "ruthless struggle and merciless blows." This method was wrong. In place of it, in criticizing "left" doctrinairism, we used a new one: to start from a desire for unity, and thrash out questions of right and wrong through criticism or argument, and so achieve a new unity on a new basis. This was the method used in the "rectification campaign" of 1942. A few years later in 1945 when the Chinese Communist Party held its Seventh National Congress, unity was thus achieved throughout the Party and the great victory of the people's revolution was assured. The essential thing is to start with a desire for unity. Without this subjective desire for unity, once the struggle starts it is liable to get out of hand. Wouldn't this then be the same as "ruthless struggle and merciless blows"? Would there be any Party unity left to speak of? It was this experience that led us to the formula: "unity—criticism—unity." Or, in other words, "take warning from the past in order to be more careful in the future," and to "treat the illness in order to save the patient." We extended this method beyond our Party. During the war it was used very successfully in the anti-Japanese bases to deal with relations between those in positions of leadership and the masses, between the army and the civilian population, between officers and men, between different units of the army and between various groups of cadres. The use of this method can be traced back to still earlier times in the history of our Party. We began to build our revolutionary armed forces and bases in the south in 1927 and ever since then we have used this method to deal with relations between the Party and the masses, between the army and the civilian population, between officers and men and in general with relations among the people. The only difference is that during the anti-Japanese war, this method was used much more purposefully. After the liberation of the country, we used this same method— "unity—criticism—unity"—in our relations with other democratic parties and industrial and commercial circles. Now our task is to continue to extend and make still better use of this method throughout the ranks of the people; we want all our factories, co-operatives, business establishments, schools, government offices, public bodies, in a word, all the six hundred million of our people, to use it in resolving contradictions among themselves. . . .

Marxism has also developed through struggle. At the beginning, Marxism was subjected to all kinds of attack and regarded as a poisonous weed. It is still being attacked and regarded as a poisonous weed in many parts of the world. However, it enjoys a different position in the socialist countries. But even in these countries, there are non-Marxist as well as anti-Marxist ideologies. It is true that in China, socialist transformation, in so far as a change in the system of ownership is concerned, has in the main been completed, and the turbulent, large-scale, mass class struggles characteristic of the revolutionary periods have in the main concluded. But remnants of the overthrown landlord and comprador classes still exist, the bourgeoisie still exists, and the petty bourgeoisie has only just begun to remold itself. Class struggle is not yet over. The class struggle between the proletariat and the bourgeoisie, the class struggle between various political forces, and the class struggle in the ideological field between the proletariat and the bourgeoisie will still be long and devious and at times may even become very acute. The proletariat seeks to transform the world according to its own world outlook, so does the bourgeoisie. In this respect, the question whether socialism or capitalism will win is still not really settled. Marxists are still a minority of the entire population as well as of the intellectuals. Marxism therefore must still develop through struggle. Marxism can only develop through struggle—this is true not only in the past and present, it is necessarily true in the future also. What is correct always develops in the course of struggle with what is wrong. The true, the good, and the beautiful always exist in comparison with the false, the evil, and the ugly, and grow in struggle with the latter. As mankind in general rejects an untruth and accepts a truth, a new truth will begin struggling with new erroneous ideas. Such struggles will never end. This is the law of development of truth and it is certainly also the law of development of Marxism. . . .

People may ask: Since Marxism is accepted by the majority of the people in our country as the guiding ideology, can it be criticized? Certainly it can. As a scientific truth, Marxism fears no criticism. If it did, and could be defeated in argument, it would be worthless. In fact, aren't the idealists criticizing Marxism every day and in all sorts of ways? As for those who harbor bourgeois and petty-bourgeois ideas and do not wish to change, aren't they also criticizing Marxism in all sorts of ways? Marxists should not be afraid of criticism from any quarter. Quite the contrary, they need to steel and improve themselves and win new positions in the teeth of criticism and the storm and stress of struggle. Fighting against wrong ideas is like being vaccinated—a man develops greater immunity from disease after the vaccine takes effect. Plants raised in hothouses are not likely to be robust. Carrying out the policy of letting a hundred flowers blossom and a hundred schools of thought contend will not weaken but strengthen the leading position of Marxism in the ideological field.

What should our policy be toward non-Marxist ideas? As far as unmistakable counterrevolutionaries and wreckers of the socialist cause are concerned, the matter is easy: we simply deprive them of their freedom of speech. But it is quite a different matter when we are faced with incorrect ideas among the people. Will it do to ban such ideas and give them no opportunity to express themselves? Certainly not. It is not only futile but very harmful to use crude and summary methods to deal with ideological questions among the people, with questions relating to the spiritual life of man. You may ban the expression of wrong ideas, but the ideas will still be there. On the other hand, correct ideas, if pampered in hothouses without being exposed to the elements or immunized from disease, will not win out against wrong ones. That is why it is only by employing methods of discussion, criticism, and reasoning that we can really foster correct ideas, overcome wrong ideas, and really settle issues.

The bourgeoisie and petty bourgeoisie are bound to give expression to their ideologies. It is inevitable that they should stubbornly persist in expressing themselves in every way possible on political and ideological questions. You can't expect them not to do so. We should not use methods of suppression to prevent them from expressing themselves, but should allow them to do so and at the same time argue with them and direct well-considered criticism at them.

There can be no doubt that we should criticize all kinds of wrong ideas. It certainly would not do to refrain from criticism and look on while wrong ideas spread unchecked and acquire their market. Mistakes should be criticized and poisonous weeds fought against wherever they crop up. But such criticism should not be doctrinaire. We should not use the metaphysical method, but strive to employ the dialetical method. What is needed is scientific analysis and fully convincing arguments. Doctrinaire criticism settles nothing. We don't want any kind of poisonous weeds, but we should carefully distinguish between what is really a poisonous weed and what is really a fragrant flower. We must learn together with the masses of the people how to make this careful distinction, and use the correct methods to fight poisonous weeds.

While criticizing doctrinairism, we should at the same time direct our attention to criticizing revisionism. Revisionism, or rightist opportunism, is a bourgeois trend of thought which is even more dangerous than doctrinairism. The revisionists, or right opportunists, pay lip service to Marxism and also attack "doctrinairism." But the real target of their attack is actually the most fundamental elements of Marxism. They oppose or distort materialism and dialectics, oppose or try to weaken the people's democratic dictatorship and the leading role of the Communist Party, oppose or try to weaken socialist transformation and socialist construction. Even after the basic victory of the socialist revolution in our country, there are still a number of people who vainly hope for a restoration of the capitalist system. They wage a struggle against the working class on every front, including the ideological front. In this struggle, their right-hand men are the revisionists.

On the surface, these two slogans—let a hundred flowers blossom and a hundred schools of thought contend—have no class character: the proletariat can turn them to account, so can the bourgeoisie and other people. But different classes, strata, and social groups each have their own views on what are fragrant flowers and what are poisonous weeds. So what, from the point of view of the broad masses of the people, should be the criteria today for distinguishing between fragrant flowers and poisonous weeds?

In the political life of our country, how are our people to determine what is right and what is wrong in our words and actions? Basing ourselves on the principles of our Constitution, the will of the overwhelming majority of our people, and the political programs jointly proclaimed on various occasions by our political parties and groups, we believe that, broadly speaking, words and actions can be judged right if they:

(1) Help to unite the people of our various nationalities, and do not divide them;

(2) Are beneficial, not harmful, to socialist transformation and socialist construction;

(3) Help to consolidate, not undermine or weaken, the people's democratic dictatorship;

(4) Help to consolidate, not undermine or weaken, democratic centralism;

(5) Tend to strengthen, not to cast off or weaken, the leadership of the Communist Party;

(6) Are beneficial, not harmful, to international socialist solidarity and the solidarity of the peace-loving peoples of the world.

Of these six criteria, the most important are the socialist path and the leadership of the Party. These criteria are put forward in order to foster, and not hinder, the free discussion of various questions among the people. Those who do not approve of these criteria can still put forward their own views and argue their case. When the majority of the people have clear-cut criteria to go by, criticism and self-criticism can be conducted along proper lines, and these criteria can be applied to people's words and actions to determine whether they are fragrant flowers or poisonous weeds.

★

CHAPTER VI
The Global Strategy

Introductory Note

The Chinese revolution, Mao has said, is an integral aspect of an epoch of world upheaval that began with the Russian October Revolution of 1917. The October Revolution, he argues, changed the course of world history and introduced the era that is destined to culminate in the world-wide victory of the proletarian revolution. The Chinese revolution extended and deepened the influence of the Russian revolution. Due to the unity of the world proletariat, the victory of the Chinese revolution "is a victory for the people of all China, and also a victory for the peoples of the whole world."[1]

The significance of the Chinese revolution, according to Mao, lies not only in carrying forward the tradition of the October Revolution but also in its special attraction for, and applicability to, other colonial and semicolonial countries. The Chinese revolution, in other words, is held up as a model to be followed in all backward countries.

In November 1949, in his opening remarks to the Asian and Australasian Trade Union Conference, Liu Shao-ch'i, then Mao's first lieutenant, stated emphatically that the road taken by the Chinese revolution "can also be the basic road for liberation of peoples of other colonial and semicolonial countries, where similar conditions exist."[2] He distilled the lessons of the Chinese revolution into four main rules to be followed in all these countries. First, he said,

[1] "Address to the Preparatory Committee of the New Political Consultative Conference" (June 1949), *Selected Works*, IV (Peking: Foreign Languages Press, 1961), p. 406.
[2] Quoted in Wang Shih et al., *A Brief History of the Chinese Communist Party*, translated under U.S. government auspices (Washington: Joint Publications Research Center, 1961), p. 305.

the working class must strive to form a united front with all other classes, parties, groups, and organizations that are willing to fight imperialism. Second, this "nationwide united front" must be built around, and led by, the working class. Third, to enable the working class to lead the revolution to victory, "it is necessary to build up through long struggles a Communist Party which is armed with Marxist-Leninist theory, understands strategy and tactics, practices self-criticism and strict discipline, and is closely linked with the masses." Fourth, it is necessary to set up revolutionary base areas and create a "national liberation army," led by the Communist Party.

On the basis of this and similar arguments, Lu Ting-yi, a member of the Politburo of the Central Committee of the Chinese Communist Party, boldly announced as early as 1951:

> The classic type of revolution in the imperialist countries is the October Revolution.
> The classic type of revolution in the colonial and semicolonial countries is the Chinese revolution, the experience of which is invaluable for the peoples of these countries.[3]

The Chinese communists have made a special attempt to apply at the international level the concept of united front. The struggle against imperialism, Mao has argued, must rely on two types of united front, one internal and the other external. There is, on the one hand, a united front of all anti-imperialist forces within the country and, on the other, a united front of all non-imperialist or anti-imperialist countries outside.

On the global level, the united front tactic takes two distinct forms, depending on the "targets" involved. An international united front policy against *imperialism in general* would presumably be limited to socialist countries and "oppressed nations." When aiming at *a specific imperialist power,* on the other hand, such a policy would presumably include a temporary alliance with any other imperialist country that may contradict the imperialist power in question. Thus, as early as 1936, Mao told Edgar Snow that "A Chinese anti-Fascist pact with capitalist democracies is perfectly possible and desirable. It is to the interest of such countries to join the anti-

[3] "The World Significance of the Chinese Revolution," *Hsueh-hsi* (Study), July 1, 1951. Quoted in Howard L. Boorman, "The Sino-Soviet Alliance: The Political Impact," in Howard L. Boorman et al., *Moscow-Peking Axis: Strengths and Strains* (New York: Harper & Brothers, 1957), p. 43.

Fascist front in self-defense."[4] Distinguishing between an "inner front," consisting of the various classes within China, and an "outer front," consisting of those nations willing to oppose Japanese imperialism, Mao said: "Ideally . . . our military strategy should be the strategy of the 'inner front.' That is, if the foreign nations, if Great Britain, America, France, and the U.S.S.R. resist the Japanese blockade, they will arrange themselves in the strategy of the 'outer front.' China would then fight in the milieu of Japanese imperialism while the other countries opposed to Japan [would fight] on the periphery."[5] In his talk with Anna Louise Strong a decade later, Mao identified a "vast zone" of colonial and semicolonial countries which he hoped to unify against "Western imperialism." In 1964, he said emphatically: "The people of countries in the socialist camp should unite, the people of the countries in Asia, Africa, and Latin America should unite, the people of the continents of the world should unite, all peace-loving countries and all countries that are subject to U.S. aggression, control, interference, and bullying should unite, and should form the broadest united front to oppose U.S. imperialist policies of aggression and war and to safeguard world peace."

Since the seizure of political power on the Chinese mainland in 1949, attempts have repeatedly been made to project on the global level the entire revolutionary strategy of Mao Tse-tung. The most authoritative attempt in this direction was undertaken by the Chinese defense minister, Lin Piao, in September 1965. In a document of major importance (see pp. 328 ff.), Marshal Lin insisted that "Mao Tse-tung's theory of establishment of rural revolutionary base areas and the encirclement of the cities from the countryside is of outstanding and universal practical significance for the present revolutionary struggles of all the oppressed nations and peoples." Lin added emphatically: "Taking the entire globe, if North America and Western Europe can be called 'the cities of the world,' then Asia, Africa, and Latin America constitute 'the rural areas of the world.' . . . In a sense, the contemporary world revolution also presents a picture of the encirclement of cities by the rural areas. In the final analysis, the whole cause of world revolution hinges on the revolu-

---

[4] Edgar Snow, *Red Star Over China* (New York: Grove Press, 1961), p. 89.

[5] Edgar Snow, "Interview with Mao Tse-tung: Communist Leader" (July 1936), in Mao Tse-tung et al., *China: The March Toward Unity* (New York: Workers Library Publishers, 1937), pp. 37–38.

tionary struggles of the Asian, African, and Latin American peoples who make up the overwhelming majority of the world's population. The socialist countries should regard it as their internationalist duty to support the people's revolutionary struggles in Asia, Africa, and Latin America."

Such is the attempt to universalize the revolutionary strategy of Mao Tse-tung. What worked in the domestic arena, Lin contends, can be extended and put to work at the international level. This leaves aside the crucial problem of China's inability to control the foreign policies of other countries and dictate a united posture vis-à-vis the "imperialist powers." It overlooks the forces of nationalism within individual countries and the system of international relations which imposes limitations on what nations can and cannot do if they are to maximize their own national welfare.

Readings

IMPERIALIST STRATEGY
TOWARD OTHER COUNTRIES

Imperialism, the Soviet Union, and the Intermediate Countries

From: "Talk with the American Correspondent Anna Louise Strong" (August 1946), *Selected Works,* IV (Peking: Foreign Languages Press, 1961), pp. 97–101.

STRONG: What do you think of the possibility of the United States starting a war against the Soviet Union?

MAO: There are two aspects to the propaganda about an anti-Soviet war. On the one hand, U.S. imperialism is indeed preparing a war against the Soviet Union; the current propaganda about an anti-Soviet war, as well as other anti-Soviet propaganda, is political preparation for such a war. On the other hand, this propaganda is a smoke screen put up by the U.S. reactionaries to cover many actual contradictions immediately confronting U.S. imperialism. These are the contradictions between the U.S. reactionaries and the American people and the contradictions of U.S. imperialism with other capitalist countries and with the colonial and semicolonial countries. At present, the actual significance of the U.S. slogan of waging an anti-

Soviet war is the oppression of the American people and the expansion of the U.S. forces of aggression in the rest of the capitalist world. As you know, both Hitler and his partners, the Japanese warlords, used anti-Soviet slogans for a long time as a pretext for enslavement of the people at home and aggression against other countries. Now the U.S. reactionaries are acting in exactly the same way.

To start a war, the U.S. reactionaries must first attack the American people. They are already attacking the American people—oppressing the workers and democratic circles in the United States politically and economically and preparing to impose fascism there. The people of the United States should stand up and resist the attacks of the U.S. reactionaries. I believe they will.

The United States and the Soviet Union are separated by a vast zone which includes many capitalist, colonial, and semicolonial countries in Europe, Asia, and Africa. Before the U.S. reactionaries have subjugated these countries, an attack on the Soviet Union is out of the question. In the Pacific the United States now controls areas larger than all the former British spheres of influence there put together; it controls Japan, that part of China under Kuomintang rule, half of Korea, and the South Pacific. It has long controlled Central and South America. It seeks also to control the whole of the British Empire and Western Europe. Using various pretexts, the United States is making large-scale military arrangements and setting up military bases in many countries. The U.S. reactionaries say that the military bases they have set up and are preparing to set up all over the world are aimed against the Soviet Union. True, these military bases are directed against the Soviet Union. At present, however, it is not the Soviet Union but the countries in which these military bases are located that are the first to suffer U.S aggression. I believe it won't be long before these countries come to realize who is really oppressing them, the Soviet Union or the United States. The day will come when the U.S. reactionaries find themselves opposed by the people of the whole world.

Of course, I do not mean to say that the U.S. reactionaries have no intention of attacking the Soviet Union. The Soviet Union is a defender of world peace and a powerful factor preventing the domination of the world by the U.S. reactionaries. Because of the existence of the Soviet Union, it is absolutely impossible for the reactionaries in the United States and the world to realize their ambitions. That is why the U.S. reactionaries rabidly hate the Soviet Union and actually dream of destroying this socialist state. But the fact that the U.S. reactionaries are now trumpeting so loudly about a U.S.-Soviet war and creating a foul atmosphere, so soon after the end of World War II, compels us to take a look at their real aims. It turns out that under the cover of anti-Soviet slogans they are frantically attacking the workers and democratic circles in the United States and turning all the countries which are the targets of U.S. external expansion into U.S. dependencies. I think the American people and the peoples of all countries menaced by U.S. aggression should unite and struggle against the attacks of the U.S. reactionaries and their running dogs in these countries. Only by victory in this struggle can a third world war be avoided; otherwise it is unavoidable.

STRONG: That is very clear. But suppose the United States uses the atom bomb? Suppose the United States bombs the Soviet Union from its bases in Iceland, Okinawa, and China?

MAO: The atom bomb is a paper tiger which the U.S. reactionaries use to scare people. It looks terrible, but in fact it isn't. Of course, the atom bomb is a weapon of mass slaughter, but the outcome of a war is decided by the people, not by one or two new types of weapon.

All reactionaries are paper tigers. In appearance, the reactionaries are terrifying, but in reality they are not so powerful. From a long-term point of view, it is not the reactionaries but the people who are really powerful. In Russia, before the February Revolution in 1917, which side was really strong? On the surface the tsar was strong but he was swept away by a single gust of wind in the February Revolution. In the final analysis, the strength in Russia was on the side of the Soviets of Workers, Peasants, and Soldiers. The tsar was just a paper tiger. Wasn't Hitler once considered very strong? But history proved that he was a paper tiger. So was Mussolini, so was Japanese imperialism. On the contrary, the strength of the Soviet Union and of the people in all countries who loved democracy and freedom proved much greater than had been foreseen.

Chiang Kai-shek and his supporters, the U.S. reactionaries, are all paper tigers too. Speaking of U.S. imperialism, people seem to feel that it is terrifically strong. Chinese reactionaries are using the "strength" of the United States to frighten the Chinese people. But it will be proved that the U.S. reactionaries, like all the reactionaries in history, do not have much strength. In the United States there are others who are really strong—the American people.

Take the case of China. We have only millet plus rifles to rely on, but history will finally prove that our millet plus rifles is more powerful than Chiang Kai-shek's airplanes plus tanks. Although the Chinese people still face many difficulties and will long suffer hardships from the joint attacks of U.S. imperialism and the Chinese reactionaries, the day will come when these reactionaries are defeated and we are victorious. The reason is simply this: the reactionaries represent reaction, we represent progress.

Imperialism in Southeast Asia

From: "Statement Opposing Aggression Against Southern Vietnam and Slaughter of Its People by the U.S.-Ngo Dinh Diem Clique" (August 1963) in *Statements by Mao Tse-tung* (Peking: Foreign Languages Press, 1964), pp. 8–9.

U.S. imperialism has violated the agreements reached at the first Geneva Conference by obstructing the unification of Vietnam, conducting open armed aggression against southern Vietnam and engaging in so-called special warfare over many years. It has also violated the agreements of the second Geneva Conference by its flagrant intervention in Laos in an attempt to rekindle the civil war there. Apart from those who are deliberately deceiving the people or are utterly naïve, no one will believe that a treaty can make U.S. imperialism lay down its butcher's knife and suddenly become a Buddha, or even behave itself a little better.

The oppressed people and oppressed nations must not entrust their liberation to the "wisdom" of imperialism and its lackeys. Only by strengthening their unity and persevering in their struggle will they triumph. This is what the people of southern Vietnam have been doing.

Imperialism in the Far East

From: "Statement Expressing the Chinese People's Support for the Japanese People's Great Patriotic Struggle" (January 1964) in *Statements by Mao Tse-tung* (Peking: Foreign Languages Press, 1964), pp. 14–16.

The massive anti-U.S. demonstration by the Japanese people on January 26 is a great patriotic movement. On behalf of the Chinese people, I wish to express deep respect for the heroic Japanese people.

Recently, a large-scale mass movement has started throughout

Japan to oppose the entry and stationing in Japan of U.S. F-105D aircraft carrying nuclear weapons and nuclear submarines and to demand the dismantling of all U.S. military bases, the withdrawal of U.S. armed forces, the return of Japan's territory of Okinawa, the abrogation of the Japan-U.S. "Security Treaty," etc. All this reflects the will and aspirations of the entire Japanese people. The Chinese people wholeheartedly support the just struggle of the Japanese people.

Ever since the end of World War II, Japan has been subjected to U.S. imperialist political, economic, and military oppression. The U.S. imperialists have not only oppressed the workers, peasants, students, intellectuals, urban petty bourgeoisie, religious circles, and medium and small entrepreneurs of Japan; they have also brought many big Japanese entrepreneurs under their control, interfered in Japan's foreign policy, and treated Japan as a dependency. U.S. imperialism is the most ferocious enemy of the Japanese nation.

Japan is a great nation. It will certainly not allow U.S. imperialism to ride roughshod over it for long. The last few years have seen the constant broadening of the patriotic united front of all strata of the Japanese people against U.S. imperialist aggression, oppression, and control. This is the surest guarantee of victory in their patriotic, anti-U.S. struggle. The Chinese people are convinced beyond a shadow of a doubt that the Japanese people will be able to drive the U.S. imperialists from their soil and realize their aspirations for independence, democracy, peace, and neutrality.

The Chinese and Japanese peoples should unite, the people of various Asian countries should unite, all oppressed people and nations of the world should unite, all peace-loving countries should unite, all countries and individuals subjected to U.S. imperialist aggression, control, interference, and bullying should unite and form a broad united front against U.S. imperialism to frustrate its plans for aggression and war and to safeguard world peace.

U.S. imperialism, get out of Japan, get out of the Western Pacific, get out of Asia, get out of Africa and Latin America, get out of Europe and Oceania, get out of the countries and places subjected to U.S. aggression, control, interference, and bullying!

Imperialism Around the World

From: "Statement Expressing the Chinese People's Firm Support for the Panamanian People's Just Patriotic Struggle" (January 1964) in *Statements by Mao Tse-tung* (Peking: Foreign Languages Press, 1964), pp. 11–13.

The heroic struggle now being waged by the people of Panama against U.S. aggression and in defense of their national sovereignty is a great and patriotic struggle. The Chinese people stand firmly on the side of the Panamanian people and fully support their just action in opposing the U.S. aggressors and seeking to regain sovereignty over the Panama Canal Zone.

U.S. imperialism is the most ferocious enemy of the people of the world.

It has not only committed the grave crime of aggression against the Panamanian people and deliberately and stubbornly plotted to strangle socialist Cuba, but has also never ceased to plunder and trample on the people of the Latin American countries and suppress their national-democratic revolutionary struggles.

In Asia, U.S. imperialism has forcibly occupied China's Taiwan, converted the southern parts of Korea and of Vietnam into its colonies, kept Japan under its control and semioccupied by its armed forces, undermined the peace, neutrality, and independence of Laos, plotted to subvert the Royal Government of Cambodia, and perpetrated intervention and aggression against other Asian countries. More recently, it has decided to send a U.S. fleet into the Indian Ocean, menacing the security of the Southeast Asian countries.

In Africa, U.S. imperialism is feverishly pursuing its neocolonialist policies, actively seeking to replace the old colonialists, plunder and enslave the peoples of Africa, and undermine and stamp out their national-liberation movements.

The aggressive and bellicose policies of U.S. imperialism also seriously threaten the Soviet Union, China, and the other socialist countries. Moreover, it is energetically striving to push its policy of "peaceful evolution" in the socialist countries, in order to restore capitalism in and disintegrate the socialist camp.

U.S. imperialism is even pursuing a jungle law policy toward its own allies in Western Europe, North America, and Oceania, trying hard to trample them underfoot.

The aggressive plans of U.S. imperialism to dominate the whole world run in a continuous line from Truman, through Eisenhower and Kennedy, to Johnson.

The people of the countries in the socialist camp should unite, the people of the countries in Asia, Africa, and Latin America should unite, the people of the continents of the world should unite, all peace-loving countries and all countries subjected to U.S. aggression, control, interference, and bullying should unite, and should form the broadest united front to oppose the U.S. imperialist policies of aggression and war and to safeguard world peace.

Riding roughshod everywhere, U.S. imperialism has made itself the enemy of the people the world over and has increasingly isolated itself. The atom bombs and hydrogen bombs in the hands of the U.S. imperialists can never cow anyone who refuses to be enslaved. The raging tide of the people of the world in opposition to the U.S. aggressors is irresistible. The struggle of the people of the world against U.S. imperialism and its lackeys will assuredly win still greater victories.

COMMUNIST STRATEGY
TOWARD IMPERIALIST COUNTRIES

"The Spirit of Internationalism"

From: "In Memory of Norman Bethune" (December 1939), *Selected Works*, II (Peking: Foreign Languages Press, 1965), p. 337.

Comrade Norman Bethune, a member of the Communist Party of Canada, was around fifty when he was sent by the Communist Parties of Canada and the United States to China; he made light of traveling thousands of miles to help us in our War of Resistance Against Japan. He arrived in Yenan in the spring of last year, went to work in the Wutai mountains, and to our great sorrow died a martyr at his post. What kind of spirit is this that makes a foreigner selflessly adopt the cause of the Chinese people's liberation as his own? It is the spirit of internationalism, the spirit of communism, from which every Chinese Communist must learn. Leninism teaches that the world revolution can only succeed if the proletariat of the capitalist countries supports the struggle for liberation of the colonial and semicolonial peoples and if the proletariat of the colonies and semicolonies supports that of the proletariat of the capitalist countries. Comrade Bethune put this Leninist line into practice. We

Chinese Communists must also follow this line in our practice. We must unite with the proletariat of all the capitalist countries, with the proletariat of Japan, Britain, the United States, Germany, Italy, and all other capitalist countries, for this is the only way to overthrow imperialism, to liberate our nation and people and to liberate the other nations and peoples of the world. This is our internationalism, the internationalism with which we oppose both narrow nationalism and narrow patriotism.

The United Front Against Fascism

From: "On the International United Front Against Fascism" (June 1941), *Selected Works*, III (Peking: Foreign Languages Press, 1965), p. 29.

On June 22 the fascist rulers of Germany attacked the Soviet Union. This is a perfidious crime of aggression not only against the Soviet Union but against the freedom and independence of all nations. The Soviet Union's sacred war of resistance against fascist aggression is being waged not only in its own defense but in defense of all the nations struggling to liberate themselves from fascist enslavement.

For Communists throughout the world the task now is to mobilize the people of all countries and organize an international united front to fight fascism and defend the Soviet Union, defend China, and defend the freedom and independence of all nations. In the present period, every effort must be concentrated on combating fascist enslavement.

For the Chinese Communist Party the tasks throughout the country are as follows:

1. Persevere in the national united front against Japan, persevere in Kuomintang-Communist co-operation, drive the Japanese imperialists out of China, and by these means assist the Soviet Union.

2. Resolutely combat all the anti-Soviet and anti-Communist activities of the reactionaries among the big bourgeoisie.

3. In foreign relations unite against the common foe with everybody in Britain, the United States, and other countries who is opposed to the fascist rulers of Germany, Italy, and Japan.

"A New Front of Revolutions"

From: "Revolutionary Forces of the World Unite, Fight Against Imperialist Aggression!" (November 1948), *Selected Works*, IV (Peking: Foreign Languages Press, 1961), pp. 283–85.

At this time, when the awakened working class and all genuine revolutionaries of the world are jubilantly celebrating the thirty-first anniversary of the Great October Socialist Revolution of the Soviet Union, I recall a well-known article by Stalin, written in 1918 on the first anniversary of that revolution. In that article Stalin said:

The great world-wide significance of the October Revolution chiefly consists in the fact that:

1) It has widened the scope of the national question and converted it from the particular question of combating national oppression in Europe into the general question of emancipating the oppressed peoples, colonies, and semicolonies from imperialism;

2) It has opened up wide possibilities for their emancipation and the right paths toward it, has thereby greatly facilitated the cause of the emancipation of the oppressed peoples of the West and the East, and has drawn them into the common current of the victorious struggle against imperialism;

3) *It has thereby erected a bridge between the socialist West and the enslaved East,* having created a new front of revolutions *against* world imperialism, extending from the proletarians of the West, through the Russian revolution, to the oppressed peoples of the East.

History has developed in the direction pointed out by Stalin. The October Revolution has opened up wide possibilities for the emancipation of the peoples of the world and opened up the realistic paths toward it; it has created a new front of revolutions against world imperialism, extending from the proletarians of the West, through the Russian revolution, to the oppressed peoples of the East. This front of revolutions has been created and developed under the brilliant guidance of Lenin and, after Lenin's death, of Stalin. . . .

The world revolutionary united front, with the Soviet Union at its head, defeated fascist Germany, Italy, and Japan. This was a result of the October Revolution. If there had been no October Revolution, if there had been no Communist Party of the Soviet Union, no Soviet Union, and no anti-imperialist revolutionary united front in the West and in the East led by the Soviet Union, could one con-

ceive of victory over fascist Germany, Italy, Japan, and their running dogs? If the October Revolution opened up wide possibilities
for the emancipation of the working class and the oppressed peoples
of the world and opened up realistic paths toward it, then the victory
of the anti-fascist Second World War has opened up still wider possibilities for the emancipation of the working class and the oppressed
peoples of the world and has opened up still more realistic paths
toward it. It will be a very great mistake to underestimate the significance of the victory of World War II.

Since the victory of World War II, U.S. imperialism and its running dogs in various countries have taken the place of fascist Germany, Italy, and Japan and are frantically preparing a new world
war and menacing the whole world; this reflects the utter decay of
the capitalist world and its fear of imminent doom. This enemy still
has strength; therefore, all the revolutionary forces of each country
must unite, and the revolutionary forces of all countries must likewise unite, must form an anti-imperialist united front headed by the
Soviet Union and follow correct policies; otherwise, victory will be
impossible. This enemy has a weak and fragile foundation, he is
disintegrating internally, he is alienated from the people, he is confronted with inextricable economic crises; therefore, he can be defeated. It will be a very great mistake to overestimate the enemy's
strength and underestimate the strength of the revolutionary forces.

"Leaning to One Side"

From: "On the People's Democratic Dictatorship" (June 1949), *Selected Works,*
IV (Peking: Foreign Languages Press, 1961), pp. 414–17.

The vanguard of the Chinese proletariat learned Marxism-
Leninism after the October Revolution and founded the Communist
Party of China. It entered at once into political struggles and only
now, after a tortuous course of twenty-eight years, has it won basic
victory. From our twenty-eight years' experience we have drawn a
conclusion similar to the one Sun Yat-sen drew in his testament
from his "experience of forty years"; that is, we are deeply convinced that to win victory, "we must arouse the masses of the people
and unite in a common struggle with those nations of the world
which treat us as equals." Sun Yat-sen had a world outlook different
from ours and started from a different class standpoint in studying
and tackling problems; yet, in the 1920s he reached a conclusion

basically the same as ours on the question of how to struggle against imperialism.

Twenty-four years have passed since Sun Yat-sen's death, and the Chinese revolution, led by the Communist Party of China, has made tremendous advances both in theory and practice and has radically changed the face of China. Up to now the principal and fundamental experience the Chinese people have gained is twofold:

(1) Internally, arouse the masses of the people. That is, unite the working class, the peasantry, the urban petty bourgeoisie, and the national bourgeoisie, form a domestic united front under the leadership of the working class, and advance from this to the establishment of a state which is a people's democratic dictatorship under the leadership of the working class and based on the alliance of workers and peasants.

(2) Externally, unite in a common struggle with those nations of the world which treat us as equals and unite with the peoples of all countries. That is, ally ourselves with the Soviet Union, with the People's Democracies, and with the proletariat and the broad masses of the people in all other countries, and form an international united front.

"You are leaning to one side." Exactly. The forty years' experience of Sun Yat-sen and the twenty-eight years' experience of the Communist Party have taught us to lean to one side, and we are firmly convinced that in order to win victory and consolidate it we must lean to one side. In the light of the experiences accumulated in these forty years and these twenty-eight years, all Chinese without exception must lean either to the side of imperialism or to the side of socialism. Sitting on the fence will not do, nor is there a third road. We oppose the Chiang Kai-shek reactionaries who lean to the side of imperialism, and we also oppose the illusions about a third road.

"You are too irritating." We are talking about how to deal with domestic and foreign reactionaries, the imperialists and their running dogs, not about how to deal with anyone else. With regard to such reactionaries, the question of irritating them or not does not arise. Irritated or not irritated, they will remain the same because they are reactionaries. Only if we draw a clear line between reactionaries and revolutionaries, expose the intrigues and plots of the reactionaries, arouse the vigilance and attention of the revolutionary ranks, heighten our will to fight and crush the enemy's arrogance can we isolate the reactionaries, vanquish them, or supersede them. We must not show the slightest timidity before a wild beast. . . .

"We want to do business." Quite right, business will be done. We are against no one except the domestic and foreign reactionaries who hinder us from doing business. Everybody should know that it is none other than the imperialists and their running dogs, the Chiang Kai-shek reactionaries, who hinder us from doing business and also from establishing diplomatic relations with foreign countries. When we have beaten the internal and external reactionaries by uniting all domestic and international forces, we shall be able to do business and establish diplomatic relations with all foreign countries on the basis of equality, mutual benefit, and mutual respect for territorial integrity and sovereignty.

"Victory is possible even without international help." This is a mistaken idea. In the epoch in which imperialism exists, it is impossible for a genuine people's revolution to win victory in any country without various forms of help from the international revolutionary forces, and even if victory were won, it could not be consolidated. This was the case with the victory and consolidation of the great October Revolution, as Lenin and Stalin told us long ago. This was also the case with the overthrow of the three imperialist powers in World War II and the establishment of the People's Democracies. And this is also the case with the present and the future of People's China. Just imagine! If the Soviet Union had not existed, if there had been no victory in the anti-fascist Second World War, if Japanese imperialism had not been defeated, if the People's Democracies had not come into being, if the oppressed nations of the East were not rising in struggle, and if there were no struggle of the masses of the people against their reactionary rulers in the United States, Britain, France, Germany, Italy, Japan, and other capitalist countries—if not for all these in combination, the international reactionary forces bearing down upon us would certainly be many times greater than now. In such circumstances, could we have won victory? Obviously not. And even with victory, there could be no consolidation. The Chinese people have had more than enough experience of this kind. This experience was reflected long ago in Sun Yat-sen's deathbed statement on the necessity of uniting with the international revolutionary forces.

"We need help from the British and U.S. governments." This, too, is a naïve idea in these times. Would the present rulers of Britain and the United States, who are imperialists, help a people's state? Why do these countries do business with us and, supposing they might be willing to lend us money on terms of mutual benefit in the future, why would they do so? Because their capitalists want to make money and their bankers want to earn interest to extricate themselves from their own crisis—it is not a matter of helping the Chinese people. The Communist Parties and progressive groups in these countries are urging their governments to establish trade and even diplomatic relations with us. This is good will, this is help, this cannot be mentioned in the same breath with the conduct of the bourgeoisie in the same countries. Throughout his life, Sun Yat-sen appealed countless times to the capitalist countries for help and got nothing but heartless rebuffs. Only once in his whole life did Sun Yat-sen receive foreign help, and that was Soviet help. Let readers refer to Dr. Sun Yat-sen's Testament; his earnest advice was not to look for help from the imperialist countries but to "unite with those nations of the world which treat us as equals." Dr. Sun had experience; he had suffered, he had been deceived. We should remember his words and not allow ourselves to be deceived again. Internationally, we belong to the side of the anti-imperialist front headed by the Soviet Union, and so we can turn only to this side for genuine and friendly help, not to the side of the imperialist front.

A New Storm Against Imperialism

From: "Statement by Comrade Mao Tse-tung, Chairman of the Central Committee of the Communist Party of China, in Support of the Afro-American Struggle Against Violent Repression" (April 16, 1968), *Peking Review,* April 19, 1968, pp. 5–6.

Some days ago, Martin Luther King, the Afro-American clergyman, was suddenly assassinated by the U.S. imperialists. Martin Luther King was an exponent of nonviolence. Nevertheless, the U.S. imperialists did not on that account show any tolerance toward him, but used counterrevolutionary violence and killed him in cold blood. This has taught the broad masses of the Black people in the United States a profound lesson. It has touched off a new storm in their struggle against violent repression sweeping well over a hundred cities in the United States, a storm such as has never taken place before in the history of that country. It shows that an extremely powerful revolutionary force is latent in the more than twenty million Black Americans.

The storm of Afro-American struggle taking place within the United States is a striking manifestation of the comprehensive political and economic crisis now gripping U.S. imperialism. It is dealing a telling blow to U.S. imperialism, which is beset with difficulties at home and abroad.

The Afro-American struggle is not only a struggle waged by the exploited and oppressed Black people for freedom and emancipation, it is also a new clarion call to all the exploited and oppressed people of the United States to fight against the barbarous rule of the monopoly capitalist class. It is a tremendous aid and inspiration to the struggle of the people throughout the world against U.S. imperialism and to the struggle of the Vietnamese people against U.S. imperialism. On behalf of the Chinese people, I hereby express resolute support for the just struggle of the Black people in the United States.

Racial discrimination in the United States is a product of the colonialist and imperialist system. The contradiction between the Black masses in the United States and the U.S. ruling circles is a class contradiction. Only by overthrowing the reactionary rule of the U.S. monopoly capitalist class and destroying the colonialist and imperialist system can the Black people in the United States win complete emancipation. The Black masses and the masses of white working people in the United States have common interests and common objectives to struggle for. Therefore, the Afro-American struggle is winning sympathy and support from increasing numbers of white working people and progressives in the United States. The struggle of the Black people in the United States is bound to merge with the American workers' movement, and this will eventually end the criminal rule of the U.S. monopoly capitalist class.

In 1963, in the "Statement Supporting the Afro-Americans in Their Just Struggle Against Racial Discrimination by U.S. Imperialism," I said that "the evil system of colonialism and imperialism arose and throve with the enslavement of Negroes and the trade in Negroes, and it will surely come to its end with the complete emancipation of the Black people." I still maintain this view.

At present, the world revolution has entered a great new era. The struggle of the Black people in the United States for emancipation is a component part of the general struggle of all the people of the world against U.S. imperialism, a component part of the contemporary world revolution. I call on the workers, peasants, and revolutionary intellectuals of all countries and all who are willing to fight against U.S. imperialism to take action and extend strong support to the struggle of the Black people in the United States! People of the whole world, unite still more closely and launch a sustained and vigorous offensive against our common enemy, U.S. imperialism, and its accomplices! It can be said with certainty that the complete collapse of colonialism, imperialism, and all systems of exploitation, and the complete emancipation of all the oppressed peoples and nations of the world are not far off.

A People's War in Vietnam

From: "Great Leader Chairman Mao's Message of Greetings to President Nguyen Huu Tho [of the Presidium of the Central Committee of the South Vietnam Front for Liberation]" (December 19, 1967), *Peking Review*, December 25, 1967, p. 5.

President Nguyen Huu Tho of the Presidium of the Central Committee of the South Vietnam National Front for Liberation:

On the occasion of the seventh anniversary of the founding of the South Vietnam National Front for Liberation, I extend the warmest congratulations to the fighting people of southern Vietnam on behalf of the Chinese people.

You are putting up a good fight! Relying on your own strength, you have under most difficult conditions badly battered U.S. imperialism, the most ferocious imperialism in the world, and landed it in an impasse. This is a great victory. The Chinese people salute you.

Your victory once again demonstrates that a nation, big or small, can defeat any enemy, however powerful, so long as it fully arouses its people, firmly relies on them, and wages a people's war. By their war against U.S. aggression and for national salvation under the wise leadership of great leader President Ho Chi Minh, the Vietnamese people have set a brilliant example for the oppressed peoples and oppressed nations the world over in their struggle for liberation.

The days of the U.S. aggressors in Vietnam are numbered. However, all reactionary forces on the verge of extinction invariably conduct desperate struggles. They are bound to resort to military adventure and political deception in all their forms in order to save themselves from extinction. And the revolutionary people are bound to meet with all kinds of difficulties before final victory. Nevertheless, these difficulties can all be surmounted and no difficulty can ever obstruct the advance of the revolutionary people. Perseverance means victory. I am deeply convinced that by persevering in protracted war the Vietnamese people will surely drive the U.S. aggressors out of their country.

We firmly support you. We are neighboring countries as closely related as the lips and the teeth. Our two peoples are brothers sharing weal and woe. The fraternal South Vietnamese people and the entire fraternal Vietnamese people can rest assured that their struggle is our struggle. The seven hundred million Chinese people provide a powerful backing for the Vietnamese people; the vast expanse of China's territory is their reliable rear area. In the face of the solid militant unity of our two peoples, all military adventures and political deceptions by U.S. imperialism are doomed to fail.

Victory will definitely belong to the heroic Vietnamese people!

Mao Tse-tung
December 19, 1967

The International Significance of People's War

From: Lin Piao, *Long Live the Victory of People's War!* (September 1965) (Peking: Foreign Languages Press, 1966), pp. 1–4, 42–58.

Full twenty years have elapsed since our victory in the great War of Resistance Against Japan.

After a long period of heroic struggle, the Chinese people, under the leadership of the Communist Party of China and Comrade Mao Tse-tung, won final victory two decades ago in their war against the Japanese imperialists who had attempted to subjugate China and swallow up the whole of Asia.

The Chinese people's War of Resistance was an important part of the world war against German, Japanese, and Italian fascism. The Chinese people received support from the people and the anti-fascist forces all over the world. And in their turn, the Chinese people made an important contribution to victory in the anti-fascist war as a whole.

Of the innumerable anti-imperialist wars waged by the Chinese people in the past hundred years, the War of Resistance Against Japan was the first to end in complete victory. It occupies an extremely important place in the annals of war, in the annals of both the revolutionary wars of the Chinese people and the wars of the oppressed nations of the world against imperialist aggression.

It was a war in which a weak semicolonial and semifeudal country triumphed over a strong imperialist country. For a long period after the invasion of China's northeastern provinces by the Japanese imperialists, the Kuomintang followed a policy of non-resistance. In the early stage of the War of Resistance, the Japanese imperialists exploited their military superiority to drive deep into China and occupy half her territory. In the face of the massive attacks of the aggressors and the anti-Japanese upsurge of the people throughout the country, the Kuomintang was compelled to take part in the War of Resistance, but soon afterward it adopted the policy of passive resistance to Japan and active opposition to the Communist Party. The heavy responsibility of combating Japanese imperialism thus fell on the shoulders of the Eighth Route Army, the New Fourth Army, and the people of the liberated areas, all led by the Communist Party. At the outbreak of the war, the Eighth Route and New Fourth Armies had only a few tens of thousands of men and suffered from extreme inferiority in both arms and equipment, and for a long time they were under the cross fire of the Japanese imperialists on the one hand and the Kuomintang troops on the other. But they grew stronger and stronger in the course of the war and became the main force in defeating Japanese imperialism.

How was it possible for a weak country finally to defeat a strong country? How was it possible for a seemingly weak army to become the main force in the war?

The basic reasons were that the War of Resistance Against Japan was a genuine people's war led by the Communist Party of China and Comrade Mao Tse-tung, a war in which the correct Marxist-Leninist political and military lines were put into effect; and that the Eighth Route and New Fourth Armies were genuine people's armies which applied the whole range of strategy and tactics of people's war as formulated by Comrade Mao Tse-tung.

Comrade Mao Tse-tung's theory of and policies for people's war have creatively enriched and developed Marxism-Leninism. The Chinese people's victory in the anti-Japanese war was a victory for people's war, Marxism-Leninism, and the thought of Mao Tse-tung.

Prior to the war against Japan, the Communist Party of China had gone through the First Revolutionary Civil War of 1924–27 and the Second Revolutionary Civil War of 1927–36 and summed up the experience and lessons of the successes and failures in those wars, and the leading role of Mao Tse-tung's thought had become established within the Party. This was the fundamental guarantee of the Party's ability to lead the Chinese people to victory in the War of Resistance.

The Chinese people's victory in the War of Resistance paved the way for their seizure of state power throughout the country. When the Kuomintang reactionaries, backed by the U.S. imperialists, launched a nationwide civil war in 1946, the Communist Party of China and Comrade Mao Tse-tung further developed the theory of people's war, led the Chinese people in waging a people's war on a still larger scale, and in the space of a little over three years the great victory of the People's Liberation War was won, the rule of imperialism, feudalism, and bureaucrat-capitalism in our country ended, and the People's Republic of China founded.

The victory of the Chinese people's revolutionary war breached the imperialist front in the East, wrought a great change in the world balance of forces, and accelerated the revolutionary movement among the people of all countries. From then on, the national liberation movement in Asia, Africa, and Latin America entered a new historical period.

Today, the U.S. imperialists are repeating on a world-wide scale the past actions of the Japanese imperialists in China and other parts of Asia. It has become an urgent necessity for the people in many countries to master and use people's war as a weapon against U.S. imperialism and its lackeys. In every conceivable way U.S. imperialism and its lackeys are trying to extinguish the revolutionary flames of people's war. The Khrushchev revisionists, fearing people's war like the plague, are heaping abuse on it. The two are colluding to prevent and sabotage people's war.

The International Significance of Comrade Mao Tse-tung's Theory of People's War

The Chinese revolution is a continuation of the great October Revolution. The road of the October Revolution is the common road for all people's revolutions. The Chinese revolution and the October Revolution have in common the following basic characteristics: (1) Both were led by the working class with a Marxist-Leninist party as its nucleus. (2) Both were based on the worker-peasant alliance. (3) In both cases state power was seized through violent revolution and the dictatorship of the proletariat was established. (4) In both cases the socialist system was built after victory in the revolution. (5) Both were component parts of the proletarian world revolution.

Naturally, the Chinese revolution had its own peculiar characteristics. The October Revolution took place in imperialist Russia, but the Chinese revolution broke out in a semicolonial and semifeudal country. The former was a proletarian socialist revolution, while the latter developed into a socialist revolution after the complete victory of the new-democratic revolution. The October Revolution began with armed uprisings in the cities and then spread to the countryside, while the Chinese revolution won nationwide victory through the encirclement of the cities from the rural areas and the final capture of the cities.

Comrade Mao Tse-tung's great merit lies in the fact that he has succeeded in integrating the universal truth of Marxism-Leninism with the concrete practice of the Chinese revolution and has enriched and developed Marxism-Leninism by his masterly generalization and summation of the experience gained during the Chinese people's protracted revolutionary struggle.

Comrade Mao Tse-tung's theory of people's war has been proved by the long practice of the Chinese revolution to be in accord with the objective laws of such wars and to be invincible. It has not only been valid for China, it is a great contribution to the revolutionary struggles of the oppressed nations and peoples throughout the world.

The people's war led by the Chinese Communist Party, comprising the War of Resistance and the Revolutionary Civil Wars, lasted for twenty-two years. It constitutes the most drawn-out and most complex people's war led by the proletariat in modern history, and it has been the richest in experience.

In the last analysis, the Marxist-Leninist theory of proletarian revolution is the theory of the seizure of state power by revolutionary violence, the theory of countering war against the people by people's war. As Marx so aptly put it, "Force is the midwife of every old society pregnant with a new one."

It was on the basis of the lessons derived from the people's wars in China that Comrade Mao Tse-tung, using the simplest and the most vivid language, advanced the famous thesis that "political power grows out of the barrel of a gun." . . .

War is the product of imperialism and the system of exploitation of man by man. Lenin said that "war is always and everywhere begun by the exploiters themselves, by the ruling and oppressing classes." So long as imperialism and the system of exploitation of man by man exist, the imperialists and reactionaries will invariably rely on armed force to maintain their reactionary rule and impose war on the oppressed nations and peoples. This is an objective law independent of man's will.

In the world today, all the imperialists headed by the United States and their lackeys, without exception, are strengthening their state machinery, and especially their armed forces. U.S. imperialism, in particular, is carrying out armed aggression and suppression everywhere.

What should the oppressed nations and the oppressed people do in the face of wars of aggression and armed suppression by the imperialists and their lackeys? Should they submit and remain slaves in perpetuity? Or should they rise in resistance and fight for their liberation?

Comrade Mao Tse-tung answered this question in vivid terms. He said that after long investigation and study the Chinese people discovered that all the imperialists and their lackeys "have swords in their hands and are out to kill. The people have come to understand this and so act after the same fashion." This is called doing unto them what they do unto us.

In the last analysis, whether one dares to wage a tit-for-tat struggle against armed aggression and suppression by the imperialists and their lackeys, whether one dares to fight a people's war against them, means whether one dares to embark on revolution. This is the most effective touchstone for distinguishing genuine from fake revolutionaries and Marxist-Leninists.

In view of the fact that some people were afflicted with the fear of the imperialists and reactionaries, Comrade Mao Tse-tung put forward his famous thesis that "the imperialists and all reactionaries are paper tigers." . . .

The history of people's war in China and other countries provides conclusive evidence that the growth of the people's revolutionary forces from weak and small beginnings into strong and large forces is a universal law of development of class struggle, a universal law of development of people's war. A people's war inevitably meets with many difficulties, with ups and downs and setbacks in the course of its development, but no force can alter its general trend toward inevitable triumph.

Comrade Mao Tse-tung points out that we must despise the enemy strategically and take full account of him tactically.

To despise the enemy strategically is an elementary requirement for a revolutionary. Without the courage to despise the enemy and without daring to win, it will be simply impossible to make revolution and wage a people's war, let alone to achieve victory.

It is also very important for revolutionaries to take full account of the enemy tactically. It is likewise impossible to win victory in a people's war without taking full account of the enemy tactically, and without examining the concrete conditions, without being prudent and giving great attention to the study of the art of struggle, and without adopting appropriate forms of struggle in the concrete practice of the revolution in each country and with regard to each concrete problem of struggle.

Dialectical and historical materialism teaches us that what is important primarily is not that which at the given moment seems to be durable and yet is already beginning to die away, but that which is arising and developing, even though at the given moment it may not appear to be durable, for only that which is arising and developing is invincible.

Why can the apparently weak newborn forces always triumph over the decadent forces which appear so powerful? The reason is that truth is on their side and that the masses are on their side, while the reactionary classes are always divorced from the masses and set themselves against the masses.

This has been borne out by the victory of the Chinese revolution, by the history of all revolutions, the whole history of class struggle, and the entire history of mankind.

The imperialists are extremely afraid of Comrade Mao Tse-tung's thesis that "imperialism and all reactionaries are paper tigers," and the revisionists are extremely hostile to it. They all oppose and attack this thesis and the Philistines follow suit by ridiculing it. But all this cannot in the least diminish its importance. The light of truth cannot be dimmed by anybody.

Comrade Mao Tse-tung's theory of people's war solves not only the problem of daring to fight a people's war, but also that of how to wage it.

Comrade Mao Tse-tung is a great statesman and military scientist, proficient at directing war in accordance with its laws. By the line and policies, the strategy and tactics he formulated for the people's war, he led the Chinese people in steering the ship of the people's war past all hidden reefs to the shores of victory in most complicated and difficult conditions.

It must be emphasized that Comrade Mao Tse-tung's theory of the establishment of rural revolutionary base areas and the encirclement of the cities from the countryside is of outstanding and universal practical importance for the present revolutionary struggles of all the oppressed nations and peoples, and particularly for the revolutionary struggles of the oppressed nations and peoples in Asia, Africa, and Latin America against imperialism and its lackeys.

Many countries and peoples in Asia, Africa, and Latin America are now being subjected to aggression and enslavement on a serious scale by the imperialists headed by the United States and their lackeys. The basic political and economic conditions in many of these countries have many similarities to those that prevailed in old China. As in China, the peasant question is extremely important in these regions. The peasants constitute the main force of the national-democratic revolution against the imperialists and their lackeys. In committing aggression against these countries, the imperialists usually begin by seizing the big cities and the main lines of communication, but they are unable to bring the vast countryside completely under their control. The countryside, and the countryside alone, can provide the broad areas in which the revolutionaries can maneuver freely. The countryside, and the countryside alone, can provide the revolutionary bases from which the revolutionaries can go forward to final victory. Precisely for this reason, Comrade Mao Tse-tung's theory of establishing revolutionary base areas in the rural districts and encircling the cities from the countryside is attracting more and more attention among the people in these regions.

Taking the entire globe, if North America and Western Europe can be called "the cities of the world," then Asia, Africa, and Latin America constitute "the rural areas of the world." Since World War II, the proletarian revolutionary movement has for various reasons been temporarily held back in the North American and West European capitalist countries, while the people's revolutionary movement in Asia, Africa, and Latin America has been growing vigorously. In a sense, the contemporary world revolution also presents a picture of the encirclement of cities by the rural areas. In the final analysis, the whole cause of world revolution hinges on the revolutionary struggles of the Asian, African, and Latin American peoples who make up the overwhelming majority of the world's population. The socialist countries should regard it as their internationalist duty to support the people's revolutionary struggles in Asia, Africa, and Latin America.

The October Revolution opened up a new era in the revolution of the oppressed nations. The victory of the October Revolution built a bridge between the socialist revolution of the proletariat of the West and the national-democratic revolution of the colonial and semicolonial countries of the East. The Chinese revolution has successfully solved the problem of how to link up the national-democratic with the socialist revolution in the colonial and semicolonial countries.

Comrade Mao Tse-tung has pointed out that, in the epoch since the October Revolution, anti-imperialist revolution in any colonial or semicolonial country is no longer part of the old bourgeois or capitalist world revolution, but is part of the new world revolution, the proletarian-socialist world revolution.

Comrade Mao Tse-tung has formulated a complete theory of the new-democratic revolution. He indicated that this revolution, which is different from all others, can only be, nay must be, a revolution against imperialism, feudalism, and bureaucrat-capitalism waged by the broad masses of the people under the leadership of the proletariat.

This means that the revolution can only be, nay must be, led by the proletariat and the genuinely revolutionary party armed with Marxism-Leninism, and by no other class or party.

This means that the revolution embraces in its ranks not only the workers, peasants, and the urban petty bourgeoisie, but also the national bourgeoisie and other patriotic and anti-imperialist democrats.

This means, finally, that the revolution is directed against imperialism, feudalism, and bureaucrat-capitalism.

The new-democratic revolution leads to socialism, and not to capitalism.

Comrade Mao Tse-tung's theory of the new-democratic revolution is the Marxist-Leninist theory of revolution by stages as well as the Marxist-Leninist theory of uninterrupted revolution.

Comrade Mao Tse-tung made a correct distinction between the two revolutionary stages, i.e., the national-democratic and the socialist revolutions; at the same time he correctly and closely linked the two. The national-democratic revolution is the necessary preparation for the socialist revolution, and the socialist revolution is the inevitable sequel to the national-democratic revolution. There is no Great Wall between the two revolutionary stages. But the socialist revolution is only possible after the completion of the national-democratic revolution. The more thorough the national-democratic revolution, the better the conditions for the socialist revolution.

The experience of the Chinese revolution shows that the tasks of the national-democratic revolution can be fulfilled only through long and tortuous struggles. In this stage of revolution, imperialism and its lackeys are the principal enemy. In the struggle against imperialism and its lackeys, it is necessary to rally all anti-imperialist patriotic forces, including the national bourgeoisie and all patriotic personages. All those patriotic personages from among the bourgeoisie and other exploiting classes who join the anti-imperialist struggle play a progressive historical role; they are not tolerated by imperialism but are welcomed by the proletariat.

It is very harmful to confuse the two stages, that is, the national-democratic and the socialist revolutions. Comrade Mao Tse-tung criticized the wrong idea of "accomplishing both at one stroke," and pointed out that this utopian idea could only weaken the struggle against imperialism and its lackeys, the most urgent task at that time. The Kuomintang reactionaries and the Trotskyites they hired during the War of Resistance deliberately confused these two stages of the Chinese revolution, proclaiming the "theory of a single revolution" and preaching so-called "socialism" without any Communist Party. With this preposterous theory they attempted to swallow up the Communist Party, wipe out any revolution, and prevent the advance of the national-democratic revolution, and they used it as a pretext for their non-resistance and capitulation to imperialism. This reactionary theory was buried long ago by the history of the Chinese revolution.

The Khrushchev revisionists are now actively preaching that socialism can be built without the proletariat and without a genuinely revolutionary party armed with the advanced proletarian ideology, and they have cast the fundamental tenets of Marxism-Leninism to the four winds. The revisionists' purpose is solely to divert the oppressed nations from their struggle against imperialism and sabotage their national-democratic revolution, all in the service of imperialism.

The Chinese revolution provides a successful lesson for making a thoroughgoing national-democratic revolution under the leadership of the proletariat; it likewise provides a successful lesson for the timely transition from the national-democratic revolution to the socialist revolution under the leadership of the proletariat.

Mao Tse-tung's thought has been the guide to the victory of the

Chinese revolution. It has integrated the universal truth of Marxism-Leninism with the concrete practice of the Chinese revolution and creatively developed Marxism-Leninism, thus adding new weapons to the arsenal of Marxism-Leninism.

Ours is the epoch in which world capitalism and imperialism are heading for their doom and socialism and communism are marching to victory. Comrade Mao Tse-tung's theory of people's war is not only a product of the Chinese revolution, but has also the characteristics of our epoch. The new experience gained in the people's revolutionary struggles in various countries since World War II has provided continuous evidence that Mao Tse-tung's thought is a common asset of the revolutionary people of the whole world. This is the great international significance of the thought of Mao Tse-tung.

Defeat U.S. Imperialism and Its Lackeys by People's War

Since World War II, U.S. imperialism has stepped into the shoes of German, Japanese, and Italian fascism and has been trying to build a great American empire by dominating and enslaving the whole world. It is actively fostering Japanese and West German militarism as its chief accomplices in unleashing a world war. Like a vicious wolf, it is bullying and enslaving various peoples, plundering their wealth, encroaching upon their countries' sovereignty, and interfering in their internal affairs. It is the most rabid aggressor in human history and the most ferocious common enemy of the people of the world. Every people or country in the world that wants revolution, independence, and peace cannot but direct the spearhead of its struggle against U.S. imperialism.

Just as the Japanese imperialists' policy of subjugating China made it possible for the Chinese people to form the broadest possible united front against them, so the U.S. imperialists' policy of seeking world domination makes it possible for the people throughout the world to unite all the forces that can be united and form the broadest possible united front for a converging attack on U.S. imperialism.

At present, the main battlefield of the fierce struggle between the people of the world on the one side and U.S. imperialism and its lackeys on the other is the vast area of Asia, Africa, and Latin America. In the world as a whole, this is the area where the people suffer worst from imperialist oppression and where imperialist rule is most vulnerable. Since World War II, revolutionary storms have been rising in this area, and today they have become the most important force directly pounding U.S. imperialism. The contradiction between the revolutionary peoples of Asia, Africa, and Latin America and the imperialists headed by the United States is the principal contradiction in the contemporary world. The development of this contradiction is promoting the struggle of the people of the whole world against U.S. imperialism and its lackeys.

Since World War II, people's war has increasingly demonstrated its power in Asia, Africa, and Latin America. The peoples of China, Korea, Vietnam, Laos, Cuba, Indonesia, Algeria, and other countries have waged people's wars against the imperialists and their lackeys and won great victories. The classes leading these people's wars may vary, and so may the breadth and depth of mass mobilization and the extent of victory, but the victories in these people's wars have very much weakened and pinned down the forces of imperialism, upset the U.S. imperialist plan to launch a world war, and become mighty factors defending world peace.

Today, the conditions are more favorable than ever before for the waging of people's wars by the revolutionary peoples of Asia, Africa, and Latin America against U.S. imperialism and its lackeys.

Since World War II and the succeeding years of revolutionary upsurge, there has been a great rise in the level of political consciousness and the degree of organization of the people in all countries, and the resources available to them for mutual support and aid have greatly increased. The whole capitalist-imperialist system has become drastically weaker and is in the process of increasing convulsion and disintegration. After World War I, the imperialists lacked the power to destroy the newborn socialist Soviet state, but they were still able to suppress the people's revolutionary movements in some countries in the parts of the world under their own rule and so maintain a short period of comparative stability. Since World War II, however, not only have they been unable to stop a number of countries from taking the socialist road, but they are no longer capable of holding back the surging tide of the people's revolutionary movements in the areas under their own rule.

U.S. imperialism is stronger, but also more vulnerable, than any imperialism of the past. It sets itself against the people of the whole world, including the people of the United States. Its human, military, material, and financial resources are far from sufficient for the realization of its ambition of dominating the whole world. U.S. imperialism has further weakened itself by occupying so many places in the world, overreaching itself, stretching its fingers out wide, and dispersing its strength, with its rear so far away and its supply lines so long. As Comrade Mao Tse-tung has said, "Wherever it commits aggression, it puts a new noose around its neck. It is besieged ring upon ring by the people of the whole world."

When committing aggression in a foreign country, U.S. imperialism can only employ part of its forces, which are sent to fight an unjust war far from their native land and therefore have a low morale, and so U.S. imperialism is beset with great difficulties. The people subjected to its aggression are having a trial of strength with U.S. imperialism neither in Washington nor New York, neither in Honolulu nor Florida, but are fighting for independence and freedom on their own soil. Once they are mobilized on a broad scale, they will have inexhaustible strength. Thus superiority will belong not to the United States but to the people subjected to its aggression. The latter, though apparently weak and small, are really more powerful than U.S. imperialism.

The struggles waged by the different peoples against U.S. imperialism reinforce each other and merge into a torrential, worldwide tide of opposition to U.S. imperialism. The more successful the development of people's war in a given region, the larger the number of U.S. imperialist forces that can be pinned down and depleted there. When the U.S. aggressors are hard pressed in one place, they have no alternative but to loosen their grip on others. Therefore, the conditions become more favorable for the people elsewhere to wage struggles against U.S. imperialism and its lackeys.

Everything is divisible. And so is this colossus of U.S. imperialism. It can be split up and defeated. The peoples of Asia, Africa, Latin America, and other regions can destroy it piece by piece, some striking at its head and others at its feet. That is why the greatest fear of U.S. imperialism is that people's wars will be launched in different parts of the world, and particularly in Asia, Africa, and Latin America, and why it regards people's war as a mortal danger.

U.S. imperialism relies solely on its nuclear weapons to intimidate people. But these weapons cannot save U.S. imperialism from its doom. Nuclear weapons cannot be used lightly. U.S. imperialism has been condemned by the people of the whole world for its towering crime of dropping two atom bombs on Japan. If it uses nuclear weapons again, it will become isolated in the extreme. Moreover, the U.S. monopoly of nuclear weapons has long been broken; U.S. imperialism has these weapons, but others have them too. If it threatens other countries with nuclear weapons, U.S. imperialism will expose its own country to the same threat. For this reason, it will meet with strong opposition not only from the people elsewhere but also inevitably from the people in its own country. Even if U.S. imperialism brazenly uses nuclear weapons, it cannot conquer the people, who are indomitable.

However highly developed modern weapons and technical equipment may be and however complicated the methods of modern warfare, in the final analysis the outcome of a war will be decided by the sustained fighting of the ground forces, by the fighting at close quarters on battlefields, by the political consciousness of the men, by their courage and spirit of sacrifice. Here the weak points of U.S. imperialism will be completely laid bare, while the superiority of the revolutionary people will be brought into full play. The reactionary troops of U.S. imperialism cannot possibly be endowed with the courage and the spirit of sacrifice possessed by the revolutionary people. The spiritual atom bomb which the revolutionary people possess is a far more powerful and useful weapon than the physical atom bomb.

Vietnam is the most convincing current example of a victim of aggression defeating U.S. imperialism by a people's war. The United States has made South Vietnam a testing ground for the suppression of people's war. It has carried on this experiment for many years, and everybody can now see that the U.S. aggressors are unable to find a way of coping with people's war. On the other hand, the Vietnamese people have brought the power of people's war into full play in their struggle against the U.S. aggressors. The U.S. aggressors are in danger of being swamped in the people's war in Vietnam. They are deeply worried that their defeat in Vietnam will lead to a chain reaction. They are expanding the war in an attempt to save themselves from defeat. But the more they expand the war, the greater will be the chain reaction. The more they escalate the war, the heavier will be their fall and the more disastrous their defeat. The people in other parts of the world will see still more clearly that U.S. imperialism can be defeated, and that what the Vietnamese people can do, they can do too.

History has proved and will go on proving that people's war is the most effective weapon against U.S. imperialism and its lackeys. All revolutionary people will learn to wage people's war against U.S. imperialism and its lackeys. They will take up arms, learn to fight battles, and become skilled in waging people's war, though they have not done so before. U.S. imperialism, like a mad bull dashing from place to place, will finally be burned to ashes in the blazing fires of the people's wars it has provoked by its own actions.

CHRONOLOGY

1839–42	Opium War erupts as a consequence of China's attempt to halt British smuggling of opium into Chinese ports.
1842	Treaty of Nanking opens China to foreign influence.
1851–64	Taiping Rebellion: mass reaction against British imperialism and Manchu oppression.
1893	December 26. Mao is born in Hunan.
1895	Sino-Japanese War over the control of Korea and Taiwan ends in China's defeat.
1898	Hundred Days of Reform fails, Manchu authoritarianism continues.
1900	Allied troops occupy Peking to quell Boxer Rebellion.
1911	October. Republican revolution is triggered by a revolt in Hankow.
1912	Revolution triumphs, Manchu dynasty is overthrown, Sun Yat-sen becomes provisional president, is succeeded by Yuan Shih-k'ai.
1915	January. Japan presents Twenty-one Demands, including assumption of German concessions in Shantung.
1917–18	Mao is active in patriotic and leftist movements in Hunan.
1918	Spring. Li Ta-chao founds first Marxist study group in Peking. September. Mao goes to Peking, works as assistant in Peking University library, meets Li Ta-chao and other leftists.
1919	May. May 4 Movement begins in Peking, spirit of nationalism quickly spreads to students and intellectuals.
1920	Mao becomes a confirmed Marxist and organizes first communist group in Hunan, Communist International focuses attention on China.
1921	July. Chinese Communist Party (CCP) is founded in Shanghai, Mao is among twelve or thirteen in attendance. October. CCP establishes branch in Hunan; Mao is its secretary.

1922   July. Second CCP congress is held in Shanghai, Mao does not attend.

August. CCP decides to co-operate with Kuomintang (KMT).

1923   May. Mao works in CCP headquarters in Shanghai.

June. Mao attends third CCP congress in Canton, is elected to the Central Committee.

1924   January. First KMT congress is held in Canton, Communists are admitted to regular membership, Mao is elected an alternate member of KMT Central Executive Committee, Sun Yat-sen presents his Three People's Principles of "nationalism," "democracy," and "people's welfare."

May. Whampoa Military Academy is founded with Soviet assistance, Chiang Kai-shek is director.

1925   January. Fourth CCP congress meets in Canton, Mao loses his position in Central Committee.

March. Sun Yat-sen dies, is succeeded by Chiang Kai-shek.

May. Anti-imperialist May 30 Movement breaks out in Shanghai.

Summer. Mao begins to organize peasant movement in Hunan.

1926   March. Mao heads CCP peasant department in Shanghai, Chiang purges Communists in KMT.

1926–27   Stalin and Trotsky clash over revolutionary strategy in China.

1927   January. Mao returns to organize the peasants in Hunan.

April. Chiang conducts anti-Communist terror, CCP holds fifth congress in Wuhan, Mao is censured for his unorthodox views.

July. CCP ends co-operation with KMT.

September. Mao leads abortive uprising in Hunan.

November. Mao sets up soviets in Hunan, organizes Workers' and Peasants' Revolutionary Army.

1928   April–May. Mao and Chu Teh establish the Red Army.

July. CCP holds sixth congress.

1929   January–December. Mao and Chu Teh are active militarily, Red troops control a number of areas, Mao and Li Li-san clash over questions of revolutionary strategy.

1930   June. Li Li-san line prevails in the CCP, Communists concentrate on urban areas.

December. Red Army beats back Chiang's first encirclement campaign.

1931   Spring. Chiang's second encirclement campaign ends in defeat.

September. Japanese armies invade Manchuria ("Mukden Incident"), Chiang withdraws third encirclement.

November. Central Soviet Congress holds first meeting.

December. Mao becomes chairman of Central Soviet Republic.

1932   April. Central Soviet Republic declares war on Japan and calls for a united front with KMT.

Winter. Chiang conducts fourth encirclement campaign, is turned back.

1933   October. Chiang launches fifth encirclement, successfully surrounds Central Soviet area.

1934   January. Second Central Soviet congress is convened, Mao continues as chairman.

October. Red Army breaks through Chiang's blockade, begins Long March.

1935   January. Mao crushes opposition at Tsunyi conference, emerges as CCP chairman.

May–June. Japanese demand and receive administrative authority in northern China ("Northern China Incident").

October. Long March ends, Communists establish new base in Yenan.

1936   July. Mao is interviewed by Edgar Snow.

December. Chiang is abducted and held until he agrees to CCP-KMT united front against Japan ("Sian Incident").

1937   July. Japan intensifies invasion of China ("Lukouchiao Incident").

September. Red Army is reorganized into Eighth Route Army and New Fourth Army.

November–December. Japanese armies take Shanghai, Nanking, other cities.

1939   April–June. Clashes occur between CCP and KMT troops.

1941 January. KMT troops attack New Fourth Army ("South Anhwei Incident").

April. Mao begins party rectification campaign.

1943 February. CCP-KMT discuss problems of united front.

1944 November. CCP-KMT discuss coalition government.

1945 April–June. CCP holds seventh congress in Yenan, Mao discusses coalition government.

August. Japan surrenders.

August–October. Mao and Chiang meet to work out coalition government, reaching little agreement.

October. CCP-KMT clashes renewed.

December. General George C. Marshall is sent to China as a special Presidential envoy.

1946 January. Marshall arranges a cease-fire, a political consultative conference is convened.

July. Civil war breaks out.

1947 March. KMT troops occupy Yenan.

July. KMT government orders general mobilization.

1948 April. CCP troops recapture Yenan.

November. Red Army (now called People's Liberation Army or PLA) victorious in Manchuria.

1949 January–September. Communist troops rapidly occupy all of mainland China.

August. U. S. State Department publishes *United States Relations with China* (White Paper).

October. Mao proclaims establishment of the People's Republic of China.

November. KMT government flees to Taiwan.

December. Mao visits Moscow.

1950 February. China concludes Treaty of Friendship, Alliance, and Mutual Aid with U.S.S.R.

June. Korean War erupts, President Truman dispatches Seventh Fleet to Taiwan Straits.

October. China enters Korean conflict.

1951 February. UN General Assembly declares Peking an "aggressor."

1952 October. CCP completes land reform program.

1953 January. First Five-Year Plan is inaugurated.

December. CCP announces creation of agricultural producers co-operatives.

1954 September. First National People's Congress is held, a Constitution is proclaimed, Khrushchev visits Peking.

1955 April. Bandung Conference is held, China seems willing to relax militant international policy.

December. CCP presses on with co-operativization movement.

1956 February. Khrushchev delivers "de-Stalinization" speech.

May. CCP contemplates "Hundred Flowers" policy of inviting popular criticism.

1957 February. Mao delivers Hundred Flowers-Contradictions speech.

Spring–Summer. Regime clamps down on mounting popular criticism, rectification is launched.

June. Mao's February speech is published.

October. U.S.S.R. launches sputnik.

November. Mao visits Moscow, delivers a speech stating that the "East wind is prevailing over the West wind."

1958 January–December. CCP launches "Great Leap Forward."

August. Formation of communes is announced.

December. CCP announces slowdown of commune movement, economic crisis begins, Mao resigns as chairman of People's Republic of China.

1959 April. Liu Shao-ch'i is named chairman of People's Republic of China.

1960 January–December. Sino-Soviet polemics begin, commune movement is consolidated.

August. Soviet technicians leave China, economic assistance is terminated.

1961 January–December. Sino-Soviet polemics worsen, economic crisis continues.

1962 September. CCP denounces U.S.S.R.'s "modern revisionism."

October. Cuban crisis unfolds, Chinese troops attack Indian forces.

1963 January–December. Sino-Soviet conflict intensifies and becomes fully public.

July. Sino-Soviet formal talks on ideological problems end in disagreement.

August. Nuclear test-ban treaty is concluded, China refuses to sign.

1964   January. France extends recognition to Peking.

June–December. United States becomes increasingly involved in Vietnam.

October. Khrushchev falls, China explodes first atomic bomb.

1965   May. China explodes second atomic bomb.

September. Chinese press publishes Lin Piao's *Long Live the Victory of People's War.*

1966   January–December. "Great Proletarian Cultural Revolution" is formally launched and gains momentum.

June. Peking mayor P'eng Chen is purged, as are other officials; schools are closed down.

August. Red Guards are formed to carry out the cultural revolution, Liu Shao-ch'i's name is dropped from second to eighth place on CCP roster, Lin Piao emerges as Mao's "closest comrade-in-arms."

November–December. Liu Shao-ch'i is criticized by the Red Guards, as are other high-ranking officials.

1967   February–March. Elementary and secondary schools reopen, Red Guards are called upon to prepare for spring farm work.

April. Chinese press denounces "top party person in authority taking the capitalist road" and "China's Khrushchev," both epithets apparently referring to Liu Shaoch'i.

Spring–Summer. Cultural revolution faces serious oposition, large-scale civil war erupts in many areas, Mao appears to have lost his complete control of the army.

June. China explodes first hydrogen device, announces unqualified support for the Arabs in their struggle with Israel.

September–December. Cultural revolution is toned down, the regime stresses its "successes" and "achievements," attention is turned to "production," China's universities are reopened, Lin Piao is reaffirmed as "best successor" to Mao Tse-tung.

1968   Winter–Spring. "Revolutionary committees" are formed in many areas representing an alliance between Mao's forces, other CCP factions, and military elements; the army continues to hold pivotal position.

April. Purge of high-ranking army officials appears intended to undermine military predominance and reassert CCP supremacy in the cultural revolution; Mao issues statement applauding American civil rights riots following Martin Luther King's assassination.

May–June. Chinese press insists that workers' strikes and student revolts in France and elsewhere reveal the impact of "Mao Tse-tung's thought" and the cultural revolution.

Summer. Party rebuilding confronts difficulties as new violence erupts, Chinese press denounces Soviet "betrayal" in the U.S.-U.S.S.R. nuclear non-proliferation treaty and in the U.S.-U.S.S.R. decision to discuss possibility of reducing offensive and defensive missile systems.

August. The Peking regime condemns Soviet invasion of Czechoslovakia.

October. Liu Shao-ch'i is publicly stripped of his CCP rank.

FURTHER READINGS

NOTE: This bibliography contains for the most part secondary and interpretive works that place in varying perspectives the material presented in this volume.

Anonymous, *Communist China, 1955–1959: Policy Documents with Analysis,* Cambridge: Harvard University Press, 1962.

Barnett, A. Doak, *Communist China and Asia,* New York: Harper & Brothers, 1960.

———, *Communist China in Perspective,* New York: Frederick A. Praeger, 1962.

Boorman, Howard L., "Mao Tse-tung: The Lacquered Image," *The China Quarterly,* 16 (October–December 1963), pp. 1–55.

Brandt, Conrad, *Stalin's Failure in China, 1924–1927,* Cambridge: Harvard University Press, 1958.

Brandt, Conrad, Benjamin Schwartz, and John K. Fairbank, *A Documentary History of Chinese Communism,* Cambridge: Harvard University Press, 1952.

Chao Kuo-chun, "Leadership in the Chinese Communist Party," *The Annals,* 321 (January 1959), pp. 40–50.

Ch'en Kung-po, *The Communist Movement in China* (written in 1924), edited with an introduction by C. Martin Wilbur, New York: East Asian Institute, Columbia University, 1960.

Ch'en, Jerome, *Mao and the Chinese Revolution,* New York: Oxford University Press, 1964.

Ch'en Po-ta, *Mao Tse-tung on the Chinese Revolution,* Peking: Foreign Languages Press, 1953.

———, *Stalin on the Chinese Revolution,* Peking: Foreign Languages Press, 1953.

Chen, Theodore H. E., *The Thought Reform of the Chinese Intellectuals,* Hong Kong: Hong Kong University Press, 1960.

Chou En-lai, *A Great Decade,* Peking: Foreign Languages Press, 1959.

———, *Report on the Question of Intellectuals,* Peking: Foreign Languages Press, 1956.

———, *Report on the Work of the Government,* Peking: Foreign Languages Press, 1959.

Chou Yang, *A Great Debate on the Literary Front,* Peking: Foreign Languages Press, 1958.

———, *The Path of Socialist Literature and Art in China,* Peking: Foreign Languages Press, 1960.

Chu Teh, *On the Battlefronts of the Liberated Areas,* Peking: Foreign Languages Press, 1952.

Chu Teh et al., *China's Revolutionary Wars,* Peking: Foreign Languages Press, 1951.

Clubb, O. Edmund, *Twentieth Century China,* New York: Columbia University Press, 1964.

Cohen, Arthur A., *The Communism of Mao Tse-tung,* Chicago: University of Chicago Press, 1964.

Department of State, *United States Relations with China* (White Paper), Washington: Government Printing Office, 1949.

Elegant, Robert S., *China's Red Masters: Political Biographies of the Chinese Communist Leaders,* New York: Twayne Publishers, 1951.

———, *The Centre of the World: Communism and the Mind of China,* London: Methuen and Co., 1963.

Emi Siao, *Mao Tse-tung: His Childhood and Youth,* Bombay: People's Publishing House, 1953.

Fairbank, John K., *China: The People's Middle Kingdom and the U.S.A.,* Cambridge: Harvard University Press, 1967.

———, *The United States and China,* Cambridge: Harvard University Press, revised edition, 1958.

Fitzgerald, C. P., *Flood Tide in China,* London: Cresset Press, 1958.

———, *Revolution in China,* London: Cresset Press, 1952.

Fizman, Joseph R., "The Appeals of Maoism in Pre-Industrial, Semi-Colonial Political Cultures," *Political Science Quarterly,* 74:1 (March 1959), pp. 71–88.

Griffith, Samuel B., *The Chinese People's Liberation Army,* New York: McGraw-Hill, 1967.

———, *Mao Tse-tung on Guerrilla Warfare,* New York: Frederick A. Praeger, 1961.

Hsiao Tso-liang, *Power Relations within the Chinese Communist Movement, 1930–1934,* Seattle: University of Washington Press, 1961.

Hsueh Mu-chiao et al., *The Socialist Transformation of National Economy in China,* Peking: Foreign Languages Press, 1960.

Hu Chiao-mu, *Thirty Years of the Communist Party of China,* Peking: Foreign Languages Press, 1959.

Isaacs, Harold S., *The Tragedy of the Chinese Revolution,* Stanford: Stanford University Press, 1961.

Johnson, Chalmers A., *Communist Policies Toward the Intellectual Class,* Hong Kong: Union Research Institute, 1959.

———, *Peasant Nationalism and Communist Power: The Emergence of Revolutionary China, 1937–1945,* Stanford: Stanford University Press, 1962.

Katzenbach, Edward L., and Gene Z. Hanrahan, "The Revolutionary Strategy of Mao Tse-tung," *Political Science Quarterly*, 70:3 (September 1955), pp. 321–40.

Lewis, John W., *Leadership in Communist China*, Ithaca: Cornell University Press, 1963.

Li Wei-han, *The Struggle for Proletarian Leadership in the Period of the New-Democratic Revolution in China*, Peking: Foreign Languages Press, 1962.

Lifton, Robert Jay, *Revolutionary Immortality: Mao Tse-tung and the Cultural Revolution*, New York: Random House, 1968.

Lin Piao, "The Victory of the Chinese People's Revolutionary War Is the Victory of the Thought of Mao Tse-tung," special supplement to *China Reconstructs*, December 1960.

Liu Shao-ch'i, *How to Be a Good Communist*, New York: New Century Publishers, 1952.

——, *Internationalism and Nationalism*, Peking: Foreign Languages Press, 1951.

——, *On the Party*, Peking: Foreign Languages Press, revised edition, 1952.

——, *The Victory of Marxism-Leninism in China*, Peking: Foreign Languages Press, 1959.

Long Live Leninism, Peking: Foreign Languages Press, 1960.

Lowe, Donald M., *The Function of "China" in Marx, Lenin, and Mao*, Berkeley and Los Angeles: University of California Press, 1966.

Lu Ting-yi, *Education Must Be Combined with Productive Labor*, Peking: Foreign Languages Press, 1958.

MacFarquhar, Roderick, ed., *The Hundred Flowers*, London: Stevens, 1960.

MacGregor-Hastie, Roy, *The Red Barbarians: The Life and Times of Mao Tse-tung*, London: Boardman, 1961.

Mao's China: Party Reform Documents, 1942–1944, translated with an introduction by Boyd Compton, Seattle: University of Washington Press, 1952.

"Maoism: A Symposium," *Problems of Communism*, 15:5 (September–October 1966), pp. 1–30.

Meisner, Maurice, *Li Ta-chao and the Origins of Chinese Marxism*, Cambridge: Harvard University Press, 1967.

More on the Historical Experience of the Dictatorship of the Proletariat, Peking: Foreign Languages Press, 1957.

Mu Fu-sheng, *The Wilting of the Hundred Flowers*, London: Heineman, 1962.

North, Robert C., *Chinese Communism*, New York: McGraw-Hill, 1966.

——, "The Chinese Communist Elite," *The Annals*, 277 (September 1951), pp. 67–75.

———, *Moscow and the Chinese Communists,* Stanford: Stanford University Press, 1953.

North, Robert C., and Ithiel de Sola Pool, *Kuomintang and the Chinese Communist Elites,* Stanford: Stanford University Press, 1952.

North, Robert C., and Xenia J. Eudin, *M. N. Roy's Mission to China: The Communist-Kuomintang Split of 1927,* Berkeley and Los Angeles: University of California Press, 1963.

O'Ballance, Edgar, *The Red Army of China,* London: Faber & Faber, 1962.

On the Historical Experience of the Dictatorship of the Proletariat, Peking: Foreign Languages Press, 1956.

Paloczi-Horvath, George, *Mao Tse-tung: The Emperor of the Blue Ants,* London: Secker and Warburg, 1962.

Payne, Robert, *Portrait of a Revolutionary: Mao Tse-tung,* London: Abelard-Schuman, 1961.

Pye, Lucian, *The Spirit of Chinese Politics,* Cambridge: M.I.T. Press, 1968.

Rejai, M., "Communist China and the United Nations," *Orbis,* 10:3 (Fall 1966), pp. 823–38.

———, "Redefinition of 'Maoism,'" *Journal of Asian and African Studies,* 2:3–4 (July and October 1967), pp. 186–91.

Rostow, W. W., *The Prospects for Communist China,* New York: Technology Press of MIT and John Wiley, 1954.

Rue, John E., *Mao Tse-tung in Opposition, 1927–1935,* Stanford: Stanford University Press, 1966.

Schram, Stuart R., "Chinese and Leninist Components in the Personality of Mao Tse-tung," *Asian Survey,* 3:6 (June 1963), pp. 259–73.

———, *Mao Tse-tung,* Baltimore, Md.: Penguin Books, 1967.

———, "The 'Military Deviation' of Mao Tse-tung," *Problems of Communism,* 13:1 (January–February 1964), pp. 49–56.

———, *The Political Thought of Mao Tse-tung,* New York: Frederick A. Praeger, 1963.

Schurmann, Franz, *Ideology and Organization in Communist China,* Berkeley and Los Angeles: University of California Press, 1966.

Schurmann, Franz, and Orville Schell, *The China Reader,* 3 vols., New York: Random House, 1967.

Schwartz, Benjamin I., *Chinese Communism and the Rise of Mao,* Cambridge: Harvard University Press, 1952.

———, "The Legend of the 'Legend of "Maoism,"'" *The China Quarterly,* 2 (April–June 1960), pp. 35–42.

———, "New Trends in Maoism?" *Problems of Communism,* 4:6 (July–August 1957), pp. 1–8.

———, "On the 'Originality' of Mao Tse-tung," *Foreign Affairs,* 34:1 (October 1955), pp. 67–76.

Snow, Edgar, "Interview with Mao Tse-tung," *The New Republic,* February 27, 1965, pp. 17–23.

Snow, Edgar, *The Other Side of the River: Red China Today,* New York: Random House, 1962.

——, *Red Star over China,* New York: Grove Press, 1961.

Steele, A. T., *The American People and China,* New York: McGraw-Hill, 1966.

Steiner, H. Arthur, "Constitutionalism in Communist China," *The American Political Science Review,* 49:1 (March 1955), pp. 1–21.

——, "Ideology and Politics in Communist China," *The Annals,* 321 (January 1959), pp. 29–39.

——, " 'On the Record' with Mao and His Regime," *The Journal of Asian Studies,* 17:2 (February 1958), pp. 215–23.

——, "On the People's Democratic Dictatorship in China," *The Western Political Quarterly,* 3:1 (March 1950), pp. 37–50.

——, "The Role of the Chinese Communist Party," *The Annals,* 277 (September 1951), pp. 56–66.

Strong, Anna Louise, *The Chinese Conquer China,* New York: Doubleday & Co., 1949.

——, "The Thought of Mao Tse-tung," *Amerasia,* 11:6 (June 1947), pp. 161–74.

Tang, Peter S. H., *Communist China as a Developmental Model for Underdeveloped Countries,* Washington: Research Institute on the Sino-Soviet Bloc, 1960.

——, *Communist China Today: Domestic and Foreign Policies,* New York: Frederick A. Praeger, revised edition, 1961.

Tang Tsou, *America's Failure in China, 1941–1950,* Chicago: University of Chicago Press, 1963.

Tang Tsou and Morton H. Halperin, "Mao Tse-tung's Revolutionary Strategy and Peking's International Behavior," *The American Political Science Review,* 59:1 (March 1965), pp. 80–99.

Townsend, James R., *Political Participation in Communist China,* Berkeley and Los Angeles: University of California Press, 1967.

Walker, Richard L., *China Under Communism: The First Five Years,* New Haven: Yale University Press, 1955.

——, *The Continuing Struggle: Communist China and the Free World,* New York: Athene, 1958.

Whitting, Allen S., *Soviet Policies in China, 1917–1924,* New York: Columbia University Press, 1954.

Wilbur, C. Martin, and Julie Lien-ying How, eds., *Documents on Communism, Nationalism and Soviet Advisers in China, 1918–1927,* New York: Columbia University Press, 1956.

Wittfogel, Karl A., "The Influence of Leninism-Stalinism on China," *The Annals,* 277 (September 1951), pp. 22–34.

——, "The Legend of 'Maoism,' " Parts 1 & 2, *The China Quarterly,* 1 (January–March 1960), pp. 72–86, and 2 (April–June 1960), pp. 16–34.

INDEX

This index is keyed for the most part to the author's introductions, notes, bibliography and references and is intended as a guide to the major themes of Mao's work.